EMPIRES

Cornell Studies in Comparative History

George Fredrickson and Theda Skocpol, *editors*

Empires, by Michael W. Doyle

EMPIRES

Michael W. Doyle

CORNELL UNIVERSITY PRESS

ITHACA AND LONDON

First published 1986 by Cornell University Press.

International Standard Book Number 0–8014–1756–2
International Standard Book Number 0-8014-9334-X (paper)
Library of Congress Catalog Card Number 85-24257

Printed in the United States of America

*Librarians: Library of Congress cataloging information appears
on the last page of the book.*

*The paper in this book is acid-free and meets the guidelines for
permanence and durability of the Committee on Production Guidelines
for Book Longevity of the Council on Library Resources.*

For my parents
Marie C. and
William F. Doyle

Contents

Preface 11

1 Imperialism and Empire 19

Explaining Imperialism 22
Defining Empire 30

I HISTORICAL SOCIOLOGY OF EMPIRES

2 Introduction to Part I 51

3 Athens and Sparta: Empire and Hegemony 54

Athenian Empire 55
Spartan Hegemony 58
Sources of Imperial Control 60
The Metropolitan Thresholds of Empire and Hegemony 70
The Peripheral Threshold of Subordination 76

4 Rome 82

The Rise of Empire 83
The Persistence of Empire 92
Decline and Fall 98

5 The Ottoman, Spanish, and English Empires   104

The Puzzle of Tribal Empire 105
Imperialism, Colonialism, and the Nation-State 108

6 The Sociology of Empires: Hypotheses   123

The Inadequacy of Theories of Empire 123
Hypotheses on Empire 128

II THE SCRAMBLE FOR AFRICA: NINETEENTH-CENTURY IMPERIALISM

7 Introduction to Part II   141

8 Tribal Peripheries and Formal Empire   162

Tribal Society 163
Transnational Relations 167
The Niger, 1808–1885 179
Caliban's Lament 191
Pericentric Theory 195

9 Patrimonial Peripheries and Informal Empire   198

Patrimonial Society 198
Transnational Relations 201
The Nile, 1800– 1885 208
Avoidance and Resistance 218
Collaboration and Informal Rule 226
Pericentric Theory Again 229

10 The International System and Nineteenth-Century Imperialism   232

The Three International Systems of the Nineteenth Century 234
The Colonialization of the Diplomatic System, 1879–1890 248
International Systemic Theory 254

11 Greater Britain   257

The Transnational Economy 258
The Politics of Imperial Strategy 275
The Political Economy of Metropolitan Imperialism 295

12 France, Germany, and Spain   306

French Imperialism 306
German Imperialism 319

The Collapse of Spanish Imperialism *331*
Metrocentric Theory *335*

13 The Politics of Nineteenth-Century Imperialism 339

Comparative Statics, or the Forms of Empire *341*
Dynamics of the Scramble *344*

III CONCLUSION

14 Imperial Development: The End of Empire? 353

The Gold Coast and Imperial Control *354*
Zanzibar and Decolonization *358*
The Growth of Imperial Control *361*
The Stages of Imperial Development *364*
Decolonization *369*

Bibliography 373

Index 399

Preface

Imperialism is not a word for scholars.
Lord Hailey, 1940

Imperialism was not in the mainstream of scholarly literature on world politics when Hailey, author of the monumental *African Survey*, made his remark, nor is it today. Historians have studied individual empires and colonies, but most abjure an "ism," a general process and theory. International relations scholars, for their part, tend to place imperialism in a minor position, as one of many possible policies that a powerful state can pursue.

This relative neglect has several sources. Imperial rule involves not only international relations but also the domestic politics of both the subject country (the periphery) and the ruling state (the metropole). In the study of imperialism, therefore, international politics blends into comparative politics. Equally disorienting for current scholarship, empire turns on their heads the central insights of international relations theorists. Imperialism's foundation is not anarchy, but *order*, albeit an order imposed and strained. Comparative politics, on the other hand, concerned with independent political units, recognizes imperialism as at best one minor influence among many in shaping a state. Empire and imperialism are indeed not "words" for scholars in these disciplinary traditions.

Lord Hailey's statement is unassailable in practical terms. It is clear, however, that he strongly intended his "is not" to mean "ought not to be." And that normative statement, which represents the view of many historians and political scientists even today, is highly debatable.

It is true that when Hailey wrote, the contending approaches of the leading theorists of imperialism—John Hobson, Nikolai Lenin, and Joseph Schumpeter—were exceptionally programmatic exercises in political writing. Moreover, and perhaps more tellingly, the programs they were pursuing—the condemnation or defense of capitalism—related only indirectly to the purported object of their analysis, imperialism. The results were not scholarly, at least not in the sense of being careful and complete explanations.

But Hailey's "ought not" was and is unacceptable if imperialism is taken to mean the actual process by which empires are formed and maintained. Empires have been key actors in world politics for millennia. They helped create the interdependent civilizations of Europe, India, the Americas, Africa, and East Asia which form much of our cultural heritage. They shaped the political development of practically all the states of the modern world. Before empires became disquieting subjects for scholarly analysis, they stimulated great literary works, and their historical and theoretical importance once made empire a word for scholars. Historians have steadily expanded our knowledge of individual empires. Social scientists have contributed studies of particular sources of imperialism. They are making empires and imperialism words for scholars once again. We have no reason now to exclude the subject from our study of the theory of world politics, and in this book I attempt to combine the insights of the historians and social scientists in a systematic explanation.

Empire, I shall argue, is a system of interaction between two political entities, one of which, the dominant metropole, exerts political control over the internal and external policy—the effective sovereignty— of the other, the subordinate periphery. To understand this interaction it is quite as necessary to explain the weakness of the periphery as it is to explain the strength and motives of the metropole.

This definition sets empire apart from the types of power characteristic of domestic and international politics. One subject with which empire can easily be confused is international inequality, and I will take pains to dissociate the two. To name two important examples of international inequality, a *hegemonic* power, as opposed to a metropole, controls much or all of the external, but little or none of the internal, policy of other states, and a *dependent* state, as opposed to an imperialized periphery, is a state subject to limited constraints on its economic, social, and (indirectly) political autonomy.

Although such distinctions are important, the study of empires shares much ground with the study of international relations, both in method and in conception. In the study of international relations one seeks the general causes of war and peace as well as the causes of particularly war-prone periods and specific wars, alliances, and foreign policies. Similarly, in the study of empires one wants to know the sources of empire and independence as well as the conditions that gave rise to especially imperialistic ages and of monarchical or democratic empires, and the reasons for the growth, persistence, and decline of empires. Understanding in both cases demands study at various levels of specificity. As I shall show, empires, like international politics, do exhibit some regularities across the millennia; but bearing in mind that broad analogies can yield illusory similarities as readily as illusory differences, I ground my work in an examination of individual empires and specific historical experience. The conclusions that I draw in this book are thus the product of theoretical argument joined to historical illustrations and are best understood as hypotheses in the scientific sense.

Generalization and theory are not, of course, sufficient for an understanding of the evolution of empire. It is impossible to address the question of how empires were established and maintained, and how they fell, without resort to historical narration. What follows does indeed contain such narration—description as disciplined by plot as I have been able to make it. But in a field in which Hobson warned about the use of "masked words" to rally bemused intellectual support for brutal policies, in which Lenin feared the impact of jingoistic ideas on a labor aristocracy bought by imperialistic gold, and in which Schumpeter discussed the use of imperialism itself as a "catchword," one has to be especially careful not to contribute to obfuscation. Because the scientific idiom is well adapted to an explicit presentation of arguments which lays bare any analytical weaknesses, I have used it in the theoretical sections of the book. I believe it is valuable as a pattern for argument even though no sociopolitical study can ever lay credible claim to "hard" scientific conclusions. General historical propositions are always heavily contingent, and my "general theory" is no exception. It does not build from basic axioms about human nature to propositions about imperial behavior. Instead, it begins with thoroughly contingent propositions of social science and extends them into connections—combined explanations—that shed light on aspects of the experience of empires. Such trains of explanation, unscientifically obtained though they are, are nonetheless susceptible to a useful scientific presentation in the form of statements that can be disconfirmed.

I start with an overview of the three perspectives on empires which are already well established and with a discussion of the meaning of empire. Part I, containing broad comparisons of the Athenian, Roman, Ottoman, Spanish, and English empires, focuses on the general structural conditions that explain empires, particularly those conditions which distinguish imperial metropoles from imperialized peripheries. Part II focuses more narrowly on the processes of imperialism that account for the Scramble for Africa of the 1880s.

This work began many years ago, in discussions of the war in Vietnam. We described it as an "imperialistic" war, and I wondered what that label could mean. Understanding empires proved much more difficult than I had imagined it would be. Some of the difficulty came from trying to live up to the exacting though very different standards of scholarship set by two excellent teachers with whom I studied as an undergraduate. Even though I eventually admitted to myself that I could not satisfy both Leo Gross's demand for "simple solutions" and James Kurth's admonition to produce "complete explanations," much of what is valuable in this book comes from having tried.

In the many years it has taken me to complete this book, I have benefited from much advice. I received generous and considerate advice from Joseph Nye and Jorge Dominguez, who gave me a good sense of the challenge I was undertaking if I was going to make a book worth reading. Drawing on his own wide familiarity with the subject, Tony Smith made many helpful suggestions for revision. W. A. Lewis, Harry Hirsch, and Robert Gilpin gave me advice on what eventually became Chapter 6. Richard Bernal, Richard Caves, Judith Hughes, and S. B. Saul corrected early drafts of parts of Chapters 11 and 12. Martin Kilson similarly corrected a version of Chapter 14. John Waterbury and Bernard Lewis helped me on Egypt and the Ottoman empire; Glen Bowersock valiantly tried to save me from error in my discussion of the Roman Empire; Stuart Schwartz improved my discussion of the Spanish empire; and Robert Connor advised me on Athenian imperialism and let me read his path-breaking *Thucydides* in draft. Kenneth Regan, Clara Else, and Michael Mastanduno provided indefatigable research assistance and many substantive suggestions. Roger Haydon performed wonders editing the final draft, showing me that here too, less can be more. Brian Keeling also helped improve my prose. My students at Princeton and Johns Hopkins universities have not shied away from telling me when they found my remarks on empires less than convincing; they have been my most powerful incentives for reformulation.

Fred Hirsch, my first colleague, listened to the argument in the course we taught together, made many suggestions, and inspired me with the sense that all the trying work that scholarship entailed could be a worthwhile way to spend one's life. Arno Mayer offered encouragement as well as suggestions on how to draw out my themes. Robert Keohane read the work with painstaking care and helped me to organize a considerably clearer presentation. To them, I am particularly grateful.

Edna Lloyd, Suzanne Cox, Amy Valis, Peg Clarke, Lynda Emery, Joyce McGowan, Margaret Van Sant, and Catherine Grover graciously typed and later keyboarded messy drafts with inexplicable and gratefully received good cheer.

Helpful librarians guided my searches, beginning at Widener Library (Harvard University) and later at the London School of Economics, the Public Record Office (U.K.), Firestone Library (Princeton University), M. S. Eisenhower Library (Johns Hopkins University), and McKeldrin Library (University of Maryland).

I doubt that I could have imagined a place in which to write a final draft more hospitable than the Institute for Advanced Study in Princeton. For generous financial assistance, I thank the Institute, the John Parker Compton Fellowship, the Center of International Studies and the Woodrow Wilson School of Princeton University, the Ford Foundation, the Exxon Foundation, and the National Endowment for the Humanities.

For parts of Chapter 10, I draw on material first published in my "Histoire des structures," *Revue Internationale d'histoire de la Banque* 19 (1980), 69-110. Chapters 8 and 9 draw on my "Metropole, Periphery, and System: Empire on the Niger and the Nile," in Peter Evans, Dietrich Rueschemeyer, and Evelyne Huber Stephens, eds., *States versus Markets in the World System* (Beverly Hills: Sage, 1985). I thank the publishers for allowing me to use revisions of those essays.

I feel a special gratitude to Amy Gutmann for wise counsel, loving support, and frequent encouragement. I also appreciated the patience of Abigail Gutmann Doyle who sat, drawing, for many hours while I typed on the computer. Now she is asking for her own time on the screen.

MICHAEL W. DOYLE

Baltimore, Maryland

EMPIRES

CHAPTER 1

Imperialism and Empire

Empires are relationships of political control imposed by some political societies over the effective sovereignty of other political societies. They include more than just formally annexed territories, but they encompass less than the sum of all forms of international inequality. Imperialism is the process of establishing and maintaining an empire.

To explain empires and understand imperialism, we need to combine insights from several sources. Both the opportunities that give rise to imperialism and the motives that drive it are to be found in a fourfold interaction among metropoles, peripheries, transnational forces, and international systemic incentives.

Certain states have centralized government, differentiated economies, and a shared political loyalty. These attributes permit and encourage the states concerned to dominate other political societies, and define imperial metropoles. Other societies are vulnerable to domination and collaboration. These "imperializable peripheries" have no or at best highly divided governments, undifferentiated economies, and absent or highly divided political loyalties. The forces and institutions that drive and shape imperialism, moreover, are neither primarily economic nor primarily military; they are both economic and military, and also political, social, and cultural. When these forces and institutions actually connect the societies of metropoles with the societies of peripheries, they generate opportunities and incentives for domination by the metropole as well as vulnerabilities to conquest and incentives for collaboration in the periphery. The structure of the international system—whether unipolar, bipolar, or multipolar—has an influence, though not a determining one, on imperialism. Variations in the fourfold interaction account for the varying forms that empires have taken, whether effective political control is achieved through formal annexation or through informal domination, and why empires rise, persist, and fall.

This summary is not uncontroversial. Empires have conventionally been defined in narrow terms as the formal annexations of conquered territory, marked on maps in red, blue, and yellow. They have also been defined broadly as any form of international economic inequality, as international power, as international exploitation, and as international order—even as the extension of civilization (presumably that of the conquerors). Some commentators have shunted aside the study of empires altogether in favor of exposing "imperialism"—the expansionist tendencies of the monopoly stage of capitalism or of the latest stage of atavistic militarism.

These various definitions have located the sources of empires and of imperialism in three different and exclusive areas, and empire as a subject of study for historians and social scientists has been dominated by three major views. The first uses a metropolitan, dispositional model. The second is based on an emphasis on the periphery. The third rests on the systemic model accepted by many contemporary analysts of international power politics.

To Hobson, Lenin, Schumpeter, and their followers, empire is imperialism. A product of internal, metropolitan drives to external expansion, imperialism is to them an essentially metropolitan disposition to satisfy the lust for profit of financiers, the necessities for growth of monopoly capital, the objectless drives of militaristic elites. Related approaches generalize from metropolitan observation, arguing for example that imperialism is needed to sustain industrialism or, more modestly, that it temporarily solves domestic political or economic instabilities. The focus on the disposition of metropoles has had such a strong effect that it is common for critics of imperialism to begin and end their discussion of empire with a refutation of Hobson's or Lenin's views or of what they see as related "devil theory."[1]

---

1. The criticism is from Hans Morgenthau, *Politics among Nations* (New York, 1975), pp. 52–53.

In reaction, it seems, to this fixation on the metropoles, the new historians of empire led by John Gallagher and Ronald Robinson have focused their attention on the peripheries. They discover in crises engendered in Africa, Asia, and Latin America, far from the European capitals of empire, the true roots of imperial expansion.[2] The weakness and collapse of these subordinate societies, they argue, accounts for empire. (A more recent group of historians, responding in turn to the fixations of these pericentric historians, has rediscovered the true sources of imperial dynamism in Bismarck's Germany, Disraeli's England, or European industrialism.)

Also reacting to the heat of the debate ignited by the dispositionalists, and neglecting much of the debate among historians, many social and political scientists have rejected the view that empires can be traced to particular social structures, whether of the metropoles or of the peripheries. Instead, they have argued that empire is imperial power—a natural consequence of differences in power among states in a competitive and anarchic international system.[3] Stronger states dominate weaker states.

Within each of these perspectives, wherever they locate the source of imperialism, some observers hold that empire is the product primarily of economic forces; others put strategic and military forces at the center of their explanations.

Each of these views has helped us analyze the expansion and decline of empires. Together they have generated valuable hypotheses concerning, for example, the role of trade, domestic coalitions, and diplomatic rivalries in imperial expansion. But is any one of these models adequate, or sufficient, to explain the historical similarities and varieties of empires?

A definition of empire as political control over effective sovereignty, I shall argue, raises more of the questions that theories of empires need to take into account. And just as this definition differs from those of the three current views, so too will its explanation.

2. The founding statement was John Gallagher and Ronald Robinson, "The Imperialism of Free Trade," *Economic History Review*, 2d ser., 6, 1 (1953), 1–15, which developed both the concept of informal empire and the peripheral sources of empire. Equally important were K. O. Dike, *Trade and Politics in the Niger Delta* (Oxford, 1956) and J. S. Furnivall, *Colonial Policy and Practice* (Cambridge, 1948). See also William R. Louis, ed., *Imperialism: The Robinson and Gallagher Controversy* (New York, 1976).

3. The most systematic expression of this view is Benjamin Cohen, *The Question of Imperialism* (New York, 1973). A. J. P. Taylor, *Germany's First Bid for Colonies, 1884–1885* (New York, 1970), focuses on the diplomatic sources of imperialism.

Explaining Imperialism

Metrocentric Views

Hobson's *Imperialism* is an important moment in the intellectual tradition of thinking on imperialism.[4] Here empire, considered as international expansion, became imperialism, the disposition of a metropolitan society to expand its rule. Here, too, the dispositional mode of analysis which came to characterize an entire tradition received its first coherent statement.

Hobson's decision to cast his study as an examination of imperialism rather than of empires or the British empire has a significance that the onrush of social science with its many "isms" has in large part extinguished. Hobson was a social scientist, and his decision was quite conscious:

> Those who see one set of problems in Egypt, another in China, a third in South America, a fourth in South Africa, or trace their connexion merely through the old political relations between nations, will be subjected to a rough awakening as their calculations, based on this old Separatist view, are everywhere upset. Without seeking to ignore or to disparage the special factors, physical, economic, and political, which rightly assign a certain peculiarity to each case, I would insist upon the supreme importance of recognising the dominance everywhere exercised by the new confederacy and interplay of two sets of forces, conveniently designated by the titles International Capitalism and Imperialism.[5]

He soon transformed his object of explanation, however, from this abstraction into the more measurable concept of "annexed territory," which later scholars have called formal imperialism. Annexed territory he then further focused, on territory Britain had acquired after 1870—tropical lands "painted red" on the atlas.[6]

4. John A. Hobson, *Imperialism: A Study* (1902; Ann Arbor, 1965).
5. Ibid., p. 368. Hobson's other work includes "Capitalism and Imperialism in South Africa," *Contemporary Review*, January 1900, pp. 1–17, and *Confessions of an Economic Heretic* (London, 1938). Important secondary sources are B. Porter, *Critics of Empire* (London, 1968); D. K. Fieldhouse, "Imperialism: An Historigraphical Revision," *Economic History Review*, 2d ser., 14, 2 (1961); E. E. Nemmers, *Hobson and Underconsumption* (Amsterdam, 1956), chap. 6; H. Stretton, *Policy Sciences* (New York, 1969), pp. 95–102; Mark Blaug, "Economic Imperialism Revisited," in K. Boulding and T. Mukerjee, eds., *Economic Imperialism* (Ann Arbor, 1972); and Giovanni Arrighi, *The Geometry of Imperialism,* trans. P. Camiller (London, 1978)—a fascinating updating of the Hobson paradigm.
6. Hobson, *Imperialism: A Study*, pp. 15–17. Before radically simplifying his defi-

Hobson portrayed British imperialism as the result of forces emanating from metropolitan Britain. Special interests, led by the financiers, encouraged an expansionist foreign policy designed to promote the needs of capitalist investors for investment outlets. These interests succeeded in manipulating the metropolitan politics of parliamentary Britain through their influence over the press and educational institutions, which provided them with imperialistic propaganda.[7]

Lenin and Schumpeter, too, offered dispositional, metrocentric explanations of imperialism, although both differed from Hobson in a number of respects. Lenin defined modern imperialism as the monopoly stage of capitalism which he also argued, explained it. The territorial division of the world (one aspect of Lenin's definition of imperialism) broadened Hobson's concept of formal territorial annexation to include the exercise of controlling influence by economic means—what is now called informal imperialism. For Lenin, imperialism was not the product of the special interests of high finance, it was capitalism in its monopoly, financial, and final stage, driven to search for overseas profits, raw materials, and markets. The connection between capitalism and imperialism was neither marginal nor mistaken, nor was it, as Hobson argued, subject to democratic reform; it was vital and necessary to capitalism as a whole.[8]

Schumpeter, conversely, held that pure capitalism and imperialism were not only unrelated, they were antithetical to each other. He defined imperialism as the objectless disposition of a state to unlimited forcible expansion (that is, formal imperialism or territorial conquest). This disposition originated in atavistic, militaristic institutions, such as the "war

---

nition, Hobson developed a sophisticated concept of imperialism that covered related aspects of world politics and included "informal" control. Nationalism he described as the establishment of political union on the basis of nationality"; genuine colonialism is "the migration of part of a nation to vacant or sparsely peopled foreign lands, the emigrants carrying with them full rights of citizenship in the mother country" (e.g., Australia and Canada); internationalism, such as was found in the Roman empire or the eighteenth-century aristocracy, is akin to a world citizenship. Imperialism is thus what the preceding items are not, "a debasement of this geniune nationalism, by attempts to overflow its natural banks and absorb the near or distant territory of reluctant and unassimilable peoples" (pp. 6, 9–11). Imperialism is not just annexation but also includes "spheres of influence" and "veiled protectorates" such as Egypt, where whatever the measure of local, often feudal, self-government, "major matters of policy are subject to the absolute rule of the British Government, or some British official" (p. 16).

7. Ibid., chaps. 4 and 6; and see the explanation of Hobson's analysis of these modern forces in my Chapter 7, below.

8. V. I. Lenin, *Imperialism: The Highest Stage of Capitalism* (1917; New York, 1939), pp. 9–10.

machine" of ancient Egypt, and in the aggressive instincts of war machines ancient and modern. Modern capitalism's only link to these ages-
old forces of imperialism lay in the historical residue of the corruption
of true capitalism by the war machines of the absolute monarchies of
seventeenth- and eighteenth-century Europe. When warped by the tariffs that mercantilistic considerations imposed on free-market capitalism,
capitalism became "export monopolism"—an economic system such as
that in modern Germany, which produced incentives for military conquest to expand closed national markets.[9]

Hobson and Lenin limited their dispositional theories to late capitalism
while Schumpeter's atavistic war machine overarched the ages. Some
scholars who share Hobson's and Lenin's predilection for historically
specific analysis have employed a similarly metrocentric, dispositional
approach to elucidate the imperialism of other ages. William Harris's
recent discussion of the metropolitan sources of Roman imperialism,
for example, specifically refers to this wider tradition of explanation
through dispositional factors. Since it was necessary for a Roman aris-
tocrat who wanted high office to demonstrate military skill, fortitude,
and success, the repeated skirmishes between Gauls and Romans became
forums for political ambition. A victory took a family one step closer
to aristocratic status; a campaign was a crucial manifestation of fitness
for higher office.[10] The career ladders of Roman officers were thus
festooned with the bodies of dead Gauls and Spaniards. By the end of
the Roman Republic the senators had become the largest landholders,
their massive estates worked by slave labor. Wars increasingly took on
the character of massive slave-hunting expeditions.

Dispositionalism, therefore, is an approach with variations and a common theme. Lenin shares with Hobson a focus on economic forces
within capitalism which lead from competitive to monopolistic organization and from monopoly to imperialism. Schumpeter shares with
Hobson a definition of imperialism limited to formal imperialism and
territorial conquest. Lenin shares with Schumpeter a basic determinism.
All three share a dispositional analysis: they see the roots of empire in
imperialism, a force emanating from the metropole like radio waves
from a transmitter.

9. Joseph Schumpeter, "The Sociology of Imperialisms," in *Imperialism and Social Classes* (Cleveland, 1955), pp. 88–89.

10. William V. Harris, *War and Imperialism in Republican Rome, 327–70 B.C.* (Oxford, 1979).

Pericentric Views

The second approach suggests that it is not in the metropoles but in the peripheries that the sources of imperialism can be discovered. The interaction of an international economy (considered as a constant factor without explanatory weight) and the social structure of collaboration or noncollaboration is the key to Gallagher and Robinson's interpretation of modern imperialism. "Imperialism, perhaps, may be defined as a sufficient political function of this process of integrating new regions into the expanding economy; its character is largely decided by the various and changing relationships between the political and economic elements of expansion in any particular region and time."[11] The relative weight of metropolitan and peripheral factors they make clear in a later essay. "The gaudy empires spatch-cocked together in Asia and Africa ... were linked only obliquely to the expansive impulses in Europe. They were not the objects of serious national attention. . . . It would be a gullible historiography which would see such gimcrack creations as necessary functions of the balance of power or as the highest stage of capitalism."[12]

One of the many successes that Gallagher and Robinson claim for the imperialism of free trade is Latin America, where "Canning's underlying objective was to clear the way for British mercantile expansion by creating a new and informal empire."[13] There, they suggest, Britain maintained informal control by means of blockade (Argentina in the 1840s), the influence of railways (Brazil), and most importantly the free-trade treaty. The last set in motion the attraction of trade itself, for it was largely by trade that foreign connections appealed to the indigenous elites whose collaboration made imperial rule possible. Formal empire is merely the continuation by other means of this informal paramountcy.[14]

A related pericentric view has shaped the work of Ernest Badian on the expansion of the Roman empire, particularly his discussion of the

11. Gallagher and Robinson, p. 5. A later development of this view is Ronald Robinson, "Non-European Foundations of European Imperialism," in R. Owen and Bob Sutcliffe, eds., *Studies in the Theory of Imperialism* (London, 1972). In his later works David Fieldhouse (e.g., *Economics and Empire, 1830–1914* [London, 1973]) shares this view. Robinson and Gallagher supplemented their analysis of the motives for imperialism with a stress on strategic factors influencing the "official mind," in *Africa and the Victorians* (London, 1961).

12. R. Robinson and J. Galagher, "The Partition of Africa," in F. H. Hinsley, ed., *Cambridge Modern History*, vol. 11 (Cambridge, 1962), p. 639.

13. Gallagher and Robinson, "Imperialism of Free Trade," p. 6.

14. Ibid., pp. 6–7.

origins of the Second Macedonian War, which established an informal Roman empire over the nominally independent states of Greece. Badian argues that while Roman motives remained traditional, the "Illyrian [peripheral] situation contains a main part of the answer to our question."[15] Finding the then-current instability of Greek cities inappropriate to the restrictions of traditional Roman international law (fetial law), which divided foreign relations into equal alliances or wars against enemies, Rome extended the practice of domestic client relations to its international dealings and made itself the "protector" of Greece. So Greece became subject to an informal empire.

Another variant of the pericentric approach is related to the imperialism of free trade, but it considers the special effects of an international boundary between different types of political societies. Nineteenth-century empires had, as Rome had, a "frontier problem": a border area was no sooner secured than a raid by a native chieftain would upset the delicate condition of law and order and require the taking of the next line of passes, the next oasis, or the next falls upriver. Eminently defensive in character, this dynamic was nonetheless expansive in effect. A metropolitan international system may be marked by equal rights for its members and a sense of community, but at the borders of international systems there are conflicts with polities neither equal nor similar to the central members. There, conventional diplomatic and mercantile practices fail to produce orderly interaction, and metropoles try to isolate their interests by extraterritorial means. Where isolation fails, metropoles feel compelled to impose imperial rule.[16]

Systemic Views

Many contemporary social scientists find metrocentric, dispositional views unconvincing. The single most persuasive account of imperial control can be found, they believe, in the Realist, international-systemic explanation of empire—in the theory of international power politics. Disparities in power provide both opportunities and motives for the establishment of empires.

In a general criticism of reductionist (dispositional) approaches to

15. Ernest Badian, *Foreign Clientelae, 264–70 B.C.* (Oxford, 1967), pp. 62–75.

16. A number of analyses of imperialism share this formulation. Among them are G. Balandier, "The Colonial Situation," in I. Wallerstein, ed., *Social Change: The Colonial Situation* (New York, 1969); V. G. Kiernan, *The Lords of Human Kind* (Boston, 1969); James Kurth, "Modernity and Hegemony: The American Way of Foreign Policy" (paper presented at the Harvard Center for International Affairs, Cambridge, Mass., 1971); and Tony Smith, *The Pattern of Imperialism* (New York, 1981), chap. 2.

understanding the sources of imperialism, Kenneth Waltz argues that we must concentrate our attention on the opportunities for imperial control which are present within an international system. Reductionist approaches must give way to systemic approaches.[17] Motives for empire vary, according to Waltz, though imperialist movements generally pursue three surpluses—of people, of goods, and of capital—which lead to the imperialisms of swarming, of free trade, and of monopoly capitalism.[18] These three imperialisms are compatible with many different types of regime, ranging from republics (Rome) through absolute monarchies (Bourbon France) to modern democracies (the United States). What does not vary is the enormous disparity in power between the dominant and the subordinate state. Waltz summarizes imperialism thus: "Where gross imbalances of power exist, and where the means of transportation permit the export of goods and of the instruments of rule, the more capable people ordinarily exert a considerable influence over those less able to produce surpluses."[19]

The anarchic structure of the international system also gives rise to regularities of motive, Benjamin Cohen and other scholars argue, which together produce empire. In a competition among relatively impermeable states (the common metaphor is of billiard balls), each jealously watches the power resources of the others. Each state rationally and identically strives to increase power because each realizes that the international game is a battle of relative weight: to fail to grow is to decline.[20] The characteristic result of this struggle is the balance of power, wherein statesmen register their perceptions of states' strivings and reckon new strategies of competition. Colonies or "colonial peripheries" are states struggling to maximize their independence and security, but they lack the power to resist effectively. Powerful states (metropoles), following implicit rules explained by Morton Kaplan, conquer these (presumably inessential) actors to gain additional resources in the interstate contest over the balance of power.[21]

The idea that there is a structural dynamic of international politics behind modern imperialism draws substantial support from several writers on the historical balance of power. Edward Gulick, for example, considers "compensations"—the acquisition of the territory and people

---

17. Kenneth Waltz, *Theory of International Politics* (Reading, Mass., 1979), p. 37.
18. Ibid., pp. 26–27.
19. Ibid., p. 26.
20. Cohen, chap. 7. Cf. R. Aron, *Peace and War* (New York, 1968), pt. 1, chap. 1.
21. M. Kaplan, *System and Process* (New York, 1957), p. 23.

of smaller, weaker states—to be a normal manifestation of the balance of power.[22] The disappearance of Poland in the eighteenth century, partitioned repeatedly among the stronger Holy Roman Empire, Prussia, and Russia, seems to give some support to his analysis.

Cohen explicitly analyzes nineteenth-century empire, both formal and informal, as the product of a widening gyre of international competition among great powers which required the division of the small and weak powers as compensation. But the systemic view claims to cover a wider range of imperial history. In a most striking interpretation of Athenian imperialism, for example, Jacqueline de Romilly argues that motives and opportunities attributable to the anarchy of the international order are the root causes of imperial expansion.[23] She discusses three laws that governed Athenian imperialism. The first two concern Athenian motives and help account for specific features of Athenian foreign policy. The third law, the philosophical law of the necessity of force, she holds to be both general and immutable. This is the law of the Melian Dialogue (5.84-116): The strong do what they will, the weak what they must. In the course of the war with Sparta, Athens takes a small island (Melos) allied to the Spartans and offers the island's officials a choice between surrender and destruction. Athenian officers explain to the Melians that considerations of justice are not applicable between unequals because the international system leaves only two choices: being dominated or dominating.

Imperial domination, De Romilly tells us in perhaps the purest expression of the power-systemic approach, is a necessary result of relations between powerful and weak states. It is also, in the absence of an international guarantor of order, a legitimate exercise of the natural right of self-defense. Necessary and legitimate, imperial control is nothing more than a direct reflection of differences in international power.

Metropolitan disposition, the balance of power of the systemic realists, the imperialism of free trade, and the liquid frontier of the theorists of the periphery—each claims to identify features at the historical crux of the imperial relationship. Historically, as we shall see, merchants, monopolists, and war machines have clamored for expansion; changing interstate balances called for compensation; frontiers were occasionally expansive, and trade could be imperializing in unstable peripheries. But before we can examine whether any one of these explanations separately,

22. Edward Gulick, *The Classical Balance of Power* (New York, 1955), chaps. 9–11.
23. Jacqueline de Romilly, *Thucydide et l'impérialisme athénien* (Paris, 1947).

TABLE I.
Models of imperial expansion

	Metrocentric	Pericentric	Systemic
Sources	Metropolitan dispositional forces	Reactions in periphery to metropolitan, transnational forces	Metropolitan and peripheral states
Types of actors	Metropolitan dispositions, historically discrete; domestic coalitions, classes	Groups and classes, collaborating and resisting in periphery	States identical in kind differing in degrees of power
Opportunity for expansion	Presence of disposition	Social divisions leading to collaboration and crisis	Large inequality in relative power
Motives	Disposition or coalition specific (profit, political stabilization)	Particular incentives for collaboration and resistance	General; security paramount

or only all of them together, or some of them for some of the time, actually explains the occurrence of empires, we need to examine what an empire means.

Defining Empire

Definitions of empire and imperialism remain important and controversial. I favor the behavioral definition of empire as effective control, whether formal or informal, of a subordinated society by an imperial society. This definition follows popular usage. Neither popular nor scholarly usage is, however, unambiguous about whether empire denotes only territorial conquest and formal legal transfer of sovereignty or includes the informal rule of "effective sovereignty."

The idea of empire as sovereignty controlled either formally or informally by a foreign state informed the work of the founding scholars of international relations and has shaped the literature on empires and imperialism. Imperialism, it is true, retained a connotation of domestic tyranny until the early nineteenth century.[24] Its international implications, however, begin with Thucydides.

Thucydides presents a sophisticated portrait of what Athens actually meant to its subordinated "allies" in the Delian League. The relationship changed when the contributions of the allies became compulsory and withdrawal impossible. Athens' allies, though independent in name, were in fact caught in an empire—a controlled, informal, imperial relationship with Athens.[25] Caesar also emphasized the crucial significance of control rather than colonial boundaries. W. Harris argues that this understanding can be generalized to the Roman empire as a whole, "for the Roman conception of empire, as early as we know anything about it, was a realistic one: they usually thought of it not as being the area covered by the formally annexed provinces, but rather as consisting of all the places over which Rome exercised power."[26]

Both Sir Philip Sidney (in the *Arcadia*, musings upon English rule in Ireland) and Gottfried von Leibniz (in the "Entretiens de Philarète et d'Eugène sur le droit d'ambassade") resolve the issue of empire by

24. See the extensive survey by R. Koebner and H. Schmidt in *Imperialism: The Story and Significance of a Political World* (Cambridge, 1964). For a survey focused on England, see Klaus Knorr, *British Colonial Theories* (1944; Toronto, 1963).

25. Thucydides, *The Peloponnesian War*, trans. Rex Warner (London, 1954), pp. 55, 62–76.

26. Caesar, *The Conquest of Gaul*, trans. S. A. Handford (London, 1951), p. 130, and W. Harris, *War and Imperialism in Republican Rome* (Oxford, 1979), p. 105.

discussing who possesses effective sovereignty.[27] In an important but neglected study published in 1841, *On the Government of Dependencies*, Sir George Cornewall-Lewis, one-time chancellor of the exchequer, home secretary, and secretary of state for war in various Whig-Liberal governments in Britain, distinguished "dependency" from "virtual dependency" but argued that they were both forms of international "domination."[28] During the high point of European imperial rule (from the 1890s to 1939), according to the critical literature, empire was a matter of conquered territory and imperialism a deep disposition of metropolitan society (as in the works of Hobson, Lenin, and Schumpeter). E. M. Winslow, for example, asserted that imperialism is the equivalent of "aggressive nationalism" evinced in the seizure of territory.[29] After World War II, and accompanying decolonization, a wider definition of imperialism came to the fore again, this time identified with "neo-imperialism," "neocolonialism," and that variant of dependencia theory which portrayed dependency as functionally equivalent to the imperial control.[30]

27. Leibniz, *Werke*, 1st ser., 3 (Hanover, 1864), quoted in J. Herz, *International Politics in the Atomic Age* (New York, 1959). Sovereignty exists, Leibniz argues, "So long as one has the right to be master in one's own house . . . and no superior has the right to maintain ordinary garrisons [he seems to imply police forces] and to deprive one of the exercise of his right of peace, war, and alliances. . . ." Empire, for Leibniz, exists when such sovereignty in domestic and foreign policy does not exist. Legal standing is irrelevant; despite the formal independence of certain papal princes, "Should His Holiness desire to make obey the ones [the papal princes], he has merely to send out his *sbirros* (bailiffs), but in order to constrain the others, the truly sovereign, he would need an army and cannon." In short, empire reaches as far as *sbirros*. Independent, by contrast, are those states whose borders one may cross only as an army with cannon. The German princes that Leibniz describes as formally or legally dependent are in military terms masters in their own houses—they are sovereign. For my analysis, the main interest of Leibniz's essay lies in his attention to behavioral rather than legal relationships, and his thesis that it is control (effective sovereignty) that makes or unmakes an empire.

28. Sir George Cornewall-Lewis, *On the Government of Dependencies* (London, 1841), is primarily concerned with the legal nature of dependency in order to explain the odd constitutional position of partially self-governing colonies in the mid-nineteenth century. Lewis does not pretend that law is the sole currency of politics, however, and he considers the case of "virtual dependency": "But although Ireland ceased in 1782 to be legally and in form, it did not cease to be, virtually and in fact, dependent upon Great Britain. The great body of the Irish people continued to be excluded from all effective participation in the exercise of political rights; the country was managed by a native party devoted to the English interest and to the maintenance of the connection with England; and consequently, the government was substantially though covertly, directed by the English influence"(p. 338).

29. E. M. Winslow, *Pattern of Imperialism* (New York, 1948), p. 237.

30. The dependency school covers a large range of views. Sukarno expressed the general perspective well at the first conference of the nonaligned countries at Bandung,

Both before and after the highpoint of European expansion in the late nineteenth century, in sum, empire connoted effective political control. Before that era imperialism also referred to domestic tyranny, and soon after, both in academic and in popular writing, it would come to mean annexationism, as it did for Hobson and Schumpeter.

Contemporary historians debate whether empire is a matter of annexation (formal sovereignty) or of control (effective sovereignty). In 1953 Gallagher and Robinson challenged the view that an age of imperialism (the Scramble for Africa in the 1880s and for Asia in the 1890s) followed a mid-Victorian age of anti-imperialism.[31] Imperialism, they argued, could entertain both formal annexation and informal domination, often by essentially economic means. The first characterized the Scramble; the second, no less imperial, characterized the mid-Victorian period. Their work has shaped continuing controversy among historians. Many now accept their views. Others, however, for example D. C. M. Platt and Winfried Baumgart, maintain a firm and thoroughgoing rejection of the imperialism of free trade thesis.[32] The debate cannot be

---

in 1955: "Colonialism does not just exist in the classic form. . . . It also has a modern dress in the form of economic control, intellectual control, and actual physical control by a small but alien community within the nation." See *Times* (London), 27 May 1955, and A. P. Thornton, *Doctrines of Imperialism* (New York, 1965), p. 4; Thornton says that "the essence of empire is control" (p. 36). See also J. Woodis, *Introduction to Neo-Colonialism* (New York, 1971), p. 56, and A. G. Frank, *Lumpenbourgeoisie: Lumpendevelopment* (New York, 1972), pp. 121–22.

31. Gallagher and Robinson, "Imperialism of Free Trade," pp. 1–25. For a later development of this view see Robinson, "The Non-European Foundations." Much dispute attends whether certain areas (e.g., Latin America) were in fact informally ruled or merely influenced by mutually accepted commercial ties and about the motives of imperial expansion. Nonetheless, the view that empire can be either informal or formal and that its essence in either case is a controlling relationship has won a considerable number of adherents. Perhaps the most significant convert to the importance of informal empire and to the accuracy of the continuity thesis is David Fieldhouse, in his *Economics and Empire.*

32. D. C. M. Platt has criticized Robinson and Gallagher's view that "informal rule" characterized British relations with Latin America and attempts to refute a commercial motivation for imperialism. See his "The Imperialism of Free Trade: Some Reservations," *Economic History Review*, 2d ser. 21 (August 1968), 292–306; "Further Objections to an 'Imperialism of Free Trade' (1830–1860)," ibid. 26 (February 1973), 77–91; and *Finance, Trade, and Politics in British Foreign Policy, 1815–1914* (Oxford, 1968). Hans Ulrich Wehler discussing German imperialism and Walter LaFeber (*The New Empire* [Ithaca, 1963]) discussing American imperialism accept the existence of informal and formal aspects of imperial rule. Winfried Baumgart, *Imperialism: The Idea and Reality of British and French Colonial Expansion* (New York, 1982), p. 7, adheres to the annexationist definition, pointing out that informal imperialism lacks any boundaries that could separate imperialism from influence. So does R. Zevin, who chose "rights of sovereignty" for his

resolved historiographically, for tradition supports both "control" and other definitions of empire. What are the analytical reasons for choosing a concept of empire which includes both formal and informal control?

Political control as a criterion of empire precludes neither empire considered as formal territorial conquest nor relations that have all the features of conquest but lack a conqueror's flag. Only control guarantees that the acquisition of territory has real meaning. In the 1880s Egypt and princely India were legally owned, respectively, by Turkey and the Indian princes as suzerains; Britain controlled both. Canada, on the other hand, became a dominion in 1867, but it was little dominated. If the acquisition of territory implies control, as most writers seem to intend, then control should be the subject of our analysis.

A concentration on political control or effective sovereignty does not prejudge the sources of empire, as do many dispositional definitions, or define imperialism without reference to empire.[33] One would hardly find useful studies of militarism that did not examine wars. Similarly, a definition of imperialism that does not test whether imperialism actually led to the postulated outcome, empires, is not acceptable. Defining imperialism as the disposition (such as monopoly capitalism) that purportedly causes it risks creating a simple tautology, not an explanation. And "international exploitation," another candidate for explanation, presupposes political control (but exploitation does not necessarily follow from that control).[34] Yet political control is narrower than international inequality, because inequality can cover relations between independent states that have no connection with one another (such as, say, England and Siam in the fifteenth century).[35]

definition in "An Interpretation of American Imperialism," *Journal of Economic History* 32 (March 1972), 319.

33. Identifying an empire, or imperialism, as a disposition creates a strong tendency toward circular reasoning. If imperialism is the *objectless* disposition to expand, as Schumpeter argued it was, and if empires are identified by territorial conquests lacking concrete *objects*, we have a tautology.

34. If empire and imperialism are defined as policies directed toward certain *ends*, whether "exploitation" or "civilization," the scope of imperial activity becomes unduly narrow or broad. Both ends are often better, or more easily, pursued at home. Many empires have brought neither; even exploitation, particularly if interpreted in an economic light, can be ambiguous—equivalent labor values have little meaning when technologies differ more in kind than in degree. What labor value could a commodity based on a completely different technology have?

35. Johan Galtung, "A Structural Theory of Empire," *Journal of Peace Research* 8, 2 (1971), 81-117, sets up international inequality (differences in gross national product per capita among interdependent economies) as the defining variable of empire. Unlike territory, inequality touches upon the content of an imperial relationship, specifically its

Not every form of international power can be defined as imperialism; we need to specify clearly what political control means. Otherwise, as William Langer noted: "If imperialism is to mean any vague reference to traders and bankers in the affairs of other countries, you may as well extend it to cover any form of influence. You will have to admit cultural imperialism, religious imperialism, and what not. I prefer to stick by a measurable, manageable concept."[36]

A definition of control is thus difficult to achieve. Where might imperial control fit in the conceptual catalogue of international relations? How might we avoid an assimilation of all forms of international inequality or influence into "imperialism"?

Imperial control is one form of the exercise of asymmetrical influence and power. Influence, according to Robert Dahl, can be manifest or implicit. "If A wants outcome x; if A acts with the intention of causing B to bring about x; and if as a result of A's actions, B attempts to bring about x, then A exercises *manifest* influence over B." On the other hand, "If A wants outcome x, then although A does not act with the intention of causing B to bring about x, if A's desire for x causes B to attempt to bring about x, then A exercises *implicit* influence over B." Power is a subset of influence. It can be considered the ability of the powerful actor to achieve effects that the influenced actor would not choose to have occur.[37]

Power is specific to situations. Differing "clusters" of situations, most observers agree, separate domestic from international politics and sep-

---

unbalanced character. But it is not clear that in his correlations of GNP Galtung has found the best indicator of imperial inequality. He cannot distinguish externally, imperially induced inequality from internally, peripherally, and self-induced inequality. In addition, he has to meet the problem of economically equal but politically unequal imperial relationships. An unintended but significant irony of his definition of imperialism is that an economic depression in the metropole could itself "lessen" imperialism. Galtung's economic variable provides something closer to a related symptom than to either a sign or a description of the nature of the imperial relationship.

36. William L. Langer, "Critique of Imperialism,"*Foreign Affairs* 14 (October 1935), 103. The indeterminancy of "power" as a definition of empire led Baumgart to reject informal imperialism and choose formal imperialism (annexation of territory) as the appropriate definition. But this choice led to equally ambiguous formulations about protectorates and spheres of influence, which Baumgart calls instances of "partial imperialism" (*Imperialism*, p. 8).

37. Robert Dahl, citing Jack Nagel's *The Descriptive Analysis of Power* (New Haven, 1975), in *Modern Political Analysis* (Englewood Cliffs, 1976), pp. 30–31. See also B. Barry,"An Economic Approach to the Analysis of Power and Conflict," *Government and Opposition* 9 (Spring 1974), 189–223.

arate diplomacy, interdependence, dependence, sphere of influence, hegemony, and empire one from another. An imperial cluster—amounting to foreign control over effective sovereignty—can be specified by contrasting its use of influence and power with that of the conventional categories of domestic and international politics. The five dimensions of contrast are domain, the population affected; scope, the types of behavior influenced; range, of rewards and punishments; weight, or effectiveness; and duration.[38]

Empires seem to combine aspects of both domestic and international politics. Along these five dimensions we seek what distinguishes empire from both sorts of politics. The typical conception of a domestic political system consists of first, a government, resting ultimately on the ability to exercise effective violence; second, a degree of community among individuals which permits a definition of what is acceptable; third, a society that creates habits among the population which form the basis for communication; and fourth, an economy that provides material incentives for social interaction. The domain of a domestic order is thus the individual and his or her relations to the polity. Those relations draw on interests and values shared in an economy, a society, and a cultural community, and the individuals together comprise a self-identified, separate people.[39]

Unlike the domestic order, which is characterized by the integration of its components, the international system is best understood by the independence of its elements—the states. Extreme versions portray the state in the international system as a billiard ball, an almost completely self-contained and "total" state that fully integrates polity, economy, society, and culture. Subjects or citizens of different states rarely meet except on the battlefield, and international contact is made by diplomats and soldiers.[40] More complex versions of this understanding consider international trade, travel, and culture as links between societies across national boundaries, creating ties of interdependence.[41]

38. K. Deutsch, *The Analysis of International Relations* (Englewood Cliffs, 1968), chaps. 3–4.

39. See, for general sources, Dahl, *Modern Political Analysis*; T. Parsons and E. Shils, eds., *Toward a General Theory of Action* (New York, 1951), p. 55; and R. Collins, "A Comparative Approach to Political Sociology," in R. Bendix, ed., *State and Society* (Berkeley, 1968).

40. This is often termed the Hobbesian approach.

41. J. J. Rousseau, *A Lasting Peace*, trans. C. Vaughan (London, 1917), pp. 46–47. See Stanley Hoffmann, *Gulliver's Troubles* (New York, 1968), for a modern, Rousseauesque reading of the international system. For Kant's views, see Immanuel Kant, *Perpetual*

With the domestic order, societies in an empire share the characteristic of individuals effectively subject to a single sovereign—the imperial government. With the international order, societies in an empire share the characteristic of a less-than-full integration of social interaction and cultural values—the imperial government is a sovereignty that lacks a community. Moreover, unlike both confederations and federations, the imperial state is not organized on the basis of political equality among societies or individuals.[42] The domain of empire is a people subject to unequal rule. One nation's government determines who rules another society's political life.

Domain distinguishes the relational aspect, the who and whom, of empire, separating domestic from international and imperial from both. Scope, range, and weight consider the actions under control, what is controlled and by what means.

The scope of imperial control involves the political processes and the political outcomes controlled by the metropole. Machiavelli posed the classic choice for an imperial metropole: "When those states which have

---

Peace, trans. Carl Friedrich (New York, 1949); Michael Doyle, "Kant, Liberal Legacies, and Foreign Affairs," 2 pts., *Philosophy and Public Affairs* 12 (June 1983 and October 1983); F. H. Hinsley, *Power and the Pursuit of Peace* (London, 1967), chap. 6, and K. Waltz, *Man, the State, and War* (New York, 1959), chap. 4. For the transnational approach see R. Keohane and J. Nye, eds., *Transnationalism and World Politics* (Cambridge, Mass., 1972), and their *Power and Interdependence* (Boston, 1977).

42. Regions have united under special conditions into confederations and federations, which also mix the domestic and the international. In the confederal solution, regional governments devolve authority on a central government in explicitly limited subject areas, such as defense and other, usually external matters, retaining a large portion of domestic decision making within their own jurisdictions. Federal unions, conversely, dissolve state sovereignty. Alexander Hamilton, in the *Federalist*, no. 15 (New York, 1937), p. 89, described the major difference between the confederal and federal: "The great and radical evil in the construction of the existing confederation is in the principle of *Legislation* for *States* or *Governments*, in their *Corporate* or *Collective Capacities*, and as contra-distinguished from the *individuals* of which they consist." Federal authority thus is joint and equal (independent) in a system where both domestic and foreign political functions become shared; confederal authority leaves the confederal government dependent on the states (cf. K. C. Wheare, *Federal Government* [New York, 1964], pp. 33, 54). But political expansion seems generally to have resisted cooperative extension (see H. Arendt, *The Origins of Totalitarianism* [Cleveland, 1958], pp. 126–27). Decision, unlike wheat, electricity, and heating oil, does not appear to be a fungible good, and in attempts to go beyond the nation-state, to create supranationality, the nation has proved to be both "obstinate and obsolete." It persists as the point of identification and decision, whether because of pure institutional self-preservation or because of its ability to redefine public problems as problems it can manage (see Stanley Hoffmann, "Obstinate or Obsolete," in J. Nye, ed., *International Regionalism* [Boston, 1968]). Empires seek to overcome this reluctance, establishing uncooperative extensions of sovereignty which share much less solidarity than is characteristic of federations.

been acquired are accustomed to live at liberty under their own laws, there are three ways of holding them. The first is to despoil them; the second is to go and live there in person; the third is to allow them to live under their own laws, taking tribute of them, and creating within the country a government composed of a few who will keep it friendly to you."[43] A comparison of formal empire ("living there in person") with informal empire (a "friendly" government) illustrates what is controlled and how control is exercised in each relationship.

The formal control of the effective sovereignty of a subordinate society involves controlling its political decision making, a complex process with many points of influence. The social, economic, and cultural environments of the metropole penetrate those of the periphery through metropolitan forces and actors—missionaries, merchants, soldiers, bureaucrats.[44] These actors shape peripheral demands or tastes and influence the content of domestic coalitions, classes, factions, and parties in the periphery. Some decisions can be made by "men on the spot" (the colonial bureaucrats and the colonial governor) according to established colonial precedent; others call for a decision from the metropolitan government. The decision made, the colonial bureaucrats then do what they can both to assemble support for and to implement the decision. Implementation may involve adjudication in colonial courts and, perhaps, formal appeal to metropolitan courts.[45]

Effective control of peripheral sovereignty need not require a colonial governor with all the trappings of formal imperialism. If enough of the articulation of interests in a peripheral state can be influenced, the aggregation of coalitions will be controlled; and if aggregation is thoroughly shaped, sovereign decisions will be controlled. Influence over implementation or adjudication or communication is roughly equivalent to influence over the aggregation or articulation of interests, since the

---

43. Machiavelli, "The Prince," in *The Prince and The Discourses*, trans. L. Ricci (New York, 1950), chap. 5, p. 18.

44. Penetration is the "effective presence of a *central government* [here imperial government] throughout a territory (and thus over the people inhabiting it) over which it pretends to exercise control." Penetration in this sense is control, the probability that the peripheral polity will conform to public policy enunciated by the metropolitan polity. See J. LaPalombara, "Penetration," in L. Binder et al., *Crises and Sequences in Political Development* (Princeton, 1972), pp. 206, 220, 227.

45. This is a modification of a governmental process model presented by G. Almond and G. Powell, *Comparative Politics: A Developmental Approach* (Boston, 1966), pp. 29–30.

first form of influence controls which policies can be carried out.[46] The result is informal imperial control.

Historical practice is even more complex. Peripheries exert return influence on the metropole.[47] Imperial rule over the periphery, moreover, even when formally conducted by imperial bureaucrats, requires a degree of peripheral collaboration.[48] When only the lower levels of the imperial bureaucracy are manned by "natives" of the periphery (clerks in the civilian branch, soldiers in the imperial army or police) historians of empire term the result direct (formal) rule. When the governance of extensive districts of the colony is entrusted to members of the native elite under the supervision of imperial governors, the result is indirect (formal) rule.[49]

Informal imperialism can thus effect the same results as formal imperialism; the difference lies in the process of control, which informal imperialism achieves through the collaboration of a legally independent (but actually subordinate) government in the periphery. The closer the control over actual decisions, the more efficient will foreign penetration be; alternatively, the further from the decision point that one attempts to exert influence over the decision, the larger will be the range of factors that must be controlled.[50]

Controlling influence is exemplified in the strategy of blockade which

46. Informal but effective forms of control are discussed as "setting limits" by G. Murphy, "On Satelliteship," *Journal of Economic History* 21 (December 1961), 641-51. The more general case for considering both articulation and nonarticulation (suppression) can be found in P. Bachrach and M. Baratz, "Two Faces of Power," *American Political Science Review* 56 (December 1962), 947-52.

47. Bernard Bailyn described this more complicated scheme of colonial influence: "Colonial politics operated at two levels, the level of the provincial governments and the level of the central government at 'home'; and it was the latter—more distant, less palpable, less predictable—that was more important. Americans had learned to live with this fact very early in their political history. By the mid-eighteenth century, a stable pattern of informal communications had emerged, linking political forces in America directly to the political forces in England capable of overturning decisions taken in the colonies by the resident executive." See "The Origins of American Politics," *Perspectives in American History* 1 (1967), pp. 69-70.

48. Robinson, "The Non-European Foundations." On related motives in a more general case of "patronal leadership" see K. Knorr, *Power and Wealth* (New York, 1973), pp. 26-27.

49. The classic source for the distinction between direct and indirect rule and policy is Lord Lugard, *Dual Mandate in British Tropical Africa*, 5th ed. (London, 1965), chap. 10, "Methods of Ruling Native Races." For French colonial policy see Robert Delavignette, *Service africain* (Paris, 1946).

50. G. Roth, "Personal Rulership, Patrimonialism, and Empire Building in the New States," in Bendix, pp. 581-91.

is based upon the concept of total control of the economic environment, and in the meddling ambassador, who can become the de facto governor of a weak polity through his control of aggregation and implementation. In the nineteenth century the blockade was frequently employed for informal imperial control against small African states. In the twentieth century the Nazis used *aski* marks and trade subsidies to control the economic environment of southeastern Europe.[51] The controlling ambassador can be found in the nineteenth century in the persons of Consul John Kirk and his dominance of the nominally independent state of Zanzibar and of Evelyn Baring (Earl Cromer) and his rule of Egypt.

Imperial control involves not only a process but also outputs or outcomes. In formal imperialism the outcomes are not in doubt: because the metropole controls the political institutions of the periphery, empire is as imperialism does. Both internal and external policies—treaties, alliances, decisions on war and peace, foreign trade and monetary relations, together with policies concerning taxation, education, transportation, coinage, commerce, and police—provide evidence of imperial control in their very creation by imperial bureaucrats. The metropole controls what is done and who does it.

But how can one distinguish the collaboration of a nominally independent but actually subordinate peripheral government from the cooperation of an independent ally? The material economic gain to the metropole and loss to the periphery which result from policies imposed upon the periphery provide no adequate measure of imperialism. Peripheral collaboration will need to be paid for, and so we cannot expect a zero-sum relationship. Moreover, relative economic gains by the metropole do not rule out cooperation by the periphery, nor do relative economic gains made by the periphery necessarily indicate cooperation; many schemes of cooperation, after all, yield differential returns.

American colonial experience suggests labels for two signs that together serve to identify actual control of policy outcomes. One concentrates on design, the other on resistance.

"Jefferson's Rule" is that empire can be identified by a "long train of abuses" that "evince a design" to make or keep one country subject to another. The object is distinctly political even though the means of exercising influence may be economic or cultural. Jefferson's examples included controlling western lands (America's economic future), regulating trade and shipping, appointing unrepresentative governors, a lack

51. A. Hirschman, *National Power and the Structure of Foreign Trade* (Berkeley, 1945), chap. 3.

of colonial representation in imperial policy, quartering troops, and arbitrarily interfering with the exercise of local justice.[52]

"Patrick Henry's Rule" holds that "Caesar had his Brutus, Charles the first, his Cromwell; and George the Third . . . may profit by their example." Imperial tyranny often results in widespread political resistance. In formal empires resistance leads to police actions or the replacement of rebellious collaborators. In informal empires it leads to indirect constraints (threats of embargoes, blockades, etc.) or to military intervention. A successful response to peripheral resistance is a sign of effective imperialism, and effective empires control (constitute or can change) the political regime of the periphery.[53]

A final useful distinction is between imperialism and hegemony. Reflecting important differences in world politics, the analytical separation of foreign policy from domestic policy helps define imperial outcomes. Control of both foreign and domestic policy characterizes empire; control of only foreign policy, hegemony.[54] Thucydides first drew this distinction, noting that Sparta's "allies," despite their subjection to Spartan hegemony during the Peloponnesian War, exercised a considerable degree of domestic autonomy—unlike the imperialized "allies" subject to Athens.

In sum, the scope of imperial control involves both the process of control and its outcomes. Control is achieved either formally (directly or indirectly) or informally through influence over the periphery's environment, political articulation, aggregation, decision making, adjudication, and implementation, and usually with the collaboration of local peripheral elites. The scope of the outcomes covers both internal and external issues—who rules and what rules. Hegemony, by contrast, denotes control over external policy alone.

The weight of power is measured by the probability of achieving a desired outcome. The range of power is the difference between the greatest possible reward and the worst possible punishment. Tradition-

---

52. Jefferson's remarks are, of course, drawn from the U.S. Declaration of Independence, an early and thorough exposition of the behavioral significance of imperialism.

53. Patrick Henry's remark comes from his "Speech on the Stamp Act, 1765," in William Wirt, *Patrick Henry, Life, Correspondence, and Speeches* (New York, 1891), p. 86.

54. James Kurth in his 1972 paper develops a concept of hegemony that mixes foreign and domestic control. Other more current uses of hegemony employ the word to mean controlling leadership of the international system as a whole. See Robert Gilpin, *War and Change in World Politics* (New York, 1981), and Robert Keohane, "Theory of World Politics: Structural Realism and Beyond," in Ada Finifter, ed., *Political Science: The State of the Discipline* (Washington, D.C., 1983).

ally, as Karl Deutsch notes, marrying the king's daughter and being decapitated were the extremes. Today's range of influence, as Brian Barry argues, includes the activation of commitments already made ("cashing in on moral principles"), persuasion, coercion (positive or negative—bribing, compelling, or deterring), and physical force.[55]

Within the domestic order the weight of power is enormous and the range is wide. Kings' daughters and decapitations are rarer than they once were, but the pervasive integration of polity, economy, society, and culture assures high rewards and devastating penalties in the exercise of state power over individuals. The community usually defines law abiding as a cardinal virtue. Political legitimacy is supported by the ability of the state and society to educate, to reward compliance economically, and to punish disobedience. This power is weighty for three reasons: first, it is cheap, relying mostly on moral force; second, the resources of the rebellious individual are generally small; third, the resources of the state are enormous, for they include the power of all, a power to which even the current rebel has in the past contributed.

International power carries much less weight, largely because its range is less extensive and subsystems are not so closely integrated. The statesman who fails to comply with the demand of a foreign leader will not experience much guilt nor be subject to very persuasive criticism. Coercion is possible, of course, but to the extent that the economic subsystem has some degree of autonomy or is itself interdependent with the other state's economy, coercion will lose its effectivenesses. Similarly, rewards are smaller. Foreign praise and international virtue in keeping promises are thin reeds, and even though cooperation is often more desirable than conflict, the main reward is peace — benign neglect. International power thus has less weight: coercion and force are costly, the resources of the assailed statesman tend to be large, and the resources of the assailant state are often not that much larger than those of the assailed. (The last point is especially important in light of the traditional three-to-one preponderance required for successful attack.)[56]

The range of imperial power occupies a middle ground, wider than international power but narrower than domestic power. Persuasion is

55. Barry, "Economic Approach to the Analysis of Power."

56. Though the international system appears to share these characteristics, the openness of political regimes to foreign penetration varies, as R. Cottam, *Competitive Interference and World Politics* (Pittsburgh, 1967), chap. 2, notes; and for another analysis of varying political penetrability Machiavelli's argument on the "prince and his barons" contrasted to the "prince with his servants" in *Prince*, chap. 4.

important as crucial collaborators begin to accept metropolitan values, and the Mister Johnsons of Africa, the Thomas Hutchinsons of colonial America, and the zamindars of India soon come to regard the public policy of the imperialists as both "civilized" and "correct." If they have doubts, the metropole has means by which to bribe and coerce individuals directly. Should these arts fail, gunboats are ever ready to supplement their shortcomings, and force can be exercised directly on the subject population.

The weight of imperial power should also be expected to lie in between, less than domestic, more than international. Persuasion and coercion are likely to be its most effective modes because they render force often unnecessary to achieve aims. Using less of expensive force for a given end, imperial power is likely to be more efficient than international power. Although imperial power lacks the influence of shared commitments, the resources of assailed individuals are extraordinarily small: they face the power of the imperial state without their own independent state for protection, and they cannot even rely on the mercy and justice that sometimes tempers power in the communal domestic order. Finally, the imperial state draws upon the resources of both the peripheral society and the metropolitan society for its power, exceeding the national resources of a state in the international system.

Imperial power is likely to be weighty. Challenged by the heavy demands of mastering the decision making of the peripheral polity, it acquires substantial advantages from its special domain—a transnational and asymmetrical influence wielded over individuals. If mastering control over the political system of the periphery requires considerable resources, the peripheral society once mastered can generate substantial resources for the imperial metropole.

Differing weights of power distinguish imperial control from suzerainty and dependence. Having already encountered the form with the reality (in formal empires) and the reality without the form (in informal empires), we should not be surprised to find the form without the reality. In suzerainty the metropole's power lacks weight in much the same way as a feudal sovereign's political power over feudal vassals would often lack effect.[57] Sovereign decisions in the periphery are completed before

---

57. Many feudal "empires" were thus suzerainties, the king being unable to determine either who ruled (due to hereditary office or fief) or what ruled (local traditions and the interests of the local ruling elite determined these issues). But some monarchical states and many aristocratic societies did establish empires, some of which are examined in John Kautsky, *The Politics of Aristocratic Empires* (Chapel Hill, 1982). Kautsky's work also

the imperial decision, making the latter an automatic ratification. Both the metropole's legitimacy and its ability to extract and thus distribute resources have been attenuated. From the narrower perspective of the political subsystem, those factors which formerly maintained the imperial political system—the metropole-directed articulation and aggregation of interests—have come under the control of the independent periphery. Whichever way we put it, a suzerain rules by form and in form alone.

Some scholars equate dependence with imperial control, but in doing so they lose important distinctions in world politics. Dependence can best be identified as constraint, or unequal influence, produced, for example, when an international division of labor relegates raw material production, less advanced manufacturing, and low income to the periphery; advanced industrial manufacturing and high income to the core. The process of dependence makes economic growth and social change in the periphery sensitive and vulnerable to changes or restrictions emanating from the core because prices, technologies, capital, and patterns of consumption generated in the core shape the development of the periphery without the periphery being able to control these external forces. Mechanisms of dependence are both external (constraining trade, financial, and technological dependence) and internal (sustaining dependent, comprador classes).[58]

Imperial control also involves unequal sensitivities and vulnerabilities. But it can be distinguished from dependent constraint by examining the outcome of peripheral resistance (Patrick Henry's Rule). Does the metropole (core or world economy) impose costs only on dissidence and divergence, or, ultimately, does it also employ force successfully against

---

covers many political societies, such as feudal France between 850 and 1100 (p. 29), which are not empires by the definition I employ here (since the effective writ of the king often did not extend beyond the Ile de France during that period).

58. For a sampling of the many types of dependency theory, see A. G. Frank, *Lumpenbourgeoisie,* and *Capitalism and Underdevelopment in Latin America* (New York, 1967); Suzanne Bodenheimer, "Dependency and Imperialism: The Roots of Latin American Underdevelopment," and Theotonio dos Santos, "The Structure of Dependence," both in K. T. Fann and D. C. Hodges, eds., *Readings in U.S. Imperialism* (Boston, 1971); Paul Baran, *The Political Economy of Growth,* 2d ed. (New York, 1967); Samir Amin, *Accumulation on a World Scale* (New York, 1974); F. Cardoso and E. Faletto, *Dependency and Development in Latin America* (Berkeley, 1979); and Peter Evans, *Dependent Development* (Princeton, 1979). Some authors stress the stagnation of the periphery (Baran, Frank) and others that dependence permits growth (Cardoso, Evans), but all share in the three features mentioned in the text. The debate over *dependencia* also raises a host of methodological disputes, for which see a special issue of *International Organization* 32 (Winter 1978).

TABLE 2.
Weight and scope of power

	Scope of power (output)	
Weight of power	Foreign and domestic policy	Foreign policy
Control	Empire (formal and informal)	Hegemony
Constraint unequal influence	Dependence	Sphere of influence
Equal influence	Interdependence	Independence, diplomacy

resistance to guarantee control of the periphery's effective sovereignty? These distinctions, it is true, still leave areas of ambiguity, including economic domination so effective that it is never resisted or that attempts to break away cause economic dislocation so severe that they force the delinking periphery to "choose" to rejoin the dependent-imperial fold. Forceful rebellions, both failing and successful, against foreign constraints are so frequent, however, that such "silent" economic empires can be expected to be rare occurrences. Imperfect as these distinctions are, they appear to be preferable to making no distinctions at all between empire and dependence and to limiting our investigation of empire to cases of formal rule.

The unequal influence of dependence can also be distinguished from the equal influence of interdependence. Interdependence, like dependence (but unlike a sphere of influence or independent diplomatic interaction), signifies transnational interactions that affect domestic as well as foreign policy. But in a condition of interdependence the outcomes of bargaining are balanced overall, with particular victories determined by asymmetrical intensities of preference or of attention, and not by unequal vulnerability or coercion.[59]

International political inequality is a continuum, ranging from diplomacy or interdependence through some middle ground of substantial foreign constraint in dependence or sphere of influence to imperial or hegemonial control.[60] If we are to attempt an explanation of any one of

59. This sort of investigation has been done by Keohane and Nye, *Power and Interdependence*, chap. 7.

60. Robert Dahl in *Polyarchy* (New Haven, 1971), pp. 190–92, draws similar distinctions among influence, "constraint," and "outright foreign domination."

these three possibilities, we need benchmarks to distinguish among them. Clearly the differences do not lie in mechanisms of influence: economic means, for example, can be and are employed to establish control, to constrain, and to bargain. They lie in the dimensions of power. Imperial control is distinguished by its domain. It controls the lives of individuals without necessarily sharing their values. It is also distinguished by its scope. It engages in politics, not merely in war or diplomacy. The agents of empire shape, formally or informally, the political life of the subordinate periphery. Those agents control both the domestic and the foreign issues that affect the populations subject to imperial rule. In governing those populations, they employ a range of rewards and punishments considerably beyond those of conventional international relations. They thereby achieve more weight than influence or constraint; they control effective sovereignty. Empire, moreover, is distinguished by duration.

How long must imperial control be exercised before an empire exists? The question is not merely one of glory, it involves a behavioral distinction suggested by the differences between a stickup and slavery. If one's concern is to control a periphery, one needs to determine whether the periphery's acquiescence is a temporary tactic adopted by an independent polity or a surrender, however reluctant, to foreign control. The former includes temporary occupations; it is the latter relationship—measured perhaps as a political generation of ten to twenty years—that identifies the entities we call empires.[61]

Empire, then, is a relationship, formal or informal, in which one state controls the effective political sovereignty of another political society. It can be achieved by force, by political collaboration, by economic, social, or cultural dependence. Imperialism is simply the process or policy of establishing or maintaining an empire.

These definitions are more significant than they might at first seem. They distinguish empires from the rest of world politics by the actual foreign control of who rules and what rules a subordinate polity. They imply that to explain the existence of empire, or a particular empire, one must first demonstrate the existence of control; second, explain why

61. A related emphasis on duration appears in Moses Finley's definition of empire: "There have been throughout history structures that belong within a single class on substantive grounds, namely, the exercise of authority (or power or control) by one state over one or more states (or communities or peoples) for an extended period of time." Finley, "The Athenian Empire: A Balance Sheet," in Brent Shaw and Richard Saller, eds., *Economy and Society in Ancient Athens* (New York, 1981), p. 42.

one party expands and establishes such control; and third, explain why the other party submits or fails to resist effectively.

Hobson, Lenin, and Schumpeter attempted only the second of these three steps, implying that the periphery is a cipher and that only a disposition on the part of a metropole is needed to explain and account for the historical instances of empire. Historians of the periphery often write as if metropolitan transnational forces form a steady background to crises determined by actors in the periphery. The international system theorists of power argue that both the dominant and the subordinate actors must be included in an explanation of empire, but they also hold that actors differ only in degree of power—both are strategic actors (states) acting to maximize their relative power and security. This book examines these various explanations against the historical experience of empires. It is organized in two main parts.

The first part examines the social and political conditions that explain the phenomenon of empire and that provide reasons for the rise and fall of empires. It focuses on two fundamental questions to distinguish empire from the diplomacy and war of regular international politics. Why are some political societies ruled by imperial metropoles when other political societies effectively resist? Why do some states create empires over their weaker neighbors when others remain isolated at home? I shall argue that none of the established models adequately explains the variety of historical empires. Rather, four interacting sources account for the imperial relationship: the metropolitan regime, its capacities and interests; the peripheral political society, its interests and weakness; the transnational system and its needs; and the international context and the incentives it creates. A survey of ancient and early modern empires provides the historical evidence on which the argument rests.

The second part explores the processes—the forces and forms—of imperialism and imperial rule which shaped the nineteenth-century European empires. Focusing on the Scramble for Africa, it portrays the operation of metrocentric, pericentric, transnational, and systemic forces in imperialism, examining in each case the relative weight of economic and strategic factors. Political weakness in the periphery led to collapse and collaboration, and the sources of this weakness can be traced to characteristics of tribal and patrimonial societies. By way of counter-example, Ethiopia successfully resisted imperial conquest and Argentina, while economically dependent, did not become a subordinate part of empire. I shall discuss the international systemic context and its effects on the competition for empire, as well as the driving motives and the resources generated by Britain's transnational economy and metropolitan politics. A survey of the imperialisms of France and Germany includes as a counterexample the metropolitan sources of Spain's imperial collapse. These separate strands, when woven together, account for the accelerated expansion of formal empire that characterized the Scramble for Africa.

Empires have been with mankind for millennia. The conclusion discusses imperial development and one possible end to empire, decolonization.

PART I

HISTORICAL
SOCIOLOGY
OF EMPIRES

CHAPTER 2

Introduction to Part I

Empires are relationships of political control over a people. Control usually originates with a state, though control can be established, if rarely, by some nonstate body, such as a religious order or a corporation.[1] Control exists in and is defined by its behavioral effects on those who are controlled. It is this control that must be explained. Part I of this book is designed to explain why empire have arisen, why some empires persisted longer than others, and why empires have fallen. I attempt sociological answers to the question of what produces control by specifying what conditions must be present for control to exist.

From the time of Sumer and the ancient Egyptian and Chinese empires, imperial control stretches through history, many say, to the present day. "Empires," in the dramatic phrasing of Irwin St. John Tucker, "are as old as history itself. When the misty curtain first parts for us upon that stage whereon the drama of life is played, emperors occupy the center of the scene. They have held the leading role ever since."[2] Before equal states could meet and communicate, the larger and more powerful absorbed their weaker neighbors, expanding until they were

1. Such nonstate bodies in effect act as states. Examples include the East India Company and the Jesuit order in Paraguay during the eighteenth century.
2. Irwin St. John Tucker, *A History of Imperialism* (New York, 1920), p. 5.

themselves absorbed or met an equal.[3] Almost every people has expanded imperially at one time or another—and has also been imperially controlled at some period in its history.

The three major models of imperialism claim to account for the continuing appearance of empires. In metropolitan disposition, peripheral collapse, or straightforward differences in international power between any two international actors, each model purports to explain empires. None does so satisfactorily.

Empire, I shall show, is a product of a special interaction between the forces and institutions of a metropole and the forces and institutions of a periphery. Imperial control, however, is not a bilateral relationship suspended in a political vacuum. Transnational agents—metropolitan merchants, for example, or missionaries—often take on a role significant in shaping the particular content of each imperial rule (whence commercial or messianic imperialisms). I also examine, more fundamentally, whether some transnational connection is needed to establish or maintain imperial rule. Nor is transnationalism the only point at issue; similarly, the international system frequently influences the character of imperial rule. I shall be inquiring whether international competition is a necessary aspect of imperialism, necessary in the sense that empires are a direct or indirect result of geopolitical competition (the balance of power).

Which of these connections is necessary, which merely contributory in explaining the existence of empire? How do empires differ from one another—why are some formal and others informal? How do empires change—rise, persist, and fall? These questions constitute, in a sense much less ambitious than their natural science referents, the statics, comparative statics, and dynamics of imperialism.[4]

The general statics of empires will not account for the particular importance of a factor in a specific case or tell us why a particular leader acted in the way he or she did. Neither can the general features of comparative statics fully illuminate the subtler differences in the forms that imperialisms take.[5] Nor will general aspects of imperial dynamics fully explain a sudden acceleration in the rate of imperial expansion.

3. See S. N. Eisenstadt, *The Political Systems of Empires* (New York, 1968), and Adda P. Bozeman, *Politics and Culture in International History* (Princeton, 1960), for arguments concerning the origins of interstate relations.

4. See J. Bhagwati, "The Pure Theory of International Trade," *Economic Journal* 74 (March 1964), 1–84.

5. Cf. Voltaire's warning to historians: "In talking of a nation, one must consider how she seemed under a particular government, in a particular year. . . ." Voltaire, *Histoire de Charles XII* (1731; Paris, 1968), p. 32.

Nonetheless, the more general features of the imperial relationship described by statics do help us understand similar sources among empires. Comparative statics help us explain widely shared differences. Both statics and comparative statics shape the evolution of imperial development. They can be employed to address the general issues of rates of growth and the timing of imperial expansion or decline.[6] They can help us identify features that tend to encourage imperial expansion or imperial decline. But empires slowly grow or quickly accelerate, persist more or less, and slowly decline or rapidly fall. One must therefore be prepared to find different sources, or combinations of sources, associated with each of these different outcomes.

Part I begins an argument about the statics of imperialism. At the same time it draws on more general insights from comparative statics and dynamics, insights that explain the forms empires take and the sources of imperial decline and fall. These arguments rest on a conspectus of a wide variety of empires, ranging from Athens in the fifth century B.C. through Rome and the Ottoman empire to Spain and England and the other early modern empires from the sixteenth to the eighteenth centuries.[7]

This conspectus addresses four main questions: What conditions appear to make an empire possible? What conditions support the expansion of empire? What conditions support imperial maintenance? What conditions lead toward the destruction of imperial control?

6. For an example of this sort of analysis applied to historical changes in the regulation of the international system—the rise and decline of systemic hegemons—see Robert Gilpin, *War and Change in World Politics* (New York, 1982).

7. M. I. Finley suggested that this group of empires is particularly appropriate for comparative investigation because they are all preindustrial and yet literate and commercial (see "Anthropology and the Classics," in his *The Use and Abuse of History* [New York, 1975], p. 119). There may have been earlier empires (Sumerian, Egyptian, Hittite, Assyrian, Chinese, etc.), but surviving records are ambiguous on whether the behavior of these states was political or merely religious with no perceived political significance. See B. J. Kemp, "Imperialism and Empire in New Kingdom Egypt," in P. D. A. Garnsey and C. R. Whittaker, eds., *Imperialism in the Ancient World* (Cambridge, 1978).

CHAPTER 3

Athens and Sparta:
Empire and Hegemony

In the *History of the Peloponnesian War*, Thucydides explains the origins and the outcome of the great war that divided the Greeks. He describes it as a contest between two unequal alliances, the Delian League headed by Athens and the Peloponnesian League headed by Sparta.[1] The first I shall argue was an empire; the second, a hegemony. The history begins with the mobilization of Sparta's hegemonic alliance to meet the preeminent power of the Athenian empire and ends with the slow fall of the Athenian empire to final defeat as Athens' overseas possessions revolt and the city breaks apart in civil war. (Incomplete, the history does not cover the final disasters.)

Thucydides compares two political coalitions—Athens' empire and Sparta's hegemony—and he sets forth cogent and clear reasons for their growth and decline (their dynamics). But we have to infer from his history the general conditions that make empire possible and influence its character, the statics and comparative statics of empire and hegemony. Before examining the general conditions that can help account for the existence and particular character of Athens' empire and Sparta's hegemony, I propose to follow Thucydides by describing the two coalitions and by reviewing his explanation for their growth.

1. Thucydides, *History of the Peloponnesian War*, trans. Rex Warner (London, 1954). Subsequent references are to this edition, and most are given in the text.

Athenian Empire

Thucydides relates the origin of the Athenian empire in a long digression. The growth of Athenian power began in 478 B.C. with an equal and joint alliance of the Hellenic states against the Persian invader. After the Greek victory at Salamis, a combined force under the command of the Spartan Pausanias reestablished Greek power and liberated Greek colonies in the Aegean from Persian rule. Pausanias, despite military successes, alienated other states by his dictatorial manner, and the cities appealed to Athens to provide a replacement for the Spartan leader. Athens then led the Hellenic League to victory over the remaining Persian and Phoenician forces at Eurymedon in 466, and this and other victories liberated Ionia from the Persian yoke. With its allies' approval, Athens proceeded to reorganize the alliance in 454, establishing a joint treasury at Delos and allocating contributions in ships and money among the allies. Thucydides characterizes what had become the Delian League at this stage as follows:

> So Athens took over the leadership, and the allies, because of their dislike of Pausanias, were glad to see her do so. Next the Athenians assessed the various contributions to be made for the war against Persia, and decided which states should furnish money and which states should sent ships—the object being to compensate themselves for their losses by ravaging the territory of the King of Persia. At this time the officials known as "Hellenic Treasurers" were first appointed by the Athenians. These officials received the tribute which was the name given to the contributions in money. The original sum fixed for the tribute was 460 talents. The treasury of the League was at Delos, and representative meetings were held in the temple there. The leadership was Athenian, but the allies were originally independent states who reached their decisions in general congress. (1.97)

Alliance evolved into empire in three stages. When the Delian League captured cities, the populations were enslaved and the land colonized by Athenians—the leading though not yet dominating members of the league. Second, members of the league itself were coerced when they rebelled against Athenian exactions. Naxos was the first city to revolt and it was invaded and forced back into the league—forced to continue its membership and contributions (now in the form of a money tribute to Athens, where the treasury had been moved, rather than in ships to the league). Both developments accentuated Athenian strength relative to that of the rest of the allies. In the third stage, emissaries (*hellenotamiai*) were sent out to supervise the payment of tribute and to supervise, indirectly, the policies of the weakest cities.[2]

The Delian League thus became an empire in which Athens exercised imperial control, largely by informal means. The allies, including those Thucydides calls the "allies of the tribute-paying class" (2.8), each had a legally independent, formally sovereign government, generally a democratic assembly. Athens nonetheless determined both their foreign relations and their significant domestic policies. It was Athens, for example, which decided the policy of the Delian League on all the interstate disputes leading up to the outbreak of the Peloponnesian War. Athens ensured with force that the constitutions of its tributary allies, with the exception of Chios, Lesbos, and Samos, were democratic.[3] Moreover, Athens unilaterally set the level of tribute paid by all those allies not providing ships and it sent out Athenian magistrates (the *hellenotamiai*, who had once been league officials) to supervise the collection of this tax. Subordinate members of the league were required to try all cases involving the death penalty in Athens' courts and to employ Athenian currency in their commerical dealings.[4] (The former generated court fees and the latter seigniorage.) Recalcitrant allies, such as Mitylene in 427, were forced to cede part of their land for an Athenian colony (*cleruchy*). These colonies, as Plutarch notes of Pericles' colonial policy, "relieved the city of a large number of idlers and agitators, raised the standards of the poorest classes, and, by installing garrisons among the allies, implemented at the same time a fear of rebellion."[5]

This informal empire was sustained by two primary means. The first was military intervention. Each of the subordinate allies was aware that the Athenian fleet lay over the horizon, and no subordinate capital was more than a day's march from the sea. No single ally could match the Athenian fleet, partly because each of the allies contributed either money or ships to maintain it. Moreover, no combination of two or three major allies, potentially a counterweight to Athenian control, managed to acquire the allegiance of the large number of very small city-states which

2. Ibid., p. 67; cf. Jacqueline de Romilly, *Thucydide et l'Impérialisme athénien* (Paris, 1947), pp. 79–80.

3. J. B. Bury et al., *The Cambridge Ancient History*, vol. 5 (Cambridge, 1927), pp. 94–97.

4. Russell Meiggs, *The Athenian Empire* (London, 1972), pp. 167–68.

5. Plutarch, "Pericles," in *The Rise and Fall of Athens: Nine Greek Lives*, trans. I. Scott-Kilvert (Harmondsworth, 1960), p. 177.

depended, for reasons of size alone, on the security that the Athenian fleet provided. Military interventions resulted in either the restoration of a pro-Athenian (usually democratic) faction, the total depopulation of the land and its repopulation with Athenian settlers, or a confiscation of land for the purpose of establishing a garrison colony—a cleruchy. Each result served to promote Athenian imperial control.[6]

The second factor that sustained, at the same time as it threatened, the stability of the Athenian empire was the mixture of popularity and unpopularity which Athenian democratic imperialism evoked among subordinate citizens. Thucydides tells us that Athens was both feared and hated (3.37) and at the same time was an "education to Greece" (3.47), revered by the democrats of almost all of the city-states. Hatred stemmed from economic exploitation and imperial restrictions on the political autonomy of the polis. The political restrictions were perceived as particularly irksome, though preferable to the external threat of Persia and the internal threat of oligarchy. Economic exploitation took the form of the substitute naval tribute, seizures of land, and restrictions on trade that excluded nonmembers from the markets of the Delian League.[7] Conversely, the reverence and respect stemmed from an awareness that economic exploitation also conferred benefits, among them integration into the Athenian market, Athens' suppression of piracy, and other imperially provided, international "collective goods."

Athenian political restrictions on allied democracy were worse than every feasible alternative but one: the absence of Athenian protection for a democracy threatened externally by Persia and later by Sparta, and internally by domestic or exiled oligarchic enemies. As William Scott Ferguson notes, "Dependence on Sparta or Athens was, in fact, regarded by none of their allies except as the less of two evils: the greater was dependence on their domestic foes." This political dependence was most

---

6. Donald Kagan, *The Outbreak of the Peloponnesian War* (Ithaca, 1969), p. 43.

7. G. E. M. de Ste. Croix, "The Character of the Athenian Empire," *Historia* 3 (1954–55), and *The Origins of the Peloponnesian War* (Ithaca, 1972), chap. 7, on the Megarian Decree, and Donald Bradeen, "The Popularity of the Athenian Empire," *Historia* 9 (1960). Ste. Croix argues that the empire was popular and that Thucydides' history provides evidence for this view even though Thucydides "editorializes" that the empire was a tyranny. Bradeen supports the conventional view that the empire was unpopular. Both articles appear in Donald Kagan, ed., *Problems in Ancient History*, vol. 1 (New York, 1975), pp. 395–411. I have found most persuasive the view of M. I. Finley, "The Fifth Century Athenian Empire: A Balance Sheet," in P. D. A. Garnsey and C. R. Whittaker, eds., *Imperialism in the Ancient World* (Cambridge, 1978), pp. 103–26.

keenly felt by the local *proxenoi*, the informal leaders of the democratic faction and the appointed representatives of Athenian interests.[8]

One striking feature of Athenian imperialism was its instability. Fully in place in 445, the Athenian empire was short-lived by the measure of all the empires we shall be examining, collapsing in 405. Rebellions and defections were frequent—Naxos, Samos, and Mitylene are only the major revolts discussed by Thucydides. Athens, acutely aware of this instability, regarded each instance of imperial policy as a precedent or rule that could affect its relations with its allies. The debate between Cleon and Diodotus on how to punish and deter or deter and pacify Mitylene responds to these concerns, as did the horrifying repression of Melos (3.36–51, 5.87–116).

Instability and violence grew from defections and the near-equality in the material culture of Athens and its allied subordinates. When exiled factions, whether oligarchic or traditionally aristocratic, won control of democratic Athenian allies, defection followed to the military-monarchical aristocracy of Sparta in order to acquire security. Civil wars became international, international conflict spilled over into civil war, and each made the other worse. The total civil war on Corcyra was a conflict so extreme that it appears to have inspired Hobbes's later portrait of the state of nature, in which there is brutal war of all against all (3.80–84). When Athenian vigilance relaxed or when Athens was defeated, resentful cities would denounce heavy Athenian taxes and slaughter the Athenian settler-garrisons. The Greek islanders of the Aegean and the Greek settlers of Ionia, Sicily, and Thessaly perceived themselves to be similar, socially and economically, to Athens. They thus felt that Athenian rule reflected no natural (or technical) superiority but was a control exercised by those who "should" have been equal.

Spartan Hegemony

Athens ruled a league that was an informal empire, an empire sustained by sea power and democratic collaboration and rocked by near-constant turmoil. Sparta's alliance, the Peloponnesian League, was different. The Spartans regularly drew a distinction between a free Spartan alliance and the Athenian empire, and they portrayed the outbreak of the war as a Greek war of liberation against Athens. "Sparta wants peace. Peace is

8. William Scott Ferguson, *Greek Imperialism* (Boston, 1913), p. 24, and Meiggs, pp. 384, 411. For a humorous portrait of the activities of the *proxenoi*, see Aristophanes, *The Birds*, 1021–1057.

still possible if you [Athens] will give the Hellenes their freedom," one Spartan ultimatum threatened (1.139).

Prior to the outbreak of the war both leagues were in constitutional terms alliances of seemingly equal city-states, although neither was in fact. But they differed substantially in the forms that international political inequality took.[9] Athens collected tribute, Sparta did not; Athens imposed the jurisdiction of its courts, Sparta did not; Athens regulated the commerce of its allies, Sparta did not. In effect, Athens controlled the domestic as well as the foreign relations of its subject allies, but Sparta, despite Thucydides' comment that Sparta made sure its allies were oligarchies, did not wield quite the same control. Sparta had no effect on its allies' domestic societies other than to guarantee their preexisting oligarchic constitutions; oligarchy was the traditional form of society in early fifth-century Greece, particularly among the cities that were members of the Peloponnesian League.[10] Sparta thus generally supported an indigenous tradition of government. Athens, conversely, encouraged, sustained, and protected recent democratic revolutions (products of the demise of the Persian empire) and then actively controlled them. These democratic societies appeared to be less stable than were Sparta's oligarchic dependents, and consequently they seemed to require more active control.

Sparta was relatively unconcerned with the domestic affairs of the Peloponnesian League while Athens continuously intervened in the domestic affairs of the Delian League. The difference is greater than one of mere degree, even though Sparta intervened more as the war became more encompassing. Athens was an empire in that it regularly controlled the domestic *and* the foreign affairs of its allies, Sparta a hegemon in that it controlled the foreign relations of its allies.

Spartan influence amounted to near-control over the foreign policy of the Peloponnesian League; it derived from Sparta's superior military record and capacity, which was due more to the quality of its ground forces than to their quantity. Sparta's military preponderance, even relative to Corinth, ensured that it exercised general control over the league's external policy. Prior to the beginning of the Peloponnesian War Sparta had acquired a recognized position of leadership, and its agree-

9. Fliess argues that the two leagues differed only in degree and that they soon became basically identical: "The line between empire and alliance increasingly slurred on both sides and eventually the Spartan and Athenian alliances became empires in fact." Peter J. Fliess, *Thucydides and the Politics of Bipolarity* (Baton Rouge, 1966), p. 91.

10. Ferguson, pp. 20–21; Meiggs, p. 212.

ment was formally necessary to all league policy. All members formally agreed to follow Sparta in defensive wars and in those nondefensive wars to which the members agreed. Some of the later signatories of the league treaty even agreed to "follow wherever the Spartans might lead."[11] Furthermore, only Sparta could call a meeting of the league, the league being nothing more than a series of bilateral alliances with Sparta.[12]

Yet Spartan hegemony was not unbridled. The Peloponnesian League, which originated in the Hellenic League formed to resist Persian aggression, retained a defensive character. Unlike in the Delian League, members retained a right to participate in all league decisions and to keep their own military forces. Indeed, Sparta needed to be particularly sensitive to Corinthian interests, if only because Corinth had the league's largest navy and controlled the crucial isthmus linking the Peloponnese to mainland Greece. While Pausanias had tried to establish an empire on the Athenian model, Sparta failed to establish a settled imperial rule and revealed, according to one scholar, a "lack of a whole-hearted will to empire."[13]

Sources of Imperial Control

Metropolitan Motives

Many scholars in the "systemic" school argue that nothing distinguishes the sources of imperialism from those of diplomacy and war other than simple differences in fungible power. Others in the metrocentric school favor a difference in motives. Imperialist states desire to "swarm"—their people, trade, or investments—or to change the status quo, or to promote the special interests of slaveholders.[14] Objectless expansion, financial imperialism, the search for raw materials, and the clamor for glory are the special motives that separate imperial states from other states. Neither school, I shall suggest, fully captures the metropolitan sources of imperialism.

Thucydides, in his discussion of the Athenian imperialists, focuses

11. W. G. Forrest, *A History of Sparta* (London, 1968), p. 88.

12. Kagan, p. 19; Ste. Croix, *Origins*, pp. 101–23.

13. A. Andrewes, "Spartan Imperialism?" in Garnsey and Whittaker, p. 101.

14. Kenneth Waltz, *Theory of International Politics* (Reading, Mass., 1979), p. 26; Hans Morgenthau, *Politics among Nations*, 5th ed. (New York, 1975), p. 51; Perry Anderson, *Passages from Antiquity to Feudalism* (London, 1974), chaps. 1–2. For a more general statement of the thesis that domestic pressure, the search for resources to further economic growth under population pressure, generates imperialism, see N. Choucri and R. North, *Nations in Conflict* (San Francisco, 1975), pp. 15–20.

upon no single motive. To Thucydides, observing the origins of the Peloponnesian War and recalling the events that shaped the expansion of the Athenian empire, not one but three motives drew the Athenians out from their city to expand and protect their empire. "We have done nothing extraordinary, nothing contrary to human nature in accepting an empire when it was offered to us and then in refusing to give it up. Three very powerful motives prevent us from doing so—security, honor, and self-interest. And we were not the first to act in this way. It has always been a rule that the weak should be subject to the strong; and besides, we consider that we are worthy of our power" (1.76).

During the debate at Sparta at which Athenian envoys attempted to answer Corinthian charges against Athens, the envoys declared that "fear of Persia was our chief motive." That fear compelled Athens, they argued, to engage in imperial rule (1.74). Following the defeat of the Persian expeditionary force at Salamis much of the Aegean remained under Persian control, and Persia remained a great and threatening power. Following Pausanias' alienation of the allies, the Greeks called in the Athenians to help liberate the Aegean and Ionia. Persia remained a serious security threat until the battle at Eurymedon destroyed a large segment of the Persian navy. But as the Persian threat declined the Spartan threat rose, and this was the second facet of the Athenian security problem. Some allies, resenting greater control by Athens and feeling exploited by the naval tribute and its use in embellishing Athens, began to attempt to defect; others began to express less loyalty. Sparta emerged as a pole of attraction and potential subversion. The loss of an ally became not merely an absolute loss to the Athenian navy, it became a direct and double loss to Athenian security as the defecting ally joined the Spartans' Peloponnesian League. Athens had to rule the Delian League to avoid a direct loss to its security, to avoid, perhaps, being itself ruled by a Spartan hegemony.[15] Athenian envoys in Sicily explained this political necessity. "We say that in Hellas we rule in order not to be ruled; in Sicily we come as liberators in order not to be harmed; we are forced to intervene in many directions simply because we have to be on our guard in many directions . . . " (6.87). To this end, Athens prevented its allies from defecting by intervening against Naxos, Euboea and Mitylene, and Melos. It became "clearly no longer safe for us to risk letting our empire go; especially as any allies that left us would go over to you" (1.74).

15. This de Romilly calls the law of imperial political necessity.

Another facet of Athenian security involved protecting what had become a vital material interest. As a commercial society, Athens depended for its prosperity and for its very survival (its food supplies) on keeping the sea lanes of the Aegean open and free from the rivalry of an equal naval power. No amount of devastation inflicted on the territories of Athens in Attica or elsewhere threatened the political existence of a city protected by walls that connected it to the port of Piraeus (1.143). Conversely, one successful blockade of Piraeus would force Athens to surrender. Athens had to ensure that the route to the Black Sea granaries was free from naval threats, and at least some ships had to get through for the Athenians physically to survive. Regular traffic may also have been necessary to permit Athens to continue to enjoy its "political" life, its life as a polis. The technique-intense and labor-saving cultivation of the olive and the vine and the manufacture of pottery and weapons for export—all high value-added goods—brought Athens wealth and allowed Athenian citizens the relative social equality and the leisure required for participation in the polis.[16]

Guaranteeing these trade lines demanded a naval alliance that both excluded Persian power from the region and prevented Corinth, the second Aegean naval power, from acquiring a sufficient number of Athens' Delian (naval) allies to make the Corinthian navy equal to that of Athens. A firm hold on the Athenian empire, the Delian League, would win both contests.

The second motive was glory. Though difficult to estimate, it should not be underestimated. Pericles' "Funeral Oration" is an eloquent paean to the eternal glory of those who died to secure not only the survival but also the predominance of Athens and the spread of its "way of life" (2.36). Though fear of Persia was the chief motive, "afterwards we thought, too, of our own honor and of our own interest" (1.74). Athens, Pericles declares, is a model to others; its democracy reflects the energies and creativity of the entire people. The empire is the direct product of the courage and imagination of previous generations of Athenians; it reflects their ability and sacrifices. Imperial glory simplifies the task of ruling allies because, awed by Athenian might, they are less likely to revolt. At the same time the awed allies seek to associate themselves with Athenian glory and thus are less likely to want to revolt. In this fashion the spread of Athenian-style democracy in the empire adds to

16. William H. McNeill, *The Shape of European History* (New York, 1974), pp. 53–55.

the glory of Athens, the empire provides security for democracies threatened by oligarchic factions that can call upon Spartan aid (as did the Mitylenian oligarchs), and the spread of democracy provides security for the empire because allied democrats know that only in Athens' political support are they going to find the security they need to meet oligarchic competition.[17]

The third motive was simple material interest, which takes numerous forms. The Athenian citizenry gained court fees from cases appealed to Athens from the empire. The naval tribute added to state revenues, employed Athenian citizens in the navy, and in part was used to embellish the public buildings of Athens. The 1 percent toll levied at Piraeus on all shipping also added to public revenue. Athens seized land for public colonies (which supported the poor), and private individuals, usually the wealthy, seized land as well (which supported themselves). Athens maintained a monopoly of coinage within the empire, which generated seigniorage. The empire protected the trade that brought raw materials and food to Athens and permitted Athens to export olive oil, wine, and pottery (higher value-added goods) to the Aegean economies.[18] Imperial expansion also brought in valuable raw materials in an even more direct way, or so the conquest of Thasos and its nearby mine makes it appear (1.100–101). Finally, imperial conquest itself generated material benefits, bringing in large numbers of captured slaves to be sold as war booty and to form a labor force for the Athenian mines and Athenian estates.[19]

The Athenians seem to have been aware that these various benefits of imperialism went together. Slave agriculture, imperial tribute, and imperial mines produced monetary supremacy, which in turn produced commercial superiority, which in turn, through its stimulation of shipping, produced naval superiority, which in its turn sustained the empire. And the empire generated the slaves, the tribute, and the mines.[20]

---

17. 3.47. These were the arguments used by the moderate, Diodotus, to urge the Athenians to spare the mass of the Mitylenian population from execution (for the males) and slavery (for the women and children). Such punishments were later inflicted on the Melians, who did not have a democratic faction once allied with Athens.

18. Moses Finley, "The Athenian Empire," pp. 55–59. If the colony of Amphipolis is typical, colonial settlement may have been a considerable resource to the Athenian poor. This colony settled 10,000 Athenians and allies, according to Thucydides.

19. Anderson, pp. 40–41.

20. This is the major theme of Pericles' brilliant naval strategy designed to hold the empire on the strategic defensive and destroy the Spartans by means of a series of raids on their coast—a war of attrition designed to wear Sparta down. See Thucydides 1.140ff.

Not one but three motives define Athens' interest in imperialism. The empire is not objectless, not solely financial, not solely motivated by security, not solely a product of swarming. (Swarming created the resources needed to finance security; imperial security protected the swarming.) Imperial expansion cannot be understood by examining only motives, however, a point that Thucydides makes apparent in his discussion of Sparta.

Sparta acquired a hegemony over the Peloponnesian League, not an empire. But Sparta, too, was concerned with promoting its security, honor, and interest, and when the Athenian envoys at the debate at Sparta declared that Athens had done "nothing extraordinary" in seeking an empire, the record seemed to support their claim. Sparta sought to promote its security, particularly in its domination of the Peloponnese. Fear of Athens shaped its definition of security in the latter half of the fifth century. Sparta feared the international predominance of Athens, and it feared that the Athenian democracy would become "the sponsors of some revolutionary policy" among the subject populations of the Peloponnese (1.102). Sparta sought to protect and extend its honor, as a military leader of the Greeks, as a reliable leader of the Peloponnesian League, and as an upholder of the liberty of Greek peoples everywhere. Sparta also sought to promote its material interests, both in protecting its limited trade with Corinth and in acquiring booty in war.

Spartan motives influenced one another, as Athenian motives did, though in a fashion not quite as positive. The conquest of Messenia promoted the material interests of the Spartans and created a leisured society. Since leisure was devoted to constant training for war, the conquest also increased Spartan security and military prestige. But subversive contacts between subjugated peoples and neighboring states required further expansion and, later, control of the Peloponnesian League. None of these motives differed in kind from those which spurred Athens. It is not to a difference in motives but to a difference in opportunities that we should turn.

Metropolitan Opportunities

As a relationship of power, imperial control, as the systemic theorists argue, naturally reflects differences in the resources that make up power. But this merely restates the problem of explaining imperial control. Is imperialism the product of any net difference in the resources of power? Or are there particular factors that contribute to the resources of power and shape a specifically imperial relationship?

Although Thucydides has one of the Athenian envoys announce that the "weak should be subject to the strong," he does not imply that a simple net difference in power accounts for *imperial* subjection. Indeed, the Melian Dialogue and passages on the expedition to Sicily suggest quite different conclusions. Athenian power was not only large relative to any one of its subordinate allies in the Delian League, it was also different from that of Sparta and different from, and not just larger than, that of the subordinate allies.

Athens' power stemmed from three sources. Athens drew on the collective resources of its free allies—Chios, Lesbos, and, most prominently, Corcyra—which provided ships in time of war.[21] Signally adding to this allied source of power was Athens' empire. Unlike the allies, imperial subordinates provided continuous support, in peace and in war, for the expansion and security of Athenian commerce and colonies. They paid money into the central treasury to fund Athenian ships manned by Athenian sailors, thus financing their own subordination and sharing in the costs of Athens' security and public embellishment. (Some of the funds in the Delian treasury were used to construct the spectacular temples on the Acropolis.)[22] This imperial source of power had previously to be acquired, however, and then continuously sustained by metropolitan sources.

Thucydides finds the third source of Athens' power in its "adventurous spirit"—an attitude of mind and a repertory of actions which together create a distinctive way of life. Pericles described this adventurous spirit as the drive that "has forced an entry into every sea and into every land; and everywhere we have left behind us everlasting memorials of good done to our friends or suffering inflicted on our enemies" (2.41). Thucydides suggests that Athens' restlessness and innovativeness are not rooted deep in the psychology of the Athenian people but a national style—a way of thought associated with Athens' past and present institutions.[23] Nor is the repertory of actions an explosive, Schumpeterian machine; it is a set of institutions, policies, and practices which, though based in the city of Athens, extends Athenian

21. For an interesting discussion on the role of domestic and alliance sources of power see Lord Brougham, "Balance of Power" (January 1803), in *Works*, vol. 8 (London, 1857), pp. 1–50. For a discussion of Athenian power in these terms see J. Finley, *Thucydides* (Ann Arbor, 1963), p. 145.

22. Bury, p. 95.

23. For a discussion of national style, see Stanley Hoffmann, *Gulliver's Troubles* (New York, 1968), Pt. 1.

influence across borders and polities. Together they form the foundations of Athenian imperial expansion.

This adventurous spirit has twofold institutional roots—public-political and socioeconomic. The first institutional root is the democratic constitution of Athens. Citizens are not only equal (as are the Spartans according to the Lycurgan constitution) but also free. Political leadership is open to the most able, or at least to the choice of fellow citizens, and not restricted to a particular (e.g., oligarchical) class.[24] The relation of citizen to state is thus doubly strong. Political alienation and coercive enforcement become less likely when citizens themselves help make the laws that govern them. The state, rather than expending its political resources on controlling its citizens, draws its strength from their freely given support.[25]

A citizen of twentieth-century democracy could easily underestimate the political energy that Athenian democracy generated; it is both too familiar and too strange. Highly participatory democracy, in which each citizen is both statesman and soldier, produces an ideology of action, a ferment of policies, an attitude of aggressive problem solving—the spirit of adventure that Thucydides described as being behind Athenian expansion. Since there is no mediation between the state and the citizen, the state being the people assembled, what each citizen proposes or votes for in the assembly is both for himself and for the public. Private passions both inspire and are shaped by public honor. This is the source of the honor behind Athenian imperialism: a joint undertaking of the people of Athens, their empire is "of the people, by the people."

It is also "for the people," because interest, material and ideal, shapes the enterprise of empire. Each citizen stands to gain, on a private as well as a public basis, from expansion. The Sicilian expedition, for example, set out with these public sentiments to inspire it:

> There was a passion for the enterprise which affected everyone alike. The older men thought that they would either conquer the places against which they were sailing, or in any case, with such a large force, could come to no harm; the young had a longing for the sights and experiences of distant places, and were confident that they would return safely; the general masses and the average soldier himself saw the prospect of getting pay for the time being and of adding to the

24. Ferguson, p. 47.

25. Thucydides, 1.141. And see M. I. Finley, *Politics in the Ancient World* (New York, 1983), for this theme of democratic political stability when the material interests of citizens is fulfilled (as in expansion) and when mass participation is institutionalized.

empire so as to secure permanent paid employment in the future. (6.24)

Political democracy finds its military parallel in democratic armed forces. The navy was both a motive for expansion and a means of imperial power. When naval power relies on oared galleys, a democratic navy is inherently superior to a nondemocratic navy since the latter is likely to employ slave rowers who in the heat of battle cannot be called upon to fight.[26] Athenian naval dominance could be exercised relatively cheaply, and, as noted above, commerce, the tribute, and the fleet supported each other synergetically.

This near-Schumpeterian conjunction of those interested, those deciding, and those fighting was the institutional foundation that gave weight to the strong motives of material interest in Athenian expansion. The enlarged navy and the public buildings that the tribute made possible were literally theirs. So also were the colonies, the profits of coinage, and the pride and profit of judicial preeminence. In a democracy the imperial machine is the whole society, the process produces a substantive product, and atavism is realism.

As we seek the domestic roots of Athens' growing civic and imperial power, we need also to consider private institutions. Just as the citizen is freed from the restraint of public oligarchic rule, so the (nonslave) labor of Athens is "free and open," escaping the arbitrary authority of the overlord and thrown into the commercial economy of small-scale manufacture and exchange. Athen's great wealth derives from an international division of labor in which Athens exchanges advanced agricultural commodities (olive oil and wine), skill-intensive manufactured goods (pottery), and certain metals (silver from the slave-worked mines) for raw materials, especially grain from the Black Sea region.[27] Athens also controls a large share of Greek shipping and thus commerce, so that, as Pericles declared, "all the good things from all over the world flow in to us. So that to us it seems just as natural to enjoy foreign goods as our own local products" (2.38). John Hicks has argued that this commercial system, with its small trading firms and a relatively static technology, had a natural tendency to expand: "It is only by constant improvements in organization (which is what the expansionary forces are) that the tendency of the profit rate to fall can be offset. If the merchants fail to find new economies, so that they can trade more

26. Thucydides' sense of the superiority of the Athenian navy is expressed in 2.62.
27. Moses Finley, *The Ancient Economy* (London, 1973), p. 129, but see pp. 131–35.

efficiently in existing markets, they will find prices moving against them."[28]

Commercial expansion required imperial expansion. The protection of commerce from the depredations of pirates and rival cities called for a patrolling fleet, which in turn required naval outposts. Opening up foreign lands and their resources to commercial penetration also demanded an imperial presence when oligarchies (as did Sparta) sought to avoid commercial contact in order to prevent the mobilization of their democratically inclined middle and lower classes. Imperial expansion could also become necessary to break shipping or raw material monopolies, potential or actual. It was for this reason that Athens had to control the route to the Black Sea, and it may have been for this reason that Athens conquered Thasos, thereby gaining control of the Thracian mines.[29]

Were democracy and commerce necessary to the existence of empire? If democracy encouraged and commerce demanded empire, did empire require a metropolitan constitutional order based on democracy or a private socioeconomic drive based on commerce? Even in Athens' time there were empires that were not democratic—the recently defeated Persian empire, which would rise again soon, was a case in point. Are there then essential political foundations to imperialism, or will any form of political society suffice? Are commerce and other social and economic extensions of society necessary? These questions cannot be resolved in a two-country sample, but a comparison between Athenian imperialism and Spartan hegemony can begin to suggest answers.

Like Athens, Sparta drew upon the combined power of its allies. Sparta headed a league each of whose members had a vote in league policy, however, and while Sparta was clearly predominant in league councils (the importance of the Spartan army giving it a clear veto on league policy), the final decision for war was taken by majority vote in a congress of all the allies "both great and small." The league thus was a source of power, and Corinth's fleet was an especially welcome complement to Sparta's own land power, but the league was not as reliable as was Athens' empire.

The fundamental source of Spartan power was Sparta itself. Just as Athens' spirit is deemed adventurous by the Corinthian envoys, so Sparta's is characterized as slow and cautious: "Think of this, too: while

---

28. Sir John Hicks, *A Theory of Economic History* (London, 1969), p. 56.
29. J. Finley, p. 23; Thucydides, 1.100.

you [Sparta] are hanging back, they [Athens] never hesitate; while you stay at home, they are always abroad; for they think the farther they go the more they will get, while you think that any movement may endanger what you already have" (1.70).

These words reveal a profoundly isolationist state, one made secure by the constraining but very effective discipline of its army—a thin bronze line that almost never broke. Sparta's public institutions (there were no private institutions) were designed to sustain the quality of its army, and Spartan society resembled a military camp. At the top were two kings who, following the Lycurgan reforms of the seventh century B.C., became figureheads. The true political power in the state was the senate (*gerousia*), composed of the heads of the leading aristocratic families. This body effectively directed the assembly of all the citizen-soldiers, a small number of men who also formed a phalanx of elite infantry in the army, and played a decisive role in electing the *ephors*, the ruling public officials of the Spartan state.[30] Lacking all political rights of participation in Spartan policy were the *perioeici*. These were peoples of the Peloponnese (Laconia) conquered by Sparta early in its history and foreigners who had come to settle in the Peloponnese. They were permitted to conduct their own local government subject to Spartan approval and to engage in petty manufacturing and commerce, which were prohibited to the citizen. At the bottom, crushed under an oppressive tyranny, lay the helots, Greek inhabitants of Messenia conquered by Sparta in the seventh century B.C.

Life was totally public. Assigned a plot of land worked by helots, the soldier-citizen was by design free from all material cares (in fact, he was remarkably prone to corruption outside his homeland) in order to devote himself to military training. All economic resources were regulated by the state, and money was severely limited. The citizens took their meals in common. From earliest youth they focused all their energies on a rigorous military education designed to produce patriotic and fearless fighting men.[31] The state thus had little in the way of excess resources, for it directed most of its activity to disciplining its population and coercing the helots. But when challenged, its magnificent army repeatedly proved itself the best in Greece, achieving a preeminence on land equivalent to Athens' dominance of the sea (1.18).

30. Forrest, p. 113, and M. I. Finley, "Sparta and Spartan Society," in Shaw and Saller, p. 27.
31. M. I. Finley, "Sparta," p. 38.

The Metropolitan Thresholds of Empire and Hegemony

These, then, were the metropolitan sources of Athenian empire and Spartan hegemony. What distinguishes the sources of empire from those of hegemony? What distinguishes imperial metropoles and hegemonic metropoles (hegemons) from the subordinated and less powerful states of the international systems? It is political unity, I shall argue, that distinguishes imperial metropoles and hegemons from subordinated states and transnational extension that distinguishes empires from hegemonies.

To the Greeks of the time, the crucial difference distinguishing Athens from Sparta and Athenian imperialism from Spartan hegemony was the difference in "spirit" between the two rivals. Athens was aggressive, innovative; Sparta passive, isolationist. Athens was capable of extending her civilization, Sparta was not. Polybius, a later Greek commentator, focused on just this difference.

> For guarding their own country with absolute safety, and for preserving their own freedom, the legislation of Lycurgus was entirely sufficient; and for those who are content with these objects we must concede that there neither exists nor even has existed, a constitution and civil order preferable to that of Sparta. But if anyone is seeking aggrandizement, and believes that to be a leader and ruler and despot of numerous subjects, and to have all looking and turning to him, is a finer thing than that—in this point of view we must acknowledge that the Spartan constitution is deficient.[32]

Polybius has already explained why the Spartan constitution, although "excellent" for "securing unity among the citizens," was deficient as a foundation for imperialism.

> For as long as their ambition was confined to governing their immediate neighbors, or even the Peloponnesians only, they [the Spartans] were content with the resources and supplies provided by Laconia itself, having all material to war ready to hand, and being able without much expenditure of time to return home or convey provisions with them. But directly they took in hand to despatch naval expeditions or to go on campaigns by land outside the Peloponnese, it was evident that neither their iron currency, nor their use of crops for payment in kind, would be able to supply them with what they lacked if they abided by the legislation of Lycurgus; for such un-

32. Polybius, *Histories*, trans. Evelyn Shuckburgh (Bloomington, 1962), 1.6. 50.

dertakings required money universally current, and goods from foreign countries. Thus they were compelled to wait humbly at Persian doors, impose tribute on the islanders, and exact contributions from all the Greeks: knowing that if they abided by the laws of Lycurgus, it was impossible to advance any claim upon any outside power at all, much less upon the supremacy of Greece.[33]

Polybius does not say that Sparta was less powerful than Athens, for Athens could not defeat or subordinate Sparta or any of Sparta's allies within reach of the Spartan army. He says, rather, that Spartan power differed from that of Athens, and only the power of Athens was imperial.

The commercial society of Athens contributed to Athenian power and Athenian imperialism in four ways. Commerce contributed material resources that Athens otherwise would not have had. The trading of goods, particularly "venting the surplus" of wine, oil, and skilled manufactures, for raw materials provided a net addition to the Athenian economy and thus a resource of public power that could be taxed. (The addition of resources was not the key, however, for Sparta had resources.) Second, and much more important, Athenian commerce provided *extensible* resources. Trade accumulated money and goods that could be used to exercise influence and control at a distance. Money could bribe foreign leaders, supply armies far away from home bases, and purchase those goods which were not produced at home but were nonetheless needed to support fleets and armies abroad. Third, Athens excluded nonmembers from trading in the Delian League's markets, and Athenian commerce thereby provided benefits to others. Athenian commerce overflowed the confines of Attica, offering social, economic, and cultural links to Athens' allies and subordinates which made other democracies want association with Athens without Athens having to resort to the costly exercise of military force. Being part of Athens' alliance, part of its empire, provided *continuous*, though unequal, benefits to all parties.[34] Fourth, the extension of Athenian commerce created stakes overseas that had to be defended. Sparta too sought security, honor, and material interest in foreign expansion, but Athens was defending already expanded fragments and facets of Athenian society. Its "flag" followed its "trade," though not, of course, consistently (Melos appears to have had little contact with Athens prior to its destruction by an Athenian expedition). Trade also followed the flag, Athenian order hav-

33. Ibid., 1.6. 49.
34. M. I. Finley, "The Athenian Empire," p. 55.

ing provided security from pirates and, occasionally, the elimination of commercial competitors (as in the conquest of Thasos).[35] But trade provided a special incentive, a large and "defensive" argument for maintaining and expanding imperial rule.

Sparta, conversely, could rule only through military force, a costly enterprise for a small warrior nation. It had no substantial social fragment or facet, apart from the army, capable of expanding abroad to share the burdens and feed on the benefits of imperial rule, and it was limited to what its armies could hold in Laconia and Messenia. Indeed, holding these two regions in a state of servitude seemed to absorb all Spartan energy and to stimulate much of Sparta's fear of Athenian subversion. Yet oligarchs turned to Sparta for protection from the threat of democratic subversion inspired by Athens, and from this circumstance and from the superiority of Spartan arms, Sparta exercised a hegemony over the Peloponnesian League. But Sparta lacked the capability to extend its influence beyond external, military, political support. Failing to inspire the private allegiances that could win pervasive and continuous influence within the societies of the Greek city-states, Sparta lacked the wherewithal to establish or to hold an empire.

Imperial control required some form of *transnational* connection—not necessarily commerce, for agricultural colonies could perhaps have served as well. Schumpeter's thesis notwithstanding, it was because Sparta was only a war machine that it could not be a large-scale empire, as the factors that permitted Sparta to acquire its original empire suggest. Between the tenth and the eighth centuries B.C. Sparta conquered Laconia, and at the beginning of the seventh century B.C. it conquered Messenia. But this was a different Sparta, one that resembled Athens more closely than did the Sparta of the fifth century. Eighth-century Sparta had a rudimentary commercial system, private property, and exchangeable money; it lacked a rigorously totalitarian system of military education, and it sent out colonists. But a revolution followed on the heels of the Lycurgan reforms of the early seventh century, creating the rigorously militaristic, anticommercial, and isolated Sparta of later centuries.[36] At that point Sparta ceased being an empire. It did not imperialize the Messenians, it enslaved them. It did not even rule the Laconians, it employed them. Sparta became a hegemon within the

---

35. This general point is made by A. French, *The Growth of the Athenian Economy* (New York, 1964), p. 123 and chap. 7.

36. G. Dickins, "The True Cause of the Peloponnesian War," *Classical Quarterly* 5 (1911), excerpted in Kagan, p. 370.

Peloponnesian League. Later, following the defeat of Athens in the Peloponnesian War, Sparta, transformed by the pressures of thirty years of war, attempted to establish an empire over parts of Greece and sent out governors to rule these newly acquired provinces. Spartan rule was quickly and universally detested for, unlike the rule of Athens, it was a pure tyranny. The empire met with continuous rebellion and, costly to Sparta, it collapsed in fewer than twenty years.[37]

Athenian commerce was a particularly effective form of transnational influence, the sort of influence that, with coercive support in the background, molds an entire society. Sparta's army could do little more than threaten from a distance, sporadically and haltingly. Fear of Athens and military excellence laid the foundations for Sparta's hegemony, but they could not create the penetrating control of empire. Aristotle summarizes Sparta's failure as an empire well: "The Spartans always prevailed in war but were destroyed by empire simply because they did not know how to use the leisure they had won, because they had practiced no more fundamental skill than skill in war."[38]

Crossing the metropolitan threshold to empire requires the presence of a transnational society, based in the metropole and capable of extending itself to societies about to become subject to imperial rule. It also calls, if we can judge by the circumstances that led to the collapse of Athens' empire, for certain specifically political preconditions as well.

The greatest source of Athenian strength, democracy, was also the greatest weakness in a protracted war. Athenian democracy mobilized the resources of a united and patriotic citizenry to protect liberty and empire. The citizens, having chosen Pericles for their leader, were even prepared to allow the government strategic control over their private resources. But a state that responds to popular demands both draws forth the best in its citizens and succumbs to their worst passions. John Finley described the course of Athens' downfall as a "vicious cycle whereby war produced suffering, suffering unrest, unrest political violence, and this violence a type of leadership which sacrificed the state to its own ends."[39] Thucydides clearly focuses on the internal causes of the collapse without attributing them solely to democracy: "And in the end it was only because they had destroyed themselves by their own internal strife that finally they were forced to surrender" (2.65).

The stresses of war, beginning with the plague, compounded by the

37. Forrest, pp. 123–26.
38. Aristotle as quoted in Forrest, p. 126.
39. J. Finley, p. 305.

elite and popular hubris that was the dark side of Athenian honor, brought Athenian leaders to appeal to the basest motives of their suffering followers rather than to their love of country and sense of proportion. The people meanwhile ceased to trust in the wisdom of the leaders they had elected, and the result was the confused, emotional, and corrupt appeals of the debate preceding the Athenian expedition to Sicily (6.8–32). As democracy deteriorated, the rich, oppressed by wartime taxation and the destruction of their landed estates outside the city walls (a direct result of Pericles' maritime strategy), deserted to the enemy or formed cabals. After the disaster in Sicily the rich staged a coup and turned Athens temporarily into an oligarchy (8.45–98).

Nevertheless, it was no more oligarchy than it was democracy which destroyed the Athenian empire.[40] Successful empires could be democratic, as Athens had shown, but they could also be oligarchic, as was the Persian empire. It was disunion in the state, internal strife, that brought about the downfall of the Athenian empire.

The democratic army and fleet on Samos refused to follow the commands of the oligarchs (8.75), and the empire began to collapse as different Athenian factions competed for the allegiance of fleets and armies scattered across the empire. With parts of the Athenian fleet waging sporadic war against other parts of the Athenian fleet, Sparta (with Persian funds) launched a fleet that defeated Athens at sea. With Athenian naval power broken and with the commercial ties that bound together the empire disrupted, Athens' subordinate allies began to revolt, starting with the most recently acquired, Euboea. Alcibiades' return to Athens and assumption of popular leadership showed that even a temporary renewal of political unity was enough to stave off final defeat. The loyalty of Athens' oldest allies, Samos most particularly, demonstrated the residual solidarity and sense of mutual advantage that the empire held out.[41] These proved, however, mere diversions in a continuing slide into political disarray, disarray that culminated in final defeat and the arrival of a Spartan governor in the once-dominant metropole.

Political unity provided attributes essential to the strategic power of both Athens and Sparta. Both possessed a sense of political unity, or political community, among the governing population and both possessed an effective, centralized government. They were, in the termi-

40. Ferguson, p. 77.
41. Meiggs, pp. 371–72.

nology of social science, politically integrated and politically institutionalized.[42] Political community and effective central government enable the leaders of a polity to pursue rational, strategic behavior, encouraging them to put public before private goals. Political unity also enables political leaders to mobilize—through taxation, recruitment, requisition—the social resources needed in the exercise of diplomacy, violence, and administration of empires and hegemonies. Finally, it permits members of the ruling elite to assume at least a passive loyalty on the part of the governed population as they pursue what they believe are the foreign interests of the state. Furthermore, the governing stratum and the governed population can be expected to resist the blandishments that might accompany foreign attempts to penetrate the metropole itself.

These conditions are highly unlikely to be limited to Athenian-style democracies and to Spartan-style military aristocracies. Other types of political societies share these characteristics, and they will be examined in the remainder of this chapter and later. *Political unity*—community and centralized government—is thus another special metropolitan foundation of empire and of hegemony.

This examination of Athenian imperialism and Spartan hegemony leads us to several tentative conclusions. The special features that distinguish imperial metropoles from states that are merely large, populous, or rich are first, transnational extension and second, political unity. States with these characteristics can successfully establish empires. Politically unified states that possess superior quantities (relative to their neighbors) of the conventional resources of power—large populations, substantial armies, wealth—but lack the differentiated domestic society needed as a foundation for transnational extension can, nonetheless, establish hegemonies. But the histories of Athens and Sparta also suggest that the foundations of imperialism are not solely metropolitan. Metropoles, to be imperial metropoles, must have peripheries under their rule. We must distinguish imperial metropoles and hegemons, and indeed all independent states, from the societies, the peripheries, subject to the rule of imperial metropoles.

---

42. For political institutionalization and social mobilization, see Karl Deutsch, *Nationalism and Social Communication* (Cambridge, Mass., 1966), and Samuel Huntington, *Political Order in Changing Societies* (New Haven, 1968), and "The Change to Change," *Comparative Politics* 3, 3 (1971). These concepts are examined in my Chapters 8 and 9 below.

The Peripheral Threshold of Subordination

Had Athens all the metropolitan characteristics described above and been surrounded only by states resembling Sparta, would Athens have been the ruler of an empire? Spartan resistance suggests not, and it suggests more widely that metropolitan sources of empire appear to be insufficient to explain empire. We need to ask what sort of political society can become subject to another on a regular and stable basis. What distinguishes such states from the states that remain independent, become metropoles, or are simply destroyed in the course of resistance? It is not merely small size or poverty that condemns political societies to the peripheral fate, for history is replete with empires over wealthy and large peripheries. Rather, the major factor that appears to distinguish vulnerable political societies from imperial metropoles, and from gallant but futile resisters, is political unity.

Thucydides' comments on the sources of the weakness of the weak are as revealing as his comments on the sources of the strength of the strong. Melos was a small island off the coast of the Peloponnese. Though formally an ally of Sparta, it claimed to be neutral in the war between Athens and Sparta. The Athenians became concerned that Melos presented a strategic threat to their sea route to the west and set an example of independence which might tempt the more recalcitrant of Athens' allies. In 427–26 an Athenian military force demanded its surrender, and when the Melians refused "laid the country waste" (3.91). Ten years later a second Athenian expedition reached the island. The Melian Council, apparently an oligarchy, refused to allow Athenian generals to address the assembled people. Instead, the council met the generals who urged the Melians to avoid irrelevant appeals to international morality and recognize that they had no choice but destruction or surrender. The Melian Council, recalling seven hundred years of proud history as an independent polis, chose to resist. After a siege from a summer to a following winter which included several sorties against considerable odds—both reflect some popular support for the Melian Council—the Melians surrendered unconditionally to a reinforced besieging force. The Athenians "put to death all the men of military age whom they took, and sold the women and children as slaves" (5.116). The Melians chose to be annihilated rather than become part of the Athenian empire.

The Sicilians were more fortunate. The Athenians, in the year they first laid waste to Melos, sent an expedition to Sicily, responding to a request from Leontini and other cities of Ionian heritage which were in a conflict with Syracuse, the major city of the island and Dorian in heritage. The Athenians, ostensibly responding to a request for aid from fellow Ionians, in fact sent their twenty galleys because of the hope of cutting Sparta's grain supply and because of the opportunity for imperial expansion.[43] The Ionian allies of Athens together with the native Sicels joined with Leontini and Camarina in an attack on the Syracusan garrisons in Sicel territory (3.103). Soon thereafter an Athenian expedition arrived in Sicily, but Syracuse still retained its dominant position in the affairs of Sicily. When Sparta's defeat at Pylos appeared to guarantee Athenian predominance in Greece, however, Syracuse called the combatants in Sicily to a peace conference. Hermocrates, a Syracusan, warned the assembled Sicilians of the dangers of strife when foreign states lurked over the horizon waiting to divide the spoils:

> Now if we fight among ourselves and call in the help of the Athenians, who are only too willing to join in whether they are called for or not; if we then proceed to use our own resources in weakening ourselves, thus doing the preliminary work for their future empire, the likely thing to happen is that, when they see us exhausted, they will come here one day with larger forces and will attempt to bring all of us under their control. . . .
>
> We should realize that internal strife is the main reason for the decline of cities, and will be for Sicily too, if we, the inhabitants, who are all threatened together, still stand apart from each other, city against city. (4.60–61)

Persuaded that Hermocrates did indeed argue for the best policy for Sicily as a whole, the assembly made peace. The Athenian generals accepted the Sicilian peace and sailed for home where, ominously, the Athenian assembly banished them, accusing them of taking bribes.

Ten years later, the same year that witnessed the final destruction of Melos, the Athenians sent another expedition to Sicily with instructions to conquer the island. Again, Athens, had received a request to come to the aid of a Sicilian city (Egesta) struggling against Syracuse. Persuaded by Alcibiades' oratory and carried away by the chance of glory, employment, and booty which the expedition held out, the Athenian citizens assembled their largest and finest expeditionary force. These experienced forces initially overwhelmed the Sicilian opposition led by Syracuse. Syracuse called an assembly of her allies at Camarina where

---

43. Athens was ethnically linked to the Ionians; Sparta was a Dorian city (Thucydides, 3.86). This section is indebted to W. R. Connor, *Thucydides* (Princeton, 1984).

Hermocrates persuaded the Syracusans to remedy their lack of discipline and organization by forming a war directorate. Then he addressed the representatives of the Dorian cities of Sicily:

> We have in front of us the example of the Hellenes in the mother country who have been enslaved through not supporting each other . . . yet we are not prepared to unite and resolutely make it clear to them that what they have to deal with here is not Ionians, Hellespontians, and islanders who may change masters, but are always slaves either to the Persians or to someone else, but free Dorians from the independent Peloponnese living in Sicily. Are we waiting until we are taken over separately, city by city, . . . [by Athenians] sometimes trying to create dissension among us by their arguments, sometimes stirring up wars among us by holding out hopes of an alliance with them. . . . And when fellow Sicilians who live at a distance from us are destroyed first, do we imagine that the danger will not come to each of us. . . . (6.77)

All the independent Dorian cities, and several non-Dorian cities, joined a united defense under Syracusan leadership. With Spartan military aid the united defense defeated the hitherto-dominant Athenians both at sea and on land, the latter completely destroying the Athenian force. Thucydides adds his own explanation for the surprising Athenian defeat:

> The Athenians were now utterly disheartened; they could scarcely believe that this had happened, and they wished all the more that the expedition had never been made. These were the only cities they had come up against which were of the same type as their own, democracies like themselves, and places of considerable size, equipped with naval and cavalry forces. They had been unable to make use of the fifth column or to offer the prospect of a change in the form of government as a means for gaining power over them; nor had they been able to exploit a great superiority in material force; instead most of their efforts had been unsuccessful. . . . (7.55)

The unsuccessful resistance of Melos and the successful resistance of the Dorians of Sicily begin to suggest what makes for resistance to imperial rule. Political unity, as Thucydides states repeatedly, is crucial. It draws on a sense of community sufficient to make political societies resist collaboration (which Rex Warner, in the passage just quoted, translates as "fifth column"), and it enables societies to mobilize social resources for defense, as the Melians did during the long siege of their polis. Just as important is an effective, centralized, state institution possessed of effective authority over the political society, whether it be Melian oligarchy or the organized Sicilian democracies. Effective resistance requires more than political unity, however, it requires adequate resources, which may mean a political community larger than a single city (the "Dorians") and militarily well-equipped. In short, the resisters must begin to resemble imperial metropoles; Syracuse did have such a society and, on a petty scale, was itself an imperial metropole within Sicily.

Information on those states which actually did succumb to Athenian rule is not abundant. But they seem to have exhibited the very failings Hermocrates described, and they fell prey to the very dangers he warned against. Lesbos had long preserved a shaky independence from Athens. Taking advantage of the plague in Athens in 428 to begin a long-planned revolt, the leaders of the city of Mytilene sent for aid from Sparta. An Athenian besieging force arrived first and, as the siege tightened, the city's leadership, doubting the arrival of the Spartans, decided to issue weapons to the populace. Once armed, the people refused further obedience and the city's leaders, fearing for their lives if the populace took control with Athenian support, decided to surrender rather than negotiate. Political disunity destroyed effective resistance (3.27–28). Political disunity of another form, civil war, similarly contributed to the destruction and surrender to Athenian imperialism of once-powerful Corcyra (3.69–85).

The means by which Athens held on to its Ionian colonies in the Aegean and on the mainland of Asia Minor were more complicated. These areas had once been among the most prosperous and internally politically unified (integrated) in Greece. But Persian occupation, the Ionian revolt against Persia, and the Athenian-led liberation from Persian rule left behind truncated political societies. J. M. Cook describes their condition as follows:

> The ancient writers tell us little enough about the history of eastern Greece and nothing whatever about conditions there in the fifth century. But we may infer two distinct consequences of Athenian rule. On the one hand, though the cities had recovered their freedom [in the Delian League], the Persian land survey continued in force; so the cities, as corporate bodies, belonged to the Athenian League and paid their tribute, but the landowners seem to have paid rent to the Persian overlord for their estates. The Greeks of the Asiatic coast thus found themselves serving two masters. The landowners must maintain good relations with the satraps and grandees, and there

were times when democratic pressure instigated by Athens drove them into the arms of the Persians. In some of the cities the result of this interference was an embitterment of political strife which did not end with the collapse of the Athenian empire.[44]

The new democracies of Ionia—liberated by Athens, fearing the return of the Persians, and divided internally by the split loyalties of their landholders and their commercial classes (the former dependent on Persia, the latter dependent on the Athenian market)—were in no position to resist Athenian imperialism even if they had wanted to. The governments, for the most part democracies established with Athenian help, felt a genuine loyalty toward the Athenians. Furthermore, democracy in the Athenian colonies should neither be confused with Athens' own democracy nor, of course, with modern democracies. In a number of cases the "demos" to which Thucydides refers was itself a small faction within the larger population. The demos on Samos, for example, in 412 were three hundred in number.[45] Thus they felt a real sense of threat from the oligarchs who were allied first with Persia and later with Sparta.[46] Such considerations help explain Plato's comment that the Athenians kept their empire for seventy years "because they had friends in each of the cities."[47] This type of polity, which has commercial foundations and mobilized but highly divided popular loyalties, so that it lacks the capacity for institutionalized civic order, could be called a fractionated polity.[48]

Internally divided and politically dependent on Athens for support against domestic rivals, these polities were unable to unite internally or join with other polities against the overwhelming presence of Athens in the Delian League. Needing Athens to replace the overbearing Spartan Pausanias, they invited Athens to assume the leadership of the liberation from Persia, enabling Athens to employ the Ionians against each other

44. J. M. Cook, *The Greeks in Ionia and the East* (New York, 1963), pp. 122–23.

45. Donald Bradeen, "The Popularity of the Athenian Empire," *Historia* 9 (1960), excerpted in Kagan, p. 407.

46. Ste. Croix, pp. 37–40.

47. G. E. M. de Ste. Croix, "The Character of the Athenian Empire," excerpted in Kagan, p. 400.

48. A fractionated polity is a polity that shares the characteristics listed. These draw on some of the features described by S. Huntington in his analysis in *Political Order* of "praetorian societies" (though without presupposing that these societies always have a military dictatorship). I also draw on the description Fred Riggs gives of "prismatic societies" regulated by neither bureaucratic fiat nor pure market but by bargaining, in this case among factions. See Riggs, *Administration in Developing Countries* (Boston, 1964).

and further the growth of Athenian power. "By these methods they [Athens] first led the stronger states against the weaker ones, leaving the strongest to the last in the certainty of finding them, once all the rest had been absorbed, much less formidable to deal with" (3.11). And last, the commercial prosperity of these polities, in some cases their very survival, depended on access to the Athenian market.

The subjection of Ionia thus becomes comprehensible. Though their population was politically mobilized and self-aware, it was politically divided and, because divided, politically dependent. Politically and economically dependent, the Ionians could not unite to resist Athenian domination and were absorbed into the empire.

Empire requires both a metropole and a periphery. Trying to imperialize another "metropole," as Athens discovered when it attacked the Sicilians, succeeds, only when a much smaller polity (e.g., Melos) is simply obliterated. Nor could Sparta, not an imperial metropole because it lacked a transnational society, successfully established an empire. Sparta, however, could establish a hegemony over other metropoles smaller in size, less populous, and less militarily powerful. Empire is thus a relationship between a metropole and a periphery linked to the metropole by a transnational society based in the metropole; hegemony is a relationship between metropoles, one of which is more powerful than the other.

CHAPTER 4

Rome

A rich enemy excites their cupidity; a poor one, their lust for power. East and West alike have failed to satisfy them. They are the only people on earth to whose covetousness both riches and poverty are equally tempting. To robbery, butchery, and rapine, they give the lying name of "government," they create a desolation and call it peace.

> "Calgacus' Speech to the Assembled Britons," in Tacitus, *The Agricola*

Scholars who seek to understand empires are accustomed to living with a grim record of the exploitation, destruction, and subjugation of once-free peoples. Tacitus saw, as many since have seen, the desolation that apologists have called peace. But on rare occasions a different note enters, and the beneficence of empire is trumpeted. Gibbon's famous paean to imperial Rome sounds such a defiant note.

If a man were called to fix the period in the history of the world during which the condition of the human race was most happy and prosperous, he would, without hesitation, name that which elapsed from the death of Domitian to the accession of Commodus. The vast extent of the Roman empire was governed by absolute power, under the guidance of virtue and wisdom. The armies were restrained by the firm but gentle hand of four successive emperors whose characters and authority commanded involuntary respect. The forms of the civil administration were carefully preserved by Nerva, Trajan, Hadrian, and the Antonines, who delighted in the image of liberty, and were pleased with considering themselves as the accountable ministers of the laws. Such princes deserved the honour of restoring the republic, had the Romans of their days been capable of enjoying a rational freedom.[1]

Against the hard fate of the Jews and the Carthaginians, and the withering of Greek civilization, must be placed the progress of Gaul, Britain, North Africa, and Spain. Rome introduces to our examination of empire a challenging moral ambiguity—peace and material progress are now borne by the chariot of imperial domination.

Rome demands the attention of scholars of empire for three qualities: its size, its successful integration of diverse peoples, and its duration. It is an empire of full cycle rising over centuries to Mediterranean scope, retaining a Western predominance for at least 350 years, and declining and collapsing into ruins and memory. These features, moreover, are related, for its success and size are in part a function of its persistence, its persistence a function of its success. This chapter will examine the metropolitan factors that account for Rome's rise, its persistence and success, and its decline and fall. It will also suggest some of the sources of the political weakness that caused societies to succumb to Roman rule.

The Rise of Empire

"The principal conquests of the Romans were achieved under the republic; and the emperors, for the most part, were satisfied with preserving those dominions which had been acquired by the policy of the senate, the active emulation of the consuls, and the martial enthusiasm of the people."[2] So Gibbon summarized Rome's growth from a small village on one of the hills by the narrowing of the Tiber to the dominant power in Italy by 265 B.C., the beginning of the First Punic War. By 133 B.C., Carthage and Greece having been subdued, Rome dominated the Mediterranean.

It is at this early point that Rome crossed the metropolitan threshold. The expulsion of the Etruscan overlords, the severe challenge posed by the invasion of the Gauls, and a series of conquests in Italy appear to have engendered a civic pride and unity that made citizens impervious to foreign blandishments. In the same struggle, moreover, national political institutions were formed; they secured a means of participation

---

1. E. Gibbon, *The Decline and Fall of the Roman Empire*, ed. Dero Saunders (1776; New York, 1963), p. 107.

2. Ibid., p. 27.

and of coordinated decision making that could implement a directed, national policy. This national unity made expansion possible although limited in practice by the extent of Rome's resources and by regional rivals.[3]

The early expansion of the Roman city-state took place in alliance with small towns similarly caught between strong powers, the Etruscans and the Samnites. Through flexible diplomacy (and despite the disaster of the Gallic invasion), Rome step by step expanded its influence over allies in the Latin League, controlling the foreign policy of those internally free, sending out colonists to other areas more fully subjugated, and accepting on a nearly equal basis the citizenship of close and true friends.[4] Carthage at first supported this expansion, but soon Rome appeared more a rival than a client. The First Punic War, fought for the control of Sicily, divided the Mediterranean world into a bipolar rivalry. The Greek cities joined Rome, and Macedonia joined Carthage. Carthage's defeat brought southern Spain and Sicily to Rome as colonies to be ruled by governors and troops, not as Rome ruled the Italian allied states but as the Carthaginians themselves had ruled.

Rome next turned against Carthage's ally, Macedonia, to rescue its Greek allies of the Aetolian and Achaean leagues. Fighting for the freedom of Greece, Rome expelled Macedonia. However, both leagues soon came to resent Roman influence. The Aetolians called in the Syrians (191 B.C.), and the Achaeans joined with them to call in Macedonia against Rome. Again Rome triumphed, and the Greeks, once allies, became subjects.

Rome did not simply seize Greek territory, however, but penetrated it slowly. Rome became the "recognized guardian" of the balance of power at the request of the Greek city-states, guaranteeing freedom until a Greek ally demonstrated a disposition to carry out an independent policy.[5] Control in this situation of formal independence came through Roman military support and what now would probably be called Greek collaboration. As M. Rostovtzeff says, "The Greeks especially resented the frequent interference of Rome in the local affairs of their communities, though this interference was often invited by the complaints of one political party against another. As a rule the well-to-do class was in favor of Rome and was consistently supported by Rome against the

---

3. Tenney Frank, *Roman Imperialism* (New York, 1921), pp. 15–17.
4. Ibid., p. 34, and Ernest Badian, *Roman Imperialism in the Late Republic* (Ithaca, 1968), chap. 1.
5. Badian, pp. 3–5; M. Rostovtzeff, *Rome* (New York, 1960), pp. 70–71.

agitation of the lower class."[6] The Mediterranean was Rome's in fact, but the formal conclusion awaited the Third Punic War when Roman senators, alarmed by Carthaginian economic recovery, demanded the destruction of Carthage (146 B.C.).[7]

Roman officials stressed the role of the legal war and alliance keeping as the twin safeguards of the propriety of making war. The international context was also important, at Rome's historical cradle and at its Punic adolescence. But once these early threats had been eliminated, Rome faced no substantial external resistance until it encountered Parthia more than a century later. It is thus to Roman society and Roman politics that we must turn to discover other roots of expansion.[8]

Gibbon attributes Rome's rise to the national fidelity of its people, the military system of the legion, and the strength of its balanced government. The metropolitan roots of Rome's rise can indeed be divided into three analytical categories: social forces (social, cultural, and economic); technical and organizational means; and political institutions.

Polybius gives pride of place to the social and cultural forces of fidelity, honor, and religion. They, he argues, are the foundation of the Roman state. When the aristocratic youths of Rome honor their deceased fathers in the forum, "the chief benefit of the ceremony is that it inspires young men to shrink from no exertion for the general welfare, in the hope of obtaining the glory which awaits the brave."[9] Education and religion alike reinforced this national style of a people that Polybius, Gibbon's source, described as incapable of fear and "impatient of repose."[10] Machiavelli similarly identifies Romans as "lovers of the glory and the common good of their country" and again stresses the importance of liberty—giving vent to the ambition of individuals—as a cornerstone of Roman power. Liberty, ambition, and patriotism are conjoined,

6. Rostovtzeff, pp. 70–71.

7. George Liska, *Career of Empire: America and Imperial Expansion over Land and Sea* (Baltimore, 1978), stresses the factor of the Carthaginian threat, arguing that "an early threat to physical survival recurs historically as *the* traceable impetus to expansion on a relatively large scale" (pp. 7–8).

8. William V. Harris, *War and Imperialism in Republican Rome* (Oxford, 1979), chap. 2, which discusses the economic motives for war, lays stress on the internal sources of Roman imperialism.

9. Polybius, *Histories*, trans. E. Shuckburgh (Bloomington, 1962), 6. 54. Polybius contrasts this to the essentially commercial imperialism driving Carthage.

10. Ibid., 6. 56. For an assessment along similar lines by a contemporary scholar, see C. R. Whittaker, "Carthaginian Imperialism in the Fifth and Fourth Centuries," in P. Garnsey and Whittaker, eds., *Imperialism in the Ancient World* (Cambridge, 1978).

strengthening the state through religion, "the most necessary and assured support of any civil society."

Economic forces are equally important. Considered as a social foundation for imperialism, the productivity of Roman agriculture is second only to fidelity and patriotism. Small farms that produce adequate crops provide an economic base for a citizen army. Lacking the elaborate and delicate organization of irrigation, which would have rendered the levies of citizens for military campaigns economically disastrous, the citizens can avoid the despotism of public irrigation ("Oriental Despotism") and be free for civic participation and imperial expansion.[11]

Social forces thus buttress the power of the state: public economic resources were adequate, and national religion bound ambitious and patriotic citizens to one another and to the state. But as Machiavelli emphasizes, "The great things which Rome achieved . . . have been the work either of the government or of private individuals." Indeed, internal social forces often appeared to be driving government policy, even foreign policy, before them. Because military skill was necessary for high officialdom, constant warfare provided a regular part of the Roman career ladder. A victory was a stage in the aristocratization of a family; a campaign, evidence of fitness for election to higher office.[12] In the west the triumphant general produced a high body count; from the east he returned with booty, including the masterpieces of classical culture.

On a more mundane plain, a growing population demanded more land. That part of the population not supported by domestic agriculture (which, it appears, had always been substantial) required that its trade goods—pottery, weaponry—be protected in transit.[13] From the earliest times Rome's neighbors saw their lands confiscated and settled by Roman farmer-soldiers, whose presence secured the future loyalty and commercial accessibility of the area.

As the expanding city-state grew wealthier, its socioeconomic struc-

11. N. Machiavelli, *The Prince and the Discourses*, trans. L. Ricci (New York, 1950), pp. 120, 146–47. The public works source of "Oriental Despotism" is the theme of Karl Wittfogel, *Oriental Despotism* (New Haven, 1957).

12. Badian, pp. 11–13. For a discussion of the role of glory and the *laus imperii* see P. A. Brunt, "Laus Imperii," in Garnsey and Whittaker, *Imperialism in the Ancient World*.

13. Chester G. Starr, *The Beginnings of Imperial Rome: Rome in the Mid-Republic* (Ann Arbor, 1980), chap. 3. For the opposite view, Rome as pure consumer of the agriculture surplus, see Max Weber, *The Agrarian Society of Ancient Civilizations*, trans. R. I. Frank (London, 1976), p. 48; but for the need for male slaves as a stimulus to war, p. 55.

ture slowly changed.[14] The senators emerged as the largest landholders, their massive estates worked by slave labor. Some wars even took on the character of vast slave-hunting expeditions.[15] The plebeian small farmers, unable to compete with the efficient commercial agriculture of the large plantations, became increasingly poor and fled to the city, joining a nascent urban proletariat. In between there developed a class of merchants and moneylenders.

The plebs demanded land and free grain from the empire and were able to make their demands felt through the tribunate and in the elections of the consuls. Popular leaders such as the Gracchi, in addition to attempting a redistribution of Italian land and foreign land for colonization, sought in various acquisitions of territory an imperial patrimony for the common man.[16] The senators, slowly freeing themselves from legal restrictions on the exercise of wealth (the *lex Claudia*), invested in financial ventures to foreign cities which would be enforced by Roman troops.[17] Whole provinces became in practice clients of great senators. Carthage, its strategic power crippled, had its competitive productivity destroyed in order to guarantee the wine and olive trade to the Roman oligarchy, and Carthaginian land was itself parceled out among Rome's wealthy landowning classes. The merchants, tax collectors, and financiers followed in the immediate wake of the Roman military.[18] Transmarine agricultural enterprises of extensive scale thus linked together the economies and societies of the Roman empire.[19]

Roman society and economy imperialized itself by pursuing the welfare of its parts. The plebs became the population source of transnational colonies; the senators constructed transmarine agricultural enterprises; and the merchants formed commercial companies and tax-collection partnerships. The wealth of the Spanish mines flowed to Rome, cheap grain from Sicily lowered prices (and completed the ruination of small farmers), and provincial revenues permitted, in 167 B.C., the abolition of taxes for citizens. All helped bind together as an empire what otherwise would have been no more than a series of military adventures.

Without the technical and organizational means to support these expanding metropolitan and transnational interests, which both created

14. Rostovtzeff, p. 38.
15. P. Anderson, *Passages from Antiquity to Feudalism* (London, 1974), p. 62.
16. P. A. Brunt, *Social Conflicts in the Roman Republic* (London, 1971), pp. 85–88.
17. Harris, chap. 1, and Brunt, p. 149.
18. Badian, p. 45; Rostovtzeff, p. 146.
19. Badian, pp. 74–76.

Roman power and required its exercise, social forces could have had little impact on history. They would have been mere motives without a method. The method that did exist was, of course, the extraordinary military machine of the Roman legion. At first the army, composed of citizens called up for the duration and commanded by officers appointed by the Senate, was primarily a defensive force. Few aggressors, however, could outlast Rome's patriotic and disciplined legions. With continued success, the army became more demanding than responsive: booty made war lucrative for the survivors, and longer campaigns fought further from home engendered personal ties between commander and troops. By the first century B.C. these forces had combined to create war machines, led by Marius and Sulla, of a nearly Schumpeterian sort, fighting for the sake of the spoils victory brings in land and booty, fighting not merely Rome's enemies but the enemies the armies needed—even fellow Roman armies.[20]

The political institutions of Rome have frequently been identified as central to its imperial rise. Their stability and strength helped give direction to Rome's unleashed private energies. It can also be argued, however, that their limitations nearly destroyed the empire and thus Rome itself, and that a revolution was truly required to create permanent imperial institutions adequate to support a permanent empire.

Rome's constitution was fit for empire. It rested upon liberty (for nonslaves, of course) and thus freed the energies and ambitions of the people, who could safely be armed to guard the state. It opened its citizenship to outsiders. It relied upon the Senate for a stability of interest and as a source of high officials, educated in leisure and animated by the public concern that a life of material plenty can provide. For direction in peace and war, the consuls, nominated from the Senate and elected by the Assembly, provided the coordination indispensable to military strategy and civic emergencies. This combination of participation, patriotism, a public elite, and governmental coordination provided a striking source of political strength.[21] This was the constitutional order that Aristotle described as mixed and Machiavelli called perfect. The energies of the populace were not fettered; they were directed.[22]

Rome's Periphery

After the defeat of Carthage, Rome met no rival that threatened its own immediate security—which goes far to account for the size of the

20. Badian, pp. 76–92.
21. Machiavelli, chaps. 2–4; Anderson, p. 60.
22. Machiavelli, p. 127.

empire Rome acquired. To understand Roman expansion we need to examine the sources not only of Rome's power but of the weakness of Rome's victims. Rome's periphery involved two types of states: in the west, by and large, tribal societies or "barbarians," in the east civilized states, generally patrimonial monarchies and fractionated republics.[23] Both their weaknesses and the ways in which Rome ruled them differed.

Tacitus, though speaking of a later period, best recounts the major weakness of the tribal societies that Roman armies encountered: "Indeed nothing has helped us more in fighting against their [the Britons'] powerful nations than their inability to cooperate. It is but seldom that two or three states unite to repel a common danger; thus, fighting in separate groups, all are conquered."[24] He elaborates the point, while revealing the brutal attitudes that colored Roman war against tribal peoples, in a comment on warfare among German tribes:

> The Bructeri were defeated and almost annihilated by a coalition of neighboring tribes. Perhaps they were hated for their domineering pride; or it may have been the lure of booty, or some special favour accorded us by the gods. We were even permitted to witness the battle. More than 60,000 were killed, not by Roman swords or javelins, but—more splendid still—as a spectacle before our delighted eyes. Long, I pray, may foreign nations persist, if not in loving us, at least in hating one another, for destiny is driving our empire upon its appointed path, and fortunes can bestow us no better gift than discord among our foes.[25]

The primary weakness of the tribal societies of the west was not their lack of internal political unity—indeed, local patriotism was fierce and uncompromising. Rather, their primary weakness was a lack of social differentiation and thus their small scale. Social roles were mixed together, familial ties shaped commerce and religion, and political leaders were, indistinguishably, both public and private figures. These societies lacked the productivity to expand beyond the village. Linkages to other villages within the larger tribal affiliation were thereby tenuous since they neither shared a common economic interdependence nor, more significantly, a common state or political system. The fierce loyalties of tribal members thus extended no farther than the next hill; over the hill the next village or band was as much a rival or an enemy as the Romans. Many tribes such as the Aedui and the Remi, as Caesar recalls, aided

23. Badian, pp. 2–12.
24. Tacitus, "The Agricola," no. 12.
25. Tacitus, "The Germania," no. 33.

the Romans against their fellow Gauls. Facing fiercely combative but poorly organized tribes, Roman legions waged their wars brutally, massacring and enslaving.[26]

Political disorganization made it necessary for Rome, having conquered, to rule directly the areas it had acquired. Collaboration at the local level aided the Romans in ruling each new province, but frequent rebellions, still piecemeal, called for large garrisons and active military governors to administer law and order in the new provinces until urbanization permitted a more civilian administration.

Warfare and rule in the east was different. Just as expansion in the west reflected Roman behavior toward potential plantation slaves, so expansion toward the civilized east reflected Rome's domestic politics. Accustomed to the informal electoral alliances of city politics, the Romans exercised a similarly informal control, like that of an electoral coalition, over the peoples subject to their growing influence in Italy. Montesquieu described this informal power in these words:

> When they allowed a city to remain free, they immediately caused two factions to arise within it. One upheld the local laws and liberty, the other maintained that there was no law but the will of the Romans. And since the latter faction was always the stronger, it is easy to see that such freedom was only a name.
>
> It was a slow way of conquering. They vanquished a people and were content to weaken it. They imposed conditions on it which undermined it insensibly. If it revolted, it was reduced still further, and it became a subject people without anyone being able to say when its subjection began.[27]

This informality may have resulted from Rome's own ideology of law and freedom. Recognizing no formal status between slavery and freedom, the Romans engaged in two types of imperial expansion. Among civilized states of the east, Rome maintained the fiction of alliance as a cloak for control. Among the barbarians of the west, Rome engaged in predatory land seizures and slave hunts. But an equally important source

26. Caesar, *Gallic Wars*, trans. S. A. Handford (Baltimore, 1951), 2, 1–35, for the conquest of Belgium and the role of the Remi. Camille Jullian, a modern French historian, clearly became exasperated by the Gauls' failure to unite and repel the Romans. He declares that they were "rushing headlong into slavery" and engaging in "indifference amounting to treason," *Histoire de la Gaule* (Paris, 1908–26), 3:223 and passim. See also the biography by Gerard Walter, *Caesar*, trans. E. Crawfurd (London, 1953).

27. Montesquieu, *Considerations on the Causes of the Greatness of the Romans and Their Decline*, trans. D. Lowenthal (New York, 1968), pp. 69–70.

of this difference is that the east had political societies that could collaborate with Rome.

The first such society was the socially differentiated commercial oligarchy or democracy that was deeply divided into political factions reflecting class or ethnic differences. The Greek states, like the Ionian cities of the fifth century, were in just this condition at the time of the Macedonian wars; external Roman power helped keep Roman collaborators in power at home. The more that collaborators came to depend on external Roman support, the closer they moved toward an imperialized periphery.[28]

A related situation developed in Rome's relations with the patrimonial kingdoms of the east. Socially differentiated commercial societies of considerable scale, those kingdoms nonetheless lacked substantial political integration: the populations were either not mobilized politically or, if mobilized, were ethnically divided. The ruler, to secure his political position against domestic strife and foreign threats as well as to improve his personal finances, made himself a puppet, a client, of Rome. When populations did become politically mobilized, as did the Jews in the Province of Judea, and began political rebellion, the collaborating ruler had to be replaced with formal imperial rule.[29]

Tribal, fractionated, and patrimonial political societies met the fate of those unable to stage a vigorous resistance to Roman penetration. Unlike imperial Carthage (and later the Jews), which Rome destroyed, either these societies were too weak to threaten Roman security once overrun or their pro-Roman factions and patrimonial rulers found positive incentives to collaborate with Rome. They make up the other half of Rome's successful imperialism.

28. Polybius, 24. 11–12. Polybius recounts the message that Callicrates, a member of the pro-Roman faction, brought to the Senate: "The Romans were themselves responsible for the Greeks neglecting their orders and letters instead of obeying them. For in all the democratic states of the day there were two parties—one recommending obedience to the Roman rescripts, and holding neither law nor tablet nor anything else to be superior to the will of Rome; the other always quoting oaths and tablets, and exhorting the people to be careful about breaking them. Now the latter policy was by far the most popular in Achaia, and the most influential with the multitude; consequently the Romanisers were discredited and denounced amoung the populace—their opponents glorified. If the Senate would give some sign of their interest in the matter, the leaders, in the first place, would quickly change to the Romanizing party, and, in the next place, would be followed by the populace from fear." See G. Bowersock, *Augustus and the Greek World* (Oxford, 1963), for this and more general, including cultural, relations with the Greek world during the late republic and early empire.

29. Edward N. Luttwak, *The Grand Strategy of the Roman Empire* (Baltimore, 1976), chap. 1.

The Crisis of Republican Imperialism

The order that worked so well to protect and expand the city when its politics were based upon the general needs (so often forced upon the small and weak nation by surrounding circumstances) crumbled under the pressure of its own success.

When Roman arms removed the threats to Rome's security, the city-state mechanism of neighborhood politics broke down. The city-state constitution, sensitive in responding to particular demands, particularized policy and encouraged those less advantageously placed to make further particularistic demands. The people demanded and were able to require the state to seize land and booty; the Senate demanded estates and interest payments since the urban proletariat threatened their property. There was no recourse but expansion. The expansion required in the first century B.C., however, rendered the constitution ineffective, for if policy is to respond absolutely to the demands of all, there will not be enough for any. It is for this reason that, Machiavelli argues, there is no crueler fate than being subject to a republic, for under a republic a multitude must be satisfied, under a monarchy only one man.[30]

So the republican constitution, which had regulated the state while its national existence was threatened, succumbed to its own successes and its inability to regulate the distribution of booty and too-lucrative offices.[31] Rome, its civic constitution and empire, was seized by the dictators of the first century B.C., by Marius, by Sulla, by the triumvirate, by Caesar, and finally by Augustus. Augustus accomplished a metropolitan, imperial revolution, crossing the threshold to persistent empire.

The Persistence of Empire

Some historians have remarked upon the rapidity of Rome's rise, but almost all have marveled at the duration of Rome's empire across four centuries of Mediterranean dominion. The reasons for this persistence might be sought in Rome's international position. The international system provided no positive incentives to unity, for after Carthage, and not excluding Parthia, no enemies wielded power sufficient to unify

30. Machiavelli, pp. 286–87. And see K. Hopkins, *Conquerors and Slaves* (Cambridge, 1978), pp. 1–74.

31. See R. E. Smith, *The Failure of the Roman Republic* (London, 1955), pp. 50–53, and Ronald Syme, *The Roman Revolution* (Oxford, 1939), chap. 14, for an analysis of the proscriptions following each dictator's seizure of power.

Rome. On the negative side, however, the international system at least presented no enemies that could by force of arms have broken up the empire. The barbarians who finally brought the western empire down in the fourth and fifth centuries A.D. seem to have been no larger in number than, or superior in skill to, those defeated centuries before. It was Rome that had changed. Before we look at those changes, however, the more interesting question of why the empire lasted as long as it did presents itself.

Two major metropolitan conditions seem important to the empire's duration. First is the necessary political basis, the Augustan administrative revolution, which brought Rome over the "Augustan Threshold" into permanent empire. Second are the political, social, economic, and cultural forces and institutions that, through their extension from Italy, helped integrate on a transnational basis the disparate areas of the empire. They thus reduced the burden on the imperial administration that Augustus had created.

The Augustan Threshold

Rome in the first century B.C. was near collapse. The government had become the prize of warring factions, for reasons suggested above, and the empire and its riches were proving too great a spoil for the sensitive republican constitution to bear. The inefficiency of the republican scheme of government, its rapid turnover of offices, made the rule of a growing empire erratic. Each governor attempted to enrich himself, his family, and his clients during a short term of office. So large a prize—the spoils of empire—combined with such poor administration made it seem to each leading politician, Caesar, Pompey, and Crassus among them, that to prevent the prize going to a rival he needs must seize it for himself. Each leader attempted to create the needed coordination as keystone for the crumbling republican arch.[32]

But one leader's regulation was the usurpation of the next, provoking further revolt from the provincial armies. The chaos of the provinces required more than temporary dictatorship at the capital. A speech by Maecenas delivered before Augustus describes the dilemma of the republic before Augustus's administrative revolution:

> The cause of our troubles is the multitude of our population and the magnitude of the business of our government; for the population

---

32. W. E. Heitland, "The Roman Fate," in Donald Kagan, ed., *End of the Roman Empire* (Boston, 1978), pp. 70–91; Rostovtzeff, pp. 146, 149–52.

embraces men of every kind, in respect both of race and endowment, and both their tempers and desires are manifold; and the business of the state has become so vast that it can be administered only with the greatest difficulty.

Our city like a great merchantman manned with a crew of every race and lacking a pilot, has now for many generations been rolling and plunging, a ship as it were without ballast.[33]

Maecenas's words, of course, reflect the official version of the demise of the republic from a later and imperial viewpoint. The republic had become unmanageable nonetheless, and it desperately required administrative leadership of the sort that only an authoritarian, bureaucratic revolution could provide.

The Augustan revolution avoided the fate of Athens' empire during a similar breakdown of central authority. Augustus fundamentally changed the Roman constitution in two respects, and in so doing he established the conditions for persistent empire. S. N. Eisenstadt describes these conditions:

First, those "internal" conditions in the political sphere ... are the rulers' development of articulated political aspirations and activities which promote the development of autonomous political goals. Second, the "external" conditions ... are certain developments in the non-political institutions, in the fields of economic and cultural activity or social organization and stratification. The major such external condition is the development, within *all* the institutional spheres of society (albeit in differing measures), of certain limited levels of differentiation, together with what we call "free-floating" resources.[34]

Rome had already acquired the second condition. Its society was quite thoroughly differentiated along functional rather than ascriptive lines by the time of Augustus. The old ascriptive restrictions were in disarray, and Rome if anything suffered from a surfeit of free-floating resources. The crucial question was who was going to capture them.

The first condition touches upon the Augustan achievement. The Roman polity, by the first century, was undergoing a revolution, an overturning of the Senate's rule of the republic. It was rapidly losing its governmental centralization (as the Senate failed to control provincial

---

33. Dio Cassius, quoted in J. B. Bury, ed., *The Cambridge Ancient History*, vol. 10 (Cambridge, 1952), p. 192.

34. S. N. Eisenstadt, *The Political Systems of Empires* (New York, 1969), p. 27.

governors) and its autonomy (as the state became little more than a means of private enrichment).[35]

Augustus began to recentralize the state, now an imperial state, after his military victory over Anthony at Actium. The Augustan revolution rested on three achievements. Augustus rescued and thus won the full support of the Italian and provincial landed gentry who had suffered so directly and gained so little from the civil wars and predations of the urban oligarchy of Rome.[36] He reformed the administrative system. And he acquired a special, charismatic influence over the polity which he was able to bequeath to his successors as a monarchy in all but name.

The victory recentralized the army, the prime mover of politics in the late republic.[37] The major portion of the army was placed directly under the control of Augustus, thus removing it as a stepping stone to coups d'état. The major frontier provinces were placed under his direct administration, governors being his appointees. The provinces began economic recovery while officials governed with the long-term public interest more clearly in focus. The great and wealthy province of Egypt became a personal possession of the emperor as did an enormous estate acquired through confiscations. With his personal subsidy, the state treasury was able to fund these new administrative demands. Augustus's wealth and military leadership also helped him to reconcile the old republican order to the new bureaucratic, imperial reality. Controlling so much of the real substance of power—money and arms—he was able to leave much of the form—civic offices—in the hands of the Senate and the electoral assemblies.[38]

The removal of the empire from domestic politics created the conditions for steady imperial rule. The provinces could be efficiently ruled because the empire's strength was focused, and the empire was strong because, with the stability thus created, its economy could develop. This central, bureaucratic administration is the crucial condition for long-term empire whenever the periphery bears a significant political and economic value relative to the metropole, and herein lay the crux of Augustan reform: the development of a radically autonomous state. By removing control of the state from the city of Rome—from its senatorial

---

35. Ibid., p. 23.
36. Ronald Syme, *The Roman Revolution* (London, 1960), pp. 8, 360–65.
37. Rostovtzeff, pp. 170–72.
38. Ibid., pp. 177, 216. See also Chester G. Starr, *The Roman Empire: A Study in Survival* (New York, 1982), chap. 4, for an account of imperial administration from the period of Augustus.

oligarchy, equestrian financiers, and popular assembly—Augustus established a bureaucracy that put his, its own, and the empire's interests before any specifically Roman demands. In the absence of such an imperial bureaucracy, the periphery will be ravaged, the metropole divided, and both destroyed.

Administration alone, however, would be too costly; other foundations are needed to link the metropole and the provinces. Transnational forces support bureaucratic structure by integrating the political, social, economic, and cultural systems of the periphery and the metropole. Joining elite to mass and region to region, they provide a social basis for authority and coordination.[39]

Politically, Rome lowered administrative costs by permitting local self-government when possible and desirable (to Rome). Roman citizens, both civilians and retired legionnaires, retained their Roman rights of self-government (*communitas* and *libertas*) when they joined colonies in Gaul or Spain. Foreign cities that had aided Rome in the conquest of their country often also received the Latin rights of municipal self-government which Rome had granted its early Italian allies. Backward areas, those still tribal in character, were placed under the authority of a leading local family (e.g., the former chief) and permitted to handle much of their civic life on the basis of established local customs. A chain of promotion in legal status for provincial political communities mirrored the promotion to citizen for aspiring provincial leaders and recruits into the legions, who received citizenship after twenty-five years of service.[40]

This political integration operated at two levels: while the masses progressed from tribal *civitates* to *municipiae* to *communitates*, the elite were in effect one step ahead of the masses, since local aristocracies usually acquired full citizenship when the common provincials reached

39. Integration is a highly complex concept. It carries with it, even in general use, the following distinctions: first, it is a process and a condition. Both senses will be used here, the first being distinguished by "integrating." Either a mechanical integration (a similarity of values or of interests) or an organic integration (an interdependence of these values or interests), or both, can suffice to integrate a polity. Second, integration contains dimensions: vertical (stratum or class) and horizontal (territorial, or rather the people inhabiting various territories). I specify the dimension I intend unless both are intended. Lastly, integration has sectors: political, economic, social, and cultural. Each sector can in turn be integrated mechanically, organically, vertically, and horizontally. These distinctions can be important in clarifying integration and will be specified where the concept is not clear from the context.

40. S. A. Cook et al., eds., *The Cambridge Ancient History*, vol. 11 (Cambridge, 1936), pp. 197–99.

Latin rights. Moreover, elites could move higher than common people: Claudius inducted provincials into the Senate, and in 99 A.D. Trajan, a provincial from Spain, was accepted as emperor.[41]

Thus the empire was politically integrated. Administrative costs were kept low, and positive loyalty was elicited from provincials seeking full citizenship. The logical culmination occurred in the year 212, when the emperor Caracalla declared that all free men were citizens of Rome. Such was the progress of political integration that this edict caused little comment when enacted.

A Caracallan Threshold?

Under Caracalla, Rome became a political community in which citizens possessed attenuated but equal rights. Was Rome still an empire in the sense of one people controlling another? Rome had in fact reached an imperial apotheosis: the political distinction between peoples was removed even though inequalities based on class and regional tensions, manifested in the eastern revolt under Zenobia, survived.[42] But rather than moving toward the common freedom of a republican Rome, the peoples of the empire saw institutionalized participation in Rome decline more rapidly than it rose in the provinces. In 212 the peoples of the empire were assimilated in a common tyranny.

Equally powerful and more lasting was the extension of Roman society and culture. It is characteristic of this empire and later ones that the metropole tended to duplicate itself abroad in the colonies.[43] Rome urbanized the Mediterranean world and spread knowledge of Latin and, for an elite, Greek throughout the west. People began to feel themselves part of a common civilization, producing creative talent not just in Rome or Greece but in other parts of the west and the east. Culture bred loyalty, and loyalty increased the strength of the empire while helping keep administrative coercion down.

The transprovincial economy, another binding force, also contributed to the integration of the empire. Piracy was suppressed, military roads built, and with sea and land substantially secure, commerce spread throughout the Mediterranean. The pottery, bronze, and wine and oil

---

41. Rostovtzeff, p. 277; there followed Septimius Severus, an African from Lepcis Magna (in modern Libya), and Elagabalus, a Syrian. See Anthony Birley, *Septimius Severus: The African Emperor* (London, 1971), and also the insightful comparative study by Ronald Syme, *Colonial Elites: Rome, Spain and the Americas* (London, 1958), chap. 1.

42. Rostovtzeff, pp. 248–50.

43. Peter Brown, *The World of Late Antiquity* (London, 1971), p. 14.

of Italy were exchanged for African grain and eastern spices.[44] Economies of scale led to large productive enterprises scattered throughout what was otherwise an overwhelmingly agricultural world. These exchanges created ties of mutual interest to support the ties of mutual compliance under imperial administration. The flourishing economy, moreover, produced a sense of general well-being which made ruling, and collecting taxes, easier tasks. Commercial development was a particularly easy form of wealth to tax; harbor dues were easy to collect and since they could be passed along, not subject to great resistance. Rome revolutionized the commerce of the ancient world on a most extensive scale, and in commerce lay much of the free-floating, imperially mobilizable resources that fed and armed the legions and paid the administrators.

During the golden age of the Antonines, in the second century A.D., years could pass between sightings of a soldier in provincial towns within the borders of the empire. Rome developed an imperial bureaucracy and army and thus crossed the Augustan Threshold to persistence. Rome's signal accomplishment, however, lay in not needing administrative coercion in much of the day-to-day life of the empire. The transprovincial economy and the empirewide loyalties of a socially and politically integrated community made coercion exceptional rather than ordinary.

Decline and Fall

"The rise of a city, which swelled into an empire, may deserve, as a singular prodigy, the reflection of a philosophic mind. But the decline of Rome was the natural and inevitable product of immoderate greatness. Prosperity ripened the principle of decay: the causes of destruction multiplied with the extent of conquest; and as soon as time or accident had removed the artificial supports, the stupendous fabric yielded to the pressure of its own weight."[45] So Gibbon identified Rome's immoderate greatness as the root cause of its decline and fall. More specifically, he noted the growth in influence of the legions and the militarization of politics, and the burden of a government divided between Rome and Constantinople. The Christian religion sapped the military and civic power of the ancient world as man's aspirations turned to the saintly calling. The increase in strength of the barbarians also played a part, of

44. Rostovtzeff, pp. 175, 248.
45. Gibbon, p. 621. See Glen Bowersock, "Gibbon on Civil War and Rebellion in Rome," *Daedalus* 105, 3 (1976), 63–88; and Lionel Gossman, *The Empire Unpossess'd* (Cambridge, 1981), for Gibbon's ambiguous formulations of the decline of Roman power.

course, as did the lack of competition which allowed a hardening of imperial society's political arteries. Not needing to make constant adjustments, political and strategic, Rome atrophied. Having unified the known world, Rome came to know a greatness that was immoderate.

These are important insights; but one half of the empire, Byzantium, did *not* fall.[46] Why did the western half collapse? This decline and fall can best be understood as a slow undermining of the conditions that, Eisenstadt posited, are necessary for permanent empire. The central element of Rome's persistence was the Augustan reorganization of the internal, governmental conditions of the imperial metropole; the central element in the decline and fall was the deterioration of the external conditions of differentiation in society, culture, economy, and polity. Their various declines reduced the resources that the imperial government could mobilize.

To some extent international factors—the barbarian attacks—can be seen as an explanation for, and not just the agent of, Rome's fall. Without these external attacks, even a deteriorating empire might have continued to exist almost indefinitely, or until rebellions broke it into separate states. More importantly, its chances of eventual renewal, a return to original or new principles, would have been preserved. The barbarian attacks that swept aside the imperial edifice in the fifth century ended this possibility, and no western Justinian could restore Rome to imperial power. International strategic position also helps account for the fall of the west and the survival of the east. The northern frontier, Britannia, lay exposed to the Picts and, from across the North Sea, to the Saxons and Jutes. The entire Rhine frontier of Gaul and Rhaetia was easily bridged, opening the heart of the western empire—southern Gaul, Italy, Spain, North Africa—to further attacks. The eastern empire had only to defend itself along the Danube frontier; Egypt was protected by deserts, Asia Minor by the Black Sea and the Caucasus. Of course, Parthia fronted on Syria, but Parthia was another civilized power, doubly dangerous in war but amenable to negotiated peace. If Byzantium did suffer defeat on the Danube front, the imperial heartland of Asia Minor and the Middle East would still be secure behind the defenses of the Bosphorus.[47]

The observer who compares the barbarian attacks to Caesar's Gallic

46. N. H. Baynes, "The Decline of the Roman Empire in Western Europe: Some Modern Explanations," in Kagan, pp. 29–35.

47. A. M. Jones, *The Decline of the Ancient World* (London, 1966), pp. 362–63; Baynes, p. 84; Montesquieu, p. 179.

campaigns, or Trajan's conquest of Dacia, or Marcus Aurelius's war in Rhaetia, cannot fail to be struck by the fact that the fifth-century challenge was not on some new, disastrous scale. It was Rome, and particularly the west, which had changed. Collapse stemmed not from the hordes of Attila or the Ostrogoths but from within Rome itself.

Some classical historians now question the traditional picture of the Roman empire in a general and unrelieved decline. The military emperors of the fourth century, after all, did defend the frontiers better than their third-century predecessors had done. (Peter Brown's image of Napoleonic marshals replacing ineffective aristocrats is an arresting contrast to the usual allusions to creeping military despotism.)[48] Both aggregate and per capita economic product may not have declined.[49] Indeed, the rich were perhaps never more wealthy that they were in the twilight of the empire. Yet aspects of the Roman imperial polity, society, economy, and culture had changed, reversing Rome's political evolution. The steady loss of social and economic differentiation, of a sense of national community, of political unity, undermined the imperial integration and the imperial bureaucracy that had made the empire of Rome endure.

The strength of the permanent empire had rested on Rome's bureaucratic and military reorganization under Augustus. Now this strength became the germ of decay. Rome's political bases of persistent power lay in the political autonomy of the emperor and in participation in government. By the third century the emperor was encroaching upon urban self-government. The legions discovered that emperors could be made outside Rome, and in the post-Antonine age the army began to play a self-interested role, demanding spoils from its own political system. Rome became the army's conquered province, the emperors its tax collectors. Differentiation in the military sphere decreased, and army interests became particularistic. Thus Severus saw the need to "enrich

48. Peter Brown, *The World of Late Antiquity* (London, 1971), pp. 25–30, and his *The Making of Late Antiquity* (Cambridge, 1978). Glen Bowersock, "The Dissolution of the Roman Empire," in N. Yoffee and G. L. Cowgill, eds., *The Collapse of Ancient Civilizations* (forthcoming), stresses that decline should be viewed as a creative process of adjustment to new social and strategic tensions, a process in which boundaries had to, and did, shift.

49. Gerald Gunderson, "Economic Change in the Decline of the Roman Empire," *Explorations in Economic History* 13 (1976), 43–68, very usefully corrects some of the earlier generalizations. But his assumption of highly flexible market adjustments and neglect of the availability (or lack thereof) of discretionary capital and the social or political constraints on differing forms of investment may limit his conclusions.

the soldiers" as the first demand on the resources of the state.[50] Even Diocletian's substantial reforms were unable to reduce the influence of the army, now centered about two emperors and two caesars as personal followers—a military caste of soldiers bound to their profession and officers who acted as military entrepreneurs.

The civilian bureaucracy went through a similar evolution. First, it grew in size relative to the civic population, absorbing more functions and elaborating its own hierarchic structure. Over time the upper bureaucracy became the preserve of the very wealthy, and office became a sinecure and a property right. The bureaucracy became representative of the wealthy classes and their particularistic interests,[51] and the state lost its effectiveness and its general impartiality. The urban poor sought out the protection of strong rural landholders.

As the army and the bureaucracy both increased their particular demands, the range of self-government shrank. Faced with difficulties in tax collection, the central government made city counselors personally responsible for the payment of tax. Civic life, burdened with such penalties, naturally declined, and the bureaucracy had to grow even further to replace the political coordination once performed by city councils.

Rome was bound to weaken. The army and the bureaucracy grew to be enormous organizations supported by the declining, taxable, productive part of the population. The weight of taxation depressed rural productivity and ground the peasantry down into mass poverty, and the people developed an attitude of civic apathy.[52] Apathy made administration more difficult and local self-defense against barbarian attacks practically nonexistent. However, these traits were shared by west and east. Both experienced growing bureaucracies and armies and declining civic responsibility.[53] Both faced these same pressures, these same demands, on the political mobilization of resources. The reason for the more extensive decline and the later fall of Rome is to be found in the resources available to meet these demands. The crucial difference between east and west lies in the relative level of free-floating, mobilizable resources.[54]

50. Rostovtzeff, p. 267.

51. Cook et al., pp. 29–30, 256–58, 270–80.

52. A. Bernardi, "The Economic Problems of the Roman Empire," in C. Cipolla, ed., *The Economic Decline of Empires* (London, 1970), p. 48. In the same volume, see also M. I. Finley, "Manpower and the Decay of Rome," chap. 2, and Charles Diehl, "The Economic Decay of Byzantium," chap. 3.

53. M. I. Finley, *The Ancient Economy* (London, 1973), pp. 85–90.

54. Jones, pp. 367–68.

The west was tending to see a concentration of property and income within an ever smaller landlord class that was reorganizing economic life into near-feudal patterns. Much of the extensive trade that characterized the early empire was derived from large differences in technology. As the later technology of limited slave-based production spread, each region began to produce the full range of basic products, and trade in mass goods fell. Local self-sufficiency rose (prefiguring the medieval economy), the habit of extensive trade was forgotten, and in a smaller market, lower levels of efficiency may have prevailed. The barbarians also disturbed trade patterns, significantly increasing the risk of any merchant venture.[55] In the east, on the other hand, land remained more equally distributed and agricultural efficiency higher. Trade continued to play a larger role in the economy in part because the east was a source of the luxury goods that the rich still demanded and in part because its trade routes were more secure from barbarian attack.[56]

When the state sought resources from society in the west, it had to grant special concessions to the powerful rich who not only owned the land but staffed the bureaucracy, and each new state demand progressively increased the enfeudalization of the economy. A vicious circle of privatization and tax avoidance left the state impoverished, the rich wealthy, and the mass of the people destitute and dependent.[57]

The imperial state in the west suffered from a declining ability to mobilize resources. This failure, given the division of the empire, was critical. The wealth of the whole empire could not be used to meet the barbarian attacks. The citizenry could no longer be mobilized because, unlike the ancient Romans, they felt themselves to be mere consumers, not producers, of public order. The army and the bureaucracy themselves became privatized. Barbarians in complete tribes were brought in as entrepreneurial ventures by military leaders, and the bureaucracy became the patrimony of the wealthy. When the barbarians appeared, how many western Romans may have said "Better Genseric, or Alaric, than a revolutionary emperor"?

The Roman empire in the west lost the conditions of permanent empire and thereby lost the conditions of any empire, even the most ephemeral. Its emperors fell before repeated and increasingly frequent military revolts, its central administration shattered into local feudal

55. F. N. Walbank, *The Awful Revolution* (Toronto, 1968), p. 78.
56. Rostovtzeff, p. 256.
57. Walbank, pp. 92–96; it became more and more difficult for the small farmer, as opposed to the latifundist, to engage in tax evasion. Bernardi, pp. 81–83.

privileges, its army lost its payroll.[58] The Caracallan, Augustan, and metropolitan thresholds collapsed together. As its economy and society had progressively become less differentiated, so its sense of national community had been swamped by ethnic diversity. Its sense of a classical civilization shared by all had been overwhelmed by generations of political autocracy and corruption. The state had become a private possession of the ruling class, divided up among officials and a predatory army.

What was left of the centralized state, shrunken in resources and in influence, collapsed with barely a sound. It died with a whimper under the last western Roman emperor, Romulus Augustulus—whose very name, with its pathetic diminutive of Rome's founder and refounder, expresses the feeble condition of the last days of the Roman empire in the west.

58. Starr, p. 176; the three factors cited are the three he finds decisive in the collapse of Roman unity.

CHAPTER 5

The Ottoman, Spanish, and English Empires

Between the empires of classical antiquity and the empires of early modern Europe and the Near East there are substantial similarities. Actors recognize their imperial relationship as one people or organization ruling or controlling another. Usually this political relationship is acknowledged with satisfaction in the metropole, usually with laments in the peripheral area, but occasionally one finds a lonely voice in the metropolitan state decrying the brutality of empire, as did Las Casas in Spain. There are also similarities in technique, in style and evolution, and in the basic, metropolitan and peripheral roots of empire.

Differences, however, are also to be found. Some are matters merely of fashion and technique. Naval power, for example, becomes more efficient; advances in ocean-going technology enable maritime states to extend their influence to a degree that would have been excessively costly in the ancient world. Other differences are more important, and among them, in particular, the nature of the metropole and its evolution within an imperial framework call for closer examination. As the early modern metropoles differ from Rome or Athens, so their extensions abroad into the peripheries differ from the ancient empires. And as the periphery in the early modern era differs from the classical periphery, so its reception of imperialism also leads to different effects.

Again we shall be considering the rise, persistence, and fall of empires, and again shall be interested in particular imperial styles as well as the general roots of imperial development. I have chosen to consider the Ottomans, Spain, and England. The Ottoman exceeded other modern empires in duration, the Spanish in geographic extent; while it was during this early modern period that England laid the foundations of the greatest of nineteenth-century empires.

The Puzzle of Tribal Empire

The Arab, the Mongol, and the Ottoman empires might appear as striking anomalies to the view of empire presented in the previous chapter. They do not appear to meet the criteria suggested for a metropole: none began with a centralized state directing a differentiated society, none was characterized by substantial transnational economic extensions of domestic society. Indeed, they were tribal, or patriarchic, societies. Yet they conquered extensive land areas and ruled foreign peoples. Nevertheless, as Ibn Khaldun suggests, they are puzzles resolvable within and by the theory, exceptions that "prove" (in the original sense of "test") and do not refute the rule. Both Ibn Khaldun's account of Arab imperialism and the history of the Ottoman empire help resolve the puzzles.

Ibn Khaldun argued in his *Prolegomena* that tribal empires are normally next to impossible. "This is because they are more nomadic than other peoples, moving more freely in the deserts and, because of their simple and rough ways, stand in less need of cereals and other agricultural products [less differentiated]. This makes them less dependent on others and less ready to submit to authority. In fact their chiefs are generally dependent on them, since it is their solidarity which defends [the community]. Hence these chiefs must humor them and avoid any form of coercion, for this might cause disunion and end in the destruction of chiefs and the community."[1]

Ibn Khaldun portrays a society of limited social differentiation. Chiefs, sometimes called patriarchs, have more authority than their counterparts in a tribal band. But limited political direction and differentiation generally produce limited political power except, he argues, when these societies are galvanized by "a prophet or a saint" preaching a religion. Religion provides an "internal principle of restraint" that tames "fierce

---

1. Ibn Khaldun (1332–1406), *An Arab Philosophy of History*, trans. and ed. Charles Issawi (London, 1950), p. 59.

characters" and makes them amenable to leadership. The result is victory. The solidarity characteristic of the tribe is extended by religious association to *enlarge* the social unit and *direct* it, thus producing the power of a metropole without its sociopolitical institutions. This is the social basis that, Ibn Khaldun suggests, explains the overwhelming expansion of the Arabs. A similar if more personalistic and charismatic view also accounts for the strength of the Mongol sweep across Asia.

But Ibn Khaldun also argues that this type of expansion, this religious "metropolitanization" of tribal society, is ephemeral. Tribal solidarity, in the ruling of an extensive empire, he says soon transforms into "sovereignty"—coercion exercised by a state apparatus that is both military and bureaucratic. The conquering tribe, galvanized by religion, becomes socially differentiated and centrally directed in order to retain empire. Tribal empire is thus a significant but explicable exception soon corrected by the process of ruling.[2] Tribes can overrun and occupy, but to establish a settled imperial rule they must be transformed into metropoles.

The history of the rise and persistence of the Turks illustrates many of the forces that Ibn Khaldun described. The Turkish and Turcoman nomads who migrated into Anatolia in the eleventh century were still basically tribal or patriarchic peoples when they began to disrupt the decaying Byzantine empire. The defeat of Byzantium, however, at Manzikert in 1071 was not their victory. It was a battle won by a different Turkish people, the Seljuks led by Alp Arslan and already metropolitanized by fifty years of settled rule from Baghdad. The new invaders of Anatolia, who would become the Ottomans, inherited the Seljuks' victory when Arslan turned south to pursue a campaign against Egypt. Seljuk rule was short-lived, for soon thereafter the Crusaders, a revived Byzantine state, and the Mongols pounded the empire in succession. On the edges of the Mongol empire, however, Turkish tribesmen reestablished independent principalities beginning in about 1250. One tribe was the Osmanli.[3]

These Anatolian Turkish tribesmen were stamped with a strikingly militant culture (*ghazi* fanaticism), an Islamic equivalent of the Crusaders.[4] Indeed, after the overrunning of Anatolia by the Mongol horde, it

2. Ibid., pp. 108, 118.

3. Osman Turan, "Anatolia in the Period of the Seljuks and the Beyliks," in P. M. Holt, A. Lambton, and B. Lewis, eds., *The Cambridge History of Islam*, vol. 1 (Cambridge, 1970), pp. 232–54.

4. Paul Wittek, *The Rise of the Ottoman Empire* (London, 1963), pp. 17–20. See also Perry Anderson's survey of the significance of the Ottoman states in *Lineages of the Absolutist State* (London, 1979), chap. 7; Bernard Lewis, "The Arabs in Eclipse," in Carlo

was this powerful sense of religious mission that permitted the Turkish nomads of the region, who would become the core of the Ottoman state, to survive and, step by step, to conquer their rivals in western Anatolia and then Byzantium. Steeped in the *ghazi* spirit and yet able to use this religious drive to legitimate political unity and a powerful state, the Ottomans were uniquely placed to inherit the imperial presence that the Byzantines had once exercised at the crossroads of Europe and Asia Minor. Religion provided the unity that made a large-scale political community both possible and militarily powerful. The transnational appeal of religion to other Muslims and the crusading zeal with which it inspired the faithful helped the Ottomans transcend the limits of tribal social organization (its small scale and divisive tendencies). Military power conquered for them the resources and promoted the establishment of a state capable of directing expansion into empire.

These foundations, which rested on a religious metropolitanization of Turkish society, carried over into the administration of the empire. They also contributed to the longevity of Ottoman rule.

Ghazi fanaticism and the tribal military host both became reflected in a state that was highly autonomous from its society. Society became increasingly differentiated and sophisticated, as one would expect. Commerce and the arts flourished; peasant agriculture followed its normal pace. But the state took a different path. Law and religion combined in a distinct hierarchy of kadis, ulemas, a mass of teachers, and at the top the sheikh-ul-Islam, interpreting sacred law for all the faithful. Parallel to this hierarchy emerged a military-administrative institution. It became largely composed of slaves, recruited at birth from the Balkans conquered in the sixteenth century. (The most famous of these slave-soldiers were the Janissaries.) Trusted with the administration of the state under the sultan, these slaves held most military and almost all civil offices up to, and occasionally including, that of grand vizir.

The tribal heritage of the Ottomans appears to have encouraged them to avoid the capture of the state by society characteristic of many other metropoles. They avoided the crisis of republican imperialism which Rome experienced, "jumping" from the metropolitan threshold to the Augustan and even the Caracallan threshold and thus avoiding the crises that destroyed the Athenian empire and that nearly destroyed Rome in

---

Cipolla, ed., *The Economic Decline of Empires* (London, 1970), discusses the rise of the Seljuks.

the first century B.C. The Ottomans created a thoroughly centralized, empire-wide bureaucratic rule as soon as their conquests were established.[5] The levy of youths from the Balkan provinces soon followed. In political terms they integrated disparate parts of the empire at the same time. The slave-soldiers and bureaucrats of Albania found themselves in positions of power in Syria, in Rumania, and farther afield.

As a result, the decay of the Ottoman empire was not produced by political disunion in distant provinces (excepting Egypt). It was extremely slow, and it was reversed on several occasions. Eventual decay, which lasted well into the eighteenth and nineteenth centuries, was itself bureaucratic. It was the product not of political collapse but of slow stagnation as creative social impulses were smothered by a protective bureaucracy, leaving the Ottoman realm technically far behind rivals who possessed less disciplined but more creative societies. Eventually, the power that pushed to the gates of Vienna in 1698 became the "sick man of Europe." Subject to incessant pressure for reform along lines that European diplomats thought were progressive, the Ottomans were unable to implement reforms that were necessary but foreign to national traditions.[6]

In the meantime two equally great empires had arisen in the west. One was the Ottoman's rival in the sixteenth century; the other would be its protector and then undertaker in the nineteenth.

Imperialism, Colonialism, and the Nation-State

The Rise of the Spanish and English Empires

Between them, Spain and England took control of much of the known world. England acquired much of the North American seaboard. Spain conquered, settled, and controlled south of the English colonies and west of Portuguese Brazil; in 1580 Spain absorbed the Portuguese empire as it absorbed metropolitan Portugal, holding it until 1640.[7] During this period Spain took control of the Philippines, England established a growing influence in India. These eastern possessions were primarily entrepôts for trade; the western dominions were areas of settlement and thus production. And it is by this twofold division that empires of this

5. Halil Inalcık, "The Emergence of the Ottomans," in Holt, Lambton, and Lewis, p. 279.
6. Bernard Lewis, *The Emergence of Modern Turkey* (London, 1969), chaps. 2–3.
7. D. K. Fieldhouse, *The Colonial Empires* (New York, 1965), chap. 1.

era are marked. No classical empire saw this specialization, being oriented toward trade, some settlement, strategic predominance, and security. Spain and Britain focused on trade in the east, on settlement and production in the west, and neither acquired colonies for immediate reasons of national security.

International competition did, of course, play its part in the expansion of Spain and England. Columbus offered Spain the chance to bypass a looming Portuguese monopoly over the trade of the Far East.[8] For England, colonies appeared useful as an extension of piracy to weaken the power that Spain exercised in Europe as well as a means of reaching, through a northwest passage, the fabulous riches of the Orient.

International competition also helps explain the form that the empires took.[9] Informal imperialism was possible in the east, where only one (Portugal) or two metropoles were contesting the trade and allegiance of a periphery. Other international pressures induced formal imperialism, with colonial governor and troops. Spain, inefficient in many aspects of production and trade, was dangerously effective in finance; the financial pressure it exerted unconsciously through the gold-stimulated price revolution of the sixteenth century, and consciously through currency manipulations on the Antwerp Exchange, made colonies that produced either gold or a positive balance of trade important to the financial security of the other European monarchies.[10] In the seventeenth century international commercial competition led England, less efficient in shipping than Holland and less attractive than continental European markets for certain colonial products, to restrict its colonies' trade. These colonies had to be formally integrated into an order tailored to the metropole's needs.

Two fundamental aspects of this age of imperial development were, however, not reducible to international systemic factors. The rise of empire in America, formal and colonial, differed in method and results from empire in the east, informal and commercial. The problematic character of modern empires, moreover, begins to take shape in an age that saw the first stirrings of modern nationalism. The differences in metropoles and peripheries help explain these aspects of empire.

"In all colonization, two sets of factors are necessary for success,"

---

8. F. Braudel, *The Mediterranean* (London, 1973), 2:659.

9. E. E. Rich, "Expansion as a Concern of All Europe," in G. Potter, ed., *The New Cambridge Modern History*, vol. 1 (Cambridge, 1957); and J. H. Parry, *The Establishment of European Hegemony, 1415–1715* (New York, 1959), chap. 2.

10. Rich, p. 457.

J. H. Parry argues: "the private, spontaneous, largely economic urge; and the directing, protecting, sometimes limiting policy of government."[11] The transnational, private urges of the Spanish drove Spanish expansion. The state took the initial risks in financing Columbus's first expedition (the actual costs, despite stories of Queen Isabella pawning her jewels, were low). But soon the private initiative of Spanish gentry, merchants, priests, disbanded soldiers, and landless farmers would effect a constant spilling over of the imperial boundaries. These private forces operated more within the context of Christendom than within any specifically Spanish environment.

Colonization drew upon social movements wrapped up with crusading, freebooting or piracy, sugar planting, and commerce (occupations not very different one from another in the fifteenth and early sixteenth centuries). The voyages of Columbus, an Italian navigator employed by Spain, thus were part of a Mediterranean, Christian economy that, though limited in the quantity of goods exchanged, operated on a broad, transnational plain. The expeditions to the Indies and within the Indies resembled one more development of the crusading systems that had reconquered southern Spain.[12] Similarly the sugar plantation, which became so significant to the American colonial economy, originated in the Mediterranean and was developed in the Atlantic islands.[13] Christendom is also the proper perspective from which to view the religious drive behind the Spanish justification for empire. Colonization, in effect, was an entrepreneurial venture of Christendom, organized on a private basis by soldiers and merchants and priests, sanctioned by the pope, and coordinated by the competitive monarchs of Spain and Portugal.[14]

Given the private basis of much of this colonization, colonists were able to demand in the way of personal liberties as much as, and sometimes more than what they had enjoyed at home. Early postconquest Hispaniola, Mexico, and Peru, indeed, resembled independent constitutional monarchies with the *caudillo* as petty sovereign ruling at the head of his followers (the *compana*), rewarded with lands from his grant (the *encomienda*).

The metropolitan state did, however, have a crucial role to play. First,

11. J. H. Parry, "Colonial Development and International Rivalries: America," in R. B. Wernham, ed., *The New Cambridge Modern History*, vol. 3 (Cambridge, 1968), p. 526.

12. M. Gongara, *Studies in the Colonial History of Spanish America*, trans. R. Southern (Cambridge, 1975), p. 12.

13. James Lockhart and Stuart Schwartz, *Early Latin America* (New York, 1983), p. 27.

14. Fieldhouse, pp. 23, 36–38.

the state bore the early risks of expansion. Second, the state protected and, where possible, directed this expansion. Henry the Navigator in Portugal thus funded and directed Portuguese maritime exploration just as Spain would later support Columbus's voyages. And colonial ventures would have been easy prey for competing entrepreneurs or rival governments without Spanish naval support. The Treaty of Tordesillas of 1494 between Spain and Portugal, a treaty legitimated by Pope Alexander VI, had divided up the colonial world but did little to reduce the threat of colonial expropriation.

The Italian city-states, so much more advantageously placed with respect to commercial and scientific experience, did not support extensive colonial undertakings. Venice was preoccupied defending its eastern Mediterranean empire from Ottoman attack. The difficulty of adapting Mediterranean ships to the rough Atlantic and Pacific may have deterred some. Others lacked the unified government of a sizable society needed to sustain a colonial venture.[15] The unification and centralization of Spain was important to Spanish colonialism: the geographical unity of the kingdom and the curbing of overly powerful nobles and independent cities provided the organizational basis for the extraction of national resources and their concentration on colonial expansion.[16] In short, imperial expansion required Spain to cross the metropolitan threshold of political unity.

At the same time, the state saw colonial expansion as a means of strengthening itself at home and its national economy vis-à-vis external competitors. The colonies were a source of tax revenues not subject to the constraints of the Cortes, and the colonial empire was a source of national economic power.[17] This power was realized by two mercantilist

15. Though obviously not for lack of expertise: Columbus, Vespucci, Cabot were Italians who educated Europe in the art of ocean sailing.

16. The pledge, even if apocryphal, of the Aragonese nobles illustrates the one-time independence of the aristocracy the Spanish monarchs governed: "We who are as good as you, swear to you who are no better than we, to accept you as our king and soverign lord, provided you accept all our liberties and laws, but if not, not." This feudal pluralism was manifested in the power of the Cortes of Castile and locally in the town councils. Moreover, the crown was reduced to negotiating with powerful commercial bodies such as the Mesta, the sheepherding consortium, for financial support in return for the right to herd sheep across the farms of the Castilian plains. Before extensive colonial expansion could be undertaken, these divisive forces needed to be controlled. Otherwise, the state's political resources would have been directed toward maintaining its power at home; little would have been available for supporting colonial enterprises abroad. W. Borah, "Spanish Colonial Theory and Practice," in G. Nadel and P. Curtis, eds., *Imperialism and Colonialism* (New York, 1964), p. 45. And see Braudel, 2:670.

17. Fieldhouse, pp. 24–26.

means: first, regulating the foreign trade of the colony, by requiring exclusive trade relations with the metropole or the use of only metropolitan shipping; second, by regulating the internal production of the colony to ensure complementarity with the metropole, usually making the colony a producer of raw materials for the metropole and a consumer of the metropole's finished products. This complementarity improved the metropole's balance of trade. It avoided an outflow of gold that would weaken the metropolitan economy, and it ensured that the largest proportion of value-added processing took place in the metropole.[18]

The Spanish empire in the Americas, in sum, grew upon two foundations: the initiative of private colonial entrepreneurs, and the strategic support and direction of a united Spanish state.[19]

England's imperial growth in the seventeenth century was based upon similar foundations. Again private enterprise was active. The Virginia Company was founded by London merchants and drew upon the colonizing spirit of adventurous farmers. The Massachusetts Bay Company relied upon religious inspiration, which also played a leading role in Lord Baltimore's settlement for English Catholics in Maryland. Metropolitan liberties were transported across the ocean, making English America as much a reflection (if distorted) of the institutions and society of metropolitan England as Spanish America was of Spain. Of course, there were exceptions: Jamaica was a product of direct state conquest. Even there, however, the need for private resources to create an effective settlement translated many of the rights of Cromwellian England into rights for white colonists in a West Indian plantation economy.[20]

Again as in the Spanish case, the state offered protection for colonial settlements once the state had crossed the metropolitan threshold of central organization. English colonialism had begun following the Tudor centralization, when Henry VII commissioned Cabot's voyages, and interest in the further colonization of Ireland accelerated under the Tudor monarchs. Without this metropolitan protection the American colonies would have been destroyed by rivals.

In the east quite different conditions held. The rise of the English

18. Ibid., p. 43; Potter, p. 446; and for a contemporary English version of this argument see the account by Klaus Knorr, *British Colonial Theories* (Toronto, 1944), pp. 37–59.

19. H. Egerton, "Colonies and the Mercantile System," in Nadel and Curtis, pp. 57–66. For the more general impact of the consolidation of the Spanish state see J. H. Elliott, *Imperial Spain* (London, 1970), pp. 85–99.

20. E. E. Rich, "The European Nations and the Atlantic," in J. P. Cooper, ed., *The New Cambridge Modern History*, vol. 5 (Cambridge, 1970), p. 673.

empire in India, and the earlier Portuguese empire and later Dutch empire in India and the Spice Islands, also depended largely on quasi-private entrepreneurship, such as the East India companies of England and Holland. State chartering and naval support in European waters for Britain and Holland and in eastern waters for Portugal were also crucial. But empires of settlement did not result. The empires began as trading stations dependent on local states that provided protection in return for payment and military support in local wars. Under the impact of trans-national commerce, local rivalries, and European competition (which spilled over into local political rivalries), peripheral protectors became increasingly dependent on European support and increasingly subject to European control. They would eventually decline to the point where formal European rule became necessary to maintain the order that trade required.[21] If the metropolitan roots of empire were similar in both the west and the east, the peripheries differed.

Peripheries

Conditions in the various peripheries are significant to our under-standing of the European position outside Europe from the sixteenth to the eighteenth centuries. The Muslim world was not open to imperial domination—indeed, Europe was on the defensive against an expanding Muslim world. The Far East was not open to colonial settlement, while America was.[22]

In the east the English and the Spaniards, and earlier the Portuguese, encountered rival empires in India and China and, after the Tokugawa Restoration, a reunited and nationalistic monarchy in Japan. These were differentiated societies, also commercial, with centralized political in-stitutions and considerable political integration as well as a sense of political and cultural community within a wide stratum of the governing elite. Initially, Europeans traded on shore at local sufferance and under local regulations. Eastern states produced the trade goods that Europeans sought (spices and textiles), and they could enforce their own law against the Europeans. The establishment of treaty ports, as at Macao, Nagasaki, and Goa, appeared to be a mutually advantageous way of reducing disputes and limited European predominance to the sea.[23]

Even superiority in naval technology may have been fortuitous. Chinese

---

21. Fieldhouse, chap. 8; Parry, chap. 10; P. Mason, *The Men Who Ruled India* (New York, 1964), vol. 1.
22. Fieldhouse, pp. 9–10.
23. Carlo Cipolla, *Guns, Sails, and Empires* (New York, 1965), chap. 2.

junks commanded by Cheng Ho had penetrated the Indian Ocean in the first half of the fifteenth century, reaching the African coast. Their size alone would have rendered them formidable to the Portuguese vessels that arrived in the same waters more than half a century later. In addition, an established Chinese presence might have stopped the Portuguese, at the outer limits of a very thin supply line. The Ming Dynasty's decision to withdraw the fleets and dismantle them remains mysterious. Cultural xenophobia may have played a role, and Confucianism had no missionary drive to overcome disdain for barbarians. Ming transnational expansion appears to have been limited to the land, which Mandarin bureaucrats could control. Furthermore, intensive rice culture, unlike the extensive cultivation of wheat in Europe, provided investment opportunities that may have reduced public and private incentives for overseas enterprise.[24] Whatever the reasons, a historic moment passed. Ming rule entered an age of crisis, Japanese pirates harassed the Chinese coasts, and Europeans gained the time they needed to establish a formidable presence in the eastern seas.

The opportunity for imperial control developed in the east as the Indian Mughal empire in the seventeenth and eighteenth centuries, and the Chinese empire in the nineteenth, came to crisis, rebellion, and dismemberment. (In China the Manchu revival and a persistent bureaucratic tradition saved the country from outright foreign rule.) As an Oriental version of feudal society replaced collapsing empires, political division rendered local rulers insecure.[25] The breakdown of the imperial order reduced the scope of the market, thus reducing productivity and the taxable wealth produced by trade. Politically consequential loyalties were particularistic and pyramidal, directed toward feudal superiors and not to a sense of nationhood or a centralized and institutionalized state. Collaboration became acceptable and advantageous.[26]

The East—India and the Spice Islands—already produced and thus could trade the goods that the Europeans sought; in the Americas these goods had to be produced by colonial settlers. At first, trade was thereby limited to exotic raw materials, mainly furs, and colonial settlement was possible, advantageous, and necessary if wealth and souls were to be

24. Edwin O. Reischauer and John K. Fairbank, *East Asia: The Great Tradition* (Boston, 1958), pp. 522–23; Mark Elvin, *The Pattern of the Chinese Past* (Stanford, 1973); and I. Wallerstein, *The Modern World System* (New York, 1974), pp. 52–57.

25. Marc Bloch, *Feudal Society*, trans. L. A. Manyon (Chicago, 1961), vol. 2, discusses feudalism in this light, as does Max Weber, *Economy and Society*, ed. G. Roth and C. Wittich, trans. E. Fischoff (Berkeley, 1978).

26. Fieldhouse, chap. 8, surveys the empires in the east.

extracted. In the New World, Europeans encountered both tribal societies and patrimonial societies of vast scale.[27]

Tribal societies mounted an ineffective but protracted resistance to
English and Spanish expansion as Celtic tribes had to Roman expansion.
Strong village loyalties, minimal differentiation, and the absence of state
structures over considerable populations severely limited their effectiveness. Europeans had a mixed impact on them. On the one hand,
the introduction of the horse contributed to the flowering of the Plains
societies. European settlers, on the other hand, destroyed game, thereby
waging an indirect but ferocious form of economic warfare on the forest
societies.[28] Forest societies did not produce the "groceries" demanded
in Europe and were unable to resist effectively. When in addition they
possessed fertile soil, these tribal societies became the inevitable victim
of colonial settlement. Only in those areas which were unprofitable to
cultivate—the jungles, the desert, and the tundra—did flight save the
tribal peoples from rule or genocide.

The patrimonial societies of Aztec Mexico and Inca Peru, in which
the sovereign owned the land and the people on it, had themselves
established quasi-empires over the tribal peoples surrounding the Valley
of Mexico and the Andean highlands. These patrimonial societies rested
on a social demand for irrigation and roads in difficult natural environments and exercised influence resting on very little subject loyalty.[29]
Mexico and Peru may have been undergoing domestic crises when Cortez and Pizarro invaded their homelands, but the rapidity of their collapse
is nonetheless striking. Collapse must be attributed in part to the impact
of alien technology. Bernal Diaz, for example, emphasizes the startling
impression made not by Spanish guns and body armor but by mounted
warriors on Indians who had never before seen a horse.[30]

The Spaniards nonetheless met resistance, not technological stupe-
faction, and it is the quality of that resistance which explains the fall of

27. Perry Anderson, *Lineages of the Absolutist State* (London, 1974). Appendix B provides an excellent criticism of the Marxist view of the Asiatic mode of production, or
"Oriental Despotism."

28. Alexis de Tocqueville, *Democracy in America* (1835), trans. Henry Reeve (New
York, 1945), 1:351.

29. William H. McNeill, *A World History* (New York, 1967), pp. 273–76. See Eric
Wolf, *Sons of the Shaking Earth* (Chicago, 1959), and John H. Rowe, "Inca Culture at
the Time of the Spanish Conquest," pp. 198–330, and George Kubler, "The Quechua
in the Colonial World," pp. 331–410, in Julian H. Steward, ed., *Handbook of South
American Indians*, vol. 2 (New York, 1946).

30. Bernal Diaz del Castillo, *The Discovery and Conquest of Mexico* (1568), trans. A. P.
Maudslay (New York, 1956), p. 61.

the Aztec and the Inca. Once the patrimon and his immediate entourage were destroyed, political resistance ended. Even before that collapse the Spanish invaders could count upon the collaboration of large sectors of the population disaffected from, or never positively attached to, the rule of the distant patrimon. The Aztecs and the Incas had centralized power in a minimally differentiated society, but they appear to have engendered no significant loyalties to themselves or, more importantly, to their states. In the Aztec patrimony the prevalence of cannibalism no doubt accounts for some of this disaffection among the consumable, subject populations.[31] In both patrimonies the rulers were a narrow military caste. Local *caciques* were quite ready to collaborate with Spain, and Spanish *encomenderos* stepped into the position of traditional landlords until depopulation forced more land-intensive exploitation of their estates.[32]

Persistence

Among the reasons for the striking persistence of imperial Rome was the Augustan revolution, which established the politically autonomous and imperially bureaucratic state and the political, economic, and cultural integration of the provincial peoples. What reasons account for the length and strength of the Spanish and English empires in America? The former lasted for approximately three centuries (1515–1820), collapsing only after the dissolution of the metropole in a European war, the latter about half as long (1620–1770) before the American colonies rebelled against the metropole. Why did the Spanish empire last twice as long as the English? Why did both not last longer?

The English empire lasted as long as it did because it was almost exclusively an empire of settlement. Colonial settlement is a hybrid form of peripheral society. Nearly as economically differentiated as its metropole but lacking an independent state, the empire was governed by a colonial administration directed by inhabitants of the metropole. Holding together a socially mobilized society ruled by a colonial bureaucracy called for exceptionally strong communal loyalties directed toward the metropole—ties of kinship and affection for the homeland.

English settlers were integrated into the British political system because they retained a fundamental loyalty as Englishmen abroad, sharing

---

31. Ibid. Diaz describes at some length the disaffection of the Aztecs' subordinate allies, and he recalls seeing a pile of what he estimated to be 100,000 skulls near one of the temples.

32. Lockhart and Schwartz, pp. 41–42.

vicariously in England's successes and holding England to be a source of moral and cultural authority. More concrete interests were also at work. Despite (perhaps because of) mercantilist restrictions on trade, the colonies prospered, shipping their products to and buying their goods from England, which, though not the highest-priced market, was the least costly producer for most goods imported into America.[33] More importantly, England provided security from a French threat not extinguished until the defeat of France in the Seven Years' War (1756–63). America also helped, albeit indirectly, to make English imperial policy. What Bernard Bailyn has called a "stable pattern of informal communications" emerged, linking American colony and metropolitan England through professional agents such as Ferdinand Paris and English merchants who specialized in American trade and concerned themselves with their customers' political as well as commercial needs.[34]

Royal governors usually had little effective power over their colonial legislators, but fortunately for the stability of the British empire, government could generally drew on complementary interests and ties of political affection.

Persistence of the Spanish empire was quite different although there, too, the settler connection was influential. Spaniards felt as much cultural, social, and political attachment to their homeland as English settlers did for England. Spanish rule in its earliest stages was primarily maintained by that link and by the promise of honors only the metropole could offer. Spain, however, demanded more from her colonies in the way of taxes, shares in gold mining, and religious orthodoxy, and so needed a more constraining form of official influence. Spain relied on taxes because Spanish trade did not provide large returns to the metropole; she took mining shares because gold was too fungible and marketable for taxation; and she sought conversions because the Spanish state at home was founded on a crusader society. Spain demanded more, but the settlers were not prepared to cede as much: the descendants of Columbus in Hispaniola and the Pizarro brothers in Peru seemed pre-

---

33. R. Robinson, "Non-European Foundations..." in R. Owen and B. Sutcliffe, eds., *Studies in the Theory of Imperialism* (London, 1973).

34. B. Bailyn, "The Origins of American Politics," *Perspectives in American History* (1967), 69–70; Jack P. Greene, "An Uneasy Connection: An Analysis of the Preconditions of the American Revolution," in Stephen Kurtz and James Huston, eds., *Essays on the American Revolution* (Chapel Hill, 1973); and Robert W. Tucker and David C. Hendrickson, *The Fall of the First British Empire* (Baltimore, 1982), p. 203 for the perspective complementary to that of Greene.

pared to found independent states rather than see their wealth and authority taken over by the Spanish monarchy.[35]

These conflicting aims produced a crisis in the early sixteenth century: local autonomy battled against Spanish imperial centralization. The latter won, for the Spanish state was already winning the same battles for internal, autonomous power and national centralization at home. Tribunals and administrative bodies were appointed in the Americas to maintain order and ensure administrative compliance. America became an administrative province of Castile ruled by bureaucrats in the interests of Spain, with local participation in colonial councils but without local self-government.

The colonial entrepreneurs were tamed and the Spanish monarchy, free from both colonial and metropolitan constitutional restraint, crossed the Augustan, imperial bureaucratic threshold. The resources of empire, as in imperial Rome free-floating and bureaucratically autonomous, increased state autonomy at home. The Cortes lost what representative vigor it still retained when the Castilian tax burden was relieved by taxes raised in America.[36] Reciprocal self-interest supplemented bureaucratic control. Spain guaranteed the social position of the creole elite, protected them from slave and Indian rebellions and from foreign conquest, and provided some market, however unsatisfactory, for such American produce as hides and silver.[37] In return, direct bureaucratic rule from the metropole allowed Spain simply to decree the imperial reforms that, when Townsend attempted them in North America, would engender the American revolution.[38] Spain ruled by means of an effective and efficient bureaucracy and with the support of reciprocal interests in trade and cultural affinities. These were the sources of her long and stable control over the American colonies.

The Fall

The bulk of the English empire collapsed in 1776;[39] the bulk of the Spanish between 1807 and 1825, with Cuba and the Philippines not

35. *The New Cambridge Modern History*, vol. 3 (Cambridge, 1968), pp. 507–9.

36. Fieldhouse, pp. 24–25.

37. G. Elton, ed., *The New Cambridge Modern History*, vol. 2 (Cambridge, 1958), pp. 574–77.

38. Lockhart and Schwartz, pp. 349–53.

39. Even though the colonies that became the United States were the bulk of the empire in terms of population, territory, and local strategic significance, their trade value was not correspondingly large. Eric Williams in *Capitalism and Slavery* (1944; New York, 1961), has noted that Grenada alone exported in terms of value to England between 1763 and 1773 twice what the colony of New York exported between 1714 and 1773.

falling until 1898. The root cause for the collapse of the English empire in America was England's failure to cross the Augustan Threshold. Despite two attempts—one under James II, the other following the Seven Years' War in 1763—to create a politically autonomous center of empire in the metropole, no such bureaucratic autonomy was established in the English empire.[40]

The second attempt led to the American revolution. The colonists had become accustomed more to suzerainty than to empire in the eighteenth century, and Archibald Kennedy well described the weakness of a colonial governor attempting to rely on his administrative resources alone: "A governor is no sooner appointed than the first question is, into whose hands shall I throw myself? The answer is ready. Into whose but such as can best manage the Assembly. Hence prime ministers and courtiers are established, and, of course, anti-courtiers."[41] Only a governor who also controlled economic resources sufficient to manipulate the major private interests in his colony, as did Wentworth in New Hampshire, was truly in command of his colony.[42] Elsewhere the colonials resisted metropolitan political control through budgetary vetoes in the colonial legislatures and, later, revolutionary organization. They saw attempts to control as threats to traditional liberties, which aroused a sense of American nationalism. The British defeat of France removed a potent danger, and with New England's development of competing economic interests in shipping, economic reciprocity declined as an inducement to imperial patriotism.[43]

The English empire in America, never having achieved full bureaucratic control over empire, collapsed when challenged. The Spanish empire, however, *had* crossed the threshold of persistent empire. Spain's "James II" and "Townsend" won in the mid-sixteenth century when the colonials were tamed by imperial bureaucrats. The Spanish empire was organizationally more resilient than the English, and conflicts of interest between metropole and colony could be resolved—in the metropolitan interest. The colonial link did not depend on colonial acquiescence, and even if only for this reason, the superior longevity of the Spanish empire is no surprise.[44]

40. Bailyn, pp. 94–95.
41. Archibald Kennedy, *Essay on the Government of the Colonies* (1752), quoted in Bailyn, p. 99.
42. The New Hampshire example is Bailyn's, and this is the general argument of Tucker and Hendrickson, chap. 8.
43. Greene, "An Uneasy Connection."
44. J. Lindsay, ed., *The New Cambridge Modern History*, vol. 7 (Cambridge, 1957),

The reasons for its decline and fall need to be sought in competing forces. First, there was a deterioration in the efficiency and honesty of the bureaucracy. Particularism, as in Rome, led to a quasi-feudalization of bureaucratic posts as offices were sold to creole elites in order to raise immediate revenue and new offices were created to reward peninsular Spaniards with colonial spoils. The autonomy of imperial direction suffered; fewer resources could be mobilized or made available for economic development. Moreover, every attempt at reform became regarded as an attack on creole America, igniting hostility and stirring up sentiment in favor of independence. Second, the economy of some colonies tended toward ruralization and concentration of property, dissolving ties of economic reciprocity with Spain and leaving only the economic tie of taxation—a chain of servitude.[45] Third, other colonies, among them Cuba, Argentina, and Venezuela, were economically much more dynamic, and as Spain's own economy declined, the constraints of the mercantilist system proved increasingly irksome to colonials. Fourth, the creole elite perceived itself as caught between resentment of Spanish domination and fear of a slave, peasant, or Indian rising.[46]

These separate forces led to different outcomes in the colonies: Cuba remained a colony; Argentina and Venezuela rebelled early; Peru, Bolivia, Colombia, Mexico, and Ecuador rebelled later. In accounting for this pattern, we should begin by noting that rebellions occurred in reverse order to conquest, the most recently conquered areas rebelling first, the older colonies later.[47] The older colonies had had a much longer period of successful and closer political integration with Spain; they had absorbed the demands of rising creole elites within the colonial system. Political dependence on Spain also varied in degree: Venezuela and Argentina both had booming export economies for which Spain alone could not provide a large enough market while Cuba, fearing a repetition of the successful slave rebellion in nearby Haiti, found its political dependence on Spain reinforced.[48] All of these political ties were influenced

pp. 487–90; R. A. Humphreys and J. Lynch, *The Origins of the Latin American Revolutions* (New York, 1965), pp. 24–26.

45. J. H. Elliott, "The Decline of Spain," and J. Vives, "The Decline of Spain in the Seventeenth Century," both in C. Cipolla, *The Economic Decline of Empires* (London, 1970); *New Cambridge Modern History*, 4:720 and 2:378.

46. Jorge Dominguez, *Insurrection or Loyalty: The Breakdown of the Spanish American Empire* (Cambridge, Mass., 1980), chap. 13 and pp. 245–55.

47. Lockhart and Schwartz, p. 419.

48. George Reid Andrews, "Spanish American Independence: A Structural Analysis," *Latin American Perspectives* 11 (April 1984).

by the complicated evolution of American ties to the Spanish metropole during the Napoleonic Wars. Spain had suppressed rebellions in Peru and Colombia in the 1780s and 1790s, but the British blockade after 1796 and the Napoleonic invasion of Spain through 1814 prevented Spain from suppressing the early stages of the independence rebellions.

This severance of the political link to metropolitan Spain also helped stimulate the independence rebellions themselves. Bureaucrats continued to rule in Spain's name, and the colonial elite maintained allegiance; it was not until the Spanish metropole "betrayed" the American periphery by surrendering the Spanish empire to Napoleon that the links of legitimacy were truly broken and colonial nationalism triumphed over imperial bureaucracy.[49] Spain's empire, which lasted twice as long as England's and also required metropolitan collapse before it fell, had been the stronger. Much of this strength came from the political resilience generated by Spain's having crossed the Augustan threshold.

Reflecting back on the experience of Rome, one must ask why the English and Spanish empires both fell as soon as they did. Why did not a colonial emperor arise, reunite Spanish America, and claim the overall imperial throne of Spain, as frequently occurred in Roman history? Geographical factors produce a partial explanation, but geography is relative to technology and transport and they too had changed. The real difference appears to lie in integration. Approximately one century after Spain was conquered by Rome there were senators of Spanish extraction in the Roman Senate; fifty years later there was a Spanish emperor, Trajan. How many creoles, how many North American colonials returned to become leaders or rulers of *their* metropoles? In economic terms Rome had enforced mercantilistic trade restrictions on wine and olives in the early years of its growth, but with the stable establishment of its empire, Rome allowed its economic technology to spread freely throughout the Mediterranean.

The root difference is hard to pinpoint, but the operative definitions of community are important. Romans may have despised barbarians, but the colonials, whether Spaniard, African, Greek, or Gaul, were not necessarily contemptible. Once they accepted Roman law and classical civilization, they would be politically integrated into Rome.[50] By way

---

49. Humphreys and Lynch, pp. 15, 19, 142, 146; Fieldhouse, pp. 13–14.

50. Claudius inducted the first Spanish senators. National animosities did mark Rome's conflict with Carthage, but after Carthage was defeated Roman attitudes appeared strikingly non-nationalistic (although quite imperialistic). See Ronald Syme, *Colonial Elites*

of contrast, a Spanish governor of Milan, a city technically and culturally as civilized as any in Spain, commented in 1570: "These Italiams, though they are not Indians, have to be treated as such, so that they understand that we are in charge of them and not they in charge of us."[51]

The Spanish empire, and even more strongly the English empire, were not civilizations open to achievement and assimilation. Had Christendom remained the focus of Spanish colonialism things might have been different, but Spain replaced Christendom. While an Indian could become a Christian, he could not become a Spaniard. While a settler was once a Spaniard, time was making him a creole. Herein lay the seeds of the dissolution of modern national empires.

(London, 1958), chaps. 2 and 3 on Spanish and English America, including comparisons to Roman Spain.

51. H. G. Koenigsberger, "Western Europe and the Power of Spain," in *New Cambridge Modern History*, 3:238.

CHAPTER 6

The Sociology of Empires: Hypotheses

These several cases of imperial development, from Athens to Spain, tell us a good deal about the three major understandings of imperialism, and something of the sources, varieties, and development of empires. All three models suffer from general theoretical difficulties and specific analytical limitations in accounting for imperial expansion. I shall focus on the more general factors here, for apart from Joseph Schumpeter, the major dispositional theorists address nineteenth-century imperialism.

The Inadequacy of Theories of Empire

Metrocentric Theory

Metrocentric theories argue that to understand empire we need to look within the dominant metropoles and examine the internal drive to external expansion. The dispositional variant of this approach includes the works of John Hobson, Nikolai Lenin, and Schumpeter; other scholars who find domestic forces in the metropoles sufficient to explain empires fit into a wider category of new metrocentric historians. Their definition of empire as a disposition ("imperialism") creates a strong tendency toward circular reasoning. If, as Schumpeter claims, imperialism is the objectless disposition to expand and if empires are identified by territorial conquests lacking concrete objects, we are in the hands of a tautology. Similarly, if imperialism is both identified as and explained by the monopoly stage of capitalism, we are caught in a theory that may be nearly impossible to test.

Metrocentric theories also neglect important aspects of the actual experience of historical empires. Dispositional theories necessarily fail to include empires that existed before or after the dispositions were present. Lenin, for example, admits the existence of precapitalist, premonopolist empires (i.e., Rome).[1] But he neither distinguishes them from the nineteenth-century imperialism nor, more importantly, gives us any assurance that what caused past empires does not still cause the imperialism of the monopoly stage of capitalism. If stages of production were rigidly separable, the problem might not in itself be severe, but since they are not, explanation by disposition can become as arbitrary as the analyst's choice of disposition.

An equally significant analytical problem arises when the disposition is present and an empire does *not* result, as in successful resistance by the peripheral society or anti-imperial revolution by a colony. Effective resistance begins with the Sicilian defense against Athenian expansion and in the nineteenth century includes Japan, Ethiopia, and somewhat more ambiguously, Thailand, which balanced French and British influence.[2] The classical world knew few successful rebellions, but the American and Latin American revolutions exemplify anti-imperial revolts. Resistance, even against seemingly superior force, occasionally works.

A dispositional definition is an invitation to tautologous theory. This does not mean that Lenin's monopoly capitalism and Schumpeter's war machine are necessarily incorrect explanations of the metropolitan sources of imperial expansion or imperial policy. Elements of a Schumpeterian war machine do influence Athenian and Roman imperialism, for example, and in the nineteenth century dispositional ideas do help us understand some of the sources of modern imperialism. Dispositional theories are, however, at best incomplete. They can illuminate sources of imperialism, but they cannot explain either empire or imperialism.

---

1. V. I. Lenin, *Imperialism: The Highest Stage of Capitalism* (1917; New York, 1939), p. 82. For a general criticism of dispositional approaches, see D. K. Fieldhouse, "Imperialism: An Historiographical Revision," *Economic History Review*, 2d ser., 14, 2 (1961), 187–209. For an extensive critical assessment of Leninism see Bill Warren, *Imperialism: Pioneer of Capitalism* (London, 1980).

2. See Chapter 8 below.

Systemic Theory

Systemic theory does, at least, have two sides to its model of empire, and its Copernican simplicity increases its attractiveness. It combines an account of motives with a portrait of opportunities and arrives at a determinate result. Empire results from a disparity of power; world politics, as Edmund Wilson reputedly said, is a contest for survival among states which resembles a contest for survival among sea-slugs. The larger swallows the smaller, with scientific regularity.

This abstract systemic view suffers from three analytical weaknesses. First, its conception of the motives that animate the foreign relations of states is much too narrow. The international system is fraught with insecurity, but power cannot be the sole end over which states contest. Even Thucydides, putative founder of the Realist approach, finds that policies designed to promote security are challenged by policies pursued for the sake of prestige and profits.[3] Other systemic theorists do not judge security to be the sole aim of empire and even Benjamin Cohen, who focuses on systemic power as the defining characteristic of imperialism, argues only that the search for security is the fundamental source of imperialism not that it is the proximate aim of specific policies.[4] An exclusive pursuit of power reduces the state to a machine more objectless than even Schumpeter's war machine, which at least promoted the private material interests of the military caste controlling the state.[5]

Second, the systemic view is too general. The desperate search for security, which many theorists perceive at the root of imperialism, is a motivation for all international relations. The very independence of states ensures that security preoccupies them in their foreign relations, according to Raymond Aron.[6] In the absence of a global sovereign, each

---

3. Thucydides, *History of the Peloponnesian Wars*, trans. Rex Warner (Harmondsworth, 1954), 1, 76.

4. See Kenneth Waltz, *Theory of International Politics* (Reading, Mass., 1979), p. 26, the criticism of power realism in Charles Reynolds, *Modes of Imperialism* (New York: St. Martin's, 1981), chap. 2, and B. J. Cohen, *The Question of Imperialism* (New York, 1973), pp. 246–47. See Michael Walzer, *Just and Unjust Wars* (New York, 1977), chap. 1, for a criticism of realism's limitations as a moral theory.

5. J. Schumpeter, "Imperialism," in *Imperialism and Social Classes* (Cleveland, 1955), p. 97 and passim.

6. According to Raymond Aron, "The theory of international relations starts from the plurality of autonomous centers of decision, hence from the risk of war, and from this risk it deduces the necessity of the calculation of means." *Peace and War*, trans. R. Howard and A. B. Fox (New York, 1968), p. 66.

state must pursue measures of self-help which, while designed to promote its individual security, indirectly increase the insecurity of other states.[7] A spiral of increasing insecurity can motivate imperialism as a search for strategic depth or additional resources.

This is not, however, a description of the special circumstances that give rise to imperialism. It is a description of the basic condition of the international system according to a Realist systemic interpretation. Without international anarchy, we would not have imperialism (unless there were just one global empire). In this limited sense the insecurity that anarchy generates is a cause of imperialism. But, at the same time, anarchic insecurity is in this sense the cause of wars, alliances, federations, and hegemonies—each of which is conditioned and motivated by international anarchy. As a cause, international anarchy helps fully account for no single international event, and it fails to specify the circumstances within the international system that in some circumstances create imperialism and in others do not.

Third, other systemic theorists suggest that imperialism, while it may or may not share motives with general international relations, is distinguished by a set of opportunities stemming from a significant disparity of power. But this version of the systemic view is too shallow; we need to know how much disparity is enough to produce imperialism and what produces differences in power.

Theorists of international relations generally conceive of power as a complex amalgam of factors, including population, natural resources, economic productivity, strategic location, the stability of the political system, the quality of public leadership and of national morale, and the size and quality of the military forces.[8] No single factor is likely to prove determinate, and power is considered situation-specific. Furthermore, military theorists have traditionally held that military power does not translate into victory on an incremental, one-to-one scale. The attacker needs a three-to-one superiority for consistent success against a defended position.[9] Only ratios of power resources of this size or larger are likely to create a political environment in which the superior state can regularly exercise control.

Yet even with these qualifications systemic theory remains profoundly

7. Robert Jervis, "Cooperation under the Security Dilemma," *World Politics* 30 (January 1978), 167–214.

8. Hans Morgenthau, *Politics among Nations*, 5th ed. (New York, 1975), chap. 9.

9. Malcolm Hoag, "On Stability in Deterrent Races," in Robert Art and Kenneth Waltz, eds., *The Use of Force* (Boston, 1971), pp. 403–6.

ambiguous. The societies of the periphery were not passive objects of imperial expansion, nor did they have the centralized state institutions that the systemic Realists regard as the actors of international politics. Military power is not the only source of international influence, the sources of power remain unexplained, and systemic models do not tell us how to combine the elements of power into a measurement of "net power."[10] Indeed, if systemic theorists fail to account for the sources of power, their attribution of imperialism to "a gross disparity in power" merely restates in more elegant language the definition of imperialism as a relationship of control.

Pericentric Theory

Pericentric theory describes what makes empire different from other types of international relations by focusing on what makes the periphery different from other types of political society. It supplies what the metrocentric and the systemic approaches lack, a second actor. Showing how transnational forces that produce manageable trade among metropoles produce instability and crisis elsewhere, it provides an account of the weakness of one actor in a systemic relationship which helps explain the power of the metropole.

Yet pericentric theory also has significant general weaknesses. Most pericentric approaches avoid the systematic comparison involved in moving from a description to an explanation which metrocentric and systemic theorists attempt. But the most obvious general weakness in the pericentric approach has been effectively pointed out by Freda Harcourt: "By its very nature . . . imperialism implies that the motive force must come from the centre of power, not from the periphery."[11] Although some peripheries actively seek out a metropole, most unsuccessfully resist. Logically, we need to explain the pressure, whether commercial or military or other, that metropoles impose on peripheries.

Metropolitan disposition, the balance of power of the systemic Realists, the imperialism of free trade and the liquid frontier of the theorists of the periphery—each identifies features of the imperial relationship. None is an explanation of empire. The balance of the international system, or

---

10. Robert Keohane, "Theory of World Politics: Structural Realism and Beyond," in Ada W. Finifter, ed., *Political Science: The State of the Discipline* (Washington, D.C., 1983). For background on the analysis of power see the seminal essay by Jeffrey Hart, "Three Approaches to the Measurement of Power in International Relations," *International Organization* 30 (Spring 1976), 289–308.

11. Freda Harcourt, "Disraeli's Imperialism," *Historical Journal* 23, 1 (1980), p. 109.

the political economics of free trade, or frontier dynamics may in particular circumstances be a motive for imperial rule. None alone can be the foundation for a systematic theory of empire. Explaining imperialism still depends on answering the two fundamental questions that shaped the first part of this book: Why are some political societies ruled by imperial metropoles when other political societies effectively resist? Why do some states create empires over their weaker neighbors when others remain isolated at home?

Hypotheses on Empire

The histories of the Spartan hegemony and the empires of Athens, Rome, the Ottomans, Spain, and England suggest answers to those two fundamental questions. These cases also yield general conclusions about the statics, comparative statics, and dynamics of empires, which will guide our investigation of the political process of modern imperialism.

The Statics of Empire

The essential analytical starting point for the explanation of empire lies in the relationship between a metropole and a periphery, the latter penetrated by transnational forces and actors. Three essential conditions for the establishment of an imperial relationship can be conceived of as thresholds for a metropole, for transnational penetration, and for a periphery.

A metropole, one might hypothesize, demands great size or enormous population, spectacular wealth and resources or a large army. In the eighteenth century, however, Britain extended its rule over much of an India that was certainly larger, both geographically and demographically, and that by most guesses had a greater gross national product. Size, population, and wealth naturally contribute to national power and thus to the capacity of a metropole to coerce a periphery. These factors are decisive in contests between metropoles or empires (such as that between Rome and Carthage) which result in the redistribution of peripheries. At the margin, they may even decide conflicts between a relatively powerful periphery and a relatively weak metropole. But historically they were not the ordinary, determinative conditions of empires.

A metropole is constituted from three determinative elements: first, a strong, united, central government; second, a thorough sense of public legitimacy or community, widely shared among the governing population, whether elite or mass; and third, a substantial degree of social differentiation. Social differentiation helps create resources. Community ensures that citizens or subjects regard resources as (at least potentially) public. But the most important factor is strong central government. The metropole has to be capable of reaching concerted policy decisions and of mobilizing the resources that imperial policies call for.

These characteristics usually exist in effective bureaucratic regimes and in nation-states, whether authoritarian or polyarchic. The first may rely more on coercion and fear, the latter on consent, but both produce central direction and political power.

The importance of this metropolitan condition is shown in what happens when it is not observed. Just such a development, according to Thucydides, occurred during the oligarchic coup at Athens. The ensuing revolt of the democratic factions in the army and the navy was a direct consequence of the coup, which had broken the established bounds of legitimate politics and institutional central direction. Revolt divided the empire into warring factions, later destroyed both the coherence of strategy and the élan of the military, and led to the destruction of the Athenian empire by Sparta. Yet this condition, though necessary, is not sufficient: again by Thucydides' account, Sparta met the condition and existed in the same environment as imperial Athens yet was not the metropole of an empire. Sparta did attempt to guide the external policy of its allies in the war against Athens, but it did not, as did Athens its "allies," control their political systems on a long-term, general, and regular basis.

Sparta lacked the second factor necessary to establish an empire, a transnational extension of the domestic society of the metropole. Athens colonized with city-states, Rome spread an urban legal civilization, Spain recreated the liberation of Andalusia in America, and Tudor England spilled over onto the North American seaboard. The extension from the metropole of economic and sociocultural or ideological forces and the institutions that carry them provide both an incentive for metropolitan interference in peripheral politics and a means of penetrating the domestic society of the periphery. In these extensions peripheral elites find sources both of transnational, imperial loyalty (religion, ideological affinities) and of more material payments for their allegiance. Extensions are thus—from the metropolitan side—sources of considerable power over the periphery.

Indeed, it is the substantial degree of power that transnational extension can generate over the internal policy of the periphery that distinguishes empire from the lesser influence of hegemony. Transnational connections distinguished the Athenian empire, with its heralded spirit

TABLE 3.
The sociology of empire (statics)

Empire. The political control exercised by one polity (the metropole) over the domestic and foreign policy and over the domestic politics of another polity (the periphery), resulting in control over who rules and what rulers can do.

   Mode. (1) Formal — annexation and rule by a colonial governor with the collaboration of local elites.

           (2) Informal — rule through the collaboration of local rulers who are legally independent but politically dependent on the metropole.

Sources. The interaction of a metropole and a periphery joined together by transnational forces generates differences in political power which permit the metropole to control the periphery. This relationship is produced and shaped by the three necessary features, which are together sufficient. It is also influenced and shaped by the structure of the international system.

  (1) A metropole, typified by a centralized state, thorough social differentiation, and public legitimacy and communal loyalty.

  (2) A transnational extension of the economy, society, or culture of the metropole.

  (3) A periphery, which may be
     (a) tribal, typified by no central state, little social differentiation, and strong communal or village loyalty
     (b) patrimonial, typified by a central state, some social differentiation, and little communal loyalty
     (c) feudal, typified by a disaggregated state, some social differentiation, a common civilization, and pyramidal loyalties
     (d) fractionated, typified by a central state, thorough social differentiation, and a divided community with factional loyalties
     (e) settler, typified by a colonial government, thoroughly differentiated society, and a communal loyalty toward metropole

  (4) An international system, which may be unipolar, bipolar, or multipolar

---

and reality of social expansion and dynamism, from a hegemony that reflected the isolationist character of Spartan society. In the case of China many scholars believe that the Ming Dynasty halted its pursuit of overseas empire because it was reluctant to accept and lacked interest in the overseas commercial connections that imperial expansion would entail.

These two conditions constitute the metropolitan dimension of the imperial relationship; but not all states meeting these metropolitan conditions were imperial metropoles. The periphery also needs to be examined, not least because a metropole needs a periphery in order to be an imperial metropole. What sort of political society can become subject to another government on a regular and stable basis? Something must distinguish such states from those which become metropoles or are simply destroyed in the course of resistance.

Again one could explore the possibility that it is only poor states or small political societies that meet the peripheral fate, but the history of empire soon dispels such ideas. Thucydides makes the point that the inhabitants of a small poor island were able to resist the might of Athens because of their fanatical determination to remain free—they chose to be annihilated rather than Athenian. Melos as a political society was not imperialized; it fought and was destroyed. The more usual case in unequal conflicts, nevertheless, is surrender or ineffective resistance, what Tacitus described in the Roman conquest of Britain as the Britons' "inability to cooperate."[12]

The weakness of the periphery, which allows it to be conquered and indeed encourages aggression from the metropole, is a product primarily of its social organization. Technology, naturally, plays a part, but technology, too, must be explained; history is replete with examples of ill-armed but well-organized troops overcoming better-equipped opponents. Peripheral weakness stems primarily from the social behavior associated with different forms of social organization, specifically social differentiation and integration.

Differentiation, which generally signifies the specialization and separation of roles, operates to distinguish economic, cultural, and political roles and activities within a society. It also identifies the stratification of roles and ranks which distinguishes capitalists from workers, priests from laity.[13] Similarly, social integration refers to the creation of one community from geographically separate portions of the population of a state or to the communal features that mute the impact of social stratification.[14] Integration is not the same as nondifferentiation. Highly differentiated economic, political, and cultural systems can be integrated: values, rights, and duties can be shared by all or a market can create interdependent interests (what Durkheim calls "mechanical" and "organic" solidarity, respectively).[15] In these respects tribal societies differ greatly from patrimonial, feudal, fractionated, and nation-state polities.

12. Tacitus, *The Agricola and the Germania*, trans. H. Mattingly and S. A. Handford (Harmondsworth, 1970), no. 12.

13. Marion Levy, *The Structure of Society* (Princeton, 1952), pp. 307–48, discusses role differentiation, particularly on the basis of economic, political, and religious roles, the criteria of most concern here.

14. Ibid., chap. 7 on "solidarity" and the discussion of "integration" in chap. 11.

15. Emile Durkheim, *The Division of Labor in Society*, trans. George Simpson (1935; New York, 1964), pp. 129–32, uses the two forms of solidarity as constituent elements of integration.

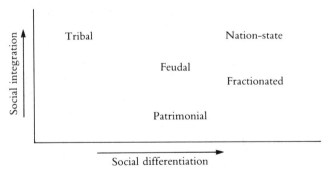

FIGURE I Social integration and social differentiation

The tribal societies of the Germanic and Celtic peoples described by Tacitus, of the Caribbean Indians encountered by Columbus, and of the North American Indians driven away by colonizing farmers were characterized by "intermittent" and nonstatal political systems. Tribal societies were both highly undifferentiated and thoroughly integrated. They lacked a centralized state—the political life of the society was not differentiated from its social life, nor was it organized in a central coercive institution—but on a local scale they were highly participatory, their inhabitants were mobilized, and their political and social institutions, mostly informal, coped fully with their needs.[16] For the most part, however, these institutions were not equipped to counteract either the metropole or its transnational forces.

The lack of social differentiation and central political direction (despite pervasive social integration at the village level) makes it difficult for tribal societies to mount extended defensive campaigns against imperial encroachment. The limited social differentiation of such societies is not conducive to the development of advanced military technologies. Just as important, their small-scale political communities preclude extensive and reliable cross-village strategic cooperation. Furthermore, small-scale

16. A survey of the general characteristics of tribal societies can be found in Gertrude Dole, "Anarchy without Chaos," in M. Schwartz, V. Turner, and A. Tuden, eds., *Political Anthropology* (Chicago, 1966), p. 85; Jacques Maquet, "African Society: Sub-Saharan Africa," *International Encyclopedia of the Social Sciences* (New York, 1968), 1:140–41; E. R. Leach, *The Political Systems of Highland Burma* (Boston, 1954), p. 12; Daryll Forde and Mary Douglas, "Primitive Economics," in George Dalton, ed., *Tribal and Peasant Economies* (Austin, 1967), pp. 13–28; Elizabeth Colson, "African Society at the Time of the Scramble," in L. H. Gann and P. Duignan, eds., *Colonialism in Africa, 1870–1960*, vol. 1 (Cambridge, 1961); E. E. Evans-Pritchard, *The Nuer* (Oxford, 1940); and Lucy Mair, *Primitive Government* (Baltimore, 1964), chap. 3.

social organization and the myriad overlap of social roles found in tribal society tend to mean that change must be total: crises are magnified, not diffused. The radically new forces of metropolitan society thus tend to provoke either domestic crisis in the periphery as society changes or intertribal hostility and conflict as the tribal regime is penetrated by metropolitan trade or metropolitan values. In either case, the result is likely to involve the metropole extending formal, direct rule to promote its goals in the periphery.

Patrimonial society, though socially more differentiated, also lacks the strong central government and the social, communitarian integration required effectively to resist an imperial metropole. Patrimonial society is capable of being closely integrated into the metropolitan-based transnational economy and of profiting from the relationship for a time. Sectors of the patrimonial society, leaders and their clienteles, become associated with the metropole in a collaboration that benefits both collaborators and metropole. In time, however, the metropolitan regime, to protect its transnational interests from patrimonial encroachment, will increase its control over the periphery step by step while the patrimonial ruler will try to avoid the erosion of essential politico-economic support. In this relationship a crisis will develop and, whether the crisis stems from bankruptcy or peripheral revolt, the metropole will step in to take full control. Patrimonial rulers are replaced by colonial governors or, if retained, rule as subordinates and reign as figureheads.[17]

Feudal peripheries, such as India after the collapse of the Mughal empire, are also prone to collaboration. Socially differentiated, the feudal state is disaggregated into a welter of small quasi sovereignties, each pursuing its own advantage. India retained a sense of shared civilization (actually two shared civilizations, Hindu and Muslim), but political loyalties were "layered" and not coextensive with a large and defensible country. Collaboration by feudal rulers violated no larger political loyalties, and it occasionally helped secure the finances and political survival

17. On patrimonial societies see Max Weber, *The Theory of Social and Economic Organizations*, ed. T. Parsons (New York, 1964), p. 347, and G. Almond and G. Powell, *Comparative Politics* (Boston, 1966), pp. 223ff. Although patrimonial systems in practice contain a large degree of traditional authority, their authority is in numerous instances supplemented by rational and charismatic supports to power. For our purposes it is the structure of politics, not the source of authority, that is of interest. See also Karl Marx, "On the Jewish Question," and "British Rule in India," in R. Tucker, ed., *Marx-Engels Reader* (New York, 1972), pp. 42 and 577–88. For a comparative discussion of feudal society (how it differs from patrimonial society) see Marc Bloch, *Feudal Society*, vol. 2, trans. L. A. Manyon (Chicago, 1964), chaps. 4, 12, and 18.

of the local potentate. Imperial rule over India continued, in Marx's words, as long as "The inhabitants gave themselves no trouble about the breaking up and division of kingdoms; while the village remains entire, they care not to which power it is transferred, or to what sovereign it devolves; its internal economy remains unchanged, the *potail* is still the head inhabitant, and still acts as the petty judge or magistrate, and collector or rentor of the village."[18]

Fractionated and settler polities are the least stable collaborators in an informal empire. Fractionated polities are highly socially differentiated and their populations are socially mobilized, making demands on a centralized government for participation, material welfare, and psychic identification. They are almost nation-states, lacking only a unified sense of public legitimacy. But caught up in fundamental factional conflict—between ethnic groups, castes, classes, regions, or ideologies—each faction can be tempted to collaborate to avoid the rule of its domestic rival. Most polities have cleavages; the fractionated polity has cleavages that overwhelm any sense of national identification and that are so politically salient as to define the coalitions that compete for political power. Settler polities are equally tenuous sources of collaboration in empire. Their government is a colonial bureaucracy staffed by natives of the metropole with which the settlers identify themselves. Loyalties are thus directed toward the mother country. Some settler polities remain loyal to the metropole because they face either international threats or domestic threats, but should metropolitan ties become economically or politically irksome, settler polities are in a politically strong condition to declare and defend their independence.[19]

Empire is thus one complement to politics between nation-states. Interstate politics, from the perspective of imperialism, involves the political relations between metropoles, just as empire involves the political relations between metropoles and peripheries which are linked by

18. Marx, "British Rule in India," p. 581.
19. By "fractionated" I intend the general distinctions drawn by S. Huntington, *Political Order and Changing Societies* (New Haven, 1968), when he uses "praetorian" policy (the reference to Rome makes it less appropriate in this context, since Rome was not fractionated, nor praetorian in a literal sense). Arend Lijphart's "consociational" polity mitigates the reinforcing cleavages I discuss by a consensus on nationalism and other cross-cutting linkages; *The Politics of Accommodation* (Berekely, 1975), chap. 5. For settler societies see J. M. Cook, *The Greeks in Ionia and the East* (New York, 1963), on Greek settlers; R. Syme, *Colonial Elites* (London, 1958); E. G. Wakefield's fascinating essays, *Letter from Sydney and Other Writings on Colonization* (New York, 1929); and for modern settlers, L. H. Gann and P. Duignan, *White Settlers in Tropical Africa* (Harmondsworth, 1962).

substantial transnational forces. This conclusion may seem much too broad, but its breadth fits the historical pervasiveness of empires. The real question is not the breadth of the theory but whether a more economical or specific theory fits the historical breadth of empires. Even the experience of Ottoman, "tribal," empire, which appears to be a significant exception to the arguments outlined above, represents the working out of basically similar forces operating in a different context.

The Comparative Statics of Empire

The two major modes of imperial rule are formal and informal. Formal empire signifies rule by annexation and government by colonial governors supported by metropolitan troops and local collaborators—the Roman pattern. Informal empire involves an Athenian pattern of control exercised indirectly, by bribes and manipulation of dependent collaborating elites, over the legally independent peripheral regime's domestic and external politics.

Specific factors within the metropole influence the form of empire: differences in ideology and ruling coalition, and the particular interests of the transnational agents that come into contact with the periphery. (These subjects will be examined in some depth in Part II below.) But the classic differences between formal and informal empires emerge in an overall comparison of the roles played by the international system and the domestic political society of the periphery. The tribal periphery tends to be associated with both formal rule (metropolitan sovereignty established by colonial governor, troops, etc.) and direct rule (colonial bureaucratic control by natives of the metropole). Patrimonial, feudal, and fractionated peripheries, on the other hand, tend toward informal rule (formal sovereignty vests in a peripheral elite); should formal rule become necessary, they tend toward indirect rule (local administration is left to the peripheral, collaborating elite).

The reasons for these different tendencies have already been suggested. In tribal peripheries, metropolitan transnational forces and organizations are highly disruptive. Metropolitan goods shift the balance of local political power, slight religious authority, even profane ritual. Furthermore, tribal societies lack established hierarchies of leadership which could serve to collaborate with the metropole. Whatever collaboration does develop is unstable, and formally institutionalized rule becomes necessary. Once established, this rule will tend to rely on the intensive bureaucracy of direct rule.

The social differentiation of patrimonial and, especially, fractionated societies, with their quasi-autonomous economic and political roles, permits collaboration without social collapse. Merchants of the periphery align themselves with metropolitan merchants, to their mutual (though not equal) advantage, as do peripheral political factions. Informal control thus is possible, advantageous, and required: possible, because collaboration is possible; advantageous, because in patrimonial peripheries it reduces administrative costs and meets with less resistance than formal rule; and required, because the metropole must, if it is to support its trade or other transnational forces, engage in political interference to match the patrimonial politicization of economic relationships.

Next to the domestic political society of the periphery as a classic determinant of the mode of empire is the structure of the international system. Multipolar systems tend to formalize or require formal institutions of imperial rule; bipolar systems tend to informalize or permit informal arrangements.

A bipolar system tends to internationalize domestic politics in a transnational extension of ideological conflict and factionalism. Bipolar informality is rooted in the clear symmetry achieved when each pole of a bipolar system becomes aligned with a particular faction within the peripheral regime. Since the periphery is ruled by either one domestic faction or the other, associated with one pole or the other, clear international alignments are expressed by domestic political arrangements. Thus stable collaboration is doubly reinforced—domestically and internationally—in a bipolar system, without the formal imposition of metropolitan rule. So, for instance, democracy and oligarchy divided the Greek world, marking by their predominance the sphere of influence or rule of Athens and Sparta.

A multipolar system, by contrast, creates incentives for formal rule. Several reasons for this observation will be developed in Part II but one straightforward reason can be found in the wider choice a multipolar system offers the peripheral regime—a choice among metropoles and thus a wider opportunity to bargain for some measure of independence. A metropole, then, if it is to exercise control to further strategic or transnational aims, must establish full and formal control over the periphery, over its day-to-day administration as well as over the general direction of its political evolution.

The Dynamics of Imperial Change

Some of the larger empires lasted a long time because, instead of disintegrating in civil wars, they crossed the Augustan threshold. Where the periphery was large relative to the resources of the metropole, empires persisted only if they were able to develop a polity that governed for the sake of the empire as a whole. The argument is most clearly illustrated in the transformation of the Roman republic into the principate by Augustus. Before Augustus the empire and its resources had become the spoils of Roman factions, and Rome seemed headed for Athens' fall. Bureaucratic reorganization enabled the Roman Empire to survive for another four hundred years. Spain crossed this threshold in the sixteenth century, creating ties and loyalties on both sides of the Atlantic that would withstand the substantial strains of mercantile restriction and foreign threat in the ensuing centuries. England, on the other hand, did not cross this threshold. Colonial spoils posed but a small problem to the operation of domestic politics, and in America England created a purely colonial empire. The weakening of transnational ties in the eighteenth century removed the sole prop of the imperial edifice and led to a colonial rebellion that neither Rome nor Spain had known.

A persistent empire presupposes imperial bureaucratic coordination and continuing transnational integration in the political, economic, and cultural spheres. This integration can merge the metropole and the periphery, as Caracalla legally integrated the two in the Roman Empire in 212. At this point an empire no longer exists, and the many peoples have become one. In the case of Rome the many were assimilated into a common despotism, but the continuing and intriguing moral attraction of the otherwise reprehensible international domination of empire lies in the possibility that all might be assimilated to a common liberty. Empire continues to attract as a road to peace, but imperialism holds a double tragedy. First, modern empires, resting upon metropolitan ethnic nationalism, may not be able to travel the whole way to integration. Second, any extensive empire, to survive long enough for integration to occur, must cross the Augustan threshold to imperial bureaucratic rule—and bureaucratizing the metropole destroys participatory government. Liberty and empire emerge, both analytically and historically, as opposites, for the periphery from the beginning and for the metropole in the end.

No empire is permanent. Some empires fell when the conditions for their persistence and growth collapsed or degenerated. When the unity of the state disappeared, they fell as quickly as did Athens. When the autonomy of the bureaucracy deteriorated or the strength of transnational society atrophied, they declined slowly. Their level of available resources fell, their resistance to foreign invasion lessened, and their ability to retain the allegiance of far-flung settlers became doubtful. Their condition in their waning days bore small resemblance to their days of glory.

Other empires were forcibly dismembered long before the metropole began to decline, when the peripheries won their independence. The periphery in the course of political development within the empire may reach a point at which further collaboration becomes unacceptable. The disaffected elite of the periphery then expels the metropole in a national, anticolonial revolt. Having awakened to a sense of national legitimacy, having mobilized and coordinated the peripheral population (as did the American Founding Fathers), and having centralized and institutionalized the polity, the former periphery joins the ranks of effectively sovereign states.

PART II

THE SCRAMBLE FOR AFRICA: NINETEENTH-CENTURY IMPERIALISM

CHAPTER 7

Introduction to Part II

One of the most important problems plaguing historians in their efforts to explain nineteenth-century imperialism is a lack of agreement about exactly what must be explained.

Early interpretations of nineteenth-century imperialism emphasized a single feature, the upsurge of imperial activity between the 1870s and 1890s—the "New Imperialism" or the "Scramble for Africa" that followed a supposed period of mid-Victorian anti-imperialism. J. A. Hobson noted the vast amounts of territory and population brought under imperial rule between 1878 and 1901 (see Table 4).[1] He saw the partitions of Africa and Asia, the former given a legal framework by the Berlin West Africa Conference of 1884-1885 and the latter operating under more haphazard arrangements, as the signal characteristics of this epoch of "modern imperialism"[2] These partitions were marked by preemptive formal annexations of territory and by competitive definitions of spheres of influence.

With the signing of a treaty often not understood by a local ruler not always legitimate, imperial powers claimed vast stretches of African land. These treaties received their only real significance on the conference

---

1. John A. Hobson, *Imperialism: A Study* (1902; Ann Arbor, 1965), p. 17. See also Table 4, "Britain's imperial expansion, 1871–1901."

2. W. L. Langer, *European Alliances and Alignments* (New York, 1931), chap. 8.

TABLE 4.
Britain's imperial expansion, 1871–1901

	Date of Acquisition	Area in Square Miles	Population
Europe			
Cyprus	1878	3,584	237,022
Africa			
Zanzibar and Pemba	1888		200,000
East Africa Protectorate	1895	1,000,000	2,500,000
Uganda Protectorate	1894–96	140,000	3,800,000
Somali Coast Protectorate	1884–85	68,000	(?)
British Central Africa Protectorate	1889	42,217	688,049
Lagos	to 1899	21,000	3,000,000
Gambia	to 1888	3,550	215,000
Ashantee	1896–1901	70,000	2,000,000
Niger Coast Protectorate	1885–98	400,000 to 500,000	25,000,000 to 40,000,000
Egypt	1882	400,000	9,734,405
Egyptian Sudan	1882	950,000	10,000,000
Griqualand West	1871–80	15,197	83,373
Zululand	1879–97	10,521	240,000
British Bechuanaland	1885	51,424	72,736
Bechuanaland Protectorate	1891	275,000	89,216
Transkei	1879–85	2,535	153,582
Tembuland	1885	4,155	180,130
Pondoland	1894	4,040	188,000
Griqualand East	1879–85	7,511	152,609
British South Africa Charter	1889	750,000	321,000
Transvaal	1900	117,732	1,354,200
Orange River Colony	1900	50,000	385,045
Asia			
Hong Kong (littoral)	1898	376	102,284
Wei-hai-wei	—	270	118,000
Socotra	1886	1,382	10,000
Upper Burma	1887	83,473	2,046,933
Baluchistan	1876–89	130,000	500,000
Sikkim	1890	2,818	30,000
Rajputana (States)		128,022	12,186,352
Burma (States)	after	62,661	785,800
Jammu and Kashmir	1881	80,000	2,543,952
Malay Protected States	1883–95	24,849	620,000
North Borneo Co.	1881	31,106	175,000
North Borneo Protectorate	1888	—	—
Sarawak	1888	50,000	500,000
British New Guinea	1888	90,540	350,000
Fiji Islands	1874	7,740	120,124

Source: J. A. Hobson, *Imperialism: A Study*, p. 17.

tables of Europe where brilliant exercises in obscure African genealogy and even more fanciful geography were required to sort out the maze of counterclaims. Meanwhile, on the African continent itself, explorers, officials, traders, and missionaries went about the slow business of making effective the paper annexations accredited in Berlin.

In Asia empire was a less dramatic event; it crept rather than ran. Imperial influence flowed and grew with the increase of trade in the valleys of China until by the time of the informal partition of the late 1890s Chinese sovereignty was shattered; ports and valleys were parceled out among the competing European and American states. To the south the French had invaded Cochin China quite early, to rescue their missionaries and establish a way station on the route to the greater riches of mainland China.[3]

The identifying feature of modern imperialism was radically reinterpreted in the early 1950s by J. Gallagher and R. E. Robinson in the now-classic article "The Imperialism of Free Trade." The two authors reevaluated both the dating and the content of imperialism. They attacked the conventional dichotomy of a pre-1870 age of anti-imperialism followed by a post-1870 age of imperialism. To them, imperial expansion was a continuous process: "Between 1841 and 1851 Great Britain acquired or annexed the Gold Coast, Labuan, Natal, the Punjab, Sind and Hong Kong. In the next twenty years British control was exerted over Berar, Oudh, Lower Burma and Kowloon, over Lagos and the neighbourhood of Sierra Leone, over Basutoland, Griqualand and the Transvaal; and the new colonies were established in Queensland and British Columbia."[4]

These annexations of the first two-thirds of the century may have been relatively minor, but they were not the only manifestation of imperialism. Our understanding of the content of imperialism, Gallagher and Robinson argued, should not be limited to formal rule. Informal imperialism, an imperialism of free trade, should be seen as equally important. Trade was often opened by force and, though pursued peacefully when and where possible, it was backed up by force. During the first half of the nineteenth century informal empire secured the routes to India and the trade of the east: "In one way or another this imperial interest demanded some kind of hold on Africa south of the Limpopo,

---

3. W. L. Langer, *The Diplomacy of Imperialism* (New York, 1935), and D. K. Fieldhouse, *Economics and Empire* (London, 1973), pp. 198–99, 205.

4. John Gallagher and Ronald Robinson, "The Imperialism of Free Trade," *Economic History Review*, 2d ser., 6 (1953), 2–3.

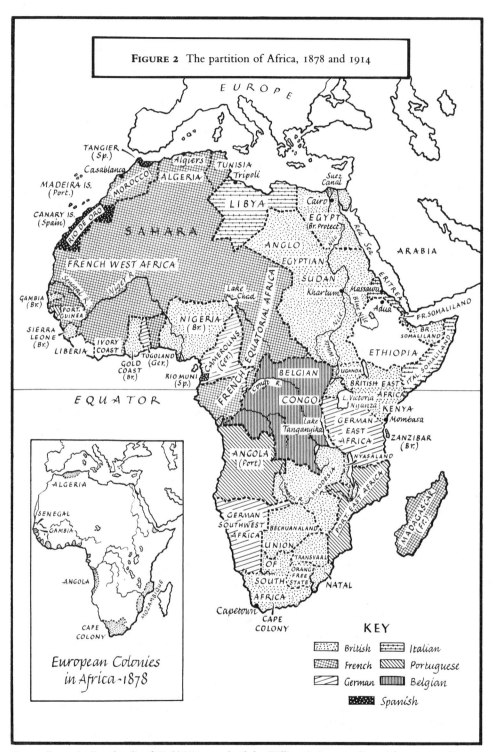

FIGURE 2 The partition of Africa, 1878 and 1914

EUROPE

TANGIER (Sp.)
Casablanca
MADEIRA IS. (Port.)
Algiers
TUNISIA
Tripoli
MOROCCO
ALGERIA
CANARY IS. (Spain)
RIO DE ORO
LIBYA
Suez Canal
Cairo
EGYPT (Br. Protect.)
SAHARA
ARABIA
FRENCH WEST AFRICA
ANGLO EGYPTIAN SUDAN
Khartum
Massawa
ERITREA
GAMBIA (Br.)
PORT. GUINEA
Senegal R.
Niger R.
Lake Chad
Khartum
Blue Nile
Adua
FR. SOMALILAND
SIERRA LEONE (Br.)
IVORY COAST
NIGERIA (Br.)
BR. SOMALILAND
LIBERIA
GOLD COAST (Br.)
TOGOLAND (Ger.)
CAMEROUNS (Ger.)
RIO MUNI (Sp.)
FRENCH EQUATORIAL AFRICA
ITAL. SOMALILAND
ETHIOPIA

EQUATOR

BELGIAN CONGO
Congo R.
UGANDA
BRITISH EAST AFRICA
L. Victoria Nyanza
KENYA
Mombasa
Lake Tanganyika
GERMAN EAST AFRICA
ZANZIBAR (Br.)
ANGOLA (Port.)
NYASALAND
RHODESIA
Zambezi R.
PORT. EAST AFRICA
MADAGASCAR (Fr.)
GERMAN SOUTHWEST AFRICA
BECHUANALAND
UNION OF SOUTH AFRICA
TRANSVAAL
ORANGE FREE STATE
NATAL
Capetown
CAPE COLONY

European Colonies in Africa · 1878

ALGERIA
SENEGAL
GAMBIA
ANGOLA
MOZAMBIQUE
CAPE COLONY

KEY

▦ British	▥ Italian	
▨ French	◩ Portuguese	
◪ German	▥ Belgian	
▓ Spanish		

Source: From *An Encyclopedia of World History*, 4th ed. by William L. Langer. Copyright 1940, 1948, 1952 and © 1968 by Houghton Mifflin Company. Reprinted by permission of Houghton Mifflin Company.

and although between 1852 and 1877 the Boer Republics were not controlled formally for this purpose by Britain, they were effectually dominated by informal paramountcy and by their dependence on British ports."[5]

Although there are many debates about specific countries, informal empire and pre-1870 expansionism did exist and empire did experience a slow formal and informal expansion throughout the nineteenth century. Raffles acquired complete but informal empire in Singapore after 1824 to safeguard the China trade of the British East India Company, MacLean dominated the hinterland of Accra in the 1840s, and the consul, aided by a Zanzibari army staffed with British officers long exercised control over Zanzibar:—all indicate an extensive and steady growth of empire before the 1870s.[6]

The third feature is, of course, the persistence of empire throughout the century. The decolonization of the continental portion of Spain's Latin American empire still left India, the Dutch East Indies, and Senegal, to name merely a few, as imperial legacies of the eighteenth century preserved and cultivated by the nineteenth.

The three features of nineteenth-century empire—persistence, the steady expansion up to the 1870s, and the acceleration of the Scramble for Africa—generated in various ways the three major interpretations of nineteenth-century imperialism. The Scramble for Africa stimulated the first two major interpretations. Although some early commentators reflected surprise at the scope of the conquest—"a mighty phenomenon" acquired in "a fit of absence of mind"—imperial publicists in Britain, France, Germany, and elsewhere soon discovered reasons for imperial expansion in commerce, strategy, finance, religion, and culture. Thus arose the first major explanation, *metrocentric* (and frequently economic) theories of imperialism. The new imperialism gave birth to theories of economic and social imperialism, to the works of Hobson, Lenin, and Schumpeter.

Second, the new imperialism became a subtheme of detailed diplomatic histories of the European balance of power before World War I, almost all informed by a *systemic* (or international power politics) perspective with states conceived of as rational, unitary strategic actors. Here, suggest Langer, Taylor, and Fieldhouse, are to be found the true

5. Ibid.
6. Fieldhouse, pp. 140, 187; R. D. Wolff, *The Economics of Colonialism* (New Haven, 1974), chap. 1; and Ronald Robinson and John Gallagher, *Africa and the Victorians* (New York, 1961), chap. 2.

sources of the Scramble for Africa. D. K. Fieldhouse, in his early work, summarizes this second attitude toward the new imperialism; it was, he says, "the extension into the periphery of the political struggle in Europe. At the center the balance was so nicely adjusted that no major change in the status or territory of any side was possible. Colonies became a means out of this impasse."[7]

During much of the generation following 1815, Britain dominated the world system so thoroughly that it could not be effectively challenged by other states. In the second half of the century Prussia rose to great-power status and transformed the international balance of power, making the balance more equal and therefore more delicate and more rigid. A strong Germany competed with a France recovering from the defeat of 1870, a Britain newly aware of foreign challenges, and an Italy unified and eager to demonstrate its newfound power on the international scene. The balance of power became "overcrowded," and expansion and compensation were no longer possible within Europe. After 1870, therefore, all the European powers sought out extra-European conquests in the global periphery where increases in territory, resources, and military bases, each adding to power and prestige, could readily be acquired.[8] For the British this impulse meant protecting the route to India through Egypt and the Suez Canal, which necessitated control over the headwaters of the Nile and a predominant position in East Africa.[9] For the French and the Germans the impulse meant acquiring "places in the sun" to demonstrate national prestige. Colonialism, according to A. J. P. Taylor, became a "move" in the European game of the balance of power.[10]

To these two interpretations, both metrocentric and systemic, the new imperialism of the late nineteenth century was a sharp break with

---

7. D. K. Fieldhouse, "Imperialism: An Historiographical Revision," *Economic History Review*, 2d ser., 14, (1961), 187–209.

8. Benjamin J. Cohen, *The Question of Imperialism* (New York, 1973), p. 16. And see Charles Reynolds, *Modes of Imperialism* (New York, 1971), for a discussion of the search for power as a source of modern imperialism.

9. Reflecting the richness of their historical work, Robinson and Gallagher are the best source for this argument even though they are the best-known scholars of the pericentric approach. See *Africa and the Victorians*, pp. 80–86. Their earlier work—"The Imperialism of Free Trade"—and their later essays of the 1970s emphasize pericentric determinants. Tony Smith, in *The Pattern of Imperialism* (Cambridge, 1981), takes an eclectic approach, attributing the imperialism of the first half of the nineteenth century largely to pericentric factors, the imperialism of the last third largely to systemic sources in the balance of power.

10. A. J. P. Taylor, *Germany's First Bid for Colonies* (New York, 1970).

the past—a radically new feature that needed to be explained by new causes emerging in the late nineteenth century.

Unlike the metrocentric and systemic interpretations of empire in the nineteenth century, the pericentric view focused on a slowly but steadily growing formal and informal empire, its growth associated with trade, frontiers, and tariff posts. Gallagher and Robinson thus describe British imperial expansion as a function of commercial expansion, "trade with informal control if possible; trade with rule when necessary."[11] Although in some of their work imperialism appears "Eurocentric" (metrocentric) in origin, the expansive aim of the "official mind," imperialism is mainly seen as a process driven by pericentric pressures from the African, Asian, and Latin American peripheries.[12] It is from this interpretation that their work derives its main impact.

Robinson and Gallagher question whether imperial Scramble should be attributed either to the great conflicts of European diplomacy or to the great thrusts of expansionary financial capitalism which the older scholarship addresses. Empires patched together and lasting but seventy-five years suggest that "the theorists of imperialism have been looking for answers in the wrong places. The crucial changes that set all working took place in Africa itself."[13] Indeed, much of the imperialism of the last quarter of the nineteenth century, in their view, was "no more than an involuntary reaction of Europe to the various proto-nationalisms of Islam."

The specifics of how one ruled via trade, however, or how free trade could be imperial, or how one responded to peripheral resistance, were not clearly defined. Many scholars have questioned whether the state played a supportive role for commerce or whether the historical cases (particularly in Latin America) actually do illustrate informal imperialism, as Gallagher and Robinson argue.[14] Others have found related,

11. Gallagher and Robinson, "Imperialism of Free Trade," pp. 2–3.
12. For the pericentric view, see R. E. Robinson, "Non-European Foundations of European Imperialism: . . . ," in E. R. J. Owen and R. B. Sutcliffe, eds., *Studies in the Theory of Imperialism* (London, 1972), chap. 5. For the Eurocentric view see Robinson and Gallagher, *Africa and the Victorians.* The controversy over Robinson and Gallagher's views together with excerpts from most of their writings can be found in Wm. Roger Louis, ed., *Imperialism: The Robinson and Gallagher Controversy* (New York, 1976).
13. R. E. Robinson and J. Gallagher, "The Partition of Africa," in *The New Cambridge Modern History,* vol. 11 (Cambridge, 1962), chap. 22, pp. 639 and 594.
14. D. C. M. Platt, "Imperialism of Free Trade: Some Reservations," *Economic History Review,* 2d ser., 21 (1968), 296–306, and his "Further Objections to an Imperialism of Free Trade," ibid., 26 (1973), 77–91. For a position supporting Robinson and Gallagher and stressing the importance of "unofficial" support for economic expansion, see D.

pericentric sources of imperialism in the "turbulent frontiers" of the peripheral tropics.[15] In South Africa, too, Britain increased its formally ruled African territory. There Boer farmers, fleeing restrictive British jurisdiction (restraints on slavery and on alien culture), trekked north, and British jurisdiction pursued them northward.[16] Colonial governments elsewhere, in search of elusive tariff revenues, found themselves shifting frontiers to include the expanding trading activities of merchants seeking to escape those same tariffs.[17]

Although the pericentric interpretation gives a valuable account of why empire steadily grew, it doesn't address the rapid and nearly simultaneous surge of interest in imperial expansion that many metropoles shared. This explanatory hiatus drew scholarship back to the metropoles and into a dialogue with the seminal views of Hobson, Lenin, and Schumpeter.

J. A. Hobson focused squarely on factors internal to the metropole as he developed his radical theory of modern imperialism. He rejected the search for land for colonial settlement and the search for markets for trade as inadequate to justify or to cause the new imperialism. Neither migrants nor trade flowed to the areas where Britain acquired new territory.[18] Instead, Hobson portrayed imperialism as the result of three

---

MacLean, "Commerce, Finance, and British Diplomatic Support in China," ibid., 26 (1973), 464–76.

15. W. D. McIntyre, *The Imperial Frontier in the Tropics, 1865–1875* (New York, 1967); John S. Galbraith, "The Turbulent Frontier," in R. Art and R. Jervis, eds., *International Politics* (Boston, 1973), p. 395; and Ira Klein, "British Expansion in Malaya," *Journal of Southeast Asian History* (1968), 53–68.

16. Robinson and Gallagher, *Africa and the Victorians*, chap. 14.

17. J. D. Hargreaves, *Prelude to the Partition* (London, 1963), chaps. 2 and 5; C. W. Newbury, *The Western Slave Coast and Its Rulers* (Oxford, 1971).

18. J. A. Hobson, *Imperialism* (London, 1902), pp 40–43. Norman Etherington, "Reconsidering Theories of Imperialism," *History and Theory* 21, 1 (1982), 1–36. extends the "mistaken identity thesis" from Lenin to Hobson, arguing (as Stokes argued for Lenin) that Hobson is not really providing a theory of imperial expansion but a theory of militarism, etc. While Etherington exposes the special role of militarism, he focuses on the investment component of underconsumption. Hobson also placed considerable emphasis on the essential role of the special interests, the role of superexports in response to underconsumption, and the actual, complicated role investment plays in imperial expansion. Hobson considered trade and emigration a decreasing factor for the British economy; moreover, what trade and emigration did exist were not going to the new tropical territories. He demonstrated that investment was increasingly important but as Etherington notes, he knew it was not flowing to the new territories. Hobson managed to reconcile these results with his support of the investment hypothesis: interference with *"powerful civilised states"* was neither possible nor needed, but when some capital does go to "small, decadent, or new countries . . . alien investments exercise a dominant power

forces: economic, political, and sociopsychological. These three forces emanate from—are the *dispositions* of—a metropolitan society such as was Great Britain. Together they produce the drive of imperial expansion.

The economic force, Hobson argued, is composed of two layers of material interest. First, special interests such as financiers, the munitions industry, certain export trades, and shipping pursue their own advantages in imperial markets and territorial expansion. They favor expansion wherever and whenever they can.[19] Second and much more significant is the financial "taproot" of imperialism, a mixture of underconsumption and oversaving. In advanced capitalist societies a few are very rich and many are very poor. The poor, who consume what they earn, lack the income to sustain effective demand for the products of modern industry. The rich, who save much of what they gain, cannot consume enough of what industry can produce. When consumption is insufficient, the savings of the rich cannot be absorbed domestically. The economy therefore needs to export goods and in particular capital in order for the rich to continue to profit from present and future investments. Investors need an outlet for investment, ideally in controlled colonial areas where the investor can both realize high rates of return and be able to repatriate profits. Desperate to invest, investors fall into the clutches of financiers; without imperialism, advanced capitalism would collapse from unequal distribution.[20]

Hobson believed that by the end of the nineteenth century the British

---

in foreign policy." These countries, Egypt among them, both permit and require such political interference "to safeguard and improve investments" (*Imperialism*, p. 54). Hobson does not assume that this growth of foreign investment was actually flowing in preponderant volume to the newly acquired colonies, but he suggests that the amount that was going to the new territories would require political control—imperialism.

19. Hobson, *Imperialism*, chap. 4. The relative importance of trade and investment in Hobson's analysis of imperialism has provoked a recent debate. P. J. Cain focuses on the importance and inadequacy of Hobson's analysis of trade flows; P. F. Clarke affirms the significance of Hobson's emphasis on finance and investment. My own interpretation stresses Hobson's arguments that suggest it is the political *combination* of trade, financial, bureaucratic, and other interests that made imperialism a potent force (and a force subject to political reform). See Cain, "J. A. Hobson, Cobdenism, and the Radical Theory of Economic Imperialism: 1898–1914,"*Economic History Review*, 2d ser. 31, 4 (1978), 565–84, and Clarke, "Hobson, Free Trade, and Imperialism," ibid. 34, 2 (1981), 308–12.

20. Hobson, *Imperialism,* chap. 6. Economic collapse and depression will eventually restore the balance between consumption and investment. But this economic "solution" is not a political solution—not, that is, a solution that the groups which Hobson argues control the state are likely to permit. Here Hobson's economic model again intersects with and is supported by his "political conspiracy" (since the latter can occur only under the circumstances explained by the model). Hobson is not an early Keynes, even though they developed somewhat similar programs.

polity was democratic and that the majority interest clearly opposed imperialism. Needing to explain how imperialism warped the manifest interest of a democratic majority, he added politics to imperialism's economics: the "Reactionary Alliance" led by the financiers solved the contradiction. The alliance included not only special economic interests but also three key actors in the state—the landed aristocracy, the civil service, and the military—which stood to gain from empire. The alliance controlled politics in a formally democratic society by manipulating political parties and the public consciousness, funding the parties' electoral campaigns, and financially controlling the press and the universities.[21]

Hobson's reforming cure corresponded to his diagnosis of the imperial syndrome.[22] Public policy that redistributed income to the poorer sectors of society through unionization and welfare payments would free capitalism from underconsumption and oversaving, he argued. To change government policy in favor of the poor would require arousing the public consciousness. Policy and consciousness could together change the disposition of the metropole from imperialism to peaceful, commercial internationalism.[23]

Lenin also offered a dispositional theory of imperialism, although he differed from Hobson in a number of respects. When Lenin discussed the "territorial division" of the world, one aspect of his definition of imperialism, he retained a concept of imperial expansion that included both the acquisition of territory by conquest (Hobson's definition) and the exercise of controlling influence by economic means (an informal imperialism). For Lenin, imperialism was not the product of the special interests of high finance; it was capitalism in its monopoly, financial, and final stage. The connection between capitalism and imperialism was neither marginal nor mistaken, nor, as Hobson had argued, subject to reform; it was vital and necessary to capitalism as a whole.[24]   Lenin's

21. Hobson, *Imperialism,* pt. 2, chaps. 1 and 3.

22. Ibid., chap. 2.

23. Ibid., p. 89. Hobson did not categorically oppose foreign control of the peoples of the periphery. A reformed, democratic metropole would practice internationalism with its fellow metropoles and a developmental trusteeship, supervised by an international organization, over the peoples of Africa and Asia. The alternatives, inviolable autonomy or private commercial exploitation, were unacceptable. The first deprived the world of needed raw materials; the second could lead to exploitation worse than under public imperialism (pp. 232–38). Hobson sought to explain and to end a special type of imperialism, one that encouraged imperial expansion and thereby stimulated militarism and other ills.

24. Lenin, *Imperialism: The Highest Stage of Capitalism* (New York, 1939). For critical reviews of Marxist and Leninist theory see Louis Fischer, *Lenin* (New York, 1964);

Imperialism was an unabashedly political explanation designed to expose the capitalist origins of World War I and to confute Kautsky's claim that capitalism could evolve peacefully. It was also an explanation of the economic and political expansion of the metropoles.[25]

Marx had left a confusing legacy on the subject of imperialism. In some works he identified it with Napoleon III's antics, in others he described it as an inevitable and progressive (if painful) economic de-

---

Wolfgang Mommsen, *Theories of Imperialism* (New York, 1980); Anthony Brewer, *Marxist Theories of Imperialism* (London, 1980), chaps. 2–5; E. M. Winslow, *The Pattern of Imperialism* (New York, 1948); T. Kemp, *Theories of Imperialism* (London, 1967); and D. K. Fieldhouse, *The Theory of Capitalist Imperialism* (London, 1967). W. L. Langer's *The Diplomacy of Imperialism* (New York, 1935), pp. 68–69, remains in a number of respects the best short critique of economic imperialism.

25. Hilferding added an emphasis on the crucial role of finance and monopoly (finance) capital, arguing that though capitalist expansion is a *policy* not a necessity of capitalist growth, the accumulation of financial capital and the formation of modern corporations leads banks to create monopolies or cartels. Just as finance capital demands protectionism at home to preserve its cartel prices, so it demands control abroad to ensure the stability of investments. Free-trade policy ended with the demise of competitive industrial capitalism. The existence of more than one center of finance capital engaging in protection leads to economic conflict, and economic conflict to war. E. M. Winslow, *The Pattern of Imperialism* (New York, 1948), chap. 7.

Rosa Luxemburg rejected the idea that imperialism was a mere policy of capitalism. Instead, she emphasized the "realization" problem—how to guarantee effective demand when capital goods expenditure itself created more consumption goods and when workers could not consume all of the final product. She concluded that to realize surplus value, exports are necessary. Furthermore, these exports must be purchased outside the capitalist economy—in underdeveloped lands abroad *or* in a country's own primitive sectors (together constituting the "external economy"). Imperialism therefore is "the political expression of the accumulation of capital in its competitive struggle for what remains still open of the non-capitalist environment." Imperialism, in short, was a competition for noncapitalist consumers (and suppliers of raw materials). See Luxemburg, *The Accumulation of Capital* (1913; London, 1951), p. 466, and Alan Hodgart, *The Economics of European Imperialism* (New York, 1977).

In 1914 Kautsky defined imperialism as "the striving of every industrial nation to annex larger and larger *agrarian* regions, irrespective of what nations inhabit them." Previously, he had stressed the role of preindustrial factors—aristocratic, military classes and their ties to banking—and a search for new land to conquer. Despite his growing appreciation of the expansive thrust of industrial and bank capitalism, Kautsky retained an emphasis on atavistic forces as causes and a (perhaps resulting) belief in a pacifist, evolutionary socialist strategy. Furthermore, he argued that imperialism did not necessarily cause war—war is a policy, not a necessity, of capitalism, for capitalist countries can combine in large international cartels to exploit the world, engaging in "ultra-imperialism." T. Kemp, *Theories of Imperialism* (London, 1966), chaps. 4–5.

Some of Lenin's animus against Kautsky becomes clearer when we note that Kautsky was not only a socialist competitor, he had the unique distinction of reaching three "incorrect" conclusions: imperialism is a policy, it has roots that are atavistic and not essentially capitalist, and capitalism can be pacific.

velopment of backward regions. It was not, however, of central significance to his theory of capitalism.[26] His general economics left room for more than one inference: exports might restrain the downward plunge of profits, foreign investment might have a similar effect, and imperialism might aid in either solution, but no specific connection was systematically argued at the theoretical level.

Lenin attempted to fill this gap in Marxist theory. He began by defining imperialism in five "essential features":

> (1) The concentration of production, and capital developed to such a high stage that it created monopolies which play a decisive role in economic life.
> (2) The merging of bank capital with industrial capital and the creation, on the basis of "financial capital," of a "financial oligarchy."
> (3) The export of capital, which has become extremely important, as distinguished from the export of commodities.
> (4) The formation of international capitalist combines which share the world among themselves.
> (5) The territorial division of the world among the greatest capitalist powers is *completed*.[27]

Lenin provided not an analysis of international politics but a description of capitalist development in its highest stage. He also argued, however, that the first features were causally anterior to the economic and territorial divisions of the world in the last stage of capitalism. Territorial division, which includes both formal and informal imperialism, is "closely associated with" and "*bound* up with" the economic division.[28]

Lenin's imperialism (the economic and political division of the world) is the product of institutions and forces. The institutions are monopoly

26. Albert O. Hirschman suggests that Marx may have been particularly reluctant to develop a theory of economic imperialism although certainly aware of Hegel's views on the role of foreign trade as a means of absorbing domestic overproduction. Foreign trade, by solving the overproduction crisis, would dim the prospects for domestic revolution. See Hirschman, "Hegel, Imperialism, and Structural Stagnation," *Journal of Development Economics* 3 (March 1976), 1–8. On Marx's view of colonialism and the changes made by later socialists, see G. Lichtheim, *Marxism* (London, 1961), pp. 310–31.

27. Lenin, *Imperialism*, p. 89.

28. Ibid., pp. 70, 75. See Eric Stokes, "Late Nineteenth-Century Colonial Expansion and the Attack on the Theory of Economic Imperialism: A Case of Mistaken Identity," *Historical Journal* 12, 2 (1969), 285–301, who argues that economic imperialism was really a theory of conflicts among industrial states. He correctly emphasizes Lenin's attention to and inclusion of industrial conflicts, public and private, in imperialism. But Lenin specifically included political division and redivision of overseas colonies as an essential feature of imperialism.

capital, composed of the merger of industrial and bank capital, and the state, a reflection of those economic institutions. The forces are exerted by and through the institutions. Lenin first outlined the growth of monopoly in concentrated production. Companies expand their capital base and merge their holdings in order to even out fluctuations in production and to weather recurrent financial crises, and large firms then become the dominant form of industrial enterprise.

Lenin developed this familiar analysis of late-19th-century monopoly growth in showing the increasing concentration of the banks themselves. These huge banks acquire funds that must be invested profitably, and in investing, they transform the usual financial services they offer corporations into distinct forms of control manifested in seats on the boards of directors of their client companies. Seeking secure investments, they demand careful management, noncompetition with their other investments, and even (where it appears safe) mergers to reduce fluctuations in stock values caused by competition. The result is a single financial oligarchy of capitalists which operates through the coordinating control that banks exercise over corporations and a new stage of capitalism—finance or monopoly capitalism.

Finance capitalism serves as a channel for three international pressures or forces. The first is the search for profitable investment necessitated by "superabundance" of capital in the advanced capitalist economies, now constucted along monopoly lines. "The necessity for exporting capital," Lenin argues, "arises from the fact that in a few countries capitalism has become 'over-ripe' and (owing to the backward state of agriculture and the impoverished state of the masses) capital cannot find 'profitable' investment."[29] Capital cannot stimulate demand from either agriculture or the masses because "investing" in them would involve lower profits for capitalists.

For his second force, Lenin followed Rosa Luxemburg's argument that underconsumption drives monopolies to seek markets in the undeveloped areas of the world. Even though trade is not the predominant form of international exploitation, concentrated industries find that exports can momentarily slow the tendency of the rate of profit to fall. Moreover, capital export complements trade by creating certain advantages for home-country exporters. When loans are tied to the purchase of home-produced goods, exports are secured for monopoly industries.

The third force is a search for control of markets and sources of raw

29. Lenin, *Imperialism*, p. 63.

materials in order to secure monopoly. Occasionally agreements divide the world market, but much more usual is a continual "struggle for redivision" such as the one characterizing the international oil industry. One of the clearest forms of this expand-or-be-absorbed monopoly pressure is the connection between colonialism and the search for raw materials. "These monopolies are most firmly established when *all* sources of raw materials are controlled by one group. . . .Colonial possession alone gives complete guarantee of success to the monopolies against all the risks that the latter will defend themselves by means of a law establishing a state monopoly," as Germany did when it established a state cartel in oil.[30]

Although bank and industrial monopolies are the crucial institutions of imperialism, the state also plays an important role. The economic foundations of the state shift toward "parasitism" (here Lenin followed Hobson). The imperialist state becomes a "rentier state," collecting interest for its dominant class of capitalist investors. The top levels of the working class— "the aristocracy of labor"—become politically subservient as they reach bourgeois status through their share in imperialist superprofits. Empire turns into a "bread and butter question"—opportunities for settlement and expanded markets that increase popular welfare and, indirectly, stave off revolution. The size and power of the state increases, transforming it as an institution. To relieve popular discontent, it employs colonial mercenary armies, and to maintain popular support it encourages "social chauvinism," or national hatreds and lusts for conquest.[31]

Lenin not only described a solution to imperialism, as Hobson did; he took the first steps toward achieving it. His solution was, of course, revolution. It was, however, somewhat more complicated than is sometimes assumed. Revolution at home is necessary to emancipate the colonies, since emancipation is " 'impracticable' under capitalism"; but national liberation abroad is also needed to stage successful revolution at home:

> The social revolution can come only in the form of an epoch in which are combined civil war by the proletariat against the bourgeoisie in the advanced countries and a *whole* series democratic and revolutionary movements, including the national liberation movement, in the undeveloped, backward and oppressed nations. Why? Because

30. Ibid., p. 82.
31. Ibid., pp. 100–109.

capitalism develops unevenly, and objective reality gives us highly developed capitalist nations side by side with a number of economically slightly developed, or totally undeveloped, nations.[32]

Lenin believed with Marx, that capitalism was both destructive and creative in colonial areas. As feudal and colonial stages of production were transformed by the world market and by international investment into industrial capitalism, so the objective foundations for a bourgeois, national revolution would be laid. In capitalist metropoles the concentration of industry and the immiseration of the working class would lead to conditions ripe for a communist-led revolution under a "dictatorship of the proletariat."

National bourgeois revolution in the colonial peripheries and communist revolution in the metropoles are sped along by the likelihood of interimperialist war.[33] Kautsky had argued that beyond imperialism, "ultra-imperialism" is possible in which capitalists form alliances to reduce economic and political competition in the world economy.[34] Lenin replied that any slackening of competition is merely a truce since capitalism develops *unevenly*. Relative forces change, and alliances cannot be maintained; states and imperialist monopolies will seek to prevent their decline or to promote their rise by war. Kautsky offered, Lenin argued, no more than a "reactionary ideal" which seeks to move from monopoly back to peaceful competition. Capitalism can neither evolve into democratic competition nor maintain peace by an alliance of national monopolies.[35]

Schumpeter did not hold capitalism responsible for imperialism; indeed, he argued, capitalism was inherently anti-imperialistic. Although Schumpeter shared with Hobson an ideological commitment to liberal

32. V. I. Lenin, "The Socialist Revolution and the Rights of Nations to Self-Determination" *Selected Works* 5 (New York, 1943), pp. 267–81; and for quotation, "A Caricature of Marxism and Imperialist Economism," *Collected Works* 23, August–October 1917 (Moscow, 1964), p. 60.

33. V. I. Lenin, *State and Revolution* (1917; New York, 1943), p. 74.

34. The best account is by John Kautsky in "J. A. Schumpeter and Karl Kautsky," *Midwest Journal of Political Science* 2 (May 1961), 108–9.

35. The propensity of the working class to succumb to the attractions of imperialist profits has worried many contemporary Marxists, particularly those in the Third World. Frantz Fanon, for example, was aware of this possible contradiction between the interests of the colonial masses and those of the metropolitan proletariat. He hoped that, if the metropolitan proletariat failed to perceive their long-run interests in the liberation of the masses in the periphery, the global depression that a peripheral rebellion and a rejection of world capitalism would engender would soon make them aware of their interdependence. See Fanon, *Wretched of the Earth* (New York, 1968), pp. 80–81.

values and to the doctrines of free trade and competitive capitalism, he nonetheless shared with Lenin a theory that is basically deterministic.[36] Schumpeter focused solely on the metropolitan sources of empire, but unlike Hobson and Lenin he developed his theory of imperialism in a sweeping historical survey.

"Imperialism," Schumpeter said, "is the objectless disposition on the part of a state to unlimited forcible expansion."[37] Dispositional, formal, and without object (that is, unlimited), Schumpeter's definition excluded those imperialisms which were what he asserted nineteenth-century England's to have been, mere "catchwords."[38]

36. See Joseph Schumpeter, "The Sociology of Imperialism," in *Imperialism and Social Classes* (Cleveland, 1955), first published in *Archiv für Sozialwissenschaft und Sozialpolitik* 46 (1919). Schumpeter may not have read Lenin before writing this essay, but he was aware of the work of two of Lenin's sources, Hilferding and Bauer. Schumpeter's later views appear in *Business Cycles* 2 (New York, 1939). He there adopted the view that imperialism could not be understood as a rational phenomenon corresponding to the interests of any one class or group, including the war machine. Instead, he argued, imperialism is a psychological manifestation of a people as a whole (even though it appears in a particularly virulent form in the lower middle class). See the discussion in E. M. Winslow, *The Pattern of Imperialism* (New York, 1948), pp. 232–36; R. Koebner and H. Schmidt, *Imperialism* (Cambridge, 1964), pp. 6–7; Cohen, pp. 73–75; and P. M. Sweezy, "Peoples' Imperialism," in S. Harris, ed., *Schumpeter: Social Scientist* (Cambridge, Mass., 1951).

37. Schumpeter, "Sociology of Imperialism," p. 6. The basic idea is quite simple, though its specification can be complicated. "Objectless" expansion is expansion for its own sake, and in Schumpeter's special use of the word it is "not concrete." Concrete interests in expansion are objects such as hunting grounds, salt deposits, the political unification of a geographically divided people, or the acquisition by a planter aristocracy of trading stations for the purchase of slaves. Nonconcrete, or objectless, interests are wars fought to increase the profits of war profiteers or to stimulate patriotism. Schumpeter stresses that "concreteness" should be assessed in relation to the objective of the war or other form of expansion, not in relation to the motives of its participants. First, "a concrete interest *must be present*"; second, "the conduct of the state which is under study must be calculated to *promote* this interest"; and third, "it must be possible to *prove* that this interest, whether avowed or not, is actually the *political driving force* behind the action." If any of these three stringent conditions is not met, the act of expansion is objectless.

38. Ibid., pp. 11, 14–15, 21. Schumpeter draws the distinction between imperialism as *word* and imperialism as *deed*. Imperialist ideas do not an imperialist make; some imperialisms, such as England's are mere political "catchwords." The imperial federation plans of the 1890s were imperialist in tone, but Britain was not imperialist in fact. Imperialism was not supported by the masses who, he says, shaped British politics from the seventeenth century onward; powerful industries and trades were pacifist; the professional army was not uncontrolled. *Anti*-imperialism rather than imperialism thus was the "level of the storm-tossed ocean." The waves of imperialism were but temporary aberrations of imperialist sentiment. If this account seems a bit confusing, it is because it is. Schumpeter established England's freedom from imperialism by demonstrating that

True imperialism, in the nineteenth century and earlier is the product of a "war machine," warlike instincts, and export monopolism. Schumpeter's typical example—Egypt—is also his oldest, for here the first war machine developed. Before the invasion of the Hyksos, Egypt was a peaceful agrarian society of peasants dominated by a provincial landlord nobility that owed loose allegiance to the pharoah. To expel the invaders Egypt needed an army, and the social changes required to support it "militarized" Egyptian society. Under the leadership of the pharoah a caste of professional soldiers evolved, organized into a military aristocracy. The pharoah and the soldier caste formed a war machine that would conquer the entire Middle East in order to maintain its social and professional position: "Created by the wars that required it, the machine now created the wars it required."[39] The very success of the Egyptian war machine in achieving national liberation destroyed its "objectful" function, and it became atavistic and pursued objectless expansion. Wars were fought merely for the acquisition of booty and glory, for the sake of warriors and monarchs.

Schumpeter believed that a war machine is a necessary and sufficient cause of imperialism. A warlike disposition, elsewhere called an "instinctual element of bloody primitivism," is the natural ideology of a war machine, but it can also exist independently. The Persians were a "warior nation" from the outset, the Assyrians exulted in bloody wars of religious extermination, and the Arabs engaged in a "popular" or a "people's imperialism." Religion was not itself the war-inducing factor.

the causes of imperialism (which he has not yet presented) were not present in England— a circular proceeding.

39. Ibid., p. 25. The expansive regimes of Louis XIV and Catherine the Great conform to the pattern as well: warlike court nobilities pressure the monarch to find employment for the aristocratic classes on the battlefield. Not all nobilities are war machines, however, and some are merely agrarian landlords, for example the German nobility of the Middle Ages. That is, the war machine is not simply a national army. "Militarism is not necessarily a foregone conclusion when a nation maintains a large army, but only when high military circles become a political power. The criterion is whether leading generals as such wield political influence and whether the responsible statesman can only act with their consent. That is possible only when the officer corps is linked to a definite social class, as in Japan, and can assimilate to its position individuals who do not belong to it by birth" (pp. 95–96). Not all imperialisms fit the model: Macedonian imperialism was the imperialism of one man, and Roman imperialism from the Punic Wars to Augustus was a product of the *class interest* of the senatorial proprietors of latifundia and of their search for new land and slaves. The senatorial order, as a class, sought to maintain its leadership of Roman politics by fostering perceptions of international danger and by conducting wars that stimulated a sense of Roman glory. Both enhanced the position of the Senate by engendering threats that called for strategic direction which only the Senate was capable of providing.

Only when religion became linked to a warlike social structure did it evolve into an instinctual support for imperialism.

The last clear-cut imperialism was that of the absolute monarchies of Louis XIV and Catherine the Great. Modern (nineteenth-century) empires represent merely the vestiges, the atavisms, of those times. Imperialism, therefore, is not and cannot be a stage or a development of modern capitalism. Schumpeter argued the proposition by explaining both the theoretical incompatibility of imperialism (in his sense) with capitalism and the actual vestiges—nineteenth-century imperialism—that plagued the international politics of his time.

Capitalism, according to Schumpeter, produces an "unwarlike disposition." The populace is "democratized, individualized, rationalized" as a consequence of the industrial revolution.[40] Capitalism individualizes as "subjective opportunities" replace the "immutable factors" of traditional, hierarchical society, and it rationalizes as the instability of industrial life necessitates constant calculation; rational individuals, moreover, demand democratic governance. As "*no* class" gains from forcible expansion when free trade prevails, no democracy (no capitalist democracy) would tolerate imperialism. In the nineteenth century, however, imperialism coexisted with the capitalist societies of the European metropoles. Schumpeter argued that nineteenth-century capitalism had been warped by export monopolies and big banks, which favored imperialism. Tariffs allow monopolies to become established since they prevent foreign competition from reducing firms to their efficient size. In a protected market the monopolist can pay low (real) wages and engage in selective pricing, and the need to find markets for monopolies protected from foreign competition results in the acquisition of colonies. Colonies similarly become attractive for the banks, providing them with an area in which to invest capital that otherwise would be invested at home and drive down the rate of return.[41]

Monopoly profits thus disrupt the peaceful logic of free trade, requiring the destruction of foreign competitors and the preemptive acquisition of colonies.[42] As "export-dependent monopoly capitalism" destroys international capitalist harmony, a bought press attempts to

40. Ibid., p. 68.

41. Ibid., pp. 95–96. "Foreign raw materials and foodstuffs are as accessible to each nation as though they were within its own territory. Where the cultural backwardness of a region makes normal economic intercourse dependent on colonization it does not matter, assuming free trade, which of the "civilized" nations undertakes the task of colonization" (pp. 75–76).

42. Ibid., pp. 82–83.

mask the public swindle. Nevertheless, Schumpeter judges, "deep down, the normal sense of business and trade prevails." The real losers from imperialism, the small capitalists and workers, know it and will react.[43]

Schumpeter's theory of imperialism is, somewhat surprisingly, quite close both to Lenin's monopoly capitalist alliance of big business and big banks and to Hobson's reactionary alliance. For Hobson and even more directly for Lenin, however, capitalism led to monopoly imperialism; for Schumpeter, no such direct connection holds. Export monopolism completely depends on tariff barriers, and tariff barriers are the product not of capitalism but of the absolute monarchy that liberal capitalism rejects. The monarch needed readily collectible revenue, and he lacked the political effectiveness to collect an income tax. The tariff was his answer, and it is the survival of the monarchy and the nobility which sets in motion export monopolism and its tendencies toward international conflict.

Nonetheless, export monopolism is not by itself a sufficient cause for imperialism. Imperialism still requires the war machine.

> But export monopolism to go a step further is not imperialism. And even if it had been able to arise without protective tariffs, it would never have developed into imperialism in the hands of an unwarlike bourgeoisie. If this did happen, it was only because the heritage included the war machine, together with its sociopsychological aura and aggressive bent, and because a class oriented toward war maintained itself in a ruling position. This class clung to its domestic interest in wars and the pro-military interests among the bougeoisie were able to ally themselves with it.[44]

The diagnosis bears its prognosis: the spread of capitalist industrialism changes the public so that it will reject the war machine, national aggression, export monopolism, and consequently, imperialism.

Hobsonian, Leninist, and Schumpeterian interpretations still vie as to which provides the most convincing explanation of the Scramble for empire. In modern revisions they shape Hans Ulrich Wehler's study of the "social imperialist" triangle of imperial Germany—a study of how imperialism becomes a countercyclical device to manage domestic class politics.[45] They also influence, among others, A. S. Kanya-Forstner's

43. Ibid., p. 85.
44. Ibid., p. 97.
45. Hans Ulrich Wehler, "Bismarck's Imperialism: 1862–90," *Past and Present* 48 (August 1970), drawn from *Bismarck und der Imperialismus* (Cologne, 1969). See Winfried

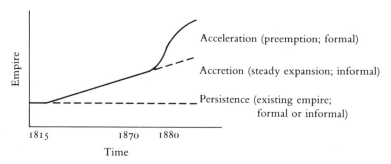

FIGURE 3 Nineteenth-century imperialism

investigation of the French military's role in colonial expansion, Freda Harcourt's study of Disraelian foreign policy, and numerous accounts of economic factors in the new imperialism.[46]

The chapters of Part II have two aims. First, we need to explain the three features of nineteenth-century imperialism. Empire in the nineteenth century mainly persisted (though the Spanish empire in America collapsed), it slowly expanded, and then it accelerated.[47] These features constitute a function of empire against time.

In Part I, I argued that neither a systemic nor a metrocentric nor a pericentric model of imperialism was in itself sufficient to explain empires. Instead, the existence of empire called for a combined explanation, one that took into account the apparently necessary roles of a metropole, a periphery, and a transnational connection. But the actual role played by metrocentric, pericentric, and systemic pressures for imperial expansion was a subject I considered only in passing. Here, drawing on arguments developed in Part I and an analysis of the new circumstances of the nineteenth century, I shall explore the role of systemic, metrocentric, and pericentric sources, as well as the transnational forces that

Baumgart, *Imperialism: The Idea and Reality of British and French Colonial Expansion, 1880–1914* (New York, 1982), for a discussion of these views.

46. A. S. Kanya-Forstner, *The Conquest of the Western Sudan* (London, 1969); Freda Harcourt, "Disraeli's Imperialism, 1866–68: A Question of Timing," *Historical Journal* 23 (1980).

47. Geoffrey Barraclough, *Introduction to Contemporary History* (Baltimore, 1967). See also M. B. Brown, *The Economics of Imperialism* (Harmondsworth, 1974), and P. J. Cain and A. G. Hopkins, "The Political Economy of British Expansionism Overseas, 1750–1914," *Economic History Review*, 2d ser., 32, 4 (1980). For a metrocentric "push" or what the authors call a "lateral pressure" account of overall nineteenth-century imperialism, see Nazli Choucri and Robert C. North, *Nations in Conflict: National Growth and International Violence* (San Francisco, 1975).

connect them, in shaping the three phase evolution of nineteenth-century imperialism.

Second, having discussed in Part I the general structural conditions (both static and dynamic) that sustain empire, I shall focus more closely on imperialism—on the process of imperial expansion. Persistence and acceleration were particularly associated with formal empire, expansion with informal empire. I shall explore the forms, the comparative statics, that expansion took and its various national styles.

CHAPTER 8

Tribal Peripheries and Formal Empire

Dear W. Gladstone,

We both your servants have met this afternoon to write you these few lines of writing trusting it may find you in a good state of life as it leaves us at present. As we heard here that you are the chief man in the House of Commons, so we write to tell you that we want to be under Her Majesty's control. We want our country to be governed by British Government. We are tired of governing this country ourselves, every dispute leads to war, and often to great loss of lives, so we think it is best thing to give up the country to you British men who no doubt will bring peace, civilization, and Christianity in the country. Do for mercy sake please lay our request before the Queen and to the rulers of the British Government. Do, Sir, for mercy sake, please to assist us in this important undertaking. We heard that you are a good Christian man, so we hope that you will do all you can in your power to see that our request is granted. We are quite willing to abolish all our heathen customs. . . . No doubt God will bless you for putting a light in our country. Please to send us an answer as quick as you can.

King Bell and King Acqua
of the Cameroons River, West Africa
6 November 1881[1]

Not every extension of empire is accompanied by a written invitation such as the one issued by kings Bell and Acqua, members of the com-

---

1. Kings Bell and Acqua to Gladstone, 6 November 1881, F.O. 403/18, Part I, in the Public Record Office, Kew, Surrey (hereafter PRO).

mercial oligarchy ruling a small town on the west coast of Africa. (Gladstone hesitated, and the Germans snapped up the Cameroons.) But the Athenian conquest of Corcyra was preceded by invitations from factions within Corcyrean society, and Rome was likewise invited into Greece and Britain by governing or dissident elites. The periphery, whether it collaborates or resists, helps determine the character of an imperial relationship and needs to be taken into account if we are to understand empire.

Even an expansive metropole does not imperialize all peoples with which it comes into contact. More fundamentally, the distinction between metropole and periphery itself needs to be accounted for. Why were Japan and Ethiopia able to remain independent; why was Britain able to control Zanzibar or West Africa or India, and why was none of the three able to control Britain?

This chapter focuses on tribal society, the first of two major types of peripheral society that European metropoles encountered in the nineteenth century. (The second, patrimonial society, is addressed in the next chapter.) Political anthropologists have called tribal societies "primitive systems with intermittent political structures."[2] And the imperial man in the street, expressing all that he knew about them, called them "the natives."

Tribal Society

Intermittent and nonstatal political systems were characteristic of the tribal societies encountered by Tacitus, Columbus, the colonizing farmers of the United States, and the missionaries and merchants of equatorial Africa.[3] In Part I, I described these tribal societies as being highly undifferentiated yet thoroughly integrated. On a local scale, moreover, they are highly participatory, their inhabitants are mobilized, and their political and social institutions—the vast majority of them informal—cope fully with the needs that the society defines.[4]

In tribal societies, religion guides and is thoroughly enmeshed with

2. G. Almond and G. B. Powell, *Comparative Politics: A Developmental Approach* (Boston, 1966), p. 217.

3. Basil Davidson, *The African Genius* (Boston, 1969), chap. 1.

4. Almond and Powell, p. 22; S. Huntington, *Political Order in Changing Societies* (New Haven, 1968), chap. 1. See also Gertrude Dole, "Anarchy without Chaos," in M. Schwartz, V. Turner, and A. Tuden, eds., *Political Anthropology* (Chicago, 1966), p. 85.

the political order: priests are rulers and rulers, priests. Economic life is part of ritual and the tending of a field, for example, becomes an act of worship, as among the Kachin tribes of Upper Burma.[5] Political leaders are the regulators of the economy as well as the font of justice, and so, as in the Ekpe societies of the Niger Delta, economic success directly qualifies the wealthy for political leadership.[6] Elizabeth Colson, in her description of African society at the time of the Scramble, offers a telling portrait of the minimally differentiated integration of tribal society: "Local economic exchanges were thus regulated by institutions which had other purposes and an ethic which emphasized the maintenance of the long-term relationship between participants rather than immediate gain. Economic activity was therefore strongly conditioned by religious beliefs which reflected the complex interweaving of multiple social relationships and pervaded most aspects of life."[7]

Similar values, rights, duties, and technologies govern the lives of the members of each individual tribal unit. The wider aggregations that have been likened to nations, such as the Ibo or the Nuer, often share only a common religious heritage manifested in common respect for a shaman (the Nuer leopard-skin chief) or an oracle (the Ibo Arochuku). These widest aggregations can be considered to be incipient nations, highly unintegrated even though the typical tribal member lives his entire life in a closely integrated village.[8]

Minimal social differentiation combines with thorough communal social integration to have important consequences for tribal political order. Tribal political order in turn shapes how tribal societies respond to foreign, metropolitan intrusions—whether, that is, tribes resist successfully or not.

In tribal societies, political conflict management is based upon the collectivity—the family and the tribe. These societies are not collections of individuals, they are aggregations of families. Moreover, these families are corporations that pass on permanent rights and duties.[9] The

---

5. E. R. Leach, *The Political Systems of Highland Burma* (Boston, 1954), p. 12; Daryll Forde and Mary Douglas, "Primitive Economics," in George Dalton, ed., *Tribal and Peasant Economies* (Austin, 1967), pp. 13–28.

6. Davidson, pp. 95–99. For similar ideas among the Barotse see M. Gluckman, *The Ideas in Barotse Jurisprudence* (New Haven, 1965), pp. 38–39.

7. Elizabeth Colson, "African Society at the Time of the Scramble," in L. H. Gann and P. Duignan, eds., *Colonialism in Africa, 1870–1960*, vol. 1 (Cambridge, 1961), p. 56.

8. E. Isichei, *The Ibo People and the Europeans* (London, 1973), p. 78. For similar arguments see E. E. Evans-Pritchard, *The Nuer* (Oxford, 1940).

9. Sir Henry Maine, *Ancient Law* (London, 1880), p. 126.

family is always supreme for it is only within the family that the person finds the meaning that is his or her place in society.[10] These families are extended, not nuclear; they group themselves into lineages and the lineages into tribes, which then establish law among themselves as a form of international law.[11]

Political control in this society is highly diffuse, exercised by no specific person or institution. Primitive society, to follow Malinowski, is regulated by a mixture of legal, moral, and religious sanctions enforced by the group. (These three sorts of sanctions are neither separate nor differentiated.) Law derives from and is enforced by socially upheld custom—habit that is taught as proper human behavior and is enforced through criticism, ostracism, and harsher means. Law is the result of centuries of slow, piecemeal adaptation to difficult environments, often embodying something like an invisible hand of inherited accommodations which tends to mute extreme conflicts.[12] Law is nonetheless attributed a divine origin, providing it with supernatural legitimacy.[13]

Illuminating examples of the functioning of political order in tribal societies are widely reported. When among the Kuikuru of the Amazon Basin a number of huts were struck by lightning, a local shaman was called in to divine the criminal. After a lengthy ritual that included a tobacco trance, the shaman singled out a particularly asocial member of the tribe as the guilty party. This public indictment resulted in the tribesman's death at the hands of a gang of enraged young men.[14] When among the Bena of Tanzania local chiefs and great men disagree, conciliation is attempted until finally the parties to a dispute agree on some statement of the facts and some means of restitution. These conciliations solve disputes and in doing so increase the influence of the local political leadership without requiring the authority of a state institution.[15]

10. Ibid., p. 129.

11. Lucy Mair, *Primitive Government* (Baltimore, 1964), chap. 3.

12. Schwartz, Turner, and Tuden, "Introduction"; Gideon Sjolberg, "Transnational Societies and the Process of Change," in J. Finkle and R. N. Gable, eds., *Political Development and Social Change* (New York, 1971), pp. 12–13.

13. For example, the oracle of the Ibo people provided one of the few means of tribal coherence. Thus shamans declared misfortunes to be divine retribution for violations of the sacred law. The diviner, playing a quasi-judicial role, channeled religious forces to specific situations and made known the will of the deity to maintain social cohesion and exorcise the "trouble" perceived by the tribe. K. O. Dike, *Trade and Politics in the Niger Delta* (Oxford, 1959), pp. 134–35; S. Simpson and J. Stone, *Cases and Readings on Law and Society* (St. Paul, Minn., 1948), chap. 2.

14. Dole, pp. 73–85.

15. M. Schwartz, "Bases for Political Compliance in Bena Villages," in Schwartz, Turner, and Tuden, pp. 89–108.

Tribal societies share many of the features of a diffuse political order because they share a low level of socioeconomic differentiation and a high level of integration. There are, however, significant variations in other aspects of the social, economic, political, and cultural life of nineteenth-century Africa. Considering varieties in economic technostructure, one sociologist has distinguished five civilizations in the African continent, and his taxonomy is useful in understanding the variations of tribal society. Jacques Maquet talks of the civilizations of the bow, the glades, the granaries, the spear, and the cities.[16]

The bow identifies the civilization of hunter-gatherer bands—societies with very little differentiation and very small scale. Each member of the band shares in all the band's functions. Economic life is intensely participatory, the headman acts according to tradition, and what few external relations exist involve reciprocal exchanges with the nearest similar band (especially for wives).

In the glades, slash-and-burn agriculture is practiced, and as in the civilization of the bow the size of the economic and political unit is severely limited by the need to move frequently. In the glades somewhat more exalted chiefs tend to emerge, but chiefs still lead only where their followers want to go. Political and social organization is often based upon lineage distinctions within a population sharing a common culture, and each lineage has a chief managing its affairs. Chiefs negotiate to settle interlineage disputes. These societies develop more complex hierarchies of rule with head chiefs in positions of formally superior authority, but these head chiefs lack effective authority and the societies lack centralized power. Tacitus's German chieftains vied with popular "assemblies"; head chiefs among the nineteenth-century Ashanti vied with influential subordinate chiefs.[17]

The civilization of the granaries, found in the savannahs of Central Africa, rests on subsistence agriculture. Chiefdoms, as among the Barotse, appear strong. Given only the slightest surplus, the chief begins to take an extra share in redistribution, and from these resources he begins to acquire differentiated political power.[18]

The spear tends to conquer the granaries. The civilization of the spear (for example, the Nuer) shares the bandlike characteristics of the bow

16. Jacques Maquet, "African Society: Sub-Saharan Africa," in *International Encyclopedia of the Social Sciences*, vol. 1 (New York, 1968), pp. 140–41.

17. Tacitus, *Agricola and Germania*, trans. H. Mattingly (Baltimore, 1970), pp. 110–11; Colson, p. 37.

18. Maquet, p. 145; Mair, pp. 108–11.

but herds cattle. Through the extensive wealth and mobility that cattle make possible, these peoples achieve substantial economic and political strength. Societies of equal warriors, they often establish themselves as the ruling aristocracy of granary peoples and create state institutions to control their peasants. In doing so, they move beyond the intermittent political system of tribal society.

The last civilization is that of the city. Some of Africa's cities, responding to opportunities for long-distance trade, developed into extensive though fragile empires that were both highly differentiated and centralized, thus extending beyond the scope of this review of tribal political systems. But in the earliest stages of urban commercial development, as the civilizations of the glade transform themselves into commercial cities, the tribal features of minimal differentiation and lack of centralization or integration survive. In these towns, secret oligarchical societies rule by means of their wealth, witchcraft, and household police.[19] Traditions are law, and the state as an institution is extremely "thin"—it consists of nothing more than a meeting of notables divorced from the continuous administration that a bureaucracy might have sustained.[20] States are grafted onto tribal societies, reflecting the influx of surplus resources that trade and the opportunity to tax it provided. But trade, both traditional long-distance exchanges within Africa and the new trade in slaves and commodities with Europeans at the coast, remained sporadic and involved few products. What is impressive was the ability of some of these thin states to manage and even to resist European pressures to penetrate their authority, acquire their resources, and transform their societies.[21]

Transnational Relations

Tribal societies were far from static. They adjusted to many changes in their physical, economic, and political environments. In the nineteenth century the pace of change accelerated, and a major source of change, following their "discovery" by intrepid (and transitory) explorers, was the arrival of a variety of transnational actors. Settlers, missionaries, merchants and commercial companies, diplomats, soldiers, and officials

19. B. Davidson and F. K. Buah, *A History of West Africa to the Nineteenth Century* (New York, 1966), pp. 224–29.

20. Colson, pp. 47, 56–59.

21. C. W. Newbury, "Trade and Authority in West Africa from 1850 to 1880," in Gann and Duignan, p. 75.

came into contact with tribal peoples; each group had different interests (material and ideal), its own mode of operation, and varying effects. All, however, became agents of imperialism.

Colonial Settlers

When we consider the impact of colonial settlement on tribal societies, we are concerned with the migrations of settlers politically and militarily supported by metropolitan governments or, on rare occasions, a church or corporation. The motives that lead colonial settlers to migrate are, of course, diverse, but since commerce and mining provide small scope for employment in tribal societies, the primary economic motive tends to be land.

Colonial settlement of an unoccupied territory by settlers retaining all their metropolitan rights (including representation with taxation) would involve no imperial control. This pattern has not, however, been the norm. Instead, colonial settlement intersects with imperial politics at a number of points. Since rights to land are deeply enmeshed in the social and religious structure of the peripheral society, colonial settlement is a highly disruptive enterprise. It needs to be backed by substantial military force or be directed against a particularly weak peripheral society. As a transnational force, consequently, colonial settlement tends to operate against tribal peoples that are militarily and politically weak.

Where land is sparsely settled by indigenous inhabitants, little military support from the metropole is required to establish colonial settlement. In temperate zones, small farms or ranches can be set up by colonists themselves at little public cost to the metropole.[22] Furthermore, local resistance tends to be ineffective—a result de Tocqueville in his discussion of the destruction of the Indians of North America attributed to the social structure of tribal hunters: "The territory of a hunting nation is ill-defined; it is the common property of the tribe and belongs to no one in particular, so that individual interests are not concerned in protecting any part of it."[23] In sparsely inhabited territory with fertile soil and a tropical climate, plantation agriculture (following the importation of slave labor) is the likely result of colonial settlement. Plantations also can be established largely by private initiative, but unlike temperate agriculture they require a considerable initial investment to create the extensive scale of operation necessary for profitable enterprise. Settle-

22. Philip Mason, *Patterns of Dominance* (London, 1971), p. 107.
23. Alexis de Tocqueville, *Democracy in America* (1835), trans. Henry Reeve and Phillips Bradley (New York, 1945), 1:351.

ment in a densely populated tropical or temperate region, on the other hand, usually requires substantial metropolitan force, and some form of enserfment or debt peonage tends to be the result.[24]

Differing patterns of colonial settlement give rise to differing forms of dependence on the metropolitan regime. Settlers, Ronald Robinson argued in a seminal article, were the "ideal pre-fabricated collaborators" with imperial rule. They share the culture, technology, and political ideology of the metropole. Barring those who emigrate due to dissidence (such as prompted English Puritans in their move to Massachusetts), they are already politically allegiant and seek to be economically dependent.[25] Settlers in sparsely populated areas tend to be the best collaborators at the beginning of an imperial relationship because they are very cheap to install and produce very rapid economic or strategic gains. They are also socially and politically integrated, however, and they thus tend to develop independent interests and demand independent political institutions to promote their interests. As colonists rapidly acquire a strong stake in the colonial status quo, metropolitan attempts to change or reform colonial society or the colonial relationship provoke effective resistance. In extreme cases, such as America in 1776 and Rhodesia in 1965, apparent metropolitan shifts of policy may stimulate unilateral declarations of independence.

In densely populated peripheral regions, another colonial relationship develops. The native population poses a constant challenge to the security of the settlers' rule on which the metropolitan regime can play to ensure the continuing loyalty of the colonial elite.[26] Where the peripheral people actually challenge the collaborating elite, the collaborators are most dependent upon and subservient to the metropole. Edmund Spenser noted this propensity in the *Faerie Queene* when Lady Irena ("harshness"—the collaborating settlers) calls for Lord Grey's protection from Grantarte (the native Irish).[27]

Colonial settlement has two different but directly imperial aims: to acquire land itself and systematically to exploit an indigenous popula-

---

24. Mason, p. 107.

25. R. Robinson, "The Non-European Foundations . . . ," in R. Owens and Bob Sutcliffe, eds., *Studies in the Theory of Imperialism* (London, 1972), pp. 117–39.

26. With respect to colonial policy and the creation of collaborating classes, see also J. Phillip, "The Function of Land in Colonial Society," *Victorian History Magazine* no. 39 (1968).

27. See also Spenser's "Views on the Present State of Ireland" (1596) and "Brief Note on Ireland" in *The Works of Edmund Spenser*, vol. 10, ed. E. Greenlaw et al. (Baltimore, 1949), pp. 43–245.

tion. The first is usually associated with settlement in sparsely populated areas, the second with settlement in densely populated areas. In the latter case, few indigenous collaborators are prepared to cede land and accommodate metropolitan interests. Settlers both seek and often require the formal political support of their metropoles—formal imperial rule.

Missionaries

Missionaries appear to have only indirectly imperial aims, but the conversion of souls in tribal societies often rested upon imperial protection and had imperial consequences. A Gikuyu proverb from East Africa reflects the relationship: "One White Man gets you down on your knees in prayer, while the other steals your land." Christianity appeared to many African tribes the ritual aspect of imperialism.[28]

The initial African contact with missionaries came through Portuguese emissaries to the kingdom of the Kongo in the fifteenth and sixteenth centuries, but the main missionary stimulus began only in the nineteenth century. It was led by Protestant evangelicals, followed soon by Catholics and secular humanitarians (medical doctors, educators, etc.). The political strength of this religious and humanitarian campaign in the metropole was reflected in the campaign against the slave trade and the establishment of Sierra Leone and Liberia as colonies for freed slaves. The effects in Africa were also revolutionary, for at one stroke the vast preponderance of foreign commerce was declared illegal. European concern was maintained throughout the century by the exploits of courageous missionaries, both religious and secular humanitarians, who captured the public imagination of Europe and spread the doctrines of Christianity and technical progress throughout the sub-Saharan continent.[29]

The missionaries had a threefold impact on tribal societies: they converted, they supported imperial conquest, and they sustained imperial development. Individual Africans may have converted out of awe for the technical skills that the Europeans were capable of teaching, out of a desire for self-esteem sought by marginal members of tribal society (just as many early Christian converts in the Roman empire were slaves), or out of specifically religious motives beyond the analysis of social science. Striking, however, is the extent of conversion. The superior

28. F. B. Welbourne, "Missionary Stimulus and African Response," in V. Turner, ed., *Colonialism in Africa*, vol. 3 (Cambridge, 1971), p. 310.

29. C.P. Groves, "Missionary and Humanitarian Aspects of Imperialism from 1870 to 1914," in Gann and Duignan, pp. 463 and 470.

technology of the metropolitan society encouraged some tribal leaders to adopt Christianity in politically "Constantinian" conversions; elsewhere the destabilizing impact of metropolitan commerce and political power created confusion and alienation from traditional tribal values. Values could not be separated from superior foreign technology in a totally integrated tribal society. Early conversions were themselves also destabilizing as the new converts rejected traditional chiefs and traditional practices, such as polygamy, and further dislocated tribal society. E. A. Ayandele describes this impact as follows: "Worst of all he [the missionary] was a disturber of society, preaching individualism in a well-knit communal society, egalitarianism among a class-ridden people where slaves and masters had their allotted place, and encouraging the low-born to rise up against their masters."[30] Christianity both stimulated a social crisis and offered a personal consolation to individuals suffering from it.

Missionaries not only converted individuals, they played an important role in the conquest of tribal societies. Sir Harry Johnston, a consul in the Niger Delta, attributed a significant place in imperial conquest to missionary endeavor: "The ease with which the white man has implanted himself in Africa, as governor, exploiter and teacher, is due more to the work of missionary societies than to the use of machine guns."[31] On occasion, missionaries so completely converted and transformed native society that conquest by the metropolitan power became a mere formality—such appears to have been the case in part of Yorubaland in the nineteenth century.

More often, missionaries were catalysts; the metropole sent troops to protect them and their converts from irate native chiefs. Missionaries also disrupted local tradition by encouraging the economic transformation of the tribal economy. Sir T. F. Buxton, a leading propagandist of missionary conversion, argued that "Africa would be redeemed by the Bible and the Spade."[32] Through "Commerce and Christianity," a related doctrine, the missionaries encouraged an economic transformation of African society which would replace slavery with agriculture and commerce. Conversions, individual plot agriculture, and capitalist commerce each destabilized tribal society. Missionaries and their supporters in the metropoles helped popularize imperial conquest; in the

---

30. E. A. Ayandele, *The Missionary Impact on Modern Nigeria, 1842–1914* (London, 1966), p. 101.
31. Ibid., p. 28.
32. Groves, p. 485.

peripheries, their activities usually provoked tribal resistance, making imperial protection—direct and formal imperial rule—necessary.

Although missionary enterprise contributed to imperial development, the missionaries were not straightforward agents of imperial expansion. They helped transform peripheral society in accordance with the needs of imperial political stability, it is true. Missionary education trained the clerks whom colonial administrators desperately required, bringing into existence a new pro-imperial, educated elite.[33] Yet the early-nineteenth-century program of Christian conversion of Africa included provisions for indigenous control—metropolitan direction and financing of each mission was designed to end as soon as local converts could assume the financial burden. By the end of the century this program of indigenous leadership had been abandoned. Racism and the threat to formal imperial rule were apparently sufficient to reverse metropolitan support for a native episcopate. Christianity later presented a focus for African nationalism in the form of Ethiopianism, a schismatic form of "Africa for the Africans" Protestantism. The missionaries, moreover, were not always prepared to acquiesce in the colonial system: Protestant missionaries helped lead a campaign against the abuse of native populations in the Congo, and Jesuits agitated against excessively high taxes in Rhodesia. Imperial Christianity, even at the height of imperialism, retained some elements of Christianity.[34]

Merchants and Commercial Companies

Accounts of economic factors have flourished in the literature on imperialism almost to the exclusion of other transnational forces. Though not the sole transnational contact, economic forces and actors certainly had a crucial impact. To examine that impact we need to consider the three main economic factors that shape a tribal periphery's transnational relations: the organizational structure of the transnational economy, the traditional economy of the tribal trade, and the economic role of political factors.

Transnational commerce and investment can be organized through a "trade diaspora" formed of metropolitan settlers in the periphery mediating intermittent exchange between metropolitan merchants and the peripheral economy.[35] (In the slave trade and the early phases of the

33. Ibid., p. 491.
34. Ayandele, pp. 176–82, 213, 263.
35. Philip D. Curtin, *Cross-Cultural Trade in World History* (Cambridge, 1984), chaps. 1, 11. For a typology of transnational organization see M. Barratt Brown, *Essays on*

palm oil, gold, and ivory trades, metropolitan factors simply purchased products or human beings from local merchants.) Alternatively, economic contact can be directly controlled from the metropole and yet operate within the peripheral economy. In this case, the firm retains its central organization in the metropole and extends itself through subordinate agents in the periphery. After colonial rule has been established, metropolitan investors can purchase portfolio investments (bonds and stocks) in commercial, extractive, or transportation firms organized in the periphery. Finally, a multinational form of organization, with semi-independent operations managed in the periphery by metropolitan and some peripheral agents and loosely coordinated at the top in the metropole, occasionally appears. The East India Company was one example, and its analogues could be found in the chartered Royal Niger Company and the Imperial East and South Africa companies.

These various forms of economic enterprise share two characteristics. On the one hand, every one is seeking to maximize profits, which engenders an expansionist dynamic. Local middlemen compete to control local supplies, and European firms have a natural incentive to leapfrog established trade areas and reach cheaper sources of supply in the hinterland. This is the logic of the expanding "trade frontier," moving beyond the limits of formally ruled colonies, and the logic of the gold rush.[36] The other common characteristic these enterprises share is their transnational contact—the fact that they both influence and are influenced by the periphery and the metropole. Yet an essential difference lay between the merchant in the trade diaspora who relied upon local middlemen and the large company, whether in commerce or mining or transportation, that penetrated the frontier and created, to all intents, its own economic environment.

In West Africa, salt and gold moved from village to village and in long-distance caravans centuries before the arrival of metropolitan merchants. Still, trade was in economic terms far less significant than agriculture, and what trade did exist differed structurally from that of the metropoles of nineteenth-century Europe. Trade was embedded in a tribal society and culture in which it tended to be a minor factor. It was conducted, therefore, according to religious ritual, extraeconomic social position, and intertribal politics. Exchange was based on social rules of symmetry (exchanging complementary goods, such as fish and meat)

Imperialism (London, 1972), p. 66; a similar categorization appears in E. Staley, *War and the Private Investor* (Chicago, 1935), p. 27.

36. Dike, p. 203.

and centricity (redistribution by a village headman).[37] Furthermore, transportation difficulties as well as social and political relations limited trade between villages—indeed, Europe's national barriers were inter-village commonplaces in Africa, and the African merchant was socially bound by noneconomic roles.

The initial response to the arrival of Europeans with exotic goods for sale could be revolutionary. Where tribal systems based on cooperative cultivation were weak and the opportunity of trade was strong, tribes became commercial oligarchies. Religion, social customs and relation-ships, and political structure reoriented themselves around the new op-portunities for trade. A number of the coastal villages of West Africa evolved toward what was called the House System—trading houses composed of chief merchants (and their slaves) who created a commercial oligarchy and acted as middlemen for European merchants. The slave trade and later palm oil trade up to 1880 were organized on this basis.[38] Trade increased stratification and moved these societies from communal participation to hierarchies of power and wealth which organized the transportation of products from the interior to the coast in a manner not that different from the traditional trade diasporas of the Sahara and the Sahel.

Where the European contact was less substantial, however, resistance, instability, and then political collapse greeted the arrival of European commerce. New products, new technologies, and new incomes, di-vorced from their social moorings, changed traditional prices: the Eu-ropeans introduced a cash nexus into a society previously based on particularistic relationships. The new commerce made the young or the outcast as rich as the chosen elders and thereby destroyed the religious basis for traditional political authority.[39] The rapid, total adaptation of the commercial city-states of the coast, moreover, disrupted the old balance of power between them and the traditional societies of the hin-

37. Karl Polanyi, *The Great Transformation* (Boston, 1944), pp. 47–49; Newbury, "Trade and Authority in West Africa from 1850 to 1880," pp. 74–75.

38. A. J. Latham, *Old Calabar, 1600–1891* (Oxford, 1973).

39. See "Ekpe Society" in Davidson, *African Genius,* p. 97; J. E. Flint, *Sir George Goldie and the Making of Nigeria* (London, 1960), pp. 20–21; Colin Newbury, "Trade and Authority in West Africa," in Gann and Duignan, p. 82; R. Robinson and J. E. Gallagher, *Africa and the Victorians* (New York, 1961), chap. 2. For an account of a different local rivalry, also disruptive and ultimately turning on the relative availability of force, between a European diaspora community of merchants and a pre-existing Muslim community of merchants in Senegal, see Philip D. Curtin, *Economic Change in Pre-Colonial Africa* (Madison, Wis., 1975), chaps. 3–4.

terland. Trade and religious wars resulted. Thus when Lagos merchants attempted to penetrate their hinterland, the king of Ijebu warned the British governor of Lagos: "The Lagos people sell to the Jebus, the Jebus or their neighbor to the neighbor to the interior and vice versa to the Coast. This is the custom of whole countries in the interior and the Governor [of Lagos] must not interfere."[40] Political organization was not as extensive as the market area required by long-distance European commerce. As wars closed sources of supply and disrupted trade and profits, European merchants demanded some form of order backed up by European force to ensure regular trade and to break the boycotts that coastal oligarchies used to increase their profits and to punish occasional European chicanery.[41]

Where the middlemen had a more dominant position with respect to the interior, in such areas as the Niger Delta, a more stable relationship evolved. British factors consigned goods in trust to native middlemen in turn for payment in palm oil months later. In these circumstances European trade added not only to the wealth of tribal society but also to its material power. In exceptional cases, among them Ashanti and Dahomey (slave-trade powers that dominated the interior of the Gold Coast), this increased power created a significant strategic rival to the European presence. But it also destabilized traditional relationships with other African communities, which then called for metropolitan protection. Each of these strengthened powers eventually provoked military conquest, but for a time European trade encouraged stable growth.[42] Trade so prospered on the west coast of Africa that between the 1850s and 1880s it more than doubled in value.[43]

It is in these nearly stable but temporary circumstances that one can observe the fundamental division between merchants and companies. The merchants, individually lacking the capital to do anything else, were committed to a symbiotic relationship with the middlemen. They competed with the middlemen to purchase lowest-cost palm oil, but they relied upon the native oligarchies for the penetration of the interior. The

40. Lord Kimberly, minute of 6 August 1872, quoted in Newbury, p. 76; P. A. Igbafe, "The Fall of Benin: A Reassessment," *Journal of African History* 2 (1970), 385–400.

41. This is a major theme of A. G. Hopkins, *An Economic History of West Africa* (New York, 1974); see especially p. 164. In the Cameroons, see Consul Hewett, Memorandum, 17 December 1883, F.O. 403/31 (PRO); Dike, pp. 99–105.

42. David Laitin, "Capitalism and Hegemony," *International Organization* 36 (1982), 687–713, also interprets Yorubaland's rise and fall from this perspective.

43. Newbury, p. 77. See also A. G. Hopkins, "Economic Imperialism in West Africa: Lagos, 1880–1892," *Economic History Review*, 2d ser., 21, 3 (1968), 580–606.

companies, extensively capitalized, had the resources to bypass the middlemen. They also had an incentive to seek out the lower-cost sources of supply in the interior. A conflict was brewing that would pit the European coastal merchant and the middlemen against the large companies. The European merchants would be able to sell out; the African middlemen would be outsold.[44]

In this economic struggle one of the decisive factors was metropolitan support. Government did not direct economic penetration, for prior to 1886 the British government's policy, like that of many European metropoles, was one of laissez-faire and compliance with the practices of international law. Rather, government determined the secure range of commercial enterprise by determining whom it would protect.[45] Until the 1880s England sought the political support commerce needed through the promotion of "strong native powers" to collaborate with British enterprise.[46] Attempts in the 1860s to restrict British commitments had failed, and in the 1870s both Liberals and Conservatives had accepted a general policy of protecting the incremental extension of commerce.[47] At the same time the British government wanted to restrict commitments in money and men, and so it rejected applications for a royal charter by the National African Company despite the company's pleas for political arrows for their commercial bow.

Governmental support shifted to a hinterland and thus a procompany policy when the growth of French competition in the late 1870s appeared to threaten the imposition of exclusionary colonial tariffs. With this political and military support, Britain's economic presence changed from coastal commerce and collaboration to company colonialism.

The shift from coastal commerce to company colonialism contributed transnational sources to the shift from informal empire over the coast to formal empire over the hinterland. Because merchants kept most of their capital as goods in stock and little in fixed form, they could adjust to the instability of trade with the coastal oligarchies. The establishment of large-scale commercial companies changed this calculus as the role

44. J. S. Galbraith, "Gordon, Mackinnon, and Leopold: The Scramble for Africa," *Victorian Studies* 14, 4 (1971), 369–88; M. Lynn, "Change and Continuity in the British Palm Oil Trade with West Africa," *Journal of African History* 33, 3 (1981), 331–48, and Curtin, *Economic Change*, chap. 11.

45. D. C. M. Platt, *Finance, Trade, and Politics in British Foreign Policy* (London, 1968), pp. 72, 148.

46. Robinson and Gallagher, chap. 2.

47. See Chapter 11 below and J. Grenville, *Lord Salisbury and Foreign Policy* (London, 1964), p. 110.

of fixed capital increased (in docks, trading stations, steamboats). With more at stake in a less flexible form, the more direct control of Africans became desirable: formal colonialism, whether by colonial bureaucracy or chartered royal company, served this need. The transnational economy thus played an important and complex role in initiating imperial rule, but transnational forces leaned on political support.

Consuls, Soldiers, and Colonial Administrators

Political control may be the essence of an imperial relationship, but the tool and its object are not always synonymous. A tool may be used for more than one purpose, and when tools are human they have their own ends and consequences. In particular, bureaucrats can engender an imperialism not sought by the metropolitan state.

Tribal areas were much too unexalted to receive a full diplomatic representative; consuls (former or current merchants and occasionally military officers) were deemed worthy to manage mutual relations. The diplomat was closely associated with the metropolitan political hierarchy or foreign ministry and thus with official policy. The consul, however, was but one step removed from the local merchants, their factions, and their interests that he was supposedly regulating and protecting. Consuls MacLean of the Gold Coast and Hewett and Johnston of the Niger Delta became the leading spirits, in fact the firebrands, of the coastal merchants.[48] Unable to wield control from a distance, the metropolitan government could only accept the excesses of an aggressive consul or find someone to replace him. In practice the doctrine of relying on the "man on the spot" often swayed official thinking.[49]

While the mercantile consul is a special product of the industrial age, the soldier has a much longer history in imperial expansion. Tribal society demands the use of force to support other transnational contacts (due to their disruptive effects) and requires a special form of warfare. Calgacus, a leader of the ancient Britons, admonished his soldiers, "It is our quarrels and disunion that have given them [the Romans] fame."[50] And indeed, the absence of extensive political and military organization in tribal societies resulted in disorganized frontier warfare, easy game

48. Robinson and Gallagher, chap. 2.

49. W. David McIntyre, *The Imperial Frontier in the Tropics, 1865–1875* (London, 1967), Conclusion.

50. Tacitus, p. 82.

for Roman victories, and slave hunts and the sort of "pacification" waged by the U.S. Cavalry in the American West.[51]

In the African context, two major military forces were at work. One was the British navy, committed by metropolitan politics to the suppression of the slave trade and the support of the consuls, which focused its effort against European slavers and indigenous coastal towns. Because the naval presence could be only sporadic, naval imperialism tried to rely upon native collaborators to create stable conditions for trade. The other, more dynamic military factor was French colonial troops in Senegal. The stalemate in French metropolitan politics gave these troops considerable independence. The incentive to gain promotions through conquests created a continually expanding military frontier: disputes with native chiefs along the indistinct colonial frontier led to conquests, which in turn drew a hazy frontier for the next dispute and the next ambitious colonel.[52] Military imperialism favored a direct presence, a colonial army of occupation.

Just as the soldier followed the consul, so the administrator followed in the wake of the soldier's conquest. One of the fixed principles of administration in nineteenth-century Africa was making a colony pay its own way in taxes or tariffs. But the merchant's equally strong incentive to avoid tariffs by trading outside the colonial boundaries created a built-in incentive for colonial expansion. The tariff frontier crept forward in search of escaping merchants, and the search for an adequate hinterland marked much of the Scramble for Africa.[53] When the boundaries north of the Gold Coast Colony came up for negotiation with the French, Monson, the British negotiator, wrote: "We wish to be most clearly understood that we do not advocate the abandonment of Mossi. In our opinion, the essence of the arrangement which may be come to with France appears to us to consist in providing the colony of the Gold Coast on the one hand and the British possessions lying to the east of Dahomey on the other hand with a sufficient hinterland for their development. . . . "[54] Each metropole sought a hinterland for its colony, and preclusive expansion followed.

51. E. Badian, *Roman Imperialism in the Late Republic* (Pretoria, 1967), chap. 1; cf. Gibbon, *Decline and Fall*, in *The Portable Gibbon*, ed. D. Saunders (New York, 1952), pp. 6, 15.

52. A. S. Kanya-Forstner, *The Conquest of the Western Sudan* (London, 1969).

53. D. K. Fieldhouse, *The Colonial Empires* (New York, 1965), p. 186. Hemming, an official of the Colonial Office, minuted the need to secure "room for the development of Trade" in any negotiations determining boundaries with the French in West Africa. 5 May 1889, C.O. 537/12, vol. 3 (PRO).

54. C.O. 537/14 (PRO).

Settlers, missionaries, merchants, and public officials were the major transnational forces at work changing tribal societies. They influenced the process of imperialism: some consciously strived for the expansion of empire, while others were caught up in imperial expansion as tribal society collapsed about them. They also influenced the form empires took. Settlers destroyed native society altogether and welcomed formal imperial rule provided it gave them a substantial voice in colonial policy. Commerce tended to create local oligarchies, which could then become the collaborating classes on which indirect rule depended. The military, which preferred direct rule, destroyed armed tribal opposition and with it many of the leaders who might have collaborated in indirect rule.

The interests of transnational forces, the structure of peripheral society, and the drives of the metropole each had only a partial effect on the process and form of imperial expansion. No single factor shaped the specific features of the colonial outcome, only their combined effect was decisive. In the histories of the Niger Delta and the African periphery we can trace this combined causation.

The Niger, 1808–1885

The evolution of the relationship between the African societies of the bights of Benin and Biafra and of the Niger Valley, on the one hand, and Britain, on the other, illustrates the effects of transnational contact and international coercion.* Between 1808 and 1885 tribal society entered general crisis as these societies adjusted to the destabilizing impact of Western commerce and gunboat diplomacy. The eventual result of this crisis was formal colonial rule. British dominance resulted from trade, religion, exploration, and military power acting within four arenas—the local African (the peripheral), the British in Africa (the transnational), the British in Britain (the metropolitan), and the intra-European (the international systemic). No single arena, no single source of contact is sufficient to account for the imperialism that developed.

A coastal mangrove swamp interlaced with myriad waterways and an interior palm forest characterize the geography of what is now south-

---

*This section is adapted from my "Metropole, Periphery, and System: Empire on the Niger and the Nile," in *States versus Markets in the World System*, ed. Peter Evans, D. Rueschemeyer, and E. Stephens (Beverly Hills, 1985), and appears by permission of Sage Publications, Inc.

ern Nigeria.[55] The coast was unsuitable for cultivation but provided
with good communications in the waterways of the Niger Delta; the
interior was quite fertile but had only one major means of transit, the
Niger flowing to the coast.[56]

Due to its infertility the coast seems to have been occupied only by
necessity, by losers in intertribal wars. The coastal tribes traded their
dried fish and salt for the root crops and palm nuts produced by the
societies that developed in the forest belt. In the interior, larger, complex
societies governed by religious monarchies grew in Oyo and Benin.
The coast developed what could best be called a merchant feudalism
(the house system) resting on the "flat," egalitarian social structure of
tribal society.[57] It depended, politically and economically, on the forest
belt.

The Portuguese were the first Europeans to arrive. In the second half
of the fifteenth century their ships came in search of a route to the
Orient—to the profits of the gold and pepper trades. The size of the
interior kingdoms, the traders' total dependence on African rulers for
the supply of commodities (gold and later slaves), and the small number
of Portuguese ships on the coast encouraged Portuguese respect for the
sovereignty of the local rulers.[58]

The higher profits possible in the slave trade overcame the early search
for gold and pepper, and Britain acquired the dominant position.[59] This
expanding trade began to have a substantial effect on inter- and intratribal
relations, for the Europeans needed the cooperation of the coast. The
small coastal settlements at Bonny, Calabar, and Lagos reversed their
dependence on and deference to the interior, becoming middlemen that

55. Great Britain did not form Nigeria as a political entity until the middle of the
twentieth century. By "Nigeria" I refer to the geographic area that comprises modern
Nigeria. For a general discussion of tribal society in the Niger region in this period, see
Isichei, *Ibo People and the Europeans*; Dike's classic *Trade and Politics in the Niger Delta*;
Davidson and Buah, pp. 224–29; Newbury, "Trade and Authority in West Africa from
1850–1880"; Latham, *Old Calabar, 1600–1891*; Hopkins, *Economic History of West Africa*;
and Colson, "African Society at the Time of the Scramble."

56. J. C. Anene, *Southern Nigeria in Transition* (Cambridge, 1966), p. 4; David Northrup, *Trade without Rulers* (Oxford, 1978), pp. 10–15.

57. Anene, p. 10. Northrup (p. 13) describes these political societies as follows: "Political units, like residential settlements, tended to be limited in size and cohesiveness.
The basic political unit was the localized patrilineage, generally a subdivision of a village,
which managed its own affairs. Matters between lineages were regulated at the village
level and the largest unit of regular political action was a group of villages claiming
ancestral ties."

58. Michael Crowder, *The Story of Nigeria* (London, 1966), p. 69.

59. Sir Alan Burns, *History of Nigeria* (London, 1963), p. 67.

conveyed slaves from the interior to the coast. European traders left the collection of slaves to the coastal tribes, who required the payment of "comey"—tariffs—from the ships anchored on their shores.[60] This revenue combined with tribal egalitarianism to articulate ranks in the house system: chief, traders, and slaves. Powerful individuals or oligarchic, collective leaderships came to dominate the house, a king such as in Bonny or the Egbo "freemasonry" in Calabar.[61]

Yet at the very height of this system, the seeds of its destruction were being sown in deepest Europe. In 1772 Granville Sharp succeeded in obtaining the *Somerset v. Knowles* decision, which ended legal recognition of slavery in England.[62] Perhaps more significantly, the trade necessities of Liverpool and Bristol were shifting from those of an entrepôt in the triangular trade—goods to Africa, slaves to the New World, sugar from the Caribbean—to those of an exporter of industrial goods and importer of tropical raw materials.[63] In 1807 Parliament made the slave trade illegal.

Britain's commitments to end the slave trade, protect missionaries, and promote commerce destabilized African society. Britain signed antislaving treaties with Spain and Portugal in 1817, stationed a naval squadron on the Gulf of Guinea, and later offered its navy large bounties (prize money) on captures of slave ships. It established a permanent naval station at Spanish Fernando Po. Yet the trade continued, and British humanitarians were disconcerted to learn that slavers drowned their human cargo on the approach of a British ship.[64] By 1839 Sir T. F. Buxton was attributing the continuation of slavery (both the trade and domestic slavery) to African causes: the lack of legitimate commerce, the lack of agriculture, the lack of "civilization." He suggested reinforcing the squadron to provide additional security, setting up "factories" (trading posts), establishing farms, and sending out missionaries.[65] His ideas rapidly took hold as the missionaries, the explorers, and the merchants combined to bring "civilization" to Africa with the "Bible and the Spade."[66]

60. Crowder, p. 72.

61. Dike, p. 7; Crowder, p. 72.

62. R. Coupland, "The Abolition of the Slave Trade," in J. H. Rose, ed., *The Cambridge History of the British Empire*, vol. 2 (Cambridge, 1940), p. 196.

63. Burns, p. 76; H. Temperley, "Capitalism, Slavery, and Ideology," *Past and Present* no. 75 (May 1977), 94–118.

64. Dike, p. 20; Burns, p. 104.

65. Sir T. F. Buxton, *The African Slave Trade and Its Remedy* (London, 1840).

66. See Donald M. McFarlan, *Calabar, The Church of Scotland Mission* (London, 1957),

The pattern of transnational contact adjusted to these new forces. The missionary Hope Waddell came from the West Indies to Calabar, preaching against the mistreatment of slaves. (In doing so, he opened the way for the slave rebellions that would undermine the political basis of the Egbo cult.) On the Niger the British government financed exploration of potential agricultural regions: in 1841 "Bible and Spade" missionaries accompanied Commander Allen, planting a model farm that they hoped would increase production and thereby stimulate trade. Malaria, however, decimated the expedition. Technology had not yet conquered the mosquito, and this fact alone restrained further penetration of the interior.[67]

Liverpool rapidly shifted its trade from slaves to palm oil, the raw material needed to lubricate the machines of Britain's new industries and wash the bodies of a growing industrial population. The illegal slave trade became a nuisance: it subtracted possible laborers from palm oil gathering and it distracted coastal middlemen from the oil trade.[68] As the trade in oil grew, supercargoes (officers in charge of a ship's trade goods) went to coastal towns to supervise the collection of oil. British merchants extended trading goods to African middlemen in return for promised future deliveries of oil. As African middlemen fell deeper into debt, British financial power resulted in an oligopsony for the large Liverpool firms. In response, the Africans employed boycotts to alter the terms of trade, the supercargoes replied by indiscriminate seizures of oil, and British merchants called for the navy.[69] The effects on delta society were at first quite minor because slaving continued apace with the new palm oil trade. As the British suppressed the slave trade, however, the African towns were forced to comply for lack of customers.

---

pp. 22–26. On the missionary impact see also Welbourne, "Missionary Stimulus and African Response"; Groves, "Missionary and Humanitarian Aspects of Imperialism from 1870–1914"; and Ayandele, *Missionary Impact on Modern Nigeria, 1842–1914.*

67. W. A. Allen and H. D. Trotter, *Expedition to the Niger* (London, 1848), pp. 94, 270; Daniel R. Headrick, *The Tools of Empire* (New York, 1981), chap. 3, an interesting study of the importance of quinine in Africa.

68. Dike, p. 53.

69. With the naval squadron went a new attitude. In 1824, Captain Owen visited Bonny in order to survey the coastline. He sent a junior officer to inform King Opubu Pepple of his visit instead of presenting his credentials in person to the sovereign, as had been the custom when the Europeans were weak. In reply, Opubu closed the market to the British. The supercargoes then conciliated the two in a "palaver," leading Owen to remark that the supercargoes treated Bonny as the "purlieus of St. James" rather than as "a Negro town on the west coast of Africa." (Owen also used "freed" slaves as laborers to build his naval station on Fernando Po; the coast's attitudes were not London's.) Crowder, p. 153.

Now the British wanted oil and, to stay solvent, the houses searched for oil.

The new palm oil trade both destabilized and increased the resources of tribal societies.[70] Increased revenues for the coast changed the system of interior markets and hence the region's intertribal balance. Formerly engaging in sporadic slave-raiding expeditions into the interior, each coastal town now established a regular hinterland—a palm oil market it guarded from rival towns and from the British. Trading canoes from the coastal towns carried oil and European trading goods back and forth. This regular trade required a security that the coast established. With war canoes in reserve, the king of Bonny used a religious authority that he derived from his position as caretaker of the JuJu, the god of both his town and his hinterland markets.[71] The Egbo society, a religious cult, likewise extended from Calabar into its hinterland.

Tension between coastal towns and the rising local power of the British increased. In 1835 a British naval vessel seized a Spanish slaver in Bonny Harbor—an unprecedented violation of Bonny sovereignty, according to the Africans. The lieutenant commanding the naval vessel explained that the seizure was legalized by an Anglo-Spanish treaty of 1835. Unimpressed, Anna Pepple, the new regent, arrested the lieutenant. The British squadron appeared, rescued the lieutenant, and forced a protection treaty on Bonny (1836) which guaranteed British subjects against interference.[72] When the regent broke an article of the treaty, the squadron returned and deposed Anna Pepple for being unprepared to uphold "law and order." The squadron installed William Dappa Pepple in his place and went on its way. British power in the delta was becoming predominant, but it could be applied only intermittently, when the patrolling squadron was present.

African success in adapting to the new trade itself sowed the seeds of social dislocation. For many years coastal societies had relied on the sale of slaves. Social stability had been enhanced by the ability to expel (sell) dangerous malcontents. Now that the slave was no longer merely a commodity for export, he was a necessarily permanent part of society and began to demand social status and power to match the wealth he

---

70. This interpretation, emphasizing both the resource-adding and the crisis-engendering results of transnational contact, differs from the general argument, stressing the resources added by trade, advanced with reference to the Yoruba by Laitin in "Capitalism and Hegemony." I interpret his model as one of the three patterns of transnational contact.

71. Dike, pp. 134–35.

72. Ibid., pp. 69, 77.

could legally earn. The old, free chiefs would not accept social status equal or inferior to that of successful ex-slaves, and this externally induced tension culminated in the slave revolts of the 1850s and 1860s.

Many separate forces came together to spur increasing numbers of interventions. Britain, having chosen to enter an age of free and expanding worldwide trade, did not want territorial expansion.[73] Intrusions in African societies, however, increasingly damaged African order without providing an imperial order with which to replace it.

The frustrations of escalating interventions that London neither desired nor could control led the House of Commons in 1849 to pass a motion withrawing the expensive squadron, a motion only barely rejected by the House of Lords. To establish closer control and to remedy the failure of intermittent naval intervention, London appointed a consul whom it instructed to coordinate British security in the region on a permanent basis. The appointment was ineffective; fifteen years later the report of the Select Committee published the results of an investigation by Parliament into the expensive disturbances on the coast of Africa. Annoyed by the uprisings of the Ashanti on the Gold Coast and the fighting in the hinterland of Lagos, which were having a disastrous effect on trade and the budgets of these colonies, the committee again attempted to set a London policy for western Africa. As expensive commitments were not popular in England at the height of the "Little England" and free trade movements, a select parliamentary committee recommended a "policy of non-extensions" and "gradual withdrawal" from everywhere but Sierra Leone.[74] At the same time, the Foreign Office gave a subsidy to encourage trade on the Niger River and reiterated its commitment to protect the "legitimate rights of trade." London had yet to realize that trade and intervention were inseparable on the Niger coast.

By the 1840s Britain's influence was becoming a regular presence. In Bonny a JuJu priest named Awanta led his followers on an anti-British rampage in 1847, destroying cargoes and attacking ships. King William Dappa Pepple would not arrest the priest, who had religious immunity, and the squadron then captured Awanta on orders from London, to protect the considerable British property at risk in Bonny.[75] According to the coast, the need for a coherent British presence was acute; so

73. J. Gallagher and R. Robinson, "The Imperialism of Free Trade," *Economic History Review*, 2d ser., 6 (1953).

74. Anene, p. 42; Dike, pp. 166–67, 168.

75. Dike, pp. 91–92.

London appointed John Beecroft, himself a trader, consul in 1849. At the same time, Lord Palmerston disclaimed any British desire "to seek to gain possession either by purchase or otherwise, of any portion of the African continent."[76] Despite the disclaimer, transnational contacts intensified and, with them, disputes. Intervention became more continuous.

African failures to deliver oil against goods already received produced many preremptory seizures in the 1840s, and the Africans instituted a very effective embargo on trade that, due to the political authority of their chiefs, was not lifted until the Europeans conceded. In the early 1850s, however, the supercargoes found an institutional remedy for their dependence on African authority (and the irregular appearance of the squadron) in the courts of equity. Established under the guns of the squadron, these courts came to be chaired by British supercargoes. Having mostly British and a few African members, they mediated disputes in a manner more favorable to Liverpool interests.[77]

The consul's "sterling diplomacy" supplemented the operation of free-trade rules on the coast. In 1852 Laird's steamship mail line opened the trade of West Africa to increased competion. King Eyo of Old Calabar attempted to send his oil directly to England, but the consul intervened. Although later rebuked by the Foreign Office, he effectively crushed the leading rival to European monopoly.[78]

The tactics of the naval squadron were not yet obsolete, but the merchants were demanding a much more substantial and thorough foreign presence to preserve law and order. Where the navy's gunboats could reach, they enforced informal imperial order, the authority of the consuls; so, for instance, the consul burned Old Town Calabar (1856) to provide a lesson to other uncooperative towns and to secure the safety of threatened missionaries.[79] Increasingly common, however, was the imperial transformation illustrated by Britain's new relationship with Lagos.

In 1851 Lagos, a city on a lagoon west of the Delta, was still engaging in the slave trade and blocking the legitimate commerce of the town of Abeokuta, which was undergoing "civilization" by the missionaries. The missionaries put pressure on Palmerston who passed the case on to Consul Beecroft. After an initial failure the naval squadron captured the

76. Quoted in ibid., p. 95.
77. Anene, pp. 45–47.
78. Dike, pp. 102, 123.
79. Crowder, p. 161.

town and installed a puppet, Akitoye. The British naval commander recalled: "I made him [Akitoye] put on his kingly robes, mount his horse, assemble all his warriors, and ride completely round the town; I went with him and made the people stop every ten minutes, and call out 'Hurrah for Akitoye'; this pleased him very much and has had a good effect."[80] Lagos was now a de facto British protectorate, under informal imperial rule. In the same year Beecroft went to Old Calabar to mediate a slave revolt by the Order of the Bloody Band against the Egbo society. Responding to pleas from the supercargoes, who feared trade disruption, Beecroft propped up the Egbo society and in 1852 supervised the election of the next king of Old Calabar.[81]

The British had become a vital internal factor for African societies. Every temporary success in European stabilization carried with it further destabilization. Tribal societies exploded from within and their established relations with neighboring tribes disintegrated, as the further history of Bonny shows. In 1852 King William Dappa Pepple had a stroke; the strong Anna Pepple house opposed his choice of regents. Sporadic fighting broke out on all sides, and William tried to divert attention by starting a war against New Calabar, but none of the sides rallied to the common cause. Beecroft was called in by the supercargoes in 1854. He deposed the monarch and the regents, and established a regency committee headed by Anna Pepple.[82] The regency lacked JuJu legitimacy, however, and thus had neither political nor religious ties with the interior; trade stagnated. In 1859 the same supercargoes requested the consul to restore King William to his throne, in order to restore trade relations with hinterland markets that Britain was neither capable nor desirous of directly ruling.[83] Stable collaborators were becoming harder to find; by 1872 the consul had moved his headquarters into the delta itself, to New Calabar, where he was newly empowered to exercise magisterial powers over all British subjects and in certain "native cases" before the courts of equity.[84]

80. Quoted in A. G. Hopkins, "Property Rights and Empire Building: Britain's Annexation of Lagos, 1861," *Journal of Economic History*, 2d ser., 40, 4 (1980), 780. See also Robert Smith, *The Lagos Consulate, 1851–1861* (London, 1978); C. W. Newbury, *The Western Slave Coast and Its Rulers* (London, 1961), pp. 53–54; and Martin Lynn, "Consul and Kings: British Policy, 'The Man on the Spot,' and the Seizure of Lagos," *Journal of Imperial and Commonwealth History* 10 (1982).

81. Crowder, p. 158.
82. Ibid., p. 159.
83. Ibid., pp. 160–62.
84. Dike, p. 201.

Changes on the coast disrupted the interior. Britain came into full possession of Lagos in 1861 when the puppet king Docemo, for a pension, ceded it to Britain to the accompaniment of African schoolchildren, conducted by missionaries, singing the British national anthem. The British governor then mounted a balance-of-power, divide-and-destroy, policy against the interior states. Abeokuta, formerly friendly to the missionaries, expelled its "westernizers" when it saw what had happened to independent Lagos and blocked the Lagos palm oil trade.[85] The governor of Lagos sent arms to the traditional enemy of Lagos, Ibadan, and encouraged it to circumvent the Abeokutan blockade with its oil. War raged in the interior. The only victors could be the British merchants, but London did not yet want the political spoils.

The interior also disrupted the coast. Technological innovations, the steamboat and quinine, had at last opened the river to British penetration. The Baikie expedition ascended the Niger in 1854, lost no lives to malaria, and set up the Lokoja mission to convert the Africans to Christianity and free trade. Trading companies soon followed.[86] On the coast Liverpool traders and African middlemen joined forces to resist the diversion of trade to the new river route. As Liverpool merchants lost profits and the middlemen lost livelihood, they encouraged African attacks on the Laird steamers. Laird sought protection, and the navy bombarded villages along the river in collective punishment.[87] Certain Liverpool firms began to shift their sphere of operations, but African middlemen were doomed to lose their markets and the economic foundations of their trading society.

Some chose to resist. For the first time political opposition was concerted by a forceful and brilliant African leader. In the first half of the nineteenth century religious fanatics had led opposition that had been curbed either by the local ruler or by the naval squadron. Now in Bonny a determined leader came into a position of power as head of the Anna Pepple house. He was JaJa. In 1867 King George of Bonny, an English-educated puppet, had promised the consul that he would accept British guidance in return for military support. JaJa had meanwhile developed

---

85. Saburi O. Biobaku, *The Egba and Their Neighbors, 1842–1872* (London, 1957), pp. 70–72.

86. Dike, p. 169. And see Rev. Samuel Crowther, *The Gospel on the Banks of the Niger: Niger Expedition, 1857–9* (1859; London, 1968), pp. 16, 30–32. This book provides a fascinating account of missionary attitudes (though Crowther was an African) toward trade and agriculture and "native uplifting." Also see Macgregor Laird's views on the linkage of trade, religion, etc., in the appendix to the same book.

87. Burns, p. 159.

exceptionally close ties with the hinterland and consequently great wealth. When the rivalry between George and JaJa became violent, George beseeched the consul for gunboat support. Before the British navy arrived, JaJa withdrew to Opobo, a city he had founded upriver athwart Bonny's route to the oil hinterland.[88]

The years from 1849 to 1879 saw significant changes in the interaction of the British and the Africans. The primary change was the introduction of permanent intervention. The naval squadron had operated intermittently; the consul, always present, had the power and the proximity to make effective his depositions of local rulers (Lagos), his playing of internal politics (Bonny), and his intertribal balance-of-power policy (western Nigeria). He encouraged traders and missionaries, insofar as they helped him, and they reciprocated. African societies on the coast felt continual pressure, and their attempts at real independence were thwarted by superior military power when political or economic tactics failed. London did not direct a policy of takeover; rather, it permitted a multifaceted expansion that would eventually demand it.

Hobson, Lenin, and some theorists of power see the era of the Scramble for Africa from 1879 to 1885 as imperialism. But Britain had already acquired effective control of the delta and Lagos, of the first through informal control, of the second through formal acquisition. The Scramble nevertheless differed from previous periods of imperial expansion: the rate of expansion accelerated, and the new era produced formal submission. New forces in Europe stimulated the acceleration of imperialism, but a new intensity in transnational competition also sped the contest for trade and control. Both factors were conditioned by the continuing crisis of tribal society.

In Europe competitive industrialism, the rise of popular national consciousness, and the amalgamation of formerly splintered states produced higher diplomatic tension. The British position in the African and Asian periphery was challenged by Germany and France, which wanted the prestige, the profits, and the power that Britain seemed to be reaping at little cost.[89] British politicians began to speak of the empire as an investment for the future in a possibly hostile, and certainly protec-

88. Dike, pp. 187–89, 198. And see S. N. Nwabara, *Iboland: A Century of Contact with Britain* (Atlantic Highlands, N.J., 1978), pp. 82–93.

89. C. W. Newbury, "The Development of French Policy on the Lower and Upper Niger, 1880–1898," *Journal of Modern History* 31, 1 (1959), 16–26; Newbury and A. S. Kanya-Forstner, "French Policy and the Origins of the Scramble for West Africa," *Journal of African History* 10, 2 (1969), 253–76.

TABLE 5.
British trade with West Africa (£ millions), 1853–82

	1853–62	1863–72	1873–82
Total trade of British West Africa	8.9	19.0	27.3
British share of total trade of British West Africa	5.7 (64%)	10.7 (56%)	13.9 (50%)
British trade with other West African ports	25.8	26.2	20.1

Source: Colin Newbury, "Trade and Authority in West Africa from 1850 to 1880," in L. H. Gann and P. Duignan, eds., *Colonialism in Africa*, vol. 1 (Cambridge, 1961).

tionist, world. Between 1850 and 1880 the total trade (both British and French) of West Africa roughly doubled, but Britain's trade with non-British markets in West Africa, though remaining large, declined in absolute terms.[90] The French colonial tariff system effectively discriminated against British trade, and only in its colonies had Britain been able to slow the decline of its market share. Early Victorian confidence had departed; competition had arrived.[91]

On the Niger River, meanwhile, transnational competition from both British and non-British corporations accelerated. British corporate competition escalated first. With the improvement in transportation, the African supply price of oil jumped after a long fall, bid up by the competition of the many small British traders newly able to reach the trade of the interior. Foreign competition, particularly French, followed soon after.

A merchant named George Goldie-Taubmann arrived in 1876 determined to end the ruinous competition, swamp the French, and establish a basis for order that would permit trade to function profitably.[92] These three aims were closely connected—violence disrupted markets, competition eliminated narrow profit margins. Tribal uprisings multiplied when foreigners supplied arms, and order could not be maintained without some means of meeting the cost of a river police force. A profitable monopolistic trade was the most readily available means with which to realize his aims.

Trade and control were of necessity wed in a tribal society experiencing crisis. Continuous fluctuations in trade prices disrupted the eco-

90. Newbury, "Trade and Authority in West Africa from 1850 to 1880," p. 77.
91. C. A. Bodelsen, *Studies in Mid-Victorian Imperialism* (London, 1966), pp. 79–83.
92. John E. Flint, *Sir George Goldie and the Making of Modern Nigeria* (London, 1960), pp. 29–38.

nomic existence of these societies and in particular destabilized their
government revenues. European trade, furthermore, altered the balance
of power among societies. Both changes encouraged violence.[93] Continuing trade required the stability of imperial rule, which in turn required funds from trade. Foreign competition merely exacerbated this
peripheral dynamic, as Goldie himself clearly perceived: "Prince Bismarck, although new to the subject, has at once grasped what Mr.
Goldie-Taubmann has been pressing on the Government for four years,
since November 1881, *viz.*, that in these uncivilized parts of the world
where the early stages of development do not admit of heavy revenues
or of indolent administration (due to native uprisings) progress and
security can only be attained by administration and commercial work
being in the same hands."[94]

Goldie sought the authority to rule the Niger with the support of the
British government against foreign interference. In 1879 he formed the
United Africa Company. Buying out his British competitors, he soon
acquired a near-monopoly on the Niger River which rapidly reduced
the supply price of oil and restored profits. Goldie's company then waged
commercial warfare against the advancing French firms. Although the
French government sponsored the French firms, Goldie managed to
force them to sell out to him.[95] With the United Africa Company commercially supreme on the river, Goldie sought a royal charter in 1881
authorizing him to impose political order on the separate Niger tribes.

Pacifying the delta had led to a "creeping imperialism," but bringing
imperial order to the Niger Valley contributed to the "leaping imperialism" of the Scramble. Atlantic gunboats could not reach the upper
Niger in the dry season, and the valley was a single economic unit that
could be blockaded by rivals unless its entire length were under one
control. Goldie aimed to provide that needed political control. Still only
the head of a private company, but with the acquiescence of London,
he began making treaties with emirs and tribal leaders in hopes of presenting the British government with a fait accompli, an administrative,
military (he formed his own gunboat squadron), and political rule that
London would have to accept and would welcome in its bargaining with
European powers.[96]

93. This is a major theme of Hopkins, *Economic History of West Africa*.
94. F.O. 403/71 Part I (PRO). For development of this argument see C.O. 537/14,
vol. 5, pp. 7–8 (PRO); Flint, chaps. 3–4; and J. S. Furnivall, *Colonial Policy and Practice*
(Cambridge, 1948), p. 518.
95. Robinson and Gallagher, *Africa and the Victorians*, pp. 166, 175.
96. Dike, pp. 210–11.

Both corporate and European imperialism escalated the continuing crisis of tribal society in the delta. Traditional leaders of tribal societies were challenged by new social forces, most of them unleashed by trade and missionaries. These challenges led to increasing domestic violence, which stimulated the pathetic yet moving plea that opens this chapter. Resistance also put independence at risk. Consul E. H. Hewett feared the growing power of JaJa, who was rapidly extending his trade throughout the delta hinterland (where British gunboats could not go). The consul appealed to London for annexation of JaJa's hinterland, an appeal that the supercargoes heartily seconded.[97]

German and French competition in West Africa compounded local crises and seemed to justify securing British interests in the whole Niger region. Preemption, Sir Percy Anderson (a Foreign Office assistant secretary who headed the Africa Section) warned on 11 June 1883, had become a serious danger: "though we have the advantage ground with the Oil Rivers Chiefs [Niger Delta], these Chiefs, if we do not within a given time accept the protectorate for which they are prepared, will unquestionably place themselves in the hands of the French."[98] London instructed Jewett to obtain treaties of protection in the delta and told Goldie to continue to do the same in the valley. The Scramble had begun. At the Congress of Berlin in 1885 the British could put forward a claim to control the Niger and its delta, though the protectorate over the delta served more as a paper device than as a program of rule.[99] Initially a means of communicating European spheres of influence, the Niger Protectorate would become the institutional excuse for the escalation of control. It led to the recruitment of a police force, which penetrated the remote interior to impose imperial order on a crippled tribal political order.

Caliban's Lament

> This island's mine by Sycorax my mother
> Which thou takest from me. When thou camest first,
> Thou strokdst me and made much of me; wouldst give me

---

97. Ibid., p. 216.

98. F.O. 403/19, Part II (PRO). See also John E. Flint, "Britain and the Partition of West Africa," in Flint and Glyndwr Williams, eds., *Perspectives of Empire* (New York, 1973), p. 102, who argues this general theme of French competition.

99. Wm. R. Louis, "Sir Percy Anderson's Grand African Strategy, 1883–1896," *English Historical Review* 81, 2 (1966), 292–314.

> Water with Berries in't; and teach me how
> To name the bigger light, and how the less,
> That burn by day, and night; and then I loved thee
> And showed thee all the qualities of the isle,
> The fresh springs, brine pits, barren place and fertile.
> Cursed be I that did so! All the charms
> Of Sycorax—toads, beetles, bats light on you!
> For I am all the subjects that you have,
> Which first was mine own king; and here you sty me
> In this hard rock, whiles you do keep from me
> The rest of the island.

The experience of a tribal periphery in contact with metropolitan transnational forces, like Caliban's, was a chronicle of false expectations and a chained reality. The first contact with tribal societies was frequently peaceful and mutually profitable, "water with berries in it" and the names of the "bigger light and the less" exchanged for the "qualities of the isle." But curses soon followed, as tribal society strained under the bewildering but attractive foreign technology and values and as communal freedom disappeared under collaborating chiefs and colonial police.

The metropole achieved imperial control through the collaboration of the few, the ineffective resistance and acquiescence of the many. Collaboration, in the sense of cooperation and mutual exchange, seems to have been the nearly universal experience of the first stages of contact. This collaboration, resulting from massive differences in technology which made European products seem exceptionally valuable to peripheral rulers, reflected the peaceful character of early commercial and missionary contacts. Early collaboration revolutionized a number of these tribal societies, and because they were undifferentiated, total collaboration was the result.

Resistance was a secondary reaction, as the revolutionary cultural impact of commerce and mission provoked crises of adjustment.[100] Where the native social structure was stronger or away from the immediate coast, domestic resistance from alarmed traditional tribal interests developed. Other tribal societies took advantage of European commerce to increase their resources, and transnational commercial contact often shifted the local balance of power, also provoking resistance from those

100. T. O. Ranger examines the connections between early collaboration, religious revivals, resistance, and later nationalism in the periphery in "Connections between 'Primary Resistance' Movements and Modern Mass Nationalism in East and Central Africa: Part I," *Journal of African History* 9, 3 (1968), 437–53.

tribes that lost relative power. Since these tribes were not of great geographical extent, this latter intertribal warfare appeared a collapse into
anarchy just as the former resistance appeared an unjustified attack on
Europeans going about their peaceful, legitimate activities.[101] Finally,
the collaborators themselves became in effect "collaboratively" redundant and in turn a fount of resistance. By this stage collaboration in
colonial armies or as "native authorities" had become the politically
significant act that laid the foundations for imperial rule.

This pattern repeated itself throughout the nineteenth-century periphery. Tribal societies were left an independent existence only in remote islands of the Pacific, in the depths of the Amazon, in the expanses
of the Saharan and Arabian deserts, and at the heights of mountain
ranges. There, a paucity of transnational contact and a determination to
resist prevailed against metropolitan forces. There, or within territories
formally defined as empires on maps (but where imperial rule had yet
to be established), tribal societies retained a political existence separate
from empire. Here survived tribes that would become famous in the
twentieth century (such as the Saudis) or would inspire nationalism
among those governed (such as the Maroons of Jamaica's Blue Moun-
tains). But most, as the Indians of North America, merely awaited the
arrival of the railroad which spelled their end or transformation.

For most tribal societies, the existence, the form, and the rate of
imperial expansion directly followed from the transnational crises they
experienced. Tribal societies could adjust to changes in trade and could
mount substantial resistance. But when trade was combined with missionary attempts to transform society and when these powerful trans-
formations were backed by sporadic force and political intervention,
tribal society entered a threefold crisis. Externally induced transfor-
mations (new religions, freed slaves, popular and particularistic demands) destabilized the traditional patterns of society. Communal
integration and lack of social differentiation made transnational contact
socially destabilizing because no aspect of contact could be socially isolated; change had to be total and, to produce stability, tribal collaboration
had to be total. This revolutionary transformation engendered domestic

101. Scholars such as D. C. M. Platt have argued that British and other metropoles
did not aggress against peripheral societies in this period. The Foreign Office confined
its policy to the international legal protection of citizens' rights and lives abroad. As a
statement of policy, this is a fair summary. But it misses the crucial fact that the distinction
between protecting what were, in effect, European revolutionaries and aggressing against
peripheral society was irrelevant, as a practical matter, in the tribal context. Platt, *Finance,
Trade, and Politics in British Foreign Policy.*

dissent from traditional religious authorities and from individuals materially and ideally attached to traditional ways, tempting the metropole to impose imperial order to protect its transnational agents and tribal collaborators.

African societies and governments had come to depend on external trade. Fluctuations in that trade, which Africans could not control, made the challenge of adjustment still more burdensome. And even total collaboration became unstable. It destabilized a tribe's relations with its near neighbors, who often reacted violently. Again the metropole was able to exploit divisions, often judging that it must exploit intertribal differences to restore order. Although resistance occurred, as in the striking example of JaJa's rule, the social structure of tribal society (its small-scale village unit) meant that the metropole rarely faced a general up-rising.

In short, general crisis allowed the metropole to call on African resources to suppress African resistance. Nevertheless, imperial rule over a tribal periphery tends to formal, and usually direct, rule. Local collaborators cannot be relied upon to provide stable law and order for commerce or conversions; none of the political units of tribal society is extensive enough to provide political order for an entire market or social region; and the weaknesses of tribal society tend to attract transnational agents who themselves prefer formal metropolitan rule. The period of stable informal empire tends to be brief. Collaboration leads to increased differentiation into class hierarchies where collaborators form an elite. But in small-scale societies with traditions of communal integration this differentiation is difficult to sustain. New strata are mobilized, disrupt the collaborative order, and lead to imperial intervention and formal rule. Formal rule with colonial bureaucrats and soldiers alone could establish the modicum of public order needed to protect the lives of Europeans who were changing the periphery. The metropole had to rule directly, sending out administrators and soldiers because the tribal periphery lacked collaborating emirs, rajas, and oligarchs. Collaboration took place, but it was at the level of bureaucratic subordinates: foot soldiers in the colonial police and clerks in the colonial administration.

Formal colonial empires use administrative mechanisms of control. The political basis of this control lay in the threat of force from a colonial police, the collaboration of newly modernized (educated and converted) elites, and the collaboration, again only at a low level, of traditional or appointed tribal leaders. Modernized elites collaborated for physical security from a traditionalist backlash and to express new metropolitan political and cultural allegiances. Traditional elites collaborated to prevent further change and social upheaval. Direct rule, which was associated with extensive changes ("assimilation") and employed most regularly by the French, relied upon the progressive collaborator. The traditional collaborator of slightly more hierarchical tribal societies acquired a key role in the British strategy of conservative indirect rule, which left more responsible administrative positions in the hands of the peripheral elite.[102]

Pericentric Theory

Pericentric theory focuses on what makes empire different from other types of international relations by focusing on what makes the periphery different from other types of political society. It supplies what metrocentric and systemic approaches lack: a second actor. Thus it can show how the transnational, metropolitan forces that produce manageable trade among metropoles can produce crisis elsewhere. Its account of the weakness of one of the actors in a systemic relationship helps explain the power of the metropole.

Pericentric theorists neglect, however, at least three active and non-pericentric determinants of empire. Metropoles and the international system can shape the form of, determine priorities in, and set the pace of imperial expansion. Transnational actors from the metropole come in different varieties; their drives are different, they demand different things of the periphery, and they have different effects on peripheral society. Explorers demand little more than free passage and only minimally disrupt tribal societies. Missionaries demand cultural revolutions and have a severely disruptive effect on tribal societies. Merchants and financiers add resources as they set loose destabilizing influences. As Britain's primary transnational agents in West Africa were merchants and missionaries, there was some substantial basis for information collaboration but also for considerable disruption. That informal collaboration should collapse into formal colonial authority was a logical outcome. France's reliance on soldiers, virtual freebooters, from the garrisons in Senegal (the *officiers soudanais*) had an equally logical result. It encouraged formal imperialism from the outset, causing relatively little social dislocation except in the political hierarchy. The sort of

102. Martin Kilson, "The Emergent Elites of Black Africa, 1900 to 1960," in L. H. Gann and P. Duignan, eds., *Colonialism in Africa*, vol. 2: *History and Politics of Colonialism, 1914–1960* (Cambridge, 1970), pp. 351–98.

transnational forces that a metropole sends out makes a difference to the stability and welfare of differing groups in the peripheral society.

The second nonpericentric determinant of empire concerns the priorities that determined imperial expansion. If we interpret pericentrism as a general theory about the destabilizing mixture of international politics and economics, then, as D. C. M. Platt writes, we have to note that the link between British foreign policy and trade and investment was particularly distant in the first three quarters of the nineteenth century.[103] Only strategic areas, such as India, received special treatment; all other regions secured only the minimum of diplomatic protection needed to ensure equality of treatment for British merchants. (It is international law, moreover, not politicoeconomic strategy, that determines diplomatic protection.)[104]

As we have seen, promoting free trade and protecting one's citizens' rights under international law were inseparable from imperial control in the Niger Valley and in other parts of the nineteenth-century periphery. There was no London policy to subjugate Nigeria, and the one clearly articulated London policy was the decision of 1865 in favor of "gradual withdrawal." Subjugation nonetheless resulted. Platt, however, has shown that not all parts of the periphery were Niger Deltas. In the United States and Argentina much less intrusive interference met metropolitan needs; elsewhere, in Mexico for example, British merchants and investors went unprotected by metropolitan sanction. Platt's arguments suggest that in West Africa we should pay special attention to the combination of missionary and mercantile interests and to the ways in which that combination, by destabilizing African society, placed British subjects in dangerous circumstances requiring naval rescue.

The third point concerns the considerable role of metropolitan and systemic factors in setting the pace of imperial expansion, even apart from the crises they helped create in the peripheries. The Niger, Delta and Valley would have fallen, slowly and piecemeal, to imperial conquest—if not to Britain or to France then to Goldie and his National African Company, as Sarawak had fallen to the Brookes in the 1840s. But in the 1880s European competition (primarily commercial) brought Britain to accept Goldie's acquisitions, provided a public guarantee against French and German seizure, and permitted him to establish a tax system

103. See Platt, *Finance, Trade, and Politics in British Foreign Policy*, pp. 50, 51.

104. D. C. M. Platt, "The Imperialism of Free Trade: Some Reservations," *Economic History Review*, 2d ser., 21, 2 (1968), 296–306, and "Further Objections to an 'Imperialism of Free Trade' (1830–1860)," ibid. 26, 1 (1973), 77–91.

that funded his speedy conquest of the northern reaches of the Niger Valley. Now French and German rivalry was shaping Britain's overseas policy, and now London perceived a threat to trade in the advance of French tariff frontiers and in the informal advantages that rule conveyed to national merchants.[105] Leaping imperialism replaced creeping imperialism, and the Scramble was on.

---

105. See Paul M. Kennedy, *The Ride of the Anglo-German Antagonism, 1860–1914* (London, 1980), pp. 57–58, for his analysis of the growing perception of international economic competition. T. V. Lister, assistant undersecretary at the Foreign Office in charge of African affairs, wrote: "Everybody seems to be agreed that the occupation of any place or river by the French is almost destructive of British trade, and it is therefore of great importance to keep them out of districts which either are or might be favourable to that trade." Minute of 24 October 1883, quoted in M. E. Chamberlain, *The Scramble for Africa* (London, 1974), p. 124.

CHAPTER 9

Patrimonial Peripheries and Informal Empire

Many of the societies that the European metropoles encountered in the nineteenth century, from the Amazon basin through sub-Saharan Africa to the highlands of Southeast Asia, were tribal. In Central America, parts of North Africa, the Western Sudan, and East Africa, however, as well as in the major societies of India, Southeast Asia, and the Far East, patrimons and feudal overlords ruled, however tentatively and sporadically.

Very limited differentiation and relatively high integration characterize tribal societies. Typically, the member of the tribe leads a life in which his social roles are interlocked: certain economic functions are attached to special authority positions and likewise to religious roles and ritual. In the least differentiated bands the tribal assembly is simultaneously the religious synod, the board of directors, and the committee of public safety. These small social units, like their larger but similar tribal counterparts, are closely integrated, share common values and technology, and depend closely upon each other for the performance of economic and political tasks.

Patrimonial Society

In patrimonial and feudal societies both of the commonplaces of tribal society undergo substantial change. There is significantly more differentiation, and there is substantially less communal integration. This social differentiation shows itself both horizontally and vertically. Horizontally, the different spheres of social action become more separate. Max Weber noted one separation in discussing the first step in the political evolution of society beyond mere ties of kinship, a step he called patrimonialism:

> With the development of a purely personal administrative staff, especially a military force under the control of the chief, traditional authority tends to develop into "patrimonialism." Where absolute authority is maximized, it may be called "Sultanism."
>
> The "members" (e.g. of the communal tribe) are now treated as "subjects." An authority of the chief which was previously treated principally as exercised on behalf of the members, now becomes his personal authority, which he appropriates in the same way as he would any ordinary object of possession.[1]

The key distinction of patrimonialism is that the *state*, or government, emerges from the communal tribe as a separate entity. At the same time there is a further differentiation of the other spheres of society: economic functions become relatively more separate, as do religious rites. From the perspective of a completely differentiated social system, patrimonial government is noteworthy for its interference (i.e., lack of complete differentiation) with the economic processes of society.[2] From the standpoint of tribal society, however, the more notable development is the separation of economics and politics to such an extent that the latter can even be seen as interfering with the former.[3] Differentiation also sepa-

---

1. Max Weber, *The Theory of Social and Economic Organizations*, ed. T. Parsons, trans. A. M. Henderson (New York, 1964), p. 347. See also G. Almond and G. Powell, *Comparative Politics* (Boston, 1966), pp. 223ff. Although partimonial systems in practice contain a large degree of traditional authority, in numerous instances that authority is supplemented by rational and charismatic supports to power. For our purposes it is the structure of politics and not the source of authority that is of interest.

2. Patrimons use, for example, "benefices" (and grants or tax monopolies) to support their rule, even though they are "irrational" in their effects on the economic order. Marx described this interpenetration of social and political life for feudal and, by analogy, the more general patrimonial society: "The old civil society (feudalism) had a *directly political* character; that is, elements of civil life such as property, the family, and types of occupation had been raised in the form of lordship, caste and guilds, to elements of political life. They determined, in this form, the relation of the individual to the *state as a whole*; that is, his *political* situation, or in other words, his separation and exclusion from the other elements of society." Karl Marx, "On the Jewish Question," in R. Tucker, ed., *The Marx-Engels Reader* (New York, 1972), p. 42.

3. Weber, pp. 357, 355.

rates society vertically—the patrimon holds the highest position, his staff come next in the social hierarchy, and the rest of the society become "subjects."

Integration, which in tribal societies was synonymous with the undifferentiated whole, becomes a problem when society differentiates. Values may no longer be shared; since subjects are no longer equal participants, they are unlikely to identify themselves with the patrimon's leadership and administrative staff and, indeed, may feel that they depend less on each other. As subjects rely on the patrimon for protection, their tribal ties of mutual enterprise may disappear into isolated family economies linked by only sporadic commerce. At the same time the arbitrary exactions of patrimonial rule frustrate the extensive and intensive economic interdependence required by true entrepreneurial capitalism.[4]

Two paths lead to patrimonialism: one endogenous and evolutionary, the other exogenous and revolutionary. In the first case, such as occurred in the Trobriand Islands, patrimonial appropriation can develop from the tribal system of redistribution and reciprocity when the band's headman begins to take a progressively larger share of the goods that he is redistributing. To sustain this corruption, a household military force emerges, in its turn sustained by corruption. In the second case, exemplified by Rwanda, conquest by a foreign tribal group leads to expropriation. A patrimonial leader and his followers seize the land, people, and resources of the conquered tribe. In both cases differentiation increases, integration decreases.[5]

Feudal society resembles patrimonial society in a number of important respects. Jacques Maquet has suggested that feudal society is little more than a systematic alliance of patrimonial regimes—an alliance of the various feudal lords (patrimons) for mutual protection—but feudalism probably would not survive if it were a mere alliance of patrimonial equals. The feudal system differs from an alliance of patrimonial regimes in three features. First, the feudatories hold loyalties to a central authority. Second, the feudal, central ruler possesses his own military staff and has the formal right to call upon other feudatories to enforce the obligation of a recalcitrant feudal vassal. Third, although western feudal society resembles patrimonial alliances in being geographically dispersed, the eastern variety is quite different in that dispersion of authority

4. Ibid., p. 357.

5. J. Maquet, "African Society: Sub-Saharan Africa," in David Sills, ed., *International Encyclopedia of Social Sciences*, vol. 1 (New York, 1968), pp. 148–49.

is functional. Tax farming, for example, is instituted as benefices for pledged political support.[6]

Feudal societies, though often large, resemble patrimonial societies in the crucial sense that they fail to amass a political power corresponding to their size. Patrimonial societies, although differentiated in social structure and centralized in authority, are normally constrained by a lack of integration. Feudal societies, although socially differentiated and, at least within the feudatory class, more socially and culturally integrated, are wracked by political division.[7] Weber explains this fatal characteristic as follows: "It goes without saying that whenever this type of feudalism (hereditary) is highly developed, the status of supreme authority is precarious. This is because it is always very dependent on the voluntary obedience and hence the purely personal loyalty of the members of the administrative staff who, by virtue of the feudal structure, are themselves in possession of the means of administration."[8] As patrimonial and feudal societies are both more differentiated and more powerful than tribal societies, their interaction with the transnational forces and institutions of the metropole was quite distinct from that of tribal society.

Transnational Relations

Transnational relations, as the preceding chapter argued, are determined by the nature, number, and size of transnational organizations, the character of the peripheral society, and the type of support which they receive from the metropole.

Settlers, who played a very important role in transnational relations with tribal society, are much less significant in relations with patrimonial and feudal societies. What settlement does take place in the initial stages of interaction with a patrimonial regime tends to be urban and on terms dictated by the indigenous society. These temporary settlers include merchants, bankers, petty clerks, and assorted providers of seaport services (nowhere better portrayed than in Conrad's *Lord Jim*). Relatively secure, they play a lucrative role in the economic development of the local society, fitting into it as the foreign contacts of local merchants

6. For a thorough discussion of feudal society see Marc Bloch, *Feudal Society*, trans. L. A. Manyon (Chicago, 1964), chaps. 4, 12, 18.

7. For example, the feudal kingdom of medieval France was divided into many *pays* and two distinct language groupings, the Langue d'Oc and Langue d'Oil. Some of the nobility and the church could communicate in Latin and the court language (Langue d'Oil); the peasantry remained culturally divided.

8. Weber, p. 376.

and clerks. They do not fundamentally challenge the basis of that society, which is sufficiently differentiated to accommodate their additional diversity. Although patrimonial differentiation has reached a point where foreign settlers do not of and in themselves threaten the entire fabric of society, however, politics and the private interests of rulers direct the legal system and economic transactions in a fashion incompatible with the independent working of market forces.

As a result, metropolitan settlers characteristically demand extraterritoriality, a demand that often struck a responsive chord in the patrimonial ruler who wished to minimize the impact of foreign forces on his control of his patrimony. From St. Paul's claim of "civis Romanus sum" against the subordinate patrimonial kingdom of Herod and the steelyard of the Hanse in London to the immunities of European settlers in Alexandria, Tunis, Constantinople, and Shanghai, the metropole has demanded extraterritorial application of metropolitan law over settlers, whether individual or corporate. The peripheral riposte has been the regulated treaty port.[9]

Almost no patrimonial societies were sparsely settled. Neither small farm settlement, which characterized the frontiers in America, South Africa, Canada, and Australia, nor plantation agriculture as it emerged in the West Indies offered itself as a possibility to emigrants from the metropole to patrimonial or feudal societies. Patrimonial societies required a concentration of population—or rather, a concentration of partly differentiated, interdependent populations required patrimonialism. Settlers had to seize or purchase land, but since land was the primary source of patrimonial power and authority, they were likely to encounter strong resistance. Unlike tribal land, patrimonial land had a committed, particularistic defender. Although militarily formidable, however, once the partimonial "prince and his servants" were defeated, political resistance at the center collapsed and the country became the patrimony of the imperial settlers. It was in this manner that Cortez and his band acquired Mexico, Pizarro Peru, and Alexander Persia.[10] A feudal regime, Machiavelli's "prince and his barons," put up a much stiffer long-term

9. D. Landes, *Bankers and Pashas* (Cambridge, Mass., 1958), pp. 92–96; J. K. Fairbank et al., *East Asia: The Modern Transformation* (Boston, 1965), pp. 340–42; D. K. Fieldhouse, *Economics and Empire* (Ithaca, 1973); and P. Curtin, *Cross-Cultural Trade in World History* (Cambridge, 1984), p. 247.

10. The metropoles of bureaucratic empires (Mexico, Peru, Persia), which rely for political unity on a narrow caste, become vulnerable when that caste splits as, for example, in a succession crisis.

resistance to foreign conquest. Feudal France, although defeated at Agincourt, merely retreated and resumed resistance.[11]

Missionaries underwent experiences somewhat similar to those of settlers. Few conversions occurred, again due to the superior political capacity of patrimonial regimes. In a differentiated society, a religious organization could confront the metropolitan missionaries, and, in an as yet unsecularized society, the patrimonial leader was concerned to prevent a rival center of power being formed about foreign converts ("a state within the state"). Any foreign religion associated with a powerful metropolitan state was thus rejected; when not so associated, it was occasionally successful. Christian success in China and Japan, for example, appears until the twentieth century to have been inversely proportional to the strength of European imperial metropoles in the Orient, where metropolitan support halted early success by igniting repression in a concerned China and Japan.[12] But if patrimonial collapse occurred, it was total: conversions were extensive after the fall of the patrimonies of Mexico and Peru.

Some of the most interesting changes in transnational relationships emerge when feudal and patrimonial societies come into contact with metropolitan merchants, companies, and financiers. Some had already influential counterparts in tribal societies, for instance merchants; others, such as financiers, were newly influential. Both groups often needed metropolitan government support to achieve their aims, for internal crises and intertribal trade warfare together demanded a rapidly escalating political and military control by metropolitan consular and military agents. The formal colonial rule thus necessitated was exercised either by the metropolitan government or by proxy, by chartered colonial company. These chartered companies, the products of the mounting competition of metropolitan trading firms, reflected the larger scale of capital resources required to provide both profit and physical security in tribal societies.

Patrimonial society provided, in contradistinction, a much more favorable environment for metropolitan commercial enterprise.[13] Because of the differentiation of patrimonial society together with the wider

11. Machiavelli, *The Prince*, trans. L. Ricci (New York, 1950), chap. 4; D. K. Fieldhouse, *The Colonial Empires* (New York, 1967), chap. 2.

12. Fairbank et al., p. 61.

13. Commercial, manufacturing, and railroad investments were the major forms of private transnational contact with patrimonial and feudal societies. For example, their respective shares of direct foreign investment in China in 1931 were 21.4%, 16.5%, and 24.8%, according to C. F. Remer, *Foreign Investment in China* (New York, 1968), p. 86.

scope of its market, metropolitan merchants found an established legal system that recognized certain minimal rights of property and contract. General social differentiation, moreover, was such that commerce did not automatically conflict with religious ritual, social hierarchy, or political procedure, as it generally did in tribal society.[14]

Metropolitan merchants could almost be assimilated as foreign versions of domestic merchants, but they could not be completely integrated into local custom and law. In part they did not choose to be. Where patrimonial leaders influenced the economy for incomprehensible, non-economic ends and bribery and coercion were everyday modes of doing business, extraterritoriality enforced metropolitan standards of property and contract. The patrimonial leader, moreover, although not unaccustomed to merchants, sought to control them as much as possible—at least to the extent of preventing their economic resources being added to those of his political rivals. The early nineteenth-century rulers of China were able to limit Western trade to a select group of Chinese merchants who were held legally responsible for the behavior of the Westerners. A contest naturally emerged: Western merchants sought maximum liberty of trade, the patrimonial regime, maximum control.[15] Whichever won, however, mercantile contact did not present a revolutionary challenge to the patrimony.

Mining and manufacturing did. Mining was revolutionary primarily because it affected the use of the land—the foundation of patrimonial society—and because it controlled the livelihood of a larger number of people more intensively that did commerce. The labor force, mobilized by cash wages, appeared to the patrimon as only tenuously under his control and particularly when foreign (though not metropolitan) labor was employed to extract the riches from the earth. For example, the Selangor Tin Company of Malaya employed Chinese labor in the 1860s and 1870s; soon an all-out rivalry developed between the mines and the local sultan who had once welcomed mining enterprises.[16] Just as capitalist mining was at least legally feasible in patrimonial society, recognizing as it did some economic rights in land, so manufacturing could

14. J. Hicks, *A Theory of Economic History* (London, 1969), chaps. 2–3.

15. R. Murphey, *Treaty Ports and China's Modernization* (Ann Arbor, 1971); A. J. Sargent, *Anglo-Chinese Commerce and Diplomacy* (Oxford, 1907), chaps. 3 and 4; and Fairbank et al., *East Asia*.

16. See Fieldhouse, *Economics and Empire*, pp. 189–95, and Joseph Conrad, *Nostromo* (London, 1904), on the mine as a too-tempting stake in quasi-patrimonial politics. See also A. G. Hopkins, "Imperial Business in Africa: Interpretations," *Journal of African History* 17 (1976), 267–90.

associate itself with handicraft. Here, too, the effects were disturbing. Again labor was mobilized out of the patrimonial order and into the influence of extraterritorially protected foreigners; local handicrafts were swamped. Direct foreign investment merely exacerbated the patrimon's inability to control these forms of foreign investment. Britain, for example, was reluctant to provide protection for mere portfolio investment in foreign-registered companies, but British companies had both a stronger legal claim (especially when they obtained a peripheral government concession) and often a stronger voice in the making of home government decisions.[17]

Investment in transportation, such as in railroads, does not appear to have been so politically revolutionary. Its indirect social and economic effects may in the long run have been very important, but their immediate market impact was incremental, requiring only increased traditional response—in agriculture, for example. A railroad, in the absence of a domestic iron industry, is a river flowing on command across the land.[18] Moreover, railroads tend to strengthen whatever political regime they run within, a surrogate, in short, for the pharaoh's Nile.[19]

Long-term loans to the patrimonial regime itself tended to subvert most thoroughly the possibility of stable relationships between the metropole and the periphery. Unlike tribal societies, patrimonial or feudal governments could obtain loans. They often did so, however, for the highly uneconomic purposes of display, or domestic political rivalry, or personal consumption, as for instance millions of pounds sterling of debt contracted by Khedive Ismail of Egypt.[20] These objects were as vital to a patrimonial regime as public water works were to a metropolitan regime; but they were the wrong objects for a loan that was one day to be repaid from increased revenue. Problems went much beyond unproductive ends, moreover; since these regimes also tended to lack effective taxing power, repayment of these uneconomic debts became increasingly difficult.

17. D. C. M. Platt, *Finance, Trade, and Politics in British Foreign Policy, 1815–1914* (London, 1968), Conclusion, and pp. 45–51.

18. See Karl Marx, "India," in Tucker, pp. 577–88, and D. C. North, *Growth and Welfare in the American Past* (Englewood Cliffs, N.J., 1974), chap. 9.

19. But one apparent exception might be downfall of Brazilian monarchy following the agricultural revolution created by the British-funded São Paulo Railroad. The railroad opened up vast new coffee lands; but this revolution was equally a product of the constraint of slave labor. With labor available, stability might well have continued. See R. Graham, *Britain and the Onset of Modernization in Brazil* (Cambridge, 1968).

20. Landes, p. 97.

A typical pattern of collecting the debts of patrimonial regimes emerged. Metropolitan regimes employed diplomatic and often forceful means to enforce the repayment of public debts, yet private lenders lending to private borrowers were assumed to bear their own risk.[21] The private sector, hungry for foreign currency, came to depend increasingly on various forms of disguised disbursements from the patrimon. And, driven by a chronic cash shortage and tempted by the overestimation of credit worthiness accorded to almost any governmental borrower, the patrimon in effect mortgaged his patrimony. Soon the metropole came to foreclose. Santo Domingo, Nicaragua, Tunis, Egypt, the Indian Princely States, China—all experienced severe debt problems as rulers sought politically motivated loans from financiers who were prepared to employ political bribery and coercion to garner financial concessions.

Transnational contact with patrimonial society does not engender the rapidly escalating crises associated with such contact with tribal society. It does, however, require constant political influence and interference to match the politicization that forms the core of patrimonial social relations. In many cases the "men on the spot"—consuls general, soldiers, colonial officers— interfere for reasons that have little connection with the official policy of the metropolitan government.

As consuls (ex-merchants) characterized official contact with tribal society and ambassadors with independent and equal metropolitan states, so consuls general characterized contact with patrimonial regimes. The consul general was usually a public official rather than a merchant, but his duties were both political and economic, designed to match the mutual interaction of these two concerns in patrimonial society. Edward Malet, Britain's consul general in Egypt prior to the occupation, was particularly influenced by Auckland Colvin, the bondholders' representative, and Malet's dependence for guidance significantly narrowed the Gladstone government's options in Egypt. Evelyn Baring, Malet's successor in Egypt and later Earl of Cromer (fittingly a member of one of the most prominent British banking families and a former official in India), and Consul John Kirk in Zanzibar were much more independent officials of this type. They were exceptionally influential in their extraterritorial communities largely because foreign interests depended on them for protection.

21. For Britain, diplomatic support was available if a debt was secured as part of a treaty. Other governments (e.g., France) were ready to intervene for more dubious claims if an influential bank was involved, according to Platt, pp. 45–51.

By its dependence on political support, economic exchange was further politicized. The consuls conceived of their role as the maintaining effective influence to protect their nationals from undue patrimonial interference and foreign competition. In Tunisia special collaborative relationships were established between competing consuls and different ministers in the patrimonial government, and the varying fortunes of these ministers marked the rise and fall of different European interests. Overall European direction operated through the bondholders' international control, which supervised Tunisian revenues to make interest payments to European creditors.[22] When consular influence and local stability failed, the metropoles employed military forces to restore the status quo. Fleets could be used to blockade patrimonial society into submission since patrimonial societies depended on trade to a much greater degree than did tribal societies.

The army played a more significant, but derivative, role during economic and therefore political crises. Independent of crisis, moreover, the military, though usually not present in patrimonial societies before they became absorbed into an empire, played a substantial and direct role in imperial expansion when garrisoned near patrimonial societies. Military motives were likely to be autonomous—promotions, for example—and campaigns were much more akin to traditional warfare than to the frontier excursions against tribal societies made famous by the American cavalry after the Civil War and the British on the Northwest Frontier. In fact, patrimonial regimes often fought conventional-style wars to maintain their frontiers.

Extensive contact with metropolitan transnational forces could lead to the economic and political dependence of patrimonial society. This dependence set the foundations of collaboration and informal imperialism. A metropole's prolonged contact with a patrimonial society, or even immediate contact with a patrimonial society in domestic crisis, could produce incentives for conquest. Once conquered, patrimonial landlords and officials lent themselves to indirect rule coordinated by quasi-diplomatic residents rather than to the direct rule by district officers which was necessary in tribal societies. Direct rule would lead to too much resistance, would be too costly, and would waste the willingness of local leaders to collaborate with a new foreign "patrimon" provided their own interests and prestige were not disturbed.[23]

22. Fieldhouse, *Economics and Empire*, pp. 115–17.
23. See D. A. Low and R. C. Pratt, "Baganda Chiefs Negotiate Special Conditions for British Occupation, 1900," in W. Cartey and M. Kilson, eds., *Colonial Africa* (New

The mechanisms of this transition from influence to force to rule are clear in a case that was crucial to imperial rivalry and expansion in North and East Africa—the establishment of informal rule over Egypt. Yet, as Ethiopia's successful resistance to empire suggests, these transitional mechanisms were not inexorable. To these two illuminating cases we now turn.

The Nile, 1800–1885

Egypt began a modernizing revival under a Muslim dynasty in the early nineteenth century and established a patrimonial state. In mid-century it enjoyed a period of prosperity, effective quasi-independence from Ottoman Turkey, its formal suzerain, and power. As the century drew to a close, however, it became subject to informal imperialism while maintaining all the forms and trappings of its quasi-independent political existence. Not only the direction of foreign policy but also the direction of domestic political life and development became subject to British control.

Napoleon's invasion of 1798–99 rudely awakened Egypt to the outside world. It not only stimulated Egyptian revival, it also established a French interest in Egypt and aroused British fears of French control over Britain's route to India.

Egypt, a land of slightly less than three million people, had remained an overwhelmingly agricultural province of the Ottoman empire throughout the eighteenth century.[24] Economically and politically it was subject to a Turco-Circassian landlord class. Once the *mameluke* mercenaries employed by earlier Ottoman sultans, this class had seized and settled a land overwhelmingly populated by the native Egyptian *fellah*. In 1805 Mehemet Ali—an officer in the force the Ottomans had sent to recover Egypt from the retreating French—seized power. Mehemet Ali's accomplishment lay in making himself supreme among these warring

---

York, 1970), pp. 57–61; they refer to the patrimonial rule of the kabaka of the kingdom of Baganda.

24. This section is adapted from my "Metropole, Periphery, and System: Empire on the Niger and the Nile," (Beverly Hills, 1985) in *States versus Markets in the World System*, ed. by Peter Evans, D. Rueschemeyer, and E. Stephens, and appears by permission of Sage Publications, Inc. For Egypt in this period see Landes, *Bankers and Pashas*; G. Baer, *A History of Landownership in Modern Egypt, 1800–1950* (London, 1962); E. R. J. Owen, *Cotton and the Egyptian Economy, 1820–1914* (London, 1969); P. M. Holt, "Egypt and the Nile Valley," in John E. Flint, ed., *The Cambridge History of Africa*, vol. 5 (London, 1976), pp. 13–50; and R. Cottam, *Foreign Policy Motivation* (Pittsburgh, 1977), pt .2.

landlords, thereby creating a single, patrimonial state of Egypt. Nominally a viceroy of the Ottoman sultan, he made Egypt effectively independent. Strengthening the army required that he reorganize taxes, to which end he employed numerous French advisers in what can best be described as a drive for national economic development. This drive focused on the introduction of new crops (particularly long-staple cotton), the construction of public infrastructure, and the establishment of state-supervised manufacturing. Mehemet Ali exercised strict supervision over European merchants, and his monopolies controlled virtually all trade. The viceroy prospered by requisitioning a significant portion of the peasants' annual crop and then selling that crop through negotiated prices to a select ring of European merchants.[25] He expanded his control over Egypt by acquiring control over its economic growth (his monopolies) and by employing the revenues of growth to reward the increasingly diverse elites that economic growth fostered.

Fatally extending his ambitions to the conquest of the Ottoman empire, he launched an attack on Syria in 1831. Britain, fearing a French-supported power in the Middle East, intervened with a naval force and required Ali to reduce his army and dissolve his industrial monopolies. A flood of cheap European imports then put a halt to the growth of local manufacturing.[26]

Determined to increase his independence of both formal Turkish authority and actual European encroachment, Ismail (1863–79), Mehemet Ali's second successor, obtained the title of khedive as a symbolic buttress to his rule. Striving to increase his revenues, he fostered cotton production, hoping to take advantage of the high prices created by the U.S. Civil War. But unlike Mehemet Ali, whose economic monopolies bolstered his political authority, Ismail's economic success was also his political undoing. As Egyptian exports boomed from 1863 to 1875, European financial and commercial houses discovered what David Landes has called the "Klondike on the Nile"—a cotton "gold rush."[27] Although debts contracted by the Egyptian government rose to £100 million by 1876, only about two-thirds of this sum ever reached the khedive due to the discount at which Egyptian bonds sold.[28] Moreover, the khedive was committed to pay nominal interest rates of about 12 percent on most of this vast principal, rising to an effective rate of 30 percent in

25. John Marlowe, *Spoiling the Egyptians* (New York, 1975), p. 18.
26. Charles Issawi, *Egypt in Revolution* (Oxford, 1963), chaps. 1–2.
27. Landes, p. 69; Fieldhouse, *Economics and Empire*, pp. 118–19.
28. Landes, p. 317.

1876 (rates for most European governments were less than 5 percent).[29] This money had been raised in Europe (in France and to a lesser extent in Britain) to pay for public works—and also to finance shortfalls in the treasury and to pay for ostentation, outrageous compensation for minor injuries to Europeans, and ministerial corruption.

A crisis ensued in Egyptian finance. It was the product of several factors. First, patrimonial regimes stimulate shallow political loyalties, and the khedive could not appeal to the native Egyptian people on national grounds to resist foreign interference. Second, class tensions were high. By dispossessing peasants and intensifying work, the khedive and his ministers grew privately rich as Egypt grew publicly poor. Although peasants received some share of the cotton boom, they received more than their share of the bust when prices fell after the American South resumed exports.[30] Third, as part of a program to gain support among the rising native middle class, the khedive expanded the army and thus the state budget while promoting a number of native Egyptian officers to the rank of colonel. (Among them was Arabi, who would later play a leading role in the movement that led to the collapse of the independent khedival state.) A fourth factor was the patrimonial method of government, which Landes, highlighting the worst abuses, describes as follows:

> This rape of the Egyptian treasury was closely connected with the pluralistic character of the society and the economy. Government was personal, centering almost entirely in the viceroy and his family, and capriciously authoritarian, with little if any concept of a continuing, sovereign body of law. Public offices were not the impersonal embodiment of public functions, but private properties exploited by their holders for whatever they would yield. In general, position and prestige depended not on achievement or merit, but on relations and background. . . .
>
> As a consequence, success in the great Egyptian concession hunt was not to the fastest or cheapest or fairest, but to the canal builder who knew the Viceroy from childhood . . . or the promoter who slept with the mistress of the minister.[31]

29. Herbert Feis, *Europe: The World's Banker* (New Haven, 1930), p. 23, and R. Robinson and J. Gallagher with Alice Denny, *Africa and the Victorians* (Garden City, N.Y., 1968), p. 81.

30. Gabriel Baer, "Social Change in Egypt, 1890–1914," in P. M. Holt, ed., *Political and Social Change in Modern Egypt* (London, 1968).

31. Landes, pp. 97–98.

Fifth, Europeans were necessary to provide the entrepreneurial skills and finances that real economic growth in an undeveloped economy required. Their role was doubly reinforced—by necessity and by chicanery—in the Egyptian economy. They became the private financial controllers of the khedival regime, in effect issuing loans and concessions to themselves.[32] Lastly, since Europeans were protected by extraterritoriality, European finance was able to take advantage of the corruption of the regime.[33] Indeed, European consuls were able to demand the fulfillment of exorbitant contracts with the implicit backing of their metropolitan governments. France may have taken the lead, but, as Evelyn Baring later deplored, Britain also threatened foreclosure.[34]

Ismail began to lose control of the Egyptian economy and of the elites whose united support he needed to retain his khedivate. The next stage in the relationship between Egypt and the Europeans saw the piecemeal decline of the khedive's effective sovereignty until, as early as 1879 (three years before the invasion), Egypt had become an informal colony jointly ruled by Britain and France.

The first steps in this direction were designed to rescue Egypt's finances. In order to provide the khedive with the cash to meet his interest payment and to prevent France's acquisition of a controlling voice, Disraeli purchased in 1875 the khedive's Suez Canal shares.[35] Soon afterward the French government and the private association of British bondholders pressed on the khedive the creation of an Anglo-French dual control and the Caisse de la Dette Publique in return for extending his loans. The Dual Control controlled the disbursement of revenues to secure the interest on the debt—that is, controlled domestic finances.[36] With one representative of the British bondholders and one representative of the French government, it controlled revenue (British) and expenditure (French). The Caisse, composed of French, Italian, German,

32. Ibid., p. 158. Their necessity, of course, was in part the product of a *political* system that could not mobilize funds on a national basis without provoking an aristocratic coup or popular revolt or European reaction.

33. Landes, p. 165.

34. Baring Memorandum to Foreign Office, 5 May 1880 F.O. 407:17, in the Public Record Office, Kew, Surrey (hereafter PRO); and M. E. Chamberlain, *The Scramble for Africa* (London, 1974), chap. 3.

35. By 1882, 82% of the canal's commerce was British, Sir Charles Dilke, under secretary in the Foreign Office, asserted in a speech in the House of Commons, 25 July 1882; *Hansard*, 3d ser., vol. 272, 1720.

36. Fieldhouse, *Economics and Empire*, p. 111; Baring Memorandum, F.O. 407:17 (PRO). See also Lord Cromer (Evelyn Baring), *Modern Egypt* (London, 1911), chap 2; John Marlowe, *Anglo-Egyptian Relations, 1800–1956*, 2d ed. (London, 1965), pp. 91–95.

Austrian, and (later) British representatives (the British had at first refused to participate in a private bondholders' dispute), controlled the funding of Egypt's foreign debt—that is, controlled the external finances of a state whose formal sovereign was the Ottoman sultan.[37] Together they established an effective Anglo-French condominium.

Despite reorganization of the external debt, khedival finances did not improve. In 1878, further to appease Western reformers, Khedive Ismail agreed to a constitutional regime with a first minister responsible to a legislative body composed of the chief landlords. The first minister, Nubar Pasha, was a strong supporter of the Franco-British (particularly the British) interest, and both British and French ministers were appointed to the cabinet.[38]

A foreign-mandated austerity drive in the same year provoked a barracks revolt that the khedive used as an excuse to dismiss the Europeans and attempt to form a more autocratic and independent government. The European reaction was swift, forcing Ismail to abdicate in favor of his malleable son, Tewfik. "Constitutional"—that is, pro-European—government was restored. The Dual Control was restored and granted an extensive mandate to reform Egyptian finances.[39] Baring, who was later to be Britain's consul general, described this system and the growing need for European influence in these terms:

> No solid improvement could be effected without the introduction of an European element into the government of the country.... It was decided, and, in my opinion wisely decided, that they should have no executive authority, but that they should act as advisers to the Government, with full powers to investigate all financial affairs. ... It had the merit of enabling European influence, properly exercised, to produce its full measure of beneficial results, whilst at the same time it impaired as little as possible the authority of the Khedive and his Ministers, for it was essential that, whilst the latter should be guided and controlled, their authority should not be unduly enfeebled.[40]

37. R. C. Mowat, "Liberalism and Imperialism: Egypt, 1875–1887," *Historical Journal* 16, 1 (1975), 113.

38. See Vivian to Salisbury, 22 August 1878, F.O. 407:10 (PRO). See also Jean Ganiage, *L'expansion coloniale et les rivalités internationales*, vol. 1 (Paris, 1964), pp. 82–90, for an account of the evolution of the Anglo-French condominium. For an account of the operation and continuing rivalry within the Caisse see G. N. Sanderson, *England, Europe, and the Upper Nile* (Edinburgh, 1965), pp. 19–21.

39. Robinson and Gallagher, *Africa and the Victorians*, pp. 85–86.

40. Memorandum by Major Evelyn Baring, 27 April 1880, F.O. 407:17, 3008 (PRO).

Both the Europeans and the Egyptians began to realize that the European presence had shifted, from interference to informal imperial control. Lord Salisbury, a leading Conservative in Britain, highly approved of this new development. "As merchants, as railway workers, as engineers, as travelers, later as employees [of the khedival government] like Gordon or McKillog or as ministers like Rivers Wilson, they [British nationals] assert the English domination not by any political privilege or military power but by right of the strongest mind."[41] Vivian, a British official in Egypt, may have been one of Salisbury's sources for this perception of growing informal influence:

> I cannot but think that by assisting the Khedive, on his application, in the selection of able Englishmen for important posts in his administration, we shall gradually acquire, by legitimate means, to which no one can fairly take exception, an influence for English interests, English views, and English voting in Egypt of which it would be difficult to overrate the importance and which, while reforming the administration of the country, will probably give us in time every security we require for the protection of our most important interests here.[42]

By 1879 Egypt had lost a substantial degree of domestic sovereignty. Its finances were subject to Anglo-French control, and the khedive had become a puppet of European interests.[43] But as the new khedive was being drawn deeper into collaboration, protonationalist groups were developing. Some were made up of liberal reformers, Nubar Pasha among them, inspired by the Europeans' own ideals, seeking constitutionalism and national self-development. Another faction represented conservative Islam, incensed by foreign interference.[44] A third included the great landowners who feared European-style taxation to pay coupons on the international debt. The fourth and most radical group was the army—hardly surprising for, as the *Times* remarked on 12 September 1881, "The Army, we must remember, is the only native institution which Egypt now owns. All else has been invaded and contested and transformed by the accredited representatives of France and England."[45]

41. Salisbury, quoted in G. N. Uzoigwe, *Britain and the Conquest of Africa* (Ann Arbor, 1974), p. 16; see also G. Cecil, *Salisbury* (1921; New York, 1971), p. 331.
42. Vivian to Salisbury, 11 May 1878, F.O. 407:10, Part 2, correspondence on the Affairs of Egypt 1878 (PRO).
43. Agatha Ramm, "Great Britain and France in Egypt, 1876–1882," in P. Gifford and W. R. Louis, eds., *France and Britain in Africa* (New Haven, 1971), p. 81.
44. See Marlowe, pp. 112–13.
45. Quoted in P. Mansfield, *The British in Egypt* (London, 1971), p. 19.

The contest that emerged between the Europeans and the nationalists was complex. The crisis came in 1881 when Colonel Arabi, leader of the army nationalists, staged a coup.[46] A national assembly was called; Nubar Pasha was overthrown; a nationalist poet became head of government; and the nationalist movement declared itself committed to constitutional government, religious toleration, and a trusting connection with England.[47] The European response soon followed, and with it a redivision of European control. The French public had a particularly large stake in Egyptian finance, and the French government was sensitive to the demands of French bondholders for regular payments on the Egyptian debt. They strongly objected to the new Egyptian assembly's interference with the Egyptian budget.[48] The government, due to political weakness in the French assembly, was eager for a demonstration against the Egyptian nationalists, provided that the demonstration was only for show.[49]

Britain, though it also had a considerable financial stake in Egypt and its own bondholders, was reluctant to interfere. Egypt was important to Britain's position in the Middle East, and the Middle East was important for Britain's strategic priority, India. Palmerston had expressed Britain's traditional policy of informal influence when he declared: "We do not want Egypt or wish it for ourselves, any more than any rational man with an estate in the north of England and a residence in the south would have wished to possess the inns on the north road. All he could want would have been that the inns should be well-kept, always accessible, and furnishing him, when he came, with mutton-chops and post-horses."[50] The Suez Canal route to India was both commercially valuable and strategically valuable (as experience during the Indian Mutiny had shown).[51]

The traditional policy of informal influence was coming unhinged, however; no "inn" could stand a powerful military onslaught. Egypt had been protected by the Ottoman empire from what the British saw as a concerted campaign of Russian intrigue from the Near East to the Far East (a campaign centered on the "Great Game" for India). With

46. F.O. 407:18, p. 1 (PRO).
47. Memorandum to Granville, 1882, F.O. 407:19 (PRO).
48. Lyons to Granville, 12 January 1882, F.O. 407:19 (PRO).
49. Chamberlain, pp. 40–41.
50. Palmerston to Lord Cowley, 25 November 1859, in A. E. M. Ashley, *Life and Correspondence of Palmerston* (London, 1879), p. 338. See also Kenneth Bourne, *The Foreign Policy of Victorian England* (Oxford, 1970).
51. Marlowe, p. 55, and Bourne, p. 115.

the Ottoman defeat in Bulgaria at Russian hands, Britain shifted its Middle Eastern strategic pivot south—first to Cyprus and second to Egypt itself, which seemed to be coming apart at the political and financial seams. Added to this, the Liberals did not freely share the Conservatives' sense of the Great Game in Asia; Gladstone was committed to national self-determination. His Liberal government was, however, prepared to enforce the international legal obligations of the Egyptian regime—the free passage of the canal and the safety of British interests from expropriation.[52]

At this point local interests—the men on the spot—and European perceptions interacted to produce a crisis in Egyptian and European relations.[53] The men on the spot (the consuls, the traders, and the public and private representatives of the bondholders) by and large represented the interests of commerce and finance. They opposed the new regime because the new Egyptian Chamber of Delegates decided to take back control of the Egyptian budget from the Anglo-French Dual Control. The men on the spot encouraged the khedive to be intransigent and placed articles in the British press describing Arabi and his associates as dangerous anti-European fanatics.[54] (The British bondholders' representative on the Dual Control was Sir Auckland Colvin, who was also the Egyptian correspondent of the *Pall Mall Gazette*, a leading Liberal paper.)

In London, Gladstone was reluctant to exercise force; he wanted nothing to do with a bondholders' war. Colonel Arabi at first appeared to be an authentic nationalist, at least according to Gladstone's informant in Egypt—W. S. Blunt.[55] But in the spring of 1882 Arabi began to seem less and less liberal and more "military despotic," and the revolution seemed to be slipping into mass anarchy.[56] When France decided to send a naval force to overawe the Egyptian nationalists, the British Cabinet joined it to avoid the Suez lifeline falling into potentially hostile European (French) hands. Following the anti-European riots in Alexandria (provoked by a naval demonstration offshore), a full-scale intervention seemed the only means to restore security for European interests. Indeed, Vis-

52. See Paul Knaplund, *Gladstone's Foreign Policy* (New York, 1935), p. 171. For Gladstone's concern for liberal principles, see Ramm, p. 100.

53. Alexander Scholch, "The 'Men on the Spot' and the English Occupation of Egypt in 1882," *Historical Journal* 19, 3 (1976), 773–85.

54. Ibid., p. 781.

55. W. S. Blunt, *Secret History of the English Occupation of Egypt* (1907; New York, 1967), pp. 385–87.

56. Robinson and Gallagher, *Africa and the Victorians*, pp. 87 and 100.

count Lyons, Britain's ambassador in Paris attempting to coordinate the Anglo-French intervention, argued that Arabi presented a dangerous threat to the European position in the whole Arab world. Arabi was challenging the prestige on which so much of European influence rested.

> For enabling our subjects to live in safety and tranquility in that country, and for securing the execution and the permanence of any arrangements we might agree upon for the organization of it, the first thing necessary was to restore the reputation and the credit of France and England, and of Europe generally, in the East. Now, in the eyes of the natives, Arabi Pasha was the champion of fanatical hostility to Europeans, and, so to speak, the symbol of resistance to France and England. To allow him to obtain a victory over them would, I thought, be a serious danger to two Powers so deeply interested as are England and France in maintaining their prestige among the Musselmans.[57]

Fearful of how they would answer to the French Chamber of Deputies for provoking a war so far from the lost provinces of Alsace and Lorraine, the French ministry withdrew the French fleet. Fearful of how they would answer Parliament for a defeat in the East at "native" hands, the Liberal ministry instructed General Wolseley to march into Egypt.[58] Sir Charles Dilke, undersecretary in the Foreign Office, explained to Parliament that Britain intervened from "necessity, from Treaty law, and from duty." Joseph Chamberlain, president of the Board of Trade, elaborated: the Liberal Cabinet had overcome its principled reluctance to intervene in order to protect the Suez Canal, to safeguard British trade and investments and the merchants lawfully conducting business, and to promote the welfare of the Egyptian populace (to save them from a despotic Arabi).[59]

Wolseley, after his victory at Tel-el-Kebir, returned Khedive Tewfik to the capital he had fled, to begin the final stage in the full-scale imposition of British informal control. All the trappings of the formal quasi-independence of Egypt and the suzerainty of Turkey survived,

---

57. Lyons to Granville, 30 June 1882, F.O. 407:21 (PRO).

58. Robinson and Gallagher, *Africa and the Victorians*, pp. 94–121; Peter Mansfield, *The British in Egypt* (London, 1970), chap. 2.

59. Dilke, in *Hansard*, 3d ser., vol. 272, 1720–21; and Joseph Chamberlain, speech in the House of Commons, 25 July 1882, ibid., 1796–98. With respect to the "duty" to intervene, Gladstone in the first reading of the supply bill for the Egyptian intervention promised to further the "noble thirst" for the blessings of civilized life whose stirrings he saw in the nationalist movement in Egypt; 24 July 1882, ibid., 1578.

but one governmental department after another slipped in effect into the position of a British colonial ward.

The first step involved the elimination of Egyptian radical nationalism. In large part nationalism had collapsed of its own accord: the nationalists had been as stunned as the Europeans by the popular response and, seeking a national liberal state, they were dismayed by the prospects of agrarian revolution. Western-educated nationalists reverted to a subservient role; Arabi, on the way to exile, even urged the British to carry on his work of reform (which on the technical side they were to do). In the second step a special collaborative relationship with the landlords was established. Support for the landlords was designed as a holding operation until pro-Western, khedival authority could again be made effective; it was also designed to create long-term cooperation in the economic stabilization and growth of the country. (The latter was necessary if the interest on the debt was to be paid and foreign interference avoided in the new British financial management of Egypt.) Thus Baring imported skilled British engineers from India to help construct irrigation canals and port works, enhancing the agricultural (landlord) sector of the Egyptian economy and indirectly improving the tax revenues of the regime that he, as consul general, now controlled.

Restored by British authority, Tewfik and future khedives realized, or soon learned, that they depended on that authority for their own security and could be deposed by it.[60] "Advisers" were seconded to those ministries central to the immediate political and financial stability of Egypt, for stability had been the purpose of the military intervention. War, finance, public works, and the khedive's court first received advisers, but up to 1920 other departments fell under British sway.[61] The courts were taken over, the Ministry of the Interior, the Education Department, and others until, as Cromer described it, "We do not govern Egypt, we only govern the governors of Egypt."[62]

Informal rule gave the British substantial control over a landlord collaborating class and bureaucratic implementation. At the very center the khedive decided Egyptian policy in the knowledge that his tenure

60. R. L. Tignor, *British Colonial Rule in Egypt, 1882–1914* (Princeton, 1966), pp. 102–5; and see Malet to Granville, 15 September 1882, in F.O. 407:23, part VI (PRO).

61. Tignor, p. 146. In one small example of informal control, Khedive Abbas, after criticizing Kitchener's management of the Egyptian army (of which Kitchener was the general) and after much maneuvering, expressions of concern, and hints of pressure from Consul General Baring, was forced to apologize publicly to Kitchener. See the account in Philip Magnus, *Kitchener: Portrait of an Imperialist* (New York, 1968), pp. 83–89.

62. Quoted by A. Al-Sayyid, *Egypt and Cromer* (New York, 1968), p. 68.

depended on British goodwill. In addition, Britain exercised influence through prestige, through fear, and through the rare but ruthless exercise of force. But the key to the whole process was the dependence of what Baring called the "collaborating class" on imperial support. Landlords who sat in the advisory chamber, merchants who sought loans and markets in Britain, civil servants who sought advancement—they were the foundations of informal rule.

The essence of the informal imperial process lay, as Ronald Robinson has argued, in maintaining a balance of political influence between imperial collaborators and nascent nationalists.[63] The more the balance tilted toward a resurgence of nationalism, the higher the military investment Britain had to make in order to retain control. The more the khedive and the landlords felt secure, the more they threatened to become independent. Britain tried to keep the first suppressed and the second insecure.

Avoidance and Resistance

Ethiopia

On 1 March 1896, near the town of Adowa, there occurred one of the most striking events in the history of modern imperialism. A well-equipped European army of 452 officers, 8,463 European troops, and 10,749 African auxiliaries was routed.[64] Six thousand were killed, more than half of them Italian, four thousand were wounded or captured. Africa had never seen an equal force pitted against a peripheral regime, and Menelik II, negus of Ethiopia, by defeating this Italian expeditionary force, preserved the independence of his country. Why did Ethiopia survive an imperialist onslaught when so many other societies succumbed to much lesser attacks?

When Menelik ordered mobilization of the Ethiopian military forces he proclaimed: "Enemies have now come upon us to ruin the country and to change our religion. . . . Our enemies have begun the affair by advancing and digging into the country like moles. With the help of God I will not deliver up my country to them. . . . Today, you who are strong, give me of your strength, and you who are weak, help me by

63. Ronald Robinson, "Non-European Foundations . . . ," in Roger Owen and Bob Sutcliffe, eds., *Studies in the Theory of Imperialism* (London, 1972).

64. H. G. Marcus, *The Life and Times of Menelik II* (London, 1975), p. 168. See also Sven Rubenson, *The Survival of Ethiopian Independence* (London, 1976), and V. G. Kiernan, *From Conquest to Collapse* (New York, 1982), pp. 85–86.

prayer."[65] In making this appeal he was asking Ethiopians—particularly the dominant Tigre-Shoa people but also the partially assimilated Galla— to recall a patriotic identification with their political system, which historical tradition claimed extended back three thousand years. Before the spread of Islam, Ethiopia had been converted to Christianity; its patriarchs were subordinates of the Coptic church in Egypt, but the negus was the recognized defender of the faith in Ethiopia. He had led the slow expulsion of Islam from this mountain kingdom and, ever since, had been strongly supported by the church.[66] Ethiopia's long isolation nurtured a sense of separate nationhood linked to a national church. The crucial political effect of this sense of identity lay in an abhorrence of collaboration with an enemy who threatened the national existence.

On occasion the regional lords of Ethiopia did accept foreign aid in their struggle with the negus. In 1867, for example, Britain sent an expeditionary force to free its seized diplomats. The negus at the time, Tewodros (Theodore) had taken the first steps toward modernizing his country, having established small-scale industries and imported foreign technicians and arms. Determined to preserve his independence, he declared: "I know the tactics of European governments when they desire to acquire an Eastern state. First they send out missionaries, then consuls to support the missionaries, then battalions to support the consuls. I am not a Rajah of Hindustan to be made a mock of in that way. I prefer to have to deal with the battalions straight away."[67] But Tewodros had also alienated a considerable portion of the feudal nobility, who stood aside as the British expedition penetrated to the capital and forced Tewodros to release the prisoners. (With remarkable foresight, the British expeditionary leader had announced that Britain had no grievance against Ethiopia, only a complaint against the negus.) Britain had neither substantial trade nor strategic interests at stake, and the British force was impressed with the defensibility of Ethiopia. As one officer commented, "Winning a battle is a vastly different matter from the pacification of so wild a country."[68]

When national existence came under threat, the same feudal lords rallied to the national cause (e.g., against Islam and the Mahdist threat in the nineteenth century). Yohannes, Tewodros's successor, was fully aware that this support was essential and that his own domestic political

65. Marcus, p. 160.
66. R. Hess, *Ethiopia* (Ithaca, 1970), p. 40.
67. Richard Greenfield, *Ethiopia* (New York, 1965), p. 79.
68. Ibid., p. 81.

survival depended on preserving all the trappings of sovereign status. He rejected British advice to cede a small strip of territory to the Italians (seeking hinterland for their colony of Massawa) and replied, "How can you say that I shall hand over to them the country which Jesus Christ gave me?"[69] Despite the feudal conflict between the next negus, Menelik, and his nobles, the Ethiopians who had allied with the Italians in hopes of overthrowing Menelik defected to Menelik just before the great battle of Adowa to take their place in the defense of the homeland.[70] It was this commitment which was to sustain Ethiopia during the Italian occupation of 1936–41. Although Mussolini was able to defeat the Ethiopian army with poison gas and aerial warfare, the Italian occupation never established control of the countryside.[71]

If national identity can be considered a fuel of continued independence, central government should be considered the engine. In the ancient past Ethiopia had been a unified patrimonial-bureaucratic state. Although it was nearly overrun by Islam in the sixteenth century, central order was restored with the aid of the Portuguese. Between 1769 and 1885, however, the power of the Ethiopian negus declined and a feudal order emerged as territorial nobles vied for the manipulation of what central authority existed.[72] Italy and France began intriguing against each other to determine which would establish control over this potentially strategic mountain kingdom. Each supported different factions in the wars of the 1880s. It was Ethiopia's good fortune that just as European rivalry mounted in the 1880s, a powerful feudal lord of the royal line, Menelik, seized the central authority and established control over the subordinate nobles. With a personal army, the substantial revenues of recently conquered provinces in the southwest, an increasingly trained and organized bureaucracy, and a charismatic appeal, he recreated a central government from the segments of Ethiopian community. But none of this would have been possible without the pre-existing strength, a sense of political identity, that its traditional religious foundation afforded Ethiopia. Italian attempts to establish a protectorate met with firm opposition. His army supplied with French arms, Menelik led it to victory at Adowa.[73]

If a sense of national community and a centralized state proved to be the keys to independence in Ethiopia, not every state institution or sense

69. Ibid., p. 93.
70. Marcus, pp. 86–87 and 169.
71. Hess, p. 67.
72. Ibid., pp. 40, 45, 47, 48.
73. Ibid., pp. 57–58; Marcus, chaps. 5 and 6.

of community suffices. For instance, many feudal societies with a common religion nonetheless became subject to "foreign" rule as parts of eleventh-century France fell to (albeit brief and unstable) Norman-English control. Similarly, in the late nineteenth century Bali—despite, perhaps even because of its strict and venerable cultural traditions—fell to Dutch imperial expansion.[74] In Bali the unity of public worship in a "theatre state" divided the community into fine but strict gradations of prestige. Each person knew his or her fixed relation to the whole, but no one showed solidarity. When the Dutch invaded, each performed the appropriate role but no one could adjust the resources of the whole to meet the novel challenge of foreign intrusion. The only role which exemplified the independence of the state was that played by the monarch and his family—they marched together into the guns of the advancing Dutch. The state was centralized, but in Clifford Geertz's phrase the central state had an extremely low "political center of gravity."[75] The theatre state had a single, centralized "play," but the resources of power (such as control over irrigation) were as widely distributed as they were in many feudal societies. The result was a state incapable of resisting the far from substantial forces that the Dutch sent to conquer the island.

Conversely, favorable international circumstances can reduce the domestic resources required for continued independence. Siam, for example, supplemented minimal central government and national identification with an astute diplomacy that played off Britain against France.[76] Diplomacy alone is insufficient, however: intense competition between Britain and France for the Western Sudan did little to sustain the independence of the sultan of Sokoto, and Anglo-Belgian rivalry around the lakes of the Rift Valley did little for the independence of Baganda. These areas, lacking national identification, were merely divided on maps in European drawing rooms. Furthermore, strong national identity can supplement, indeed encourage, the formation of central government in response to foreign threats of intervention. Such appears to have been the case in Japan in the early sixteenth and again in the mid-nineteenth centuries when European threats galvanized the Tokugawa and Meiji restorations of central control.[77]

74. Clifford Geertz, *Negara: The Theatre State in Nineteenth Century Bali* (Princeton, 1980), chaps. 1 and 4.

75. Ibid., p. 134.

76. Chandra Jesurun, "The Anglo-French Declaration of 1896 and the Independence of Siam," *Journal of the Siam Society* 58 (1970), 105–26.

77. Fairbank et al., p. 189.

The independence that permits states of the periphery to avoid or successfully to resist imperial conquest lies in the attainment of a national identity and a centralized government. These national states on the periphery remain weak and potentially dependent on the industrial metropoles, however, and their potential dependence demands our attention.

Dependency in Latin America

Although Ethiopia and Japan form the two most striking and illuminating exceptions to imperial rule, several ambiguous cases—near-empire, near-independence—also help us understand the factors that tend to produce imperial rule. In part, these cases are a true dusk between light and dark, and actual political ambiguity matches the analytical confusion that they cause. But certain of these cases help us understand and explain some of the distinctive features that separate dependency from empire.

The question of informal imperialism in Latin America is a central issue: were the Latin American republics and monarchies informally ruled by Britain in the nineteenth century?[78]

Argentina, Brazil, and Chile were much more socially differentiated than Egypt. They also had more modern, or institutionalized, governments than did Ethiopia and Japan. But like Egypt they relied on external trade and finance, and like Egypt their societies were only partially integrated, throwing their independence into question. Different from Egypt, they answered differently.

Britain had aided the Chilean revolution and had come to acquire a dominant position in merchandising its exports and in mining its nitrates. It established a clear relationship of economic dependence: the Chilean economy became both sensitive and vulnerable to the British economy. Nevertheless, many of the most important issues in the overall direction of Chilean society—its government and path of development— were determined by the native Chilean elite. It is true that Colonel North, the British "Nitrate King" of Chile, did attempt to intervene in Chilean politics, and he intrigued in the downfall of President Balmaceda in 1891, but the Chilean government took measures in direct opposition to the nitrate interest before and after 1891.[79] Chile had become an economic dependency of Europe. Its export dependence made it vul-

78. J. Gallagher and R. Robinson, "The Imperialism of Free Trade," *Economic History Review*, 2d ser., 6, 1 (1953).

79. See H. Blakemore, *British Nitrates and Chilean Politics, 1886–1896* (London, 1974), pp. 2, 110, 210–15.

nerable to the exercise of political influence, but it was not clearly an informal colony such as Egypt.

Brazil experienced similar external pressure. Britain forced Brazil to end the slave trade, and the British market shaped Brazil's agricultural export economy.[80] Furthermore, economic relations were supplemented by a more general cultural impact; as one of Brazil's nineteenth-century political leaders declared, "When I enter the Chamber [of Deputies] I am entirely under the influence of English liberalism, as if I were working under the orders of Gladstone. . . . I am an English liberal . . . in the Brazilian Parliament."[81] But although Britain provided a model for the Brazilian middle classes who overthrew Pedro II, Britain was also perceived as the most important threat to national independence. Brazil, while clearly subject to external influence, was not so clearly controlled.

Dependence, indeed, may not be equivalent to control, as the case of Argentina, often cited as an instance of informal imperialism, suggests.[82] Britain occupied Buenos Aires in 1806 and 1807, Britain and France blockaded the coast in 1838 and again between 1845 and 1850, and, as H. S. Ferns notes in his classic study of Britain's relations with Argentina, Britain repeatedly interfered in Argentine politics.[83] The aim was to create an Argentina more suitable to British interests, an Argentina that was stable, commercially and externally oriented, and capable and desirous of repaying the loan it had contracted in 1824. The eventual outcome very much suited British interests and had a long-term impact on Argentina, setting it on the track of a dependent form of economic development. Ferns puts the argument very well:

> The determination of the British Government to ally itself politically
> with the Confederation and to apply pressure to Buenos Aires Prov-

80. Stanley and Barbara Stein, *The Colonial Heritage of Latin America* (New York, 1970), p. 149; R. Graham, *Britain and the Onset of Modernization in Brazil* (Cambridge, 1968), pp. 40–41, 87, 91, 163–70.

81. Cited by Richard Graham, "Robinson and Gallagher in Latin America," in W. R. Louis, ed., *Imperialism: The Robinson and Gallagher Controversy* (New York, 1976), p. 220.

82. Tony Smith, *The Pattern of Imperialism* (New York, 1981), pp. 23–26, makes this argument. Though I come to the opposite conclusion, our difference in interpretation is not that wide. He suggests that the Argentinian relationship with Britain barely qualifies as imperial. I suggest that it just misses this condition.

83. J. F. Cady, *Foreign Intervention in the Rio de la Plata* (Philadelphia, 1929), pp. 14, 35, 159; H. S. Ferns, *Britain and Argentina in the Nineteenth Century* (Oxford, 1960), pp. 488, 296–97. See Robinson, "Non-European Foundations," for a more general discussion of the policy of "free trade imperialism" and its goal of creating an overseas collaborating class for European commerce and investments.

ince both for the purpose of altering its independent course in the direction of incorporation in the Republic and for the collection of the Loan of 1824 may be properly regarded as one of the critical events in the history of the Argentine community. Had Buenos Aires succeeded in maintaining its political independence it would have been obliged, at least in the formative stages, to undertake its own capital accumulation. The social, political, and economic consequences of this would have been profound, for it would have been the means of creating in the richest and most compact productive area of Argentina a class of financiers and entrepreneurs dominant in their own community and independent of others. On a smaller scale there would have been created a class of similar character to that which existed in the United States. . . . As it was, the eventual integration of Buenos Aires Province in the Republic placed the financial resources of the richest area at the disposal of the whole Republic, and made these resources the means of financing vast railway schemes. . . . This investment was encouraged . . . by the dominant landed interests, which saw in the process advantages to themselves both in economic benefits and political power. . . . A geographically more concentrated development confined to the Province of Buenos Aires and the southern pampas . . . would have been not only less burdensome but might have led to a more balanced economic and industrial development. As it was, saddled with a vast foreign investment, Argentina was obliged to export or go bankrupt, and this meant concentration upon a limited range of exportable staple products with all the social and political, not to mention moral and intellectual consequences of intense specialization in an agricultural and pastoral setting.[84]

Contributing to dependence is not, however, the same as exercising control. Control implies, as in Britain's relationship to Egypt in the last two decades of the nineteenth century, an ability (and not just a desire) to shape the foreign and domestic policy and the leadership of a subordinate periphery. While this shaping can be achieved without military force or the trappings of colonial rule, by economic control of the environment, Britain did not achieve actual control in Argentina.

The revolutionary hero of South America, General San Martín, reflecting on the blockade of Argentina in 1845, told the British Foreign Office that Britain and France would not succeed; the country was too vast and its political regime too nationalistic and well-entrenched to make Argentina an easy prey for commercial blackmail. In the 1850s

---

84. Ferns, pp. 290 and 314–15.

Britain favored the confederation and not the independent city of Buenos Aires, but it was the confederationists who conquered Buenos Aires. They did so without direct British aid, and they, not Britain, controlled the future of Argentina.[85]

Argentina could be unified on Argentinian terms largely because of a widely shared sense of nationalism first stirred by the expulsion of the British expeditionary force from Buenos Aires in 1807. In addition, an extensively mobilized population was settled over a wide country, and any one of Argentina's major factions could mobilize sufficient soldiers to defeat or deter foreign intervention by land. Neither Buenos Aires nor the rural confederationists, therefore, could guarantee stable collaboration to foreign interests. The sea was Britain's, but the land was Argentina's and with it national independence—as long as Argentinians were prepared to accept the burdens that foreign trade restrictions could inflict.

In Argentina, therefore, there was economic dependence but not control and collaboration. Had the khedive and the Egyptian landlords had these degrees of effective sovereignty, the former could have kept spending and the latter would have deposed him and repudiated the debt. But the khedive, his landlords, and their soldiers were a thin occupying class ruling over a mass of Egyptian peasants. When stirred, Egyptians turned against the Turkish pashas as much as against the European foreigners, and the pashas then turned to Britain. The difference between Argentina and Egypt lay not only in greater social differentiation in Latin America but also in their more extensive political integration. Argentina, Brazil, and Chile shared the historical experiences of widely supported anti-colonial revolutions in Chile and Argentina and, in Brazil, the special and strong elite identity stemming from the experience of having been both the colony and the metropole of the Portuguese-Brazilian empire.

On the other side of the globe, China was a prey to European economic exploitation but was never completely under individual or joint European imperial control. Like Egypt, China was politically weakened by the indigenous population's hostility toward a foreign ruling dynasty, the Manchu. Moreover, the country's foreign economic sector underwent repeated crises as European states secured concessions by the repeated use of force. A hundred years previously the Chinese regime had been much stronger, and the people still possessed a strong political culture. But the Chinese identity was more universalistic than national

85. Ibid., pp. 275; 318, 321.

and thus not efficacious against a powerful external threat.[86] The regime and bureaucratic coordination, moeover, had been severely strained by the White Lotus Rebellion (1796–1800) just prior to the acceleration of European contact. China's weakness was real, but formal and in large measure actual independence was nonetheless preserved by the residual power of bureaucracy and massive geographical extent.[87] China, with even less political integration than Egypt, had the resistance of a pillow: few blows left lasting effects.

Collaboration and Informal Rule

> In Sherbro our agreements with native chiefs having brought about universal disorder, we send a body of soldiers to suppress it, and presently will allege the necessity of extending our rule over a larger area. So again in Perak. A resident sent to advise becomes a resident who dictates; appoints as sultan the most plastic candidate in place of one preferred by the chiefs; arouses resistance which becomes a plea for using force; finds usurpation of the government needful; has his proclamation torn down by a native who is thereupon stabbed by the resident's servant; the resident is himself killed as a consequence; then (nothing being said of the murder of the native), the murder of the resident leads to outcries for vengeance, and a military expedition establishes British rule.[88]

Patrimonial societies and tribal societies interact differently with metropolitan transnational forces, and the differences are important. Tribal societies seem to require formal rule. The communal integration of tribal society made transnational forces difficult to accommodate. Rapid socioeconomic change destabilized tribes internally by disrupting their political authority, externally by changing their traditional relationships to their neighbors. Small and disorganized, they required formal and direct imperial rule if the transnational interests of the metropole were to be protected.

Patrimonial societies are associated with informal rule. Indeed, colonial governors and military forces are absent for much of the relationship and, when they do appear, seem to be more advisory than administrative.

---

86. Fairbank et al., p. 108.

87. R. Murphey, *Treaty Ports and China's Modernization* (Ann Arbor, 1971).

88. Herbert Spencer, *The Principles of Sociology*, vol. 1 (1883; New York, 1897), pp. 602–3. This quotation was drawn to my attention by David Weinstein.

First contact did not involve revolutionary transformation because patrimonial and feudal societies were generally more technically advanced than tribal society. Explaining the basic principles of algebra or astronomy (Caliban's "larger light and the less") might have seemed sorcerous in a tribal society, but the irony of attempting to do so in Egypt—inventor of astronomy—could not have failed to escape the notice of even the most chauvinistic European of the nineteenth century. And social differentiation provided domestic analogues for many of the agents of metropolitan society that first encountered patrimonial society. Merchants, moneylenders, manufacturing artisans already existed, and the interlopers, while different, were comprehensible.

Most importantly, the scale and organization of patrimonial and feudal societies permitted them to demand that transnational contact at first take place on the patrimon's terms. It was the local ruler who negotiated the terms of first contact. Patrimonial government shielded its subjects from the immediate impact of transnational forces. The member of the tribe confronted as a collective individual the new knowledge and new techniques of the foreigner. And the shock could be extreme.[89] In a patrimonial society the government, separated from the people, bore this shock. Its organizational capability enabled it to manipulate transnational ties, even to employ them to strengthen the regime, as did Mehemet Ali.

In the longer run, however, transnational penetration generated pressures within the periphery. Tribal societies collapsed quickly under these pressures, but patrimonial societies were only slowly taken over by these new transnational forces. At first, extraterritoriality and normal business seemed adequate for the security and promotion of transnational interest, but because politicization was characteristic of domestic patrimonial society, transnational interests soon became politically active. Rivalry with other foreign interests made political influence even more attractive; bribes were efficient in a patrimony already oriented toward benefices as rewards for services. Moreover, patrimonial societies, which lack social solidarity, pose few obstacles to collaboration. And as Lewis Coser noted, these societies are "likely to disintegrate in the face of outside conflict, although some unity may be despotically enforced."[90] Metropolitan intervention thus tends to meet relatively slight resistance.

89. Chinua Achebe, *Things Fall Apart* (Greenwich, Conn., 1959), details, from the novelist's perspective, the personal disorganization that this shock entails as a young African confronts European law and religion. The novel treats brilliantly of the scope of this personal confrontation.

90. Lewis Coser, *The Functions of Social Conflict* (New York, 1956), p. 95 and chap.

Metropolitan governments also had a strong interest to intervene if they were not prepared to allow their interests to suffer from political prejudice and corruption.[91] Metropoles exercised increasing influence on patrimonial regimes by means of blockades (as in the opening of China), commercial restrictions (as against the slave trade), or restraints on the extension of credit. When the patrimony could no longer keep up interest payments on uneconomic loans, the metropoles stepped in to manage their debt by managing patrimonial revenues. Metropolitan governments soon found themselves interfering more regularly in policy formation and even in policy implementation.

In the end the patrimony entered a state of crisis. This crisis resulted from the social change that metropolitan merchants and bankers had stimulated, which in turn weakened the local base of the patrimon's power over his subordinate landlords. (As in Egypt, foreign debt induced land taxes.) The metropoles substituted their authority for that of the patrimonial rulers, eventually leaving little more than the shell of patrimonial sovereignty. The independent sources of patrimonial rule no longer existed, and the patrimon, dependent for his very existence on foreign support, became a cash register, emitting foreign money for foreign bills.

If the metropole totally controlled any one of the components of the periphery's process of making policy, it could exercise imperial control over the periphery in the sense of being able to prevent measures hostile to metropolitan interests. Total control of the economic environment could determine the outcome of the effective sovereignty of the periphery. But in fact the metropole's transnational impact is rarely so complete or so focused. A more diffuse but general control achieves its objects by combining influence across a number of the perceptions and political actions that go into making policy.

Metropolitan influence, informally exercised, most directly affects the environment by encouraging and excluding options. As a secondary matter, it shapes the collaborators' perception of the environment through coercion and prestige, and also through personal contact and some cultural transmission. The metropole also shapes the aggregation of interests in the periphery, partly through bribery and the collaboration of foreign-oriented special interests. Influence becomes further entrenched

---

5 passim, discussing the importance of group structure to the likelihood of unified resistance or disintegration.

91. Platt, *Finance, Trade, and Politics*, pp. 45–51.

as the metropole begins to implement decisions made, though only in formal terms, by the patrimonial ruler.

The control of options and the shaping of perceptions were part of the overall process of European transnational contact. The two latter interventions—the crucial prongs of informal imperial penetration— were coordinated by Baring in Egypt and his counterparts in other countries' foreign services. They gave needed advice to bankers and merchants, maintained special links with local collaborators, and directed their compatriots who controlled the implementation of local "decisions." Although lacking the formal sovereignty, all the substance of imperial rule was here.

Pericentric Theory Again

In the analysis of tribal and patrimonial peripheries we find confirmation of the value of pericentric theory. It accounts for who imperialized whom. It thus distinguishes effective resistance and dependency from imperialism. Yet pericentric explanations of patrimonial collaboration also have weaknesses. Not only do they neglect the metropolitan motive forces of imperialism which are needed to explain all but the most exceptional cases of active peripheral surrender. They also discount at least two active and nonpericentric determinants of empire.

Metropoles and the international system, as we shall see in subsequent chapters, help determine whether an empire was formal or informal. They also set priorities and thereby help determine which metropole conquers which periphery. They establish, moreover, the pace of imperial expansion.

In Egypt differences in metropolitan priorities—often determined in the metropoles and in the rivalry among metropoles—had noticeable effects. British pressure against Mehemet Ali from 1831 to 1840 resulted less from a peripheral crisis than from a crisis in the international system. In 1838 Mehemet Ali's victories in Syria threatened the survival of the sultan's rule in Turkey; Palmerston held that Britain must protect the integrity of the Turkish empire. Britain's priority in the eastern Mediterranean was strategic, and it dictated supporting the sultan as a bulwark against Russian advance.[92] In the 1870s and 1880s Britain's private financial and public strategic interests lay in stabilizing the khedival regime. France's priorities differed; France was more willing to accom-

92. Kenneth Bourne, *Palmerston: The Early Years* (New York, 1982), pp. 576–79.

modate financial interests seeking an immediate return on threatened investments even at the cost of khedival stability, and largely for domestic political reasons.

Metropolitan and systemic factors had a considerable role in setting the pace of imperial expansion, even apart from the crises they helped create in the peripheries. Along the Nile in the 1870s the pace of political collapse reflected peripheral financial crises and consequent political ferment in the periphery. But Disraeli's purchase of the khedive's Suez Canal shares in 1876 was also a response to the exigencies of coalition building in British domestic politics and to increased threats from an European system disrupted by the effects of the Franco-Prussian War.[93] The motives for the invasion itself, moreover, are difficult to understand if they were not to intimidate the entire east (as Viscount Lyons, Britain's ambassador at Paris, averred) and to avoid France's acquiring the Nile on its own terms, as Salisbury noted in September 1881: "As to our policy—the defence of it lies in a nutshell. When you have got a neighbour and faithful ally [France] who is bent on meddling in a country in which you are deeply interested—you have three courses open to you. You may renounce—or monopolise—or share. Renouncing would have been to place the French across our road to India. Monopolising would have been very near the risk of war. So we resolved to share."[94] To Britain's surprise, the French backed out. The crisis had escalated beyond diplomatic management, and Britain had only two choices: renounce its interests to the nationalists or invade and monopolize.

If we were interested in learning only which political societies could become subject to imperial rule, what form of imperial rule they would be likely to receive, and how quickly, once contacted, they would succumb to imperial pressure, a pericentric approach would suffice. These contributions are clearly important. But they do not tell us whether international systemic or metrocentric factors can override pericentric factors nor, as importantly, do they suggest when the pace of imperial expansion will accelerate, or which metropole is likely to be the leader, or why certain forms of empire are prevalent in certain eras. Nor, lastly,

93. Freda Harcourt, "Disraeli's Imperialism: A Question of Timing," *Historical Journal* 23, 1 (1980), 87–110; and see Schumpeter's analysis of Disraeli's use of imperialism as an electoral catchword in *Imperialism and Social Classes* (Cleveland, 1955), chap. 2.

94. Quoted in Lady G. Cecil, *The Life of Robert, Marquis of Salisbury* (London, 1921–32), 2:331–32.

does a fixation on the periphery provide the historical texture we need to understand how these events took place—the driving motives and the exploited opportunities. To round out our understanding of imperialism we need the systemic and metrocentric approaches.

CHAPTER 10

The International System and Nineteenth-Century Imperialism

The nineteenth century did not discover empire in the early 1880s when the Scramble for Africa erupted. The imperial heritage of eighteenth-century empire was not only maintained between 1815 and 1880, it was expanded at a slow but steady rate, using both formal and informal relationships of political control. The academic fixation on the latter part of the century is curious even though the imperial expansion of the period is undeniably distinctive.

This distinctiveness should be viewed in the context of the evolution of empire throughout the century. Much of nineteenth-century empire, measured by either population or resources, already existed in 1815. The Indian subcontinent, for example, with its size, population, and political and economic importance, was already the greatest possession of the century's most substantial empire. The years between 1815 and 1880, moreover, witnessed the growth of imperial control, both informal and formal, as well as a spectacular dissolution of empire in Latin American independence.

The Scramble was, nonetheless, a turning point in the experience of empire. Unlike the middle phase of the century, marked by extensive informal imperialism, it revived a predominantly formal imperialism, and this period is associated with the full transfer of rights of sovereignty (usually marked by either treaty or conquest). The globe was being rapidly painted in various colors, according to rules devised partly post facto at the Berlin West Africa Conference of 1884–85.[1] The Scramble period is marked by a noticeable acceleration of imperial expansion, which is practically system-wide. Expansion, finally, has an arational, nonsubstantive quality that Schumpeter later noted (and elevated into a definition of all imperialism). The acquisition of little-known lands of manifestly "light soils"—Lord Salisbury's euphemism for the desert areas of the French Western Sudan—was necessarily based on a gamble. The chance that these lands might prove valuable in themselves or to another power outweighed the prospective costs of management, and expansion was preemptive.[2]

Can international systemic factors account for the three stages and the changing form of nineteenth-century imperialism? In Part I we discussed the limitations of the abstract systemic model, which pictures the international system as a competition among relatively impermeable states (billiard balls), each jealously watching the power resources of the others. Each rationally and identically strives to increase its power because each realizes that the international game is a battle of relative weight. To fail to grow is to decline.[3] This model does not, however, address the specific circumstances of empire. Not all actors in world politics play this game—Kings Bell and Acqua clearly did not. Power, moreover, is an indistinct measure, and the precepts of balancing power tend to conflict. It is thus difficult to tell whether a colony adds to a nation's power and whether expansion improves power or security.

Looking more closely at the international system, one sees that the abstract interaction of identical units is an inadequate characterization; the units interact not in general but in particular, relatively stable patterns. They are not indistinguishable; they take on social characteristics—some are liberal, others conservative, some small, others large. We need a sociology of international systems to distinguish empires from interstate relations and identify various types and historical features of international systems.[4] These distinctions will need to take into account not just the number of state actors but also the political and social

1. S. E. Crowe, *The Berlin West Africa Conference* (London, 1942).

2. R. Robinson and J. Gallagher, *Africa and the Victorians* (Garden City, N.Y., 1968), p. 303.

3. R. Aron, *Peace and War* (Garden City, N.Y., 1966), chap. 1, and M. Kaplan, *System and Process* (New York, 1957), p. 23.

4. For one model of such a sociology of international systems, see Richard Rosecrance, *Action and Reaction in World Politics* (Boston, 1963). An example of a sociology of a diplomatic system, or constellation, is H. Kissinger, *A World Restored* (New York, 1964).

characteristics of these states (their domestic regimes, goals, capacities, and sources of support) and the technologies that influence the means of competition.

The Three International Systems of the Nineteenth Century

The Concert: In and Out of Tune, 1815–1850

The system created for the center of world politics in 1815 reflected the genius of a number of men and, appropriately, was built upon a foundation of multilateral balancing. On the crucial strategic conception of the younger Pitt—the need for "great masses" to contain French revolutionary power or potential power—Castlereagh carefully constructed a continent-wide edifice. Metternich attended to the need for a principle of legitimacy to define both the acceptable state and acceptable behavior toward various states, thus complementing Tzar Alexander's inspirational (and hegemonic) impetus toward cooperation.[5]

To these statesmen revolution, undermining through example and perhaps action the tenuous stability of aristocratically dominated regimes, meant war. But war meant revolution, so coercion to restore aristocratic government had to be limited and multilateral, "concerted."[6] France, as much the *club politique* of Europe as England was the world's workshop, had to be contained without creating of Russia a conservative policeman so powerful as to dominate Europe. The size and resources of Germany, and its division, provided the solutions. Both Prussia and Austria-Hungary would act as shields to contain a potentially revolutionary France while both the naval (Britain) and land (Russia) swords remained in ready reserve. France, in "revolution," was contained by the whole; Russia, in peace, by the German center. The German center was prevented from dominating Europe by its internal balance of power—Austria-Hungary in competition with Prussia for leadership of the German confederation. Britain shifted its support to balance any threat of continental hegemony.

No system, not even a well-constructed system, lasts forever, and the Concert had a rather short life. After conferences at Troppau, Laibach, and Verona (1822) the Concert split in two. England, joined by France in 1830 in a Liberal Entente, rejected the extreme conservative

5. M. S. Anderson, *The Ascendancy of Europe* (London, 1972), chap. 1.
6. E. Gulick, *The Classical Balance of Power* (New York, 1955), chaps. 9–11.

doctrine and policy of counterrevolution (in Spain, Portugal, Italy, and Greece). France had not proved dangerous and other concerns—the worldwide pull of expanding trade and sea power—made their force felt when the central systemic concern of Europe appeared less than pressing.[7]

Central international systems are often accompanied by, and affect, external subsystems. In this period there were two external systems, one intense and land-oriented, the other diffuse and seaborne. Since the central balance had failed to dominate ("centralize") the international concerns of the system, these external concerns counterreacted upon the center to influence ("externalize") it.

Russia's massive and highly prestigious army (had it not appeared to push Napoleon across Europe?) gave it a special role as the guardian of reaction on the great plain of eastern Europe. The destruction of Poland was the opening move of the eastern powers in a political game of continual intervention. It extended to an interfering protection of the Austro-Hungarian monarchy (culminating in the military intervention of 1849 to preserve Austria-Hungary from a Hungarian revolution), a meddlesome protection of Christians in the crumbling Ottoman empire, and a creeping expansion eastward across the steppes.[8]

The more spectacular external system was the Pax Britannica, which endured from 1815 into the 1870s. This empire, on which the sun truly never set, rested upon mercantile and industrial supremacy, on a balance within Europe that allowed Britain to concentrate on overseas policy, and on a political system flexible enough to take advantage of the popular nationalism that was splitting continental Europe at the seams. The workshop of the world sent its wares across all the world's oceans and seas secure in the knowledge that the navy would protect the goods at the point of sale.[9]

Sometimes the navy's use was merely technical (comprehensive charting) and constabulatory (suppressing piracy). At other times the navy overawed local regimes to preserve the open trade system. As Richard Cobden commented in 1857, "the manufacturers of Yorkshire and Lancashire look upon China and India as a field of enterprise which can only be kept open by force."[10] Without the occasional use of force—the

7. Rosecrance, chap. 5.

8. Anderson, pp. 6–8.

9. Ibid., pp. 8–9.

10. Quoted in W. D. Grampp, *The Manchester School of Economics* (Stanford, 1966), p. 101.

Opium Wars, the suppression of the Indian Mutiny, the blockade of the River Plate—local potentates would either disrupt or close trade. Another use of the navy was even more important to merchants far from home: coastal policing along the shores of Africa, Burma, and Malaya preserved not merely the openness of commerce but the very lives of the merchants.[11] The gunboat just over the horizon vastly reduced the risks of trade in the remote parts of the international economy.

Naval costs were substantial but remarkably low considering the geographic scope of the seaborne Pax Britannica. No power undermined the British "two-power" standard (at least as strong as the next two naval powers put together) in part because experience was vital, as the French had discovered in the Napoleonic Wars when they had challenged British dominance with technically superior ship design but with inferior experience. With 276 ships (in 1876) to patrol the seas and an overseas army, entirely paid for by Indian taxation, of 71,000 British and 123,000 Indians (over one-half of total British forces) to control the Indian subcontinent and serve as a striking force for campaigns anywhere on the Indian Ocean,[12] Britain dominated this external system—a unipolar world peripheral system. Regions were linked and dominated, loosely or closely, by British sea power, and only Britain linked the diverse parts of the world, the hub to the spokes of the peripheral wheel.

Actually, there were two hubs, for both England and India were strategic centers of an expanding empire. England formed the strategic center of a European-American-West African arc. India was the strategic center of an eastern arc of empire, described by Leopold Amery in 1918 as "that Southern British World which runs from Cape Town through Cairo, Baghdad and Calcutta to Sydney and Wellington."[13] India was both a key to British commerce, especially to its balance of payments, and a military reservoir.

The most striking aspect of the pax was its openness to the commerce and exploration of other European states. The British navy in effect provided the "collective good" of security for the trade of all interested in exporting to or importing from the Indian subcontinent or the sea coasts of the world. Hamburg gin flowed into Africa with Lancashire

---

11. G. Graham, *Tides of Empire* (Montreal, 1972), pp. 84–85, and K. O. Dike, *Trade and Politics in the Niger Delta* (London, 1956).

12. G. Modelski, "Some Continuities in World Politics" (paper delivered at the Harvard Center for International Affairs, Cambridge, Mass., November 1973).

13. Quoted in Keith Jeffery, "The Eastern Arc of Empire: A Strategic View, 1850–1950," *Journal of Strategic Studies* 5 (December 1982), 534.

cotton piece goods. Britain was prepared to pay the costs because the gain from trade, which would not have existed otherwise, offset the costs and because the navy was Britain's essential means of national security. The others were prepared to let Britain provide international security for commerce because the security was collective, their commercial stakes were vastly smaller than Britain's, and their national security required armies.[14] Britain tolerated openness because it was of little threat to Britain's efficient industries and exports. Britain thus policed a free-trade empire composed of some areas subject to formal and informal imperial control, others subject to hegemony, and still others wherein less substantial influence was exercised.

The quiescence of France lowered the salience of the central European balance, indirectly raising the relative importance and attention given to the oceanic Pax Britannica by Canning and his successors. The success and importance of the pax similarly redounded upon the central European balance. It became, after Louis Philippe's accession to power in France in 1830, a bifurcated system: the east was the reactionary entente, the west (France and Britain) the Liberal Entente.[15] The separation into two distinct camps, according to Palmerston, was a separation "not . . . of words but of things; not the effect of caprice or of will, but produced by the force of occurrences. The three [autocratic powers] and the two think differently, and therefore they act differently."[16]

The two halves avoided conflict until the Crimean War but a contest for leadership took place within each half. Belgian independence from Holland, for example, was treated as a dispute between France and England "external" to the European balance. Spain also found itself in this "external" crossfire. Britain and British influence became identified (with Palmerston's ready encouragement) with one Liberal faction, French prestige attached itself to the other, and, as it was noted at the time, the British and French ambassadors "act as if Spanish politicians had ceased to count as governors of an independent nation."[17]

14. Paul M. Kennedy, *The Rise and Fall of British Naval Mastery* (London, 1976), chaps. 1–3; Mancur Olson, *The Logic of Collective Action* (Cambridge, Mass., 1974), pp. 34-35.

15. Rosecrance, *Action and Reaction*, pp. 81–83.

16. Palmerston's private letter to Melbourne (1836), as excerpted in Kenneth Bourne, *The Foreign Policy of Victorian England, 1830–1902* (Oxford, 1970), p. 228. For a general discussion of the effect of differing domestic regimes see Michael Doyle, "Kant, Liberal Legacies, and Foreign Affairs," pts. 1 and 2, *Philosophy and Public Affairs* 12 (June and October 1983).

17. R. Bullen, "Anglo-French Rivalry and Spanish Politics, 1846–1848," *English Historical Review* 89 (January 1974), 38.

This condition held for several reasons. First, Spanish politics could best be characterized as fractionated. "When a party governs here it governs in toto. The Army belongs to it, the Cortes belong to it, the Court belongs to it, every office small and great is filled by the party."[18] The political balance of power was held by either the court or the army. Their shifts brought in or out the parties that then absorbed the whole political system. Second, as in the rivalry between Athens and Sparta, this political instability was associated with a binary international political subsystem. Due to the exceptional isolation of the western, liberal half of the European central system, only France and Britain were relevant international actors in the Spanish cockpit. As in the Greek world of the Peloponnesian War, this particular combination of fractionated polity and bipolar rivalry in the domestic and international systems was destructive the effective, though not the formal, liberties of national politics. In this case, the queen's marriage was the gauge—there being "French" and "British" candidates for her hand and Spain's future. Luckily for Spain, the 1848 revolution that brought disaster to Louis Philippe provided the international conditions for a more nationalist policy under the strongman prime minister Manuel Narvaez.[19]

The Age of Realpolitik, 1850–1871

The next twenty years were a momentous period for European history. Peoples that had remained divided for a millennium found states, persons scattered through eastern Europe discovered they were a people. A Napoleon returned to save France from the new political mass lurking below the liberal bourgeoisie, and the liberal national revolution (so feared in 1815) began its history as a potentially conservative force.[20] The central European balance was revolutionized, and the ends of politics became more national. While the periphery reflected increased competition, the political revolution in Europe had not yet transformed the periphery, for which nations still competed along lines established in the first half of the century.

The international revolution at the center of Europe was one of visions and goals which disrupted old regimes and inspired the creation of new national states. Technological innovations in this period—iron ships, Gatling guns, quick-fire cannons, "needle guns," and railroad

18. Quoted in ibid., p. 27.
19. Ibid., pp. 37, 42.
20. A. de Tocqueville, *Recollections*, trans. George Lawrence (Garden City, N.Y., 1970), for his discussion of the June Days.

logistics among them—were the midwives of 1870.[21] The 1850s and 1860s were wracked by new ideas wielding old weapons.

New styles of leadership reflected these changes in the ends of politics. Napoleon III and Bismarck competed for the leadership of the age. Both need to be seen in the context of the revolutions of 1848; for, as A. J. P. Taylor remarked, "The success of the revolution discredited conservative ideas; the failure of the revolution discredited liberal ideas."[22] Very few liberal governments emerged, but even the pretense of restoring a "unity of conservative interests" became impossible. Leadership could win nationalism over to the state, breaking what had seemed a permanent marriage to liberalism, and when revolution and nationalism were no longer synonymous, war could be fought on a wave of national feeling that, to everyone's surprise, did not ignite liberal revolution. The tiger of the nation-state did, however, require lavish feeding. Provinces and people could no longer be treated casually as the chips of dynastic politics, they were the children of the nation. Thus as war became more efficient, unleashing the power of the whole people, so peace became more difficult.

Bismarck offered the following explanation of the new spirit of the age:

> Who rules in France or Sardinia is a matter of indifference to me once the government is recognized and only a question of fact, not of right. I stand or fall with my own Sovereign, even if in my opinion he ruins himself stupidly, but for me France will remain France, whether it is governed by Napoleon or St. Louis and Austria is for me a foreign country. . . . I know that you will reply that fact and right cannot be separated, that a properly conceived Prussian policy requires chastity in foreign affairs even from the point of view of utility. I am prepared to discuss the point of utility with you; but if you posit antinomies between right and revolution; Christianity and infidelity; God and the devil; I can argue no longer and can merely say, "I am not of your opinion and you judge in me what is not yours to judge."[23]

The preservation of conservative orthodoxy did not permit the political construction of a united Germany, while the building of Germany on

21. M. S. Anderson, pp. 243–49, and Bernard Brodie, "Technological Change, Strategic Doctrine, and Political Outcomes," in Klaus Knorr, ed., *Historical Dimensions of National Security Problems* (Lawrence, Kans., 1976), pp. 283–92.

22. Quoted in Rosecrance, p. 163.

23. Quoted in H. Kissinger, "Reflections on Bismarck," in D. Rustow, ed., *Philosophers and Kings* (New York, 1970), p. 918.

the basis of nationalism did not require liberal revolution. This two-fold insight was the basis of Bismarck's construction of Germany—a prince had been found who could respond to both Machiavellian methods and the national appeal of the *Prince*'s last chapter.

Louis Bonaparte's program was necessarily antithetical to Bismarck's, for the hegemony of France required the division of Germany where Bismarck's program required its unification, which, given Germany's population and resources, would necessarily establish German dominance of Europe.[24] Napoleon III's policy, however, paraphrased Bismarck's. It too transcended the classes to call upon the nation, or at least the masses. This Napoleon's rise to power was, as Marx realized, a revolution in reverse: beginning with a workers' social rising, it ended in Napoleon's dictatorship to preserve the forces of order. Bonaparte, like Bismarck, relied of necessity on the backing of the class whose particular interests and ideas were synonymous with those of the particular nation-state the ruler sought to create. Bonaparte's lumpenproletariat greeted him with the delightful slogan of "Vive Napoléon, vivent les saucissons!" (Long live Napoleon, long live the sausages [distributed to his followers]!). Napoleon had his army and, behind it, "the most numerous class of French society, the small-holding peasants."[25] In like manner, Bismarck had his junkers. Both, to stay in power, had to balance the forces of order (old aristocratic and now business classes, formerly the revolutionary force) and the emerging demands of the proletariat. The balance and the balancers required general appeals to the nation and the special support of the national class.[26]

The dominant ends of this system were national; they were the necessarily competing nationalisms of France and Prussia-Germany. Napoleon sought a French Europe—a united Italy under French auspices and a disunited Germany under French influence. Bismarck of course sought the unification of Germany and thus the diminution of French power. This change in ends together with the employment of new military technology (by those nationalizing powers which could call upon their peoples) then transformed the units of the European balance. Italy emerged from its medieval patchwork under Cavour and Prussia defeated Denmark, Austria, and France to unify Germany.[27]

24. Anderson, p. 284.

25. K. Marx, *The 18th Brumaire of Louis Napoleon*, in *Selected Works* (New York, 1968), pp. 99, 115, 138, 140, 171.

26. A. J. P. Taylor, *Struggle for the Mastery of Europe* (Oxford, 1954), pp. 101–2.

27. Ibid., pp. 114–24.

These changes in the goals of states had some effects on the peripheries of the European balance. Most substantially, the Napoleonic revival of French élan engendered a dispute with Russia over religious issues in the Ottoman empire. Russia attempted to create the long-awaited conservative alliance of Prussia, Austria-Hungary, and herself against the Liberal Entente of France and Britain (which would be forced to support France merely to avoid a Russian conquest of the Near East, the quickest route to India).[28] Expecting conservative gratitude for support given to Austria in 1849, Russia was disappointed. Austria-Hungary and Prussia remained neutral while France and Britain crushed tsarist armies in the Crimea and imposed a humiliating demilitarization of the Black Sea—"Chinese-style" peace terms for a quasi- European power.[29] For the next twenty years Russia would turn her diplomacy toward Europe, to the Balkans, to rebuild influence and to seek allies (especially Prussia) to overturn the humiliating Peace of Paris. Her military expansion, however, shifted to Central Asia.

Less change took place at sea. British predominance at sea, despite a naval race in new armored gunboats with France, increased as trade and investment overflowed from Britain during the mid-Victorian boom. (Britain's economic predominance can be found reflected in one statistic: up to 1870 Britain produced as much pig iron as the rest of the world combined.)[30] Fleets guarded the free flow of shipping between stations spread across the globe. With the Indian army as a strategic reserve, the British navy maintained a favorable balance of influence at the three crucial "hinges" of world commerce. First, support of Turkey and, later, Egypt, secured the eastern Mediterranean and an overland route to India. Second, patrols of the Malacca Straits protected the route to China. Third, preservation of the "imperial factor" in South Africa from Boer challenges kept the sea route to the eastern empire and eastern markets safe.[31]

One significant new factor in the 1860s and 1870s was the beginning

---

28. Paul Farner, "The Second Empire in France," in J. P. T. Bury, ed., *The New Cambridge Modern History*, vol. 10 (Cambridge, 1960), pp. 462–63.

29. Taylor, pp. 57, 70, 85.

30. Peter Mathias, *First Industrial Nation* (London, 1969), p. 250.

31. The first hinge was the most troubling. It became known as the Eastern Question. The stability of Turkey was vital to securing the isthmus route, yet the Sick Man of Europe was anything but stable and there were no natural, local heirs to the Ottoman empire (Greece and Egypt being themselves unstable) except for Russia, Britain, or France—hence the great-power competition. This question is set forth in Bourne, pp. 112–17.

of competition for markets and influence by other powers. The United States competed with Britain for predominance in Central America in order to control the route to the California gold rush. The rivalry was settled by the Clayton-Bulwar Treaty of 1850, which created a condominium of influence in the area and specified that any Central American canal would be a joint project.[32] In other areas the Pax Britannica ignored the isolated growth of influence and territory of other powers, such as French expansion in Indochina. And elsewhere competition developed for informal control, as had earlier occurred in Spain. In a scramble to collect Mexico's international debts, for example, the French intervened in the 1860s but such challenges were mere fleas on the lion's hide.

British worldwide dominion appeared, on the whole, so natural and so effortless (and was so cheap) that it aroused little concern in England, even on the rare and isolated occasions when it was challenged. Britain alone was worldwide in the scope of its activity, commercial and financial, and in its influence. It continued to provide for Europe the collective good of security for shipping, trade, and finance, even though it was now occasionally aided by France (as in the case of Mexico in 1861) in doing so.[33]

The Predominance of Germany, 1871–1914

The Concert of 1815–48 was a brilliant concoction of multilateral balancing designed to contain both a potentially revolutionary France and her containers. The next twenty years witnessed the crumbling of this delicate dual balance against France and within Germany. The revolution arrived so rapidly and simultaneously that only one reactionary intervention was possible (Russia in Hungary). When France produced another Napoleon, she obtained the aid of England, Austria-Hungary and Prussia in crushing the last truly conservative power remaining—Russia. Lastly, the balance within Germany collapsed as Prussia won control of the center of Europe.

The Europe of 1870, which was to retain its major features until 1914, was a Europe very different from that of 1815. It was almost exactly what the statesmen of 1815 feared Europe might become, though they would have been amazed to discover that many of the changes had been

---

32. D. Humphreys, "The States of Latin America," in *New Cambridge Modern History*, 10:680.

33. Ibid., pp. 676–79.

led by men of their own kind—the aristocratic (now nationalist) leaders of Prussia, England, and Russia.

The central European balance of the 1870–1914 period differed from the continually shifting balance of 1850–70 not so much in the nature of the units, or in the national ends pursued, as in the number and relative power of the competing states. In the 1850s and 1860s there were two nationalist states, Prussia and France, and one globalist liberal regime, Britain. By the middle 1870s there were four coherent national states, Germany, France, England, and Italy, and two huge but unstable states, Russia and Austria, competing for the division and control of eastern Europe.

History and God seemed to be on the side of the big battalions after 1870, and the largest battalions that could be efficiently employed belonged to Germany. Economically, Germany grew considerably faster than her European rivals, and this growth was especially marked on the most advanced and militarily strategic sectors—steel, electricity, and chemicals.[34] In education and science Bismarck's new colossus of middle Europe leapt ahead. What she did not invent she borrowed and used more efficiently than even the original inventors had. These achievements were capped by a state enjoying wide popular support, a closed, independent executive capable of manipulating that support rather than bending to it, and overwhelming military and political prestige.

At the same time Germany was surrounded by more nation-states than had ever existed in Europe. Resources, human and material, were easier to employ than ever before. Never had there been such real political equality; no part of Europe save the Balkans was a potential candidate for intervention or informal dominance as Italy, Spain, Germany, Belgium, and Portugal had been half a century before.

The international economy also emerged in full operation. By 1870 all the major states were on the gold standard; funds moved freely between Europe's financial centers, responding to adjustments in interest rates and investment opportunities. Commodities traded almost as easily.[35] After the Cobden-Chevalier Treaty between Britain and France tariffs were as low as they would be at any time in the century. This was the true age of international free trade, automatically adjusting supply and demand in almost every market.

The international system of this era constituted a nearly ideal multi-

34. Anderson, p. 46, although the French Army was larger in late 1870s; Taylor, chap. 1.

35. K. Polanyi, *The Great Transformation* (Boston, 1944), chaps. 1–2.

polar balance of power. There were at least six major actors (Britain, France, Germany, Austria-Hungary, Russia, and Italy), and each could calculate on the basis of national interest, recognizing no superior authority or principle.[36] Moreover, every state acquired the military means with which to back up its national ambitions. The army increased in size and influence in almost every state. In France the army, once reformed, was seen as the central manifestation of the nation. In Russia and England, Milyutin and Cardwell undertook far-reaching reforms; while in Germany and Italy the army basked in glories of militant national unification.[37] In addition, naval competition and innovation began on a wide scale. The escalating technological race between guns and armor forced increased building programs on the sea-going powers, and at the same time new powers joined naval competition with Britain and France—Italy in the Mediterranean, Germany in the North Sea and Baltic, and Russia, which had reversed the demilitarization of the Black Sea with German aid at the London Conference.

As the market adjusted to supply and demand, so the balance of power should have attained a new equilibrium close to what the abstract theory predicted. This historical system, unlike many international systems, actually corresponded to the assumptions underlying the pure balance. Indeed, as Louis XIV was once contained by the other monarchs of Europe, so the too rapid rise of Germany did lead to both the idea of containment and, up to a point, the actual operation of containing diplomacy. The astute Disraeli remarked in Parliament in February 1871, following the defeat of France: "This war represents the German Revolution, a greater political event than the French Revolution of last century. . . . Not a single principle on the management of our foreign affairs, accepted by all statesmen for guidance up to six months ago, any longer exists. You have a new world, new influences at work. . . . The balance of power has been completely destroyed, and the country which suffers most, and feels the effects of this great change most, is England."[38]

But the most succinct expression of the feelings of the time—the ambivalence of relief at the halting of Napoleon III's adventures and the new fear of Germany—was a diplomat's: "Europe has lost a mistress,

36. Anderson, pp. 250–52.

37. Michael Howard, "The Armed Forces," in F. H. Hinsley, ed., *The New Cambridge Modern History*, vol. 11 (Cambridge, 1962), p. 204.

38. Quoted in W. L. Langer, *European Alliances and Alignments, 1871–1890*, 2d ed. (New York, 1950), pp. 13–14.

and gained a master."[39] Partly as a product of this ambivalence, as well as of Germany's usefulness in containing Russia, Gladstone's Liberal ministry withstood the Conservative attack on its inaction while it explored the possibility of constructing the diplomatic coalition needed to moderate Bismarck.[40]

These fears and potential policies remained in the background as Europe waited to see what the German colossus would do with its new strength. In 1875, however, the War Scare illuminated the landscape of European international politics. In an attempt to isolate France as well as to safeguard his domestic position, Bismarck instituted the Kulturkampf, a campaign designed to reduce the influence of the papacy in Germany and in Europe. (Catholicism was the religion of Germany's separatists—the Poles, the Bavarians, and Alsace-Lorrainers—and its main political support was French diplomacy.) Bismarck's scheme backfired and ignited a diplomatic coalition against Germany.[41]

The Austrians recalled their humiliation at Prussian hands when their religion was also attacked. The Russians reflected on the upstart dominance of Germany and Bismarck, formerly their supplicants. The English began to doubt Bismarck's moderation and instead noticed his power over the European continent. With energetic prodding from the French minister for foreign affairs, Decazes, a joint demarche was staged in Berlin.[42] German power met its limits in cooperative containment by other European powers, and Bismarck was persuaded to back down from his campaign of sword rattling and miter baiting.[43]

The clouds, even if they did part in this Scare of 1875 to reveal the underlying threat of German power and the potential to contain it, were exceptionally dense from 1875 to 1890. The obfuscation of German power and direction was a testimony to the exceptional skill of Bismarck. His brilliant diplomacy orchestrated all the minor aspects, the exceptions and qualifications to rational calculations of national power and security, in order to construct an alliance system that made the underlying basic tensions irrelevant. Working with archaic transnational ideologies in the age of the nation-state, and merely peripheral tensions in an age when Germany had revolutionized the European balance, he turned the in-

39. Ibid., p. 15.
40. Bourne, p. 122.
41. Langer, pp. 36–37; Taylor, pp. 222–28.
42. See especially George F. Kennan, *The Decline of Bismarck's European Order* (Princeton, 1979), Prologue.
43. W. Medlicott, *Bismarck, Gladstone, and the Concert of Europe* (London, 1956), p. 8; Taylor, p. 223.

ternational system inside out. He "colonialized" the diplomatic system, as we shall see later, to render almost irrelevant the central international balance of power.

Before examining the particular diplomatic system that Bismarck created, it is worth asking what one might have expected from a multipolar national balance of power in its relations with the peripheral world. The main peripheral system, the Pax Britannica, as we have seen, evolved from the unipolar collective goods regime of 1815–50 to a version of the same arrangement combined with isolated bipolar confrontation, informal divisions of authority, and marginal formal expansions between 1850 and 1870. A multipolar national period in the center after 1871 was bound to have effects on the periphery.

Europe, now filled with coherent national states, was no longer an arena for a nationalist foreign policy of "general appeals"—the promotion of the prestige of the state through foreign, and cheap, adventures. Each of these states, moreover, acquired the means of exercising distant influence. Armies, marine detachments, and fleets grew for primarily European reasons, to enhance the relative security of the state in Europe, but these means could also be used at more distant locations. Lastly, each of these states experienced a growth of interest in foreign commerce, even if only to acquire the variety of groceries and raw materials that the tropical world could provide.[44]

The larger number of participants in trade resulted in a revolution in the operation of the Pax Britannica. Because of increased competition for peripheral markets within the pax, Britain's dominant trade position was somewhat reduced, narrowing the gap between benefits from the collective good and the total costs of providing the good, which Britain alone had funded. As Britain began to find some incentive to close the hitherto open door, the new and old "consuming" members of the pax—France, Italy, Germany, the United States—had less of an incentive to stay a free rider. They already had to maintain military power for central balance purposes; the prospects of employing that power to enhance foreign trade and offset operating costs by tariff revenues and increased national trade provided an irresistible pressure toward exclusive colonial rule.[45]

44. Graham, pp. 85–86; J. R. S. Hoffmann, *Great Britain and the German Trade Rivalry, 1875–1914* (Philadelphia, 1933), chaps. 1–3; and D. K. Fieldhouse, *Economics and Empire* (Ithaca, 1973), p. 18. Along with this rivalry, however, there was also complementary Anglo-German trade, which the overseas trade rivalry politically overwhelmed. See Paul Kennedy, *The Rise of the Anglo-German Antagonism* (London, 1980), chap. 3.

45. They would also limit Britain's capacity to favor its own products (the pax never having been a pure collective good).

In old areas of the pax, Britain's continuing informal predominance combined with trade superiority was likely to be sufficient to retain the open-door collective goods system. But elsewhere in the periphery no such inertia was at work. Where all states, rather than joining an ongoing British pax and trading emporium, entered as near-equals, who was to pay or be compensated for the costs of security?[46]

There were three possible outcomes. The most natural was for the collective goods system to break down altogether. Each state would employ its own military, already in existence as a sunk cost, and compensate itself for increased operating costs with exclusive trade concessions to its own merchants. A scramble for still unclaimed territory would divide the remaining world.[47] The other courses of action were more cooperative. A conference could distribute the task of providing the collective good: each power's military forces could be used, operational costs being compensated for by small, negotiated, equal tariffs. Each power could receive an equal slice of the territory or market. Alternatively, the powers as a group could commission a special international organization to provide the collective good and pay operating costs with a small tariff or by subscription.[48] The last option clearly demands more cooperation. Given the ignorance about tropical lands, and thus the possibility of an accidentally unequal division of market opportunities, however, it was also the cooperative method more likely to survive the test of experience. The central system of multipolar containment of German preeminence might produce the extra incentives needed for general cooperation among the other European powers engaged on the periphery.

Just such an effort was in fact made. The personal motives of the king of the Belgians do not appear to have been noticeably internationalistic (or humanitarian).[49] But Leopold's International Association of the Congo was initially accepted by the French, British, Germans, Americans, and Belgians as an organization for the provision in the Congo Basin of such international collective goods as security of trade, exploration, and the suppression of the slave trade. This effort came, however, at the end of the containment of Germany. Leopold formally established his organization in 1876, but following the War Scare of the previous year

46. J. Flint, "Britain and the Partition of West Africa," in Flint, ed., *Perspectives on Empire* (London, 1973).

47. E. Staley, *War and the Private Investor* (Garden City, N.Y., 1935), pp. 45–49.

48. This is the colonial regime J. A. Hobson recommended in the concluding section of *Imperialism: A Study* (1902; Ann Arbor, 1965). See my Chapter 7 above.

49. Neal Ascherson, *The King Incorporated* (London, 1963).

Bismarck had accelerated his colonialization of the diplomatic system, making a cooperative collective goods solution among Germany's
"containers" quite unlikely. The Congo association was the swan song
of the collective goods approach. Instead, the empires of the late nineteenth century were shaped by quite a different diplomatic system—
Bismarck's management of the international system.[50]

The Colonialization of the Diplomatic
System, 1879–1890

A diplomatic system operates (in ideal-typical terms) within the realm
of necessity, reflecting the underlying relationships of force and tension
between major states. A range of freedom can also exist in which the
course of events can be affected. The task of diplomacy consists in
recognizing the operation of overwhelming and long-term necessity
while attempting to exploit the range of freedom.

Few diplomats have been more effective than Bismarck was between
1879 and 1890.[51] His achievement lay in exploiting the non-national,
nonfoundational aspects of the international system for his diplomatic
constellations. He dredged up the Conservative Entente, which he himself had rejected in order to found Germany, and made of it an ideological
entente against both the political new socialism that the tzars feared and
the ethnic old nationalism that threatened Austria. On this shaky foundation he combined Austria and Russia (despite their desperate rivalry
in the Balkans) with Prussia (despite Austrian and Russian resentment
of German dominance) into the Three Emperors' League, removing
France's natural allies to the east. The league was tentatively instituted
in 1872, but the strain of the 1875 War Scare and then an outburst of
actual war in the Balkans led to its collapse. Bismarck reestablished it
slowly, first with Austria in 1879 and then in a full revival, the Three
Emperors' Alliance, in 1881.[52]

Bismarck realized that these arrangements rested on an appeasement
of France, impossible as long as Alsace-Lorraine was German.[53] France

---

50. J. Stengers, "The Congo Free State and the Belgian Congo before 1914," in *La
Nouvelle Clio* 2 (1950); L. H. Gann and P. Duignan, eds., *Colonialism in Africa*, vol. 1
(London, 1969), chap. 8.

51. H. Kissinger, *A World Restored* (New York, 1964), Conclusion.

52. See Medlicott, chap. 9; Kennan, pp. 72–78; and, for a more general discussion of
the management function of alliances, Paul Schroeder, "Alliances, 1815–1945: Weapons
of Power and Tools of Management," in Klaus Knorr, ed., *Historical Dimensions of
National Security Problems* (Lawrence, Kans., 1976).

53. Taylor, pp. 259–65.

was therefore to be compensated with colonies and overseas adventures, and in the Mediterranean and elsewhere French expansion was to be encouraged and diplomatically supported. Bismarck assured France: "I want to turn your eyes away from Metz and Strasbourg by helping you to find satisfaction elsewhere." As France's republicanism would keep Russia away from an alliance, so colonial expansion would help keep France isolated from western allies.[54] Colonial competition alienated England, once the sole mistress of the seas, and Italy, a Mediterranean rival for Tunis.[55] Italy gravitated toward German leadership and the Triple Alliance, with Austria, despite its serious border disputes with the Austrians. England was kept thoroughly isolated, a condition that Gladstone created, when he stumbled into Egypt and thereby trampled on French sensibilities, and that Bismarck exploited. Quarrels with liberal England were also useful in isolating and managing his domestic enemies, who were identified with the English style of politics and with the crown prince, married to Queen Victoria's daughter.[56]

When complete, this alliance system isolated France and England while combining—albeit with considerable stress—all the remaining major powers of Europe under Bismarck's leadership. Cooperation with France other than under Bismarck's direction became nearly impossible and

54. A. J. P. Taylor further argues that it was necessary to alienate England in order to convince France of German support; and to effect this alienation, Bismarck began his colonial acquisitions in the early 1880s, hoping that a colonial quarrel with England would establish German credibility in France.

55. Taylor, p. 273; A. J. P. Taylor, *Germany's Bid for Colonies, 1884–1885* (New York, 1970), pp. 31, 35; and Langer, pp. 54–55. Although F. H. Hinsley states that "European rivalries and anxieties, restrained within the Continent, were projected on to the wider canvas of the outside and undeveloped world" (p. 99), he provides a telling argument that, rather than a straightforward projection, these rivalries were refracted through the diplomatic lens that Bismarck provided. Bismarck sought to contain France, encouraged its strife with Britain over Britain's occupation of Egypt, and stimulated occasions for German conflict with England during 1884–85 in order to reassure France of its bona fides as an ally (pp. 118–19). At the same time, Hinsley adds an interesting facet: Bismarck probably preferred an alliance with England designed to contain France directly, but, despite Bismarck's support for Britain in 1882 against France in the occupation of Egypt, Gladstone fumbled Bismarck's preferred alliance (p. 119). See Hinsley, "International Rivalry in the Colonial Sphere: 1869–1885," in E. A. Benians, J. Butler, and C. E. Carrington, eds., *The Cambridge History of the British Empire* (London, 1959).

56. According to Bismarck, "When we started Colonial Policy, we had to face a long reign by the Crown Prince, during which English influence [liberal and anti-Bismarck and Prussia] would predominate. In order to forestall this, we had to launch colonial policy, which is popular and can produce conflicts with England at any moment." Quoted in Taylor, *Struggle*, p. 284.

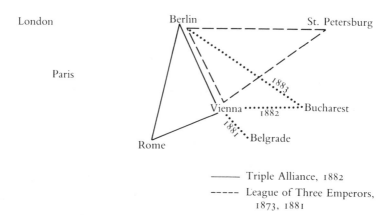

———— Triple Alliance, 1882
----- League of Three Emperors,
       1873, 1881

FIGURE 4 Bismarck's diplomatic constellation, 1879–90

(testimony to Bismarck's success) undesirable. Only Gladstone attempted a thoroughgoing diplomatic challenge.

Just as Bismarck built a coalition on issues of secondary ideology and peripheral competition, so Gladstone attempted to revive a liberal entente of *all* the great powers—a liberal Concert of Europe.[57] He hoped to produce, by multilateral methods and liberal principles, common solutions to problems such as the Balkans and colonial rivalry.[58] It was a league of nations thirty years before World War I made such an organization possible. Of necessity, it was anathema to Austria-Hungary for its adoption of liberal national rights; dangerous to Germany for its multilateralism, which would mean German containment and the threat of a French-engineered coalition; and suspicious to Russia for its radicalism and British sponsorship.[59]

Bismarck easily won the competition. In the ensuing years he did all in his power to retain the confidence of the eastern courts by moderating the hostility between Russia and Austria. He supported Russia in the east and Austria in the Balkans when doing so would not drive Russia to extreme measures. At the Congress of Berlin in 1878 he was the brilliant, "honest broker" of these various claims and interests. In the west he fostered French colonial ambitions in order to prevent a French entente with Britain. When French demands became too strong, how-

57. Langer, p. 247, and chaps. 6 and 7; Medlicott, chap. 2.
58. See especially the excerpts from Gladstone's third Midlothian campaign speech, 27 November 1879, in Bourne, pp. 420–21.
59. Medlicott, pp. 29–30.

ever, Britain applied colonial pressure on France and thus kept France aware of her diplomatic dependence on Germany. This was the theme of both German pressure on England's occupation of Egypt (through the German voting power on the Caisse) and the calling of the Berlin West Africa Conference (1884–85). The conference attempted to impose an international law, by defining the rules of expansion, on the hitherto fluid and indefinable Pax Britannica.[60]

The effect of this diplomatic constellation on the peripheries of the international system can be readily inferred. Most simply, it removed whatever European-centered incentive might have existed toward co-operation, either with a continuing Pax Britannica or with a renewed concert system. The predictable effects of a multipolar, noncollective competition on the periphery not only took their course, they were encouraged by Bismarck's policy of providing colonial compensations for France.

The result was a series of preemptive, formal annexations that, when complete, left little of the world unclaimed. Many factors contributed to this result. An increasing number of states with expanding trade now competed with the old Pax Britannica; this increase in numbers en-couraged a "gold rush." These new competitors were also armed with the means of exercising influence at a distance. Colonial tariff revenues from newly acquired areas were an attractive way to offset the operating costs of military forces that already existed for European reasons. In-creased commercial competition from newly efficient industrial powers lowered the margin between Britain's revenues in a free trade market and the costs of providing open-door security. One consequence was pressure on Britain to acquire for itself more exclusive advantages, such as the special arrangements that the Royal Niger Company would enjoy in revenue and trade control, which in turn increased the incentive of other powers to obtain exclusive advantages. Finally, no other power but Britain was so preeminent as to find it to its own advantage to maintain the open door.[61] If revenues are raised on all nations (fees) to support the mail lines of one nation (Britain), an indirect subsidy ad-vantages the one nation's shipping. Similarly, if all nations are taxed to

60. Robinson and Gallagher, p. 82.
61. Fieldhouse, p. 18, contains trade figures. On 19 May 1884 Lord Derby made this comment on the British pax: "While we have not formally claimed the bay [Angra-Pequera] we have claimed the right to exclude Foreign Powers on the general grounds of its nearness to our Settlement [in South Africa] and the absence of any other claims." Quoted in Taylor, *Germany's First Bid*, p. 37.

provide collective law and order in the periphery, the result benefits the national suppliers of the colonial government. Under the new colonial competition these benefits became important, and each nation now sought the benefits of colonial government which had once been considered a burden.

In general and theoretical terms this is what one should expect under multipolar competition. Multipolar competition was not, however, its historical source. Multipolar competition in the central international system (the strategically important system) should have led to incentives for cooperation in containing Germany, incentives that would have spilled over into cooperation in colonial expansion. Bismarck's genius lay in preserving Germany from this containment. He encouraged colonial competition in the periphery, opening the periphery up to the multipolar competitive dynamics that he had shunted aside from the containment of Germany in Europe.

A Scramble resulted. In West Africa, French projects for tapping the wealth of the Sudanese interior had long seemed to require military conquest to solve problems posed by the political instability of the Islamic states of the region. The actual timing of the Scramble, however, reflected impatience on the part of temporary holders of office in Paris. On the west coast of Africa political action became necessary as the long-term fiscal and judicial problems of small trading posts were intensified after 1880 by growing international competition and mutual fears among interested powers of exclusive protectorate and tariff treaties. In the Congo region Leopold's plans for a highly informal commercial enterprise led to formal territorial division—the French assumed that Leopold's treaty making would give him exclusive political and economic control, they staked defensive counterclaims, and other powers reacted in turn to French moves. In South-West Africa in 1884 Bismarck decided to protect Luderitz's concession, partly because he could not extract a clear British assurance of political security for this private economic venture. In East Africa Bismarck similarly supported Karl Peters's enterprise, while the British came to regard access to the lakes of the interior as a major British national interest, essential to protecting the headwaters of the Nile and thus Egypt. In south–central Africa a desire to satisfy Cape Colony imperialists, themselves primarily concerned with economic profit, constituted an essentially political motive for establishing a British sphere of interest and later protectorates.[62]

---

62. This argument is not the same as Fieldhouse's, but his description lends support

These acquisitions were overwhelmingly formal annexations, to the prevalence of which the interstate competition of the Bismarckian constellation contributed. Informal control was insufficient to impose the taxes and tariffs that would recoup operating expenses. No peripheral regime could be expected to tax its own commerce for foreigners' exclusive benefit and discriminate against other (consequently irate) foreigners without itself being under the sort of thorough foreign control that could be exercised immediately, on the spot, with colonial troops and directed by a colonial governor. Moreover, no system of informal rule could have survived the opportunities and freedoms of multipolar competition—any informally controlled regime would seek to ally itself with the next passing foreigner offering marginally better terms. Unlike the situation in a unipolar relationship where no such extra foreigner is available, or in a bipolar relationship where the one such foreigner can be equally demanding and, moreover, will probably be associated with a domestic revolutionary faction, in a multipolar balance that extra foreigner will always be just over the horizon.[63] So formal rule, which removes the technical possibility of diplomatic balancing by the peripheral regime, is necessary in a multipolar competition, and the mutual recognition of colonies reduces tensions among the major powers. Formal rule from these motives is very much an intra-European device, and it is illustrated by the rules instituted at the Berlin West Africa Conference defining the small differences, with respect to the ruled populations, between protectorates, colonies, and effective occupation.

After Bismarck "the pilot" was dropped in 1890, his brilliant and tension-ridden structure began to break apart into its more "natural" components. France discovered the strategic value of a Russian second-front threat to Germany, and Russia awoke to the harmlessness of international republicanism. Their relationship was cemented by substantial loans.[64]

But so successful had the colonialization of the diplomatic system been that France and Russia became more hostile to Britain in colonial conflicts. These colonial disputes preserved German predominance for

---

to this thesis as well (Fieldhouse, pp. 468–69). For a very interesting argument along these lines, see George N. Sanderson, "The European Partition of Africa: Coincidence or Conjuncture?" in E. F. Penrose, ed., *European Imperialism and the Partition of Africa* (London, 1975), pp. 1–54.

63. Chapter 3 above discusses the dynamics of bipolar competition in the periphery, particularly with reference to the competition between Athens and Sparta.

64. William Langer, *The Diplomacy of Imperialism*, vol. 1 (New York, 1935), chaps. 1–2.

another fourteen years, until they could be brushed aside and the Triple Entente formed. Austria, so weak relative to its cohesive neighbor to the north, was preserved. By now, however, the Triple Alliance of Austria, Italy, and Germany was caught in the maelstrom of the dissolution of the Ottoman and Austro-Hungarian empires. It proved more a source of extra tension and weakness than the linchpin of strength that Bismarck had designed.[65]

International Systemic Theory

In the 1840s the Dominican Republic attempted to give itself to Britain, France, Spain, and the United States. All refused the burden of formal rule. Later Sarawak under the aegis of the Brookes—British subjects who had through local influence become the rajahs of the area—tried to give their public estate to Britain. They were also refused. Germany refused Togo in 1874, and as late as 1876 the Colonial Office of Great Britain declined the acquisition of a large part of the Congo basin for which Lieutenant Cameron had obtained treaties of cession from African chiefs.[66] During the Scramble from 1881 to 1885 and later, however, metropolitan responses were quite different. Next to nothing was refused, and explorers were sent out at public expense to amass as many treaties as possible, even in areas such as New Guinea (hotly contested between Britain and Germany) where there had previously been little interest or transnational contact.[67]

The international political system provides some reasons for this change in behavior—not the only reasons, but some important ones. Nineteenth-century international systems evolved as an interaction between the center and an external periphery. At first the center was multilateral, multipolar, and "concerted," with conservative and liberal wings. The main periphery, the Pax Britannica, was unipolar. In the middle period the center was anarchic and increasingly national while the Pax Britannica was challenged but still basically unipolar. The last period witnessed multipolar national competition at the center, which was molded into the Bismarckian constellation, and multipolar competition across the seas.

---

65. Ibid.

66. S. Welles, *Naboth's Vineyard* (New York, 1928); N. Tarling, *Britain, the Brookes, and Brunei* (New York, 1971), pp. 127–45; and R. Rotberg, ed., *Africa and Its Explorers* (Cambridge, Mass., 1970), p. 271.

67. Robinson and Gallagher, chap. 4.

In the ancient Greek example, bipolar systems tended toward informal preemption. Now, as a complement to that tendency, we find that multipolar, nationally oriented systems that are extensive enough to contact a peripheral area in multipolar competition encourage formal preemption. This multipolar concentration accounts for the formality of imperial rule, the wide scope of its European participants, the perceived need to preempt resulting in acceleration, and the markedly non-rational quality of the Scramble—the staking out of unknown claims to which national prestige became attached. But this interpretation also has its limitations, even when it is combined with the (also powerful) pericentric interpretation.

First, multipolar competition need not logically result in formal preemption. The logic of the central balance can offset the logic of the peripheral competition. In the late nineteenth century, for example, a strict application of multipolar balancing, calculated according to national security, should have led to European containment of Germany. Containment in turn might have produced incentives for neglect or cooperation and hence slower division of the periphery. Instead, Bismarck allowed the multipolar logic to have full sway in the periphery in order to avoid containment at the center. He thereby encouraged two key characteristics of the imperial scramble—the acceleration of preemptive and preventive acquisitions, and the shift from informal to formal methods of rule.

Second, systemic concerns with security were expressed in the cases of expansion along the Niger and the Nile. French competition, primarily conceived of in commercial terms, affected Britain's decision to support Goldie, and the securing of the route to India shaped much of British strategy toward the Egyptian question.[68] Nonetheless, the security factor in neither case was clear. Britain had decided to withdraw from West Africa in 1865, presumably after assessing net interest in the region, yet did not. Despite perceived French and German threats, it took Goldie three years to persuade London to grant him a charter. Even in Egypt the canal's standing in Britain's security calculations was ambiguous. As Prime Minister Gladstone explained:

Suppose the very worst. The Canal is stopped [by the Russians]. And what then? A heavy blow will have been inflicted on the com-

---

68. Hinsley, p. 120. Chamberlain commented to Dilke: "I don't care about New Guinea and I am not afraid of German colonisation, but I don't like to be cheeked by Bismarck or anyone else." Quoted in J. L. Garvin, *Life of Joseph Chamberlain*, vol. 1 (London, 1935).

merce of the world. We, as the great carriers, and as the first commercial nation of Christendom, shall be the great losers. But it is a
question of loss and loss only. . . . What came and went quickly and
cheaply must come and go slow and dearer. . . . I turn then to the
military question and ask how much will Russia have gained? The
answer is, that she will have introduced an average delay of about
three weeks into our military communications with Bombay and
less with Calcutta. It seems to be forgotten by many, that there is a
route to India around the Cape of Good Hope, as completely as if
that route lay by the Northwest Passage. [Three weeks] will hardly
make the difference to us between life and death in the maintenance
of our Indian Empire.[69]

Security surrenders to conflicting interpretations. The decision to send
an expedition to Egypt split the Liberal Cabinet, and the majority in
favor was formed over Gladstone's objection. In the Cabinet's justification of the invasion before Parliament, Sir Charles Dilke put the same
stress on British trade as he did on strategic interests. Gladstone presented
the intervention as a means of restoring law and order and promoting
liberal progress.[70] Bondholders' committees and shipping associations
were active in mobilizing support. To see these events as driven simply
by security is to miss other motives that made odd allies out of adherents
to different security policies.

While systemic security accounts for much of the Scramble, it illuminates little of either the slow accretion before the late 1870s or the
continuance of empire, which survived no matter what the specifics of
the international system or diplomatic strategy. Empires also expanded
in regions practically devoid of metropolitan competition: the French
into Senegal, the Russians into Central Asia, and the British over the
Niger Delta before the 1870s. Moreover, not all European nations became imperial metropoles—we need to account both for the ones that
did and the ones that, as did Spain, lost their remaining imperial possessions. Imperial expansion was not vital to the national security of the
European metropoles (though some of the politicians in the metropoles
thought it was). To account for the expansion, we need also to examine
the particular and idiosyncratic interests that shape policy in the realm
of imperial choice. Such explanations must be pursued in circumstances
internal and transnational to the metropoles.

69. W. E. Gladstone, writing in *The Nineteenth Century* 2 (1877), 155–56, as quoted
in Chamberlain, p. 109.
70. Robinson and Gallagher, pp. 116–18.

CHAPTER 11

Greater Britain

In Part I we examined the structural conditions of empire. Social differentiation, political community, and state centralization together tend to produce political unity. Joined to a transnational economy, they lead to empire over tribal and patrimonial (and certain other) societies in the periphery.

In Part II we examine the process of imperialism, paying less attention to parameters and more to goals, interests, perceptions, and the actual play of historical events. In the discussion of tribal and patrimonial peripheries, I combined considerations of transnational impact and metropolitan force with those of peripheral society. I now examine the other half of the imperial relationship—the combination of transnational drives and metropolitan strategy with metropolitan politics. I investigate economic imperialism and strategic imperialism, and how both were registered and managed by metropolitan politics.

Britain's transnational economy, I show in this chapter, focused on and sustained the empire. The imperial economy also contributed motives, or drives, toward the maintenance and expansion of empire. But while the empire required the transnational economy and a metropole prepared to defend it, the economy did not require, in a strict or straightforward sense, the empire. Instead, the separate sectoral interests and actors whose interaction comprises an economy helped feed political coalitions. Nor was Britain's imperial strategy a straightforward driving force of imperialism. It too was various and subject to factional dispute. A predominant imperial coalition, conservative and imperially expansive, resulted only from the political construction of Disraeli and Salisbury. They combined groups sensitive to recent changes in the state of domestic politics, the condition of the empire (particularly Ireland), and the competitive position of Britain in the world economy and in international diplomacy with the traditional followers of the Conservative party. The Liberals, on the other hand, were not anti-imperial, but nor were they committed to the autonomous growth of empire.

Britain could have survived a loss of empire or a failure to expand, but almost any political coalition would have at least accepted expansion. The empire that Britain actually acquired reflected in part the imperial coalition that acquired it. In particular, the Conservatives needed the expansion of empire in order to dominate British politics for the last quarter of the nineteenth century.

The Transnational Economy

Early in the nineteenth century Britain became the first large, truly transnational economy, exporting manufactures and services to pay for its imports of food and raw materials. Having experienced the industrial revolution early, Britain "exported" industrialism to Europe and later to North America. This export was achieved not only through the transmission of technology and knowledge but also through the shipment of typical industrial goods, the sale of capital goods needed for production, portfolio investment, financial services, emigration, and actual overseas operation by a few English firms.

Most of the world's economic activity was domestic or national. Housing construction and services dominated investment and employment respectively (domestic service was the largest category of employment in Britain in 1850). But it was clear at the time as it is clear now that the specialization which free trade encouraged created an exchange based upon an *international* division of labor, an international economy of epic proportions. This international economy was remarkably stable—Britain produced finished manufactures and other regions sold raw materials and food to Britain. Britain's international economy began to focus increasingly on the empire, making for an *imperial* economy. In some respects these economies were separate; in others they were very much integrated.[1]

The significance of these national, international, and especially imperial economies for nineteenth-century imperial expansion has long been debated. Hobson argued (with a rigor he did not apply to investments or finance) that exports and imports provided no excuse for imperial expansion in the tropics. The "taproot," he suggested, was finance. In positions that have now become conventional benchmarks in the debate on imperialism, Lenin adapted aspects of Hobson's theory and focused the blame on monopolies. Schumpeter responded by absolving pure capitalism altogether and instead discovered the *causa causans* of international aggression in atavistic instincts and state institutions. Contemporary critics of Hobson's and Lenin's theories of economic imperialism, David Fieldhouse prominent among them, have relied upon aggregate statistics of 1904 or 1913 to demonstrate that British trade or investment was not heavily committed to the newly acquired colonial areas of Africa or Asia. This debate has been taken up in a thorough criticism of economic imperialism by B. J. Cohen, who holds that in aggregate terms no massive shift to new tropical trade or investment required an extension of the "flag."[2] More recent work has, however, revived in a careful fashion various of the arguments that were central to Lenin's thesis, and one recent essay has presented a powerful argument for a sophisticated model of British imperial expansion whose basic thrust is economic imperialism.[3]

Economic imperialism will be a major theme of the next three chapters as we explore the metropolitan roots of nineteenth-century imperialism. In this chapter I show that economic factors were a major part of the process of British expansion (though in the next I show that they were much less significant as a source of French and German imperialism). While economic factors, specifically an imperial economy, were important in British imperialism, however, a straightforward economistic

1. For a general discussion of these issues see E. Hobsbawm, *Industry and Empire* (New York, 1968), chap. 7; Alfred E. Kahn, *Great Britain in the World Economy* (New York, 1946); and Brinley Thomas, *Migration and Economic Growth* (Cambridge, 1973).

2. B. J. Cohen, *The Question of Imperialism* (New York, 1974), pp. 39–40; D. K. Fieldhouse, "Imperialism: An Historiographic Revision," *Economic History Review*, 2d ser., 14 (December 1961), 187–209.

3. See Albert Szymanski, *The Logic of Imperialism* (New York, 1981), pp. 119–21, for an argument on the dependence of imperialism on the phases of monopoly capitalism; P. J. Cain and A. G. Hopkins, "The Political Economy of British Expansion Overseas, 1750–1914," *Economic History Review*, 2d ser., 32 (November 1980), 463–90.

model of British imperialism does not serve to explain the metropolitan roots of empire. Important are some political and international factors that cannot be construed as dependent on economic drives and structures.[4]

Even if we argue that the economy did not require the new tropical territories, we still must specify the role that the economy played in empires both old and new. In order to interpret the role played by Britain's transnational economy in Britain's imperial expansion during the nineteenth century, we need to interpret economic evolution forward from 1815, rather than backward from 1913. Short-term fluctuations and perceptions as well as long-term trends in trade, investment, and finance need to be taken into account if we are going to assess the role that an extended economy played in imperial expansion.[5]

International and Imperial Trade

Britain's transnational trading economy expanded massively following the repeal of the Corn Laws and the Navigation Acts in 1846 and 1849. The rate of growth of world trade rose 80 percent in the 1850s. British exports grew 25 percent per decade before 1850 and 90 percent and 60 percent in the 1850s and 1860s.[6] The "bread and butter" sectors of this new economy were first cotton and then iron and steel (both consumed at home and exported). The free trade policy of the 1840s opened Britain to cheap food and increased dependence on foreign sources of raw material, particularly cotton from the United States, despite attempts to foster imperial sources in India and even Africa. In the 1870s a lasting and fundamental depression set in. Despite a short-lived export boom in the late 1880s, full recovery awaited the end of the century.[7]

4. Cain and Hopkins, "Political Economy," declare an allegiance to an eclectic approach, and they cite as models for their analysis "statist" theories; but their own methods of analysis appear to focus on a clearly argued and extensively supported presentation of an overwhelmingly economic argument. Another important economic theory of imperialism focusing on the demand for foreign resources in the process of economic growth is Nazli Choucri and Robert C. North, *Nations in Conflict* (San Francisco, 1975), and the earlier work by the same authors, "Dynamics of International Conflict: Some Policy Implications of Population, Resources, and Technology," in R. Tanter and R. H. Ullman, eds., *Theory and Policy in International Relations* (Princeton, 1972).

5. Kahn, chap. 3.

6. W. Rostow, *The British Economy in the Nineteenth Century* (London, 1948), chaps. 1–2.

7. The effects of the depression varied quite significantly from industry to industry. See S. B. Saul, *The Myth of the Great Depression, 1873–1896* (London, 1972); Saul, *Studies in British Overseas Trade* (Liverpool, 1960), pp. 100–113; and A. G. Ford, "Overseas Lending and Internal Fluctuations, 1890–1914," in A. R. Hall, ed., *The Export of Capital from Britain, 1870–1914* (London, 1968).

Whether in boom or depression, Britain's transnational economy had become internationalized, acquiring a surprisingly stable pattern of cotton and iron exports in return for raw materials, as Eric Hobsbawm notes:

> By the end of the eighteenth century domestic exports amounted to about thirteen percent of the national income, by the early 1870s to about twenty-two percent and thereafter they averaged between sixteen and twenty percent except in the period between the 1929 slump and the early 1950s. Until the "Great Depression" of the nineteenth century, exports normally grew faster than the real national income as a whole. In the major industries the foreign market played an even more decisive role. This is most obvious in cotton, which exported over half the total value of its output at the beginning of the nineteenth century and almost four-fifths at the end, and iron and steel, which relied on overseas markets for about forty percent of its gross production from the mid-nineteenth century.[8]

The importance of this pattern can be surmised easily: textiles and metals (including machinery) constituted over 50 percent of employment in the late nineteenth century.[9] Both sectors were the early products of the industrial revolution. The textile industry was the leader, the foundation of the eighteenth-century takeoff. Metals and machinery began in the first phase (1780–1840), creating the iron needed for early machines, and boomed in the second phase (1840–90).[10] The last two-thirds of the century truly appeared to be the age of textiles and metal—the full maturity of Britain's industrial strength lasting long, and as we shall see perhaps too long, golden years. The new industries that were to form the basis of twentieth-century industrialism (third phase, 1890–1940) and replace the "paleo-technology of coal, steam, and iron and steel," such as the "technology of physics and chemistry, scientific industrial research, electricity and petroleum, the dynamo and the internal combustion engine," were developing after 1870, but in Britain, unlike in Germany and the United States, they did not recast the economy.[11]

8. Hobsbawm, pp. 111–12.

9. Phyllis Deane and W. A. Cole, *British Economic Growth, 1688–1959* (Cambridge, 1962), p. 146; R. D. Wolff, *The Economics of Colonialism* (New Haven, 1974), p. 5.

10. Hobsbawm, chap. 6.

11. Kahn, p. 72. See also W. A. Lewis, *Growth and Fluctuations, 1870–1913* (London, 1978), pp. 128–34. Michael Beenstock, *The World Economy in Transition* (London, 1983), makes a similar argument, drawing parallels between the international crisis of the depression of the late nineteenth century and the global stagflation of the 1970s.

In the meantime other industrial states were acquiring the technology of the first industrial revolution. British commercial policy and private activities had aided the development of other industrial countries in the 1840s through the 1860s. In the late seventies and the early eighties, however, Germany, France, the United States, and others began to increase their productive efficiency and raise their domestic and imperial tariffs.[12]

Britain could no longer rely on the great industrial markets for staple exports. At the same time the underdeveloped and unprotected world—particularly the empire—increased in importance for British commercial activity. Latin America is instructive: in Mexico, Britain began to lose market share not only to the nearby United States but also to Germany. But high-quality manufactures of the sort also produced for the British and dominion markets sustained little injury in the far south of Latin America. In general terms lower-quality, though efficiently produced, goods threatened by tariffs (e.g., cotton), specialized goods, and such new products as electrical goods constituted the largest sectors of foreign competition for British exports.[13]

A stable production profile was accompanied by a shift in the geographic distribution of Britain's trade. The reasons can be found where the sector cycle and the imperial economy intersect.

Cotton goods are easy to sell, worn everywhere, and require little sophistication in their production. They are the first sector that an underdeveloped economy would purchase from abroad, and thus the first products that an industrial economy would be able to sell in volume.[14] However, cotton and other textiles, given simple production and ready market, are one of the first industries that a developing economy would establish and protect. While 73 percent of British cotton exports went to Europe and the United States in 1820, only 43 percent went to those areas in 1850.[15]

In order to pay for consumption goods such as textiles, the developing

12. Derek Aldcroft, ed., *The Development of British Industry and Foreign Competition* (London, 1968) editor's Introduction.

13. D. C. M. Platt, *Latin America and British Trade, 1806–1914* (New York, 1973), chap. 7.

14. R. Vernon, "International Investment and International Trade in the Product Cycle," *Quarterly Journal of Economics* 80 (May 1966), 199.

15. This result was primarily a product of infant-industry protection in these two countries. See F. Crouzet, "Toward an Export Economy," and J. Potter, "The Atlantic Economy," in L. S. Pressnell, ed., *Studies in the Industrial Revolution Presented to T. S. Ashton* (London, 1960).

economy will usually export bulky agricultural and mineral raw materials (both simple and profitable at a low level of technological development). In the nineteenth century this pattern often required railroads where water transport was lacking, which meant exports of iron and steel rails for Britain.[16]

If the developing economy shifts to industrial production, for instance of textiles, the next phase will witness the export of British machines to set up new factories. A three-way trade emerged. Britain's capital-intensive investment goods (machines) went to developing areas, and both capital and labor-intensive textiles went to underdeveloped areas. The first returned land-capital products such as grain and the second, labor-land products such as tropical groceries, cotton, and other raw materials.

This system of interchange could have worked well in a static world, but in the dynamic international economy of the mid-nineteenth century problems arose. Industrial progress in the developing world threatened Britain's textile industries and, a short time later, machinery industries. These two sectors, however, both heavily dependent on export sales, represented over 50 percent of British manufacturing employment in the late nineteenth century.

The free market policy response would have Britain developing new technologies of capital-rich goods to export to developed economies. These new industries could be stimulated by tariffs, subsidies, or devaluation. But there were substantial internal barriers (liberal doctrines and political coalitions benefiting from the old product mix) and international obstacles (retaliation) to those instruments of change. Moreover, the new technologies of chemicals, electrical goods, and assembly-line production were already being established in the current "developing" countries (Germany and the United States), countries that possessed the advantage of a large, continental, internal market that Britain lacked. In the old free-trading, international economic context, moreover, Britain's old staples in textiles and metals *were* profitable and would long continue to be.[17]

Another answer lay in an imperial economy founded upon an imperial policy. In the long term overall trade did increase in the empire, in part

---

16. K. E. Hansson, "A General Theory of the System of Multilateral Trade," *American Economic Review* 42 (March 1952), 59–68; M. Barratt-Brown, *After Imperialism*, rev. ed. (London, 1970), pp. 81–83; and S. G. Checkland, *The Rise of Industrial Society in England, 1815–1885* (London, 1964), pp. 56–59.

17. Lewis, pp. 131–34.

because the empire with its undeveloped tropical economies and developing agricultural dominions offered "natural" partners for the British economy. However, special imperial links were also at work. The Pax Britannica kept all undeveloped portions of the globe open to British commerce in textiles. Other colonialisms closed their undeveloped colonies with tariffs, resulting in an increased concentration by British manufacturers on the British empire—undeveloped regions whose markets were open on a free-trade basis. The British empire had in fact expanded in the tropics through preemptive annexation, in part to avoid such a closing of the undeveloped markets of Africa and Asia. The importance to the metropole of these markets now becomes somewhat clearer—they were the "Indies" for textiles, maybe even the "Americas" for investment goods of the future.

With the exception of the self-governing dominions, moreover, their markets could not be closed to British industry. When the British government in India attempted to impose a small revenue tariff in 1853–54 and again as late as 1890, the British textile industry ensured that an equivalent excise tax was imposed on the fledgling Indian manufacture of textiles.[18] Without infant industry tariffs, indigenous textile development would be restrained by British efficiency and cheap transport. (Every state that followed Britain in developing an *industrial* economy in the nineteenth century did so behind tariff walls). Preventing tariffs prevented industrial development, saving Britain's textile industry. The empire as a whole absorbed increasing proportions of these goods and India, caught between development and undevelopment, played a crucial role as market for both textiles and steel (for railroads). Indeed, Britain was the third-ranking steel trader (behind Germany and Belgium) in Europe, third in Latin America, second (behind the United States) in the Far East and Canada (a highly independent dominion). But it was first in both India and the new empire (three times and five times larger than the nearest competitor, respectively).[19]

The empire also became increasingly important for its role in meeting the balance of payments—a crucial concern for an economy dependent for its existence on the importation of food and raw materials.[20] India

18. J. Rose et al., eds., *The Cambridge History of the British Empire*, vol. 2 (Cambridge, 1940), pp. 394, 753–54; R. Moore, "Imperialism and Free Trade Policy in India, 1853–1854," *Economic History Review*, 2d ser., 17 (August 1964), 135–45; and Hobsbawm, p. 125.

19. P. L. Payne, "Iron and Steel Manufactures," in Aldcroft, p. 85.

20. Saul, *Studies*, pp. 107–9; Wolff, p. 24.

TABLE 6.
Empire share of major British exports (in percentages)

Manufacture	1870	1880	1890	1900	1913
Cotton goods	34.7	44.1	47.4	45.8	51.7
Woolen goods	14.0	25.4	20.8	29.4	33.5
Clothing	55.5	61.7	72.3	80.9	68.6
Total textiles	26.6	36.8	37.2	39.7	43.9
Iron and steel (excluding machinery)	23.0	33.0	37.0	40.0	50.0
Machinery	19.0	18.3	24.6	22.3	32.5
Vehicles					
Rail carriages	6.3	56.9	33.9	55.9	58.4
Locomotives	16.0	67.5	27.8	49.5	58.6
Motor vehicles	—	—	—	38.7	67.4
Steamships	—	—	—	7.0	20.6

Source: W. Schlote, *British Overseas Trade from 1700 to the 1930s* (Oxford: Blackwell, 1952), pp. 166–67.

TABLE 7.
Trade in semifinished and finished steel products, 1913 (in thousand metric tons)

Importers	Exporters			
	United Kingdom	United States	Germany	Belgium
Old empire (Canada)	823	1,402	212	101
India, Ceylon	573	22	197	135
New empire	117	16	8	14
Europe	373	298	2,614	645
Latin America	310	421	466	248
U.S.A.	48	—	32	7
Far East	172	169	270	99

Source: P. L. Payne, "Iron and Steel Manufactures," in D. H. Aldcroft, ed., *The Development of British Industry and Foreign Competition, 1875–1914,* (London: Allen & Unwin, 1968), p. 85.

was again crucial, exporting labor-intensive goods to land-capital intensive areas, such as the United States and Argentina (where it sent jute to pack Argentinian agricultural exports) and to capital-labor intensive areas such as Europe (where it sent luxury textiles and rice). The empire helped to balance British deficits with both these areas through the large deficit in Indian accounts with Britain (financing as much as two-fifths of Britain's total deficits), generated by the balance of trade, colonial administrative charges, and interest and return on investments.[21]

21. Hobsbawm, p. 123.

In Britain's economic evolution from the late nineteenth century into the twentieth, the empire took on an increased importance for the British economy, an importance significant for stability and welfare as a whole. Moreover, to each exporting firm these areas would have the special importance of new arenas for competition in expanding sales against those of their foreign rivals who had now conquered their own markets and were competing effectively in third-country markets. Given the need for long production runs for low costs (especially for cotton), these areas could also represent the difference between profit and loss.

But the significance of these shifts was not always clear. In the 1860s and 1870s it appeared small (Britain's dependence was not yet great), and from 1906 to 1913, during a spectacular boom in foreign trade to Europe and the United States, it appeared to be declining.[22] At other times it was equally misleading in the other direction, appearing vital for British prosperity. These changes were of some historical importance for British imperial policy.

Between the late 1870s and the late 1880s, for example, statesmen and private leaders of public opinion began to perceive the new importance of the empire. Conservatives and special interests associated with the empire led the way. In 1872 Disraeli sparked the revival of imperialism in the Conservative party with an attack on "liberal cosmopolitanism" which included a plea for an "imperial tariff" to unite the empire and its dominions. Liberals, particularly the group surrounding Gladstone, were far less enthusiastic, but even here a basic shift in attitude toward the value of empire began to alter earlier neglect and near-scorn for the imperial connection. In 1869, the *Economist*, identified with the decidedly anti-imperial wing of the Liberal party, had editorially rejected dominion requests for support and defense, demanding that the dominions pay for their alliance with London. In 1883, however, the *Economist* noted that between 1870 and 1880 British exports to the empire had risen from one-quarter to one-third of total British exports and that dominions and possessions apart from Canada took over 80 percent of their imports from Britain. Militarism and adventurism were still to be shunned, but the editors acknowledged that the empire was now a stake well worth cultivating.[23]

22. R. D. Wolff, "Modern Imperialism: The View from the Metropolis," *American Economic Association, Papers and Proceedings* 60 (May 1970), 225–30.

23. R. Blake, *Disraeli* (New York, 1967), p. 523; *Economist*, 28 August 1869, p. 1016, and 22 September 1883, p. 1104. See also an excellent article by W. G. Hynes, "British Mercantile Attitudes towards Imperial Expansion," *Historical Journal* 19, 4 (1976), 969–

In the late seventies, a time of depression and overproduction, the role of imperial trade in British trade did increase, rising from 22.7 percent of total trade by value in 1871–75 to 24.6 percent in 1876–80, and to 26.5 percent in 1881–85.[24] When the Royal Commission on the Depression of Trade and Industry (1885–86) received testimony, the threats from foreign competition and foreign tariffs were repeatedly brought to their attention. The largest chambers of commerce and the trade associations dependent on foreign trade called for the development of new markets. The Manchester, London, and Liverpool chambers in particular urged the government both "to use every effort to bring about a closer commercial union between the mother country and her colonies and dependencies" and to "encourage greater railway development in the British colonies" in order to open up new markets.[25] These trends and demands seemed to confirm the importance that France and Bismarck placed on "places in the sun," helping to make the case for preemptive annexation.

The structure of the British economy placed a premium on trade with undeveloped and developing economies, and merchants and leaders of public opinion felt that British income and employment depended on the maintenance and growth of these trades. The empire thus become a means for stabilizing the sector cycle. The mechanism by which this transformation was achieved becomes clearer as we turn to investment and finance, two additional sectors of Britain's international and imperial economy.

Investment and Finance

In dollars, the total world stock of foreign investment in 1913 was about $44 billion, of which Britain held $18 billion, France $9 billion,

---

79, where the rise of this concern is specifically identified with the early 1880s and is not found in the 1870s. Hynes makes these points more extensively in *The Economics of Empire* (London, 1979), chaps. 4–6. Lance Davis and Richard Huttenback, "The Political Economy of British Imperialism: Measures of Benefits and Support," *Journal of Economic History* 42 (March 1982), 119–32, argue that despite investor attention to overseas investment, profit rates were higher in the domestic British market. But their conclusion, that empire paid only for its investors, needs to be qualified, as Michael Edelstein suggests in his comment in ibid., pp. 131–32, by the effect of empire on overall British trade.

24. Kahn, p. 67; Saul, *Studies*, p. 104; R. Lowe, "The Value to the U.K. of the Foreign Dominions of the Crowns," *Fortnightly Review*, 1 November 1877, pp. 618–30.

25. Royal Commission Appointed to Enquire into the Depression of Trade and Industry, *Second Report*, P. P. XXI (1886), p. 390. See also B. H. Brown, *The Tariff Reform Movement in Great Britain, 1881–1895* (New York, 1943), pp. 1–28; Cain and Hopkins, p. 485.

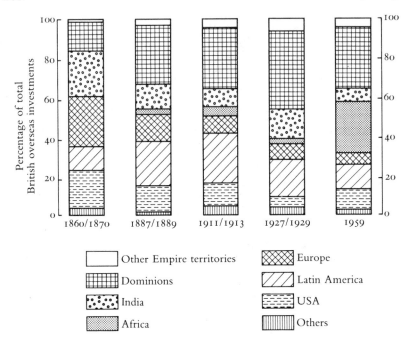

Source: E. J. Hobsbawn, *Industry and Empire* (New York: Pantheon, 1968), p. 303.

FIGURE 5 The geographical distribution of British foreign investment, 1860–1959

and Germany $6 billion.[26] Not only was Britain's position qualitatively different from that of economies of her own relative size; by World War I, Britain was receiving approximately 10 percent of national income in interest on foreign investment.[27] That investment was largely portfolio rather than direct, private as opposed to public, and going into social overhead capital.[28] A particularly large amount went into financing the infrastructure of other economies, particularly canals and later railroads.[29]

Through the early 1850s, British capital employing migratory English construction companies moved into Europe to build railroads. The returns were high, around 9 percent. This financial investment in Europe quickly assumed a more tangible form in purchases of British iron rails;

26. A. Cairncross, *Home and Foreign Investment* (Cambridge, 1953), p. 180; A. Bloomfield, *Patterns of Fluctuation in International Investment before 1914* (Princeton, 1968), p. 3.

27. Michael Edelstein, *Overseas Investment in the Age of High Imperialism* (New York, 1982), p. 18.

28. Bloomfield, p. 5.

29. Edelstein, chap. 2.

indeed, the export of capital goods from Britain doubled between 1850 and 1853.[30]

In the later 1850s a major change began to occur in the direction and nature of foreign investment. The revival of European nationalism and the creation of competitive railroad companies led the British to sell their shares in European railroads (at a considerable profit) and to shift their search for investment opportunities for this, their most efficient and characteristic "steam and iron" product, from industrial Europe to the more underdeveloped, agricultural parts of the world. The British empire, for reasons discussed below, became a preeminent location for this new search. H. S. Habbakuk describes the results of this geographical trend as follows: "In 1850 about a third of England's foreign investment was in America and the remainder in Northern Europe; in 1913 nearly fifty percent was in the Empire, twenty percent in the United States, nearly twenty percent in Central and South America and less than five percent in Europe. It is in the decades after 1850 that the geography of English foreign investment begins to assume this shape."[31]

With the shift in direction came a shift in organization: investment now came increasingly under the control of the London financial center, through direct management by English companies or through considerable formal influence in management (e.g., dual boards of directors).[32]

These long-term trends continued in the latter part of the century as capital flowed into developing, agricultural lands and into early industrial areas. The latter, as I have already argued, were also the major outlets for British capital goods. In the shorter run the trend was even more dramatic: observers in the 1880s, for example, witnessed an increased flow to Australia, the United States, and Argentina. Again, much of this new investment went into railroads, stimulating British sales of capital goods.[33]

Continuing depression in the 1890s and crises in the United States, Argentina, and Australia reduced new foreign investment in these areas and thus narrowed capital outlets. Among new outlets India, Canada, Africa, and Chile absorbed more of the reduced flow. The search for

30. L. Jenks, *The Migration of British Capital to 1875* (New York, 1927), pp. 55–69, 75, 81, 126–30, 164–74.

31. In Rose et al., 2:787.

32. Ibid., pp. 780–85, 789, and 799. These trends were particularly strong within the empire, e.g., tea plantations and construction companies.

33. Cairncross, p. 185, and Ernest A. Benians et al., ed., *The Cambridge History of the British Empire*, vol. 3: *The Empire Commonwealth, 1870–1919* (Cambridge, 1959), p. 197. Also Edelstein, chap. 13.

agricultural lands to develop assumed increased significance when the boom of 1907–13 witnessed not the expected decrease in flow to under-developed and developing areas but a relative increase. By this time over one-half of new, overseas British capital formation was going to the empire—and one-quarter of total British foreign investment was in im-perial railroads. In terms of the accumulated stock of British foreign investment in 1913, however, the international sector still predomi-nated—the United States led, followed by Canada, India, and Argentina.[34]

British investors benefited from relatively high and stable rates of return on capital, particularly when domestic investment was depressed, for booms in foreign investment alternated with booms in domestic investment.[35] Efficient exporters, especially of capital goods, gained ad-ditional markets stimulated by foreign investment.[36] Income from pre-vious international investments accounted for much of the new overseas investment in this period.[37] Britain's leadership of the gold standard permitted it to fund short-term deficits by drawing on financial reserves held not by the Bank of England but by France and by Argentinian investors whose funds rushed to England in response to slight variations in the bank rate or the gold premia.[38] So the financial costs to Britain as a whole of being an economy engaged in foreign investing were relatively low.

There may have been industrial costs, however. London, the financial governor of the British economy, faced out to sea,[39] and British industry

34. Benians et al., 3:457–58.

35. W. M. Dacey, *The British Banking Mechanism* (London, 1951), p. 59; P. L. Cottrell, *British Overseas Investment in the Nineteenth Century* (London, 1975), p. 52. H. Singer, "The Distribution of Gains between Investing and Borrowing Countries," in Richard Caves and Harry Johnson, eds., *Readings in International Economics* (Homewood, Ill., 1968), pp. 306–17, discusses the more general benefits of foreign investment for the investor. See Cairncross, p. 36; Potter, "Atlantic Economy"; Robert Fogel and S. En-german, "A Model for the Explanation of Industrial Expansion in the Nineteenth Cen-tury," *Journal of Political Economy* 77 (June 1969), 306–28; and A. G. Ford, "Notes on the Role of Exports in British Economic Fluctuations, 1870–1914," *Economic History Review*, 2d ser., 16 (December 1963), 330.

36. F. H. Hinsley, ed., *The New Cambridge Modern History*, vol. 11 (Cambridge, 1962), pp. 65–66; Cottrell, *British Overseas Investment in the Nineteenth Century*; and Albert H. Imlah, *Economic Elements in the Pax Britannica* (Cambridge, Mass., 1958), chap. 2. For the role of India in these years see the *New Cambridge Modern History*, 11:55–56.

37. C. H. Feinstein, *National Income, Output, and Expenditure of the United Kingdom* (Cambridge, 1972), cited in Barratt-Brown, p. 176.

38. Marcello de Cecco, *Money and Empire* (Totowa, N.J., 1974), chap. 4, and p. 88 for India and Argentina. See also A. G. Ford, *The Gold Standard, 1880–1914: Britain and Argentina* (Oxford, 1962), pp. 5–6.

39. E. V. Morgan and W. A. Thomas, *The Stock Exchange* (London, 1962), p. 95;

may have lacked capital for development, especially the large sums needed for creative industrial restructuring.[40] Imperial rule required railroads for imperial security, and imperial security reduced the risks of foreign investment, with the Bank of England guaranteeing and managing colonial debts.[41] In effect, the structure of the London financial market and the relative rates of profitability of the banks that composed it channeled capital outlays toward foreign and particularly imperial investment.[42]

In this fashion the late nineteenth-century English economy was thoroughly and intimately bound up with an international and more specifically an increasingly *imperial* economy. Prewar booms, with the exception of 1900–1904, were stimulated from abroad. Many of the crises—Gurney's in 1857, Baring's Argentinian crisis in 1890—also came from there.

National, International, and Imperial Economics

Britain's national economy became the "locomotive" of the international economy, and Britain's international economy became increasingly imperial. An economy that efficiently produced cotton, iron, and basic machines accumulated large profits, which were reinvested at home but especially abroad in a progressive widening of the British economy. In the later nineteenth century, technological advances of a different sort presented opportunities to continental economies (the United States, Germany, and later Russia) in efficient steel, electrical, and chemical industries. Britain, however, had a real, profitable interest in the older system. As the continental economies developed, they pushed Britain into, and Britain naturally pursued, a widening of its old path. The

Jenks, p. 87; W. F. Spalding, *The London Money Market* (London, 1922), pp. 75–76; W. Bagehot, *Lombard Street: A Description of the Money Market* (London, 1875), p. 274; P. Barrett-Whale, "The Working of the Pre-War Gold Standard," in T. S. Ashton and R. S. Sayers, eds., *Papers in English Monetary History* (Oxford, 1953), p. 154; and F. Fetter, *The Development of British Monetary Orthodoxy* (Cambridge, Mass., 1965), p. 239.

40. Cairncross, pp. 84–85; M. Edelstein, "Rigidity and Bias in the British Capital Market, 1870–1913," in D. N. McCloskey, ed., *Essays on a Mature Economy* (London, 1971); Cain and Hopkins, p. 485; and Royal Commission on the London Stock Exchange, *Report*, P. P. XIX (1878).

41. Rose et al., 2:798; Benians, 3:198.

42. The transfer of funds took place through exports and within the structure of Anglo-colonial banks, which drew capital freely both from the metropole and from the colony. Rose et al., 2:781–86; J. Baster, *Imperial Banks* (London, 1929), pp. 50 and 69; Benians et al., 3:199; Saul, *Studies*, pp. 100–113; and A. G. Ford, "Overseas Lending and Internal Fluctuations," in Hall, *The Export of Capital from Britain, 1870–1914.*

TABLE 8.
The development of the international economy

Stage	Developed	Developing		Undeveloped	
Factor intensity	Capital	Labor	Land	Land	Labor
1800	G.B.	Europe		U.S.	India
1840	G.B.	Europe	U.S.	Latin America, Australia, Canada	India, China
1870	G.B., Europe		U.S.	Australia, Latin America, Canada, Africa	India, China
1900	G.B., Europe, U.S.		Australia, Canada, Argentina, Mexico, S. Africa	Latin America, Africa	India, China

Source: Adapted from Karl Hansson, "A General Theory of the System of Multilateral Trade," *American Economic Review* 42 (March 1952), 59–88.

Europe of the 1830s and 1840s, a field of opportunity for British investment and exports, was replaced as the "agricultural" partner of industrial Britain by the American South, Australia, India, South Africa, and East Asia.

The British economy was not stagnant in the late nineteenth century, nor were iron and cotton its sole occupation. Service industries were rapidly growing, though they rested upon the foundation of gold, banks, investment, and "imperial" exports. As the traditional British economy expanded laterally, so its characteristics intensified. Investment based upon banking and a gold standard became a motor for generating exports and profits, which in turn fueled investment and cheaper raw materials for an economy becoming ever more international in nature. The dynamic effects of this development can be seen in Table 8.

The British economy, seeking to preserve a stable division of labor with a developing world, evolved a particular focus toward the empire. The empire was a particularly efficient part of its international economy: here finance worked most efficiently in turning portfolio investment into exports with the least strain on the gold standard base, and investment was most controlled and most secure. The City of London was prejudiced in this direction, politics supplemented the influence of sterling, and patriotism supplemented the purse. The economy can be deemed imperial, for the imperial connection was a large and growing faction in Britain's economy.

How much of the nineteenth-century experience of British empire does this international-imperial economy explain? An answer to this question depends on judgments about the mutual needs of empire and economy.

The extensive internationalization (and imperialization) of the British economy in the nineteenth century was crucial to integrating the disparate societies of the empire. It provided incentives for collaboration in the colonial periphery, and in the British metropole it offered motives for bearing the administrative cost that empire entails. But it could also lead to conflicts of interest. The contrasting experiences of the two centers of the first British empire—the British Caribbean and what would become the United States—are instructive. The first became economically more dependent while the second became economically independent and fractious, suggesting that circumstances special to each colony are decisive.

Regarding what empire did for the economy, however, we can draw some conclusions. Given the long-term trend in the British textile industry toward structural dependence on undeveloped markets (and assuming a continued lag in national economic innovation), one would expect a continued concern for accessible and growing markets in the undeveloped world. The expansion of the transnational economy into the undeveloped world meant an expansion of British foreign policy into these parts of the periphery.[43]

Sales in the periphery usually depended upon security that the peripheral regime could not and would not provide. The result was a continuous pressure for the expansion of at least the informal empire (control without annexation) to preserve political stability and free trade. Britain needed to exercise sufficient control so that underdeveloped areas would neither fall into anarchy nor establish protective tariffs for their own textile production.[44] Informal support (through gunboat diplomacy) for local oligarchs who supported free trade was sufficient for this end until some rival empire with its own tariffs surfaced. British

43. Choucri and North, *Nations in Conflict*, p. 19.

44. Charles Dilke, closely associated with British industry through his friend Joseph Chamberlain, described one of the threats thus: "Were we to leave India or Ceylon, they would have no customers at all, for, falling into anarchy, they would cease at once to export their goods to us and to consume our manufactures." Quoted in C. Bodelsen, *Studies in Mid-Victorian Imperialism* (1924; New York, 1968), p. 67.

statesmen were quite aware of the dangers involved. As Lord Salisbury told a Conservative public meeting in Manchester in 1884:

> You must consider this—that if you are being shut out by tariffs from civilized markets of the world, the uncivilized markets are becoming more and more precious to you, and they threaten to be the only field which will offer you a profitable business. At all events they are fields which will offer the most profitable business, and as civilization goes on, as exportation increases, these uncivilized markets will be thrown open to you, if only no foreign power is allowed to come in and interpose its hostile tariffs between you and the benefit for which you look.[45]

By themselves, however, purely economic factors do not explain the formal annexations of the late 1870s and early 1880s. British textile producers were sufficiently efficient relative to other European producers that there was no independent, metropolitan, economic force pushing for formal rule in these areas (such as would be required to export textiles if Britain were significantly inefficient in this industry). Nevertheless, an increased importance was perceived for undeveloped areas and imperial trade in those years. As a result, when free trade (the Pax Britannica) was challenged by other powers with isolating intent, Britain had good reason to defend her slice of the market by preemptive annexation. The new areas penetrated in the 1860s and 1870s in Africa and Asia (areas that would become parts of the official empire during the Scramble of the 1880s) could not match India's importance in trade. But British merchants and statesmen anticipated that they *might* be "new Indias" for the textile and other trades.[46] Textiles and trade with undeveloped regions required at least a "free-trade imperialism," though in a revised form—informal where possible (some peripheries, among them the United States, resisted), formal if rendered necessary by other metropoles' competition or by challenges from the periphery.[47]

The capital goods sector had quite different requirements. The crucial difference was that textiles could be defended informally; capital goods, however, required formal rule, a direct act of imperial preference or integration. In exporting rails and machines to developing economies, British firms were not as efficient as German or United States firms.

45. Lord Salisbury, quoted by the *Manchester Guardian*, 17 April 1884, and in Hynes, "British Mercantile Attitudes."

46. G. N. Uzoigwe, *Britain and the Conquest of Africa* (Ann Arbor, 1974), p. 27.

47. R. E. Robinson and J. Gallagher, with Alice Denny, *Africa and the Victorians* (New York, 1961), chap. 2.

The sector needed, as Birmingham manufacturers led by Joseph Chamberlain demanded, imperial "fair trade," or preferences. They needed to exclude more efficient, non-British imports and to prevent the development of dominion machinery industries just as textiles needed to prevent competing industries in undeveloped countries. Formal political mechanisms or an imperial preference would encourage governmental orders to be placed with British firms and would permit private orders to be channeled by Anglo-colonial financial ties. Only a few colonies, India among them, began to meet this need in the nineteenth century. The real independence of the dominions precluded a general solution in colonial federation, and so these industries suffered (at least until major innovations, such as motor vehicles, developed in the twentieth century).

These two central parts of the British economy required the maintenance and growth of empire. Other parts of the British economy nevertheless inclined in different directions. London-based finance was influential in the late nineteenth century and highly efficient. Although special links encouraged funds to flow to the empire, at least half of London's placements went outside the empire, pursuing higher returns that balanced increased risks. Finance was thus preeminently international, even though pleased to accommodate imperial issues. Neither innovative industries nor the traditional coal industry, meanwhile, welcomed any restrictions on trade such as imperial preference being demanded by the iron and machine trades. The new industries could take advantage of free competition in any market open to them. Imperial preference or domestic tariff protection would eventually raise their costs or lead to foreign retaliation.

No sector got what it wanted in quite the way it wanted it, suggesting that other factors need to be taken into account. The Foreign Office and the aristocratic classes still so influential in politics were, after all, disdainful of "mere" trade. The divergent pressures from other economic actors lead one to examine both domestic political forces and the pressures of international strategic competition to see how they channeled economic demands and what new independent factors they may have added in doing so. An economy, eventually "requires" too many things for full health, and politics is the art of picking the economic ailments that one can survive.

The Politics of Imperial Strategy

Many scholars have argued that nineteenth-century empires found their domestic bases in conservative nationalism. Nineteenth-century imperialism, in this view, was a modern version of the bread and circuses that Rome had found useful in distracting the masses from confiscatory social legislation.[48] Hans Ulrich Wehler, for example, observes that the German empire (both its markets and its popularity) provided one of the few countercyclical tools that Bismarck and later the kaiser could use to combat persistent overproduction and the political strains that it caused.[49] In the British case scholars have rehearsed a familiar antinomy: British imperialism was the product of the Conservative party's identification with nationalism to avoid domestic social reform, while the Liberals represented "Little Englander" anti-imperialism and, presumably, social reform.[50]

But the picture is too simple if it generally associates conservatism with imperialism, liberalism with anti-imperialism. The largest growth of formal empire occurred under Liberal auspices, between 1880 and 1886. A Conservative led the 1865 Parliamentary Commission that advocated a substantial retrenchment of existing empire and no further expansion. Some of the strongest proponents of empire and its expansion—Rosebery, Harcourt, Hartington, and Chamberlain—were Liberals or began as such.[51] Many imperialists identified themselves not as socially conservative but as social reformers (which was not the same as being a Liberal).[52] Many leading social reformers, the Fabians among them, were imperialists, and many conservatives were Little Englanders who feared the social instability that might result from ruling a large empire.[53]

Do these anomalies mean that conservatism and empire have been wrongly paired, or more widely that metropolitan politics bear little

48. R. Rosecrance, *Action and Reaction in World Politics* (Boston, 1963), chap. 6.

49. H. U. Wehler, "Bismarck's Imperialism: 1862–1890," *Past and Present* no. 48 (August 1970), 119–55.

50. Rosecrance, p. 139. See also R. Blake, *The Conservative Party* (New York, 1970), pp. 128–30.

51. S. Cooney, "The Rosecrance Model," *British Journal of International Studies* 1, 2 (1975), 131–47.

52. Ibid., pp. 141–42, but see B. Semmel, *Imperialism and Social Reform* (Cambridge, Mass., 1960), for nonliberal, including proimperial, sources of social reform. C. J. Lowe, *The Reluctant Imperialists* (New York, 1967), is a good general history of some of the differences in imperial policy, especially pp. 4–17. One of the best accounts of the party differences on imperial policy is Peter Marshall, "The Imperial Factor in the Liberal Decline, 1880–1885," in J. Flint and G. Williams, eds., *Perspectives of Empire* (London, 1973), chap. 7, though he separates ruling Ireland from imperial questions.

53. P. Fraser, *Joseph Chamberlain, Radicalism and Empire* (London, 1966); D. Winch, *Classical Political Economy and Colonies* (Cambridge, Mass., 1965), pp. 99–102; B. Semmel, *The Rise of Free Trade Imperialism* (London, 1970), p. 153.

relevance to empire? The alternative thesis is that domestic politics had no substantial effects on the rate or form of imperial development. Both political parties, this view argues, were in content or in effect imperialist. To examine these views, we must distinguish different aspects of the empire and break the conventional identity between politics and party, for politics takes place both within and between the parties. I start by sketching the evolution of imperial policies within a framework of coalition politics.[54]

Palmerstonianism

We begin at the height of Palmerstonianism, with the Whigs fully in command. The 1832 Reform Bill was their achievement, the voters it enfranchised became their voters. They combined the great landed estates with the newly enfranchised urban middle classes of commerce and industry. In this domestic context.the Don Pacifico debate of 1850, the Governor Eyre incident, and the 1865 Parliamentary Report on the colonies in Africa identify the range and distribution of midcentury views on imperial politics.[55]

The Don Pacifico incident involved the forcible protection of a merchant claiming British citizenship during a dispute in Greece. Palmerston defended protection, but Richard Cobden attacked the policy primarily as wasteful—a massive interference at large cost in a very small and dubious cause. Cobden and the Manchester Radicals were associated with the left wing of the Whig-Liberal party. The Peelite Conservatives meanwhile criticized the aggressive aspect of Palmerstonian policy, for they held the function of diplomacy to be peace. A junior member of the group, William Ewart Gladstone, took his stand on the principle of self-government, which was as applicable to Greece and its internal affairs as to any other nation—this line of reasoning would later lead him to home rule for Ireland.[56] Finally, Benjamin Disraeli spoke for the non-free-trade Conservatives, attacking intervention on the grounds of immediate practicality: intervention failed to enhance British interests overseas or to increase British prestige and power in the European balance.

Both Cobden and Disraeli criticized the aggressive pursuit of British

54. Samuel Beer, *British Politics in the Collectivist Age* (New York, 1969); Peter Gourevitch, "International Trade, Domestic Coalitions, and Liberty," *Journal of Interdisciplinary History* 8 (1977), 281–313; James Kurth, "The Political Consequences of the Product Cycle," *International Organization* 33 (Winter 1979), 1–34; and Franz Schurman, *The Logic of World Power* (New York, 1974), are important examples of this sort of analysis.

55. A. P. Thornton, *The Imperial Idea and Its Enemies* (New York, 1959), chap. 1.

56. Ibid., p. 3; P. Magnus, *Gladstone* (London, 1954), pp. 94–95.

power and liberalism.[57] Cobden found the general policy of intervention inappropriate to liberalism; Disraeli found liberalism inefficient in the pursuit of British power. Palmerston nevertheless received overwhelming support in Parliament. His policies stood for the promotion of liberal regimes like England's own, and he attempted to protect, by force if necessary, a world of free trade everywhere safe for Don Pacificos, their commerce and debts, and a political world of stability where legal rule defended the progressive role of commerce and industry and where, he believed, Britain was more than capable of holding its own.[58]

Palmerston won the support of the very large middle and conservative wing of his own party—the "national" interest group concerned with British power and material welfare. He also received the less welcome support of radicals who were agitating in favor of social reform and colonial self-government. They advocated both a forcible expansion of the area of trade (as in the Opium War) and active measures for the promotion of emigration (for the welfare of the British working class). In the first they anticipated Palmerston, in the second they went far beyond what the national party sought.[59]

As early as 1850, therefore, one can see that imperialism—even in its liberal, free-trade form—was an issue that divided parties, including the Liberal party. Fifteen years later the American Civil War highlighted new fissures in domestic imperial politics, pitting property against liberty. For the Palmerstonian party, the South respected property, trade, and the rule of law. The North was something more and something worse: it was liberal and popular, but it was under the rule of the mob rather than gentlemen. The patrons of Whiggish liberty—the Conservative party and the conservative Whigs, who included Clubdom, Society, the *Times*, *Punch*, and Palmerston himself—took their stand with Dixie. On the other side were the forces of democratic liberalism: Cobden, Bright, Mill, Goldwin, Smith, and others. Strangely, perhaps,

---

57. Thornton, p. 5.

58. Jasper Ridley, *Lord Palmerston* (London, 1970), chap. 3. Commenting on the question of China in 1837, Palmerston told Lord Minto that "We certainly have no right to meddle with what the Americans do, so long as they do not interfere with our possessions; and as to the idea that we are to prevent any and every nation in the world from having settlements to the East of the Cape, it is founded in a jealousy which is in a great degree mistaken, and in an assumption of political power which we do not possess. . . . The more civilization and commerce are extended among savage races, the better for all civilized and trading nations." Quoted in Kenneth Bourne, *Palmerston: The Early Years* (New York, 1982), p. 625.

59. Semmel, *Rise of Free Trade Imperialism*, pp. 150–53.

Gladstone (now a Liberal) was cross-pressured, for the South was also a "small nation struggling to be free." The effects of slavery were largely unknown to him, his supporters later said, even though the Gladstone family had had large investments in Caribbean plantations. Gladstone wavered throughout the war, not perceiving the virtues of northern, liberal democracy until later in the 1860s.[60]

In 1865 Governor Eyre of Jamaica suppressed a rising of ex-slaves with brutal efficiency. John Stuart Mill led the attack on him in Parliament and the drive for prosecution in the courts. Self-identified progressives divided: Eyre's defenders upheld his actions on grounds of national efficiency and power, while his prosecutors stood on abstract principle. Eyre's defenders won the support of much of the national party and of the two juries before which Eyre's case was tried,[61] but the collision of property liberalism with democratic liberalism, of utilitarian with categorical ethics, produced critical fault lines.

The central political question of the time was who or what group was going to combine a majority of what interests and what feelings into a governing coalition of some stability. Would the governing coalition be imperialist or anti-imperialist? Some of the range of choice was revealed in the commission appointed to inquire into Britain's possessions in West Africa. The Parliamentary Commission of 1865 combined Conservative isolationism with Liberal free-trade Little Englanders. But even this committee, the most anti-imperial coalition formed in British politics before World War I, was prepared to recommend a cessation only of formal expansion. It encouraged British informal influence and a trade-supporting alliance with the native powers on the coast of West Africa.[62]

Gladstone's Liberal Crusade, 1868–1874

In his first, great reforming ministry Gladstone founded his foreign policy on the bedrock principles of liberalism. The domestic political system was to be the product of the free vote of the mass of the nation, and to this end he pressed for extensions of the franchise in the 1860s. The economy was to be the outcome of the free interaction between consumer and producer (Cobden was the Liberal economic prophet of

---

60. R. Shannon, *The Crisis of Imperialism* (London, 1974); Magnus, pp. 152–55.
61. Shannon, pp. 37–38.
62. J. D. Hargreaves, *Prelude to the Partition of West Africa* (London, 1963), pp. 70–78.

the age).[63] And the international order was to be governed by the free cooperation of the states of Europe (a concept of the Concert which Gladstone derived from Aberdeen). Naturally, he assumed that the three were compatible: the mass of the nation would support a liberal economy and the Concert, and the Concert principles of nonintervention and cooperation were compatible with the maintenance of free trade and British security. Gladstone joined the liberal and radical opposition to Palmerston in a coalition led by the Liberals. They rejected the national position of self-interested interference in favor of vigorously promoting conservative liberalism overseas.

In his first ministry (1868–74) Gladstone resisted expansion in the South Pacific and Malaya. He criticized Bismarck's absorption of Alsace-Lorraine not only because it altered the balance of power but also because Bismarck had failed to consult the wishes of the inhabitants of the two provinces. He agreed to the arbitration of the *Alabama* dispute with the Americans and accepted an adverse judgment and a financial penalty by doing so. He tolerated the revision in Russia's favor of the "unjust" Black Sea clauses of the Treaty of Paris, the treaty that had ended the Crimean War.[64] Finally, troops were recalled from the self-governing colonies, which were expected to provide their own local defense and be attached to Britain by sentiments, not regiments.[65]

Yet these decisions and programs do not indicate a fundamental anti-imperialism on the part of Gladstone or the Liberal party. Gladstone defended the existing empire whenever profitable and protected the lives and property of British merchants whenever they had a reasonable case for protection. In the search for "strong native powers" who could protect British trade, his commitment to expanding trade led inevitably to some "frontier expansion." Gladstone, however, tolerated only an incremental growth of empire in defense of the liberal conception of trade and the international rights of hospitality and settlement. Disraeli's position, as we shall see, was quite different.[66]

Gladstone's first ministry witnessed three great domestic initiatives.

63. F. H. Hinsley, *Power and the Pursuit of Peace* (London, 1963), pt. 2; Shannon, pp. 47, 55. See also W. N. Medlicott, *Bismarck, Gladstone, and the Concert of Europe* (London, 1956), pp. 17–34, as well as Karl Polanyi, *The Great Transformation* (1944; Boston, 1957).

64. P. Knaplund, *Gladstone's Foreign Policy* (New York, 1935), p. 56. Gladstone's comment reflects his commitment to an ideological foreign policy; Disraeli would have regarded the "unjust" treaty as merely a strategic advantage for Britain.

65. Shannon, pp. 51–52, 83–84.

66. W. D. McIntyre, *The Imperial Frontier in the Tropics* (London, 1967), pp. 18–19, 20–24.

The Liberals' first electoral bill of 1867 sought to bring into electoral politics the top strata of the working class, for they had proved their liberal, "responsible" character. The Liberals disestablished the Irish church, which did not represent the majority of the population. And, most controversially, the Gladstonians passed an education bill supplementing, with public funds, church education (primarily Anglican) and establishing local, state-supported schools.[67]

With the passage of these measures Gladstone had done much to create his liberal order—internationally and domestically. But he had also trampled upon his massive liberal support in the process. His "Concert-ed" foreign policy of cooperation (which necessarily meant a certain amount of appeasement, as of the United States in the *Alabama* dispute) had alienated the national image that liberalism had inherited from the Palmerstonian Whigs. His attempt to encourage a freer Ireland, which he assumed would then become British and Liberal, awakened fears among the Whigs who saw his appeasement of agrarian radicalism as a threat to property in general and to their own holdings in Ireland in particular. And his education bill, through its support for church schools, angered the Dissenters, the single most powerful, well-organized, and hitherto thoroughly Gladstonian faction in the Liberal party.

Disraeli's Imperial Idea, 1874–1880

Disraeli's strategy was to court every interest that Gladstone alienated and that might also align itself with the still aristocratically dominated Tory party. He had begun to stake the party's claim to these interests in 1872, in his speeches at the Manchester Free Trade Hall and at the Crystal Palace.[68] At Manchester he offered the audience a choice between a "national" and a "cosmopolitan" foreign policy, urging them to reject Gladstone's general principles of international cooperation within the Concert. Further, he asked the assembled crowds in Manchester "whether

67. The 1870 Education Act; see Shannon, p. 90.
68. For an argument that Disraeli actually made the first moves toward creating a Conservative imperial coalition in 1866–68 by adopting the Reform Bill and sending an expedition to Abyssinia, see Freda Harcourt, "Disraeli's Imperialism, 1866–68," *Historical Journal* 23, 1 (1980), 87–109. The Abyssinian expedition, however, conveys much more the flavor of late Palmerston than early imperialism; nor does the Reform Bill integrate the social question in quite the way the speeches of the early 1870s do. Although Harcourt does suggest that the idea of a coalition drawing in the masses to an imperial and Conservative program may have been in Disraeli's plans considerably before the Crystal Palace speech, Disraeli as late as 1866 was quite skeptical of the value of imperialism in general and limited his appreciation to India (see Blake, *Disraeli*, p. 455).

you will be content to be a comfortable England modelled and moulded upon continental principles and meeting in due course an inevitable fate, or whether you will be a great country, an imperial country, a country where your sons when they rise, rise to prominent positions, and obtain, not merely the esteem of your countrymen but command the respect of the world."[69] Here can be traced the germ of the imperial idea as it was to appear in the Scramble for formal empire: it was national in a world of foreign rivals, it was calculating in the pursuit of advantage, and it rejected cosmopolitanism and abstract principles of general right.

At the Crystal Palace Disraeli developed a broader program in a contrast between liberalism and conservatism. Having reaffirmed Tory faith in the values of an established landed society, he added commitments to social reform and empire. He sought a social reform that would unite all classes under the leadership of the landed aristocracy—quite different from Gladstone's social reform. Gladstone sought to expand the middle of political spectrum, integrating the working class into middle-class democracy and economy. Disraeli sought an alliance of the extremes, land and the working class (those "angels in marble" he discerned so perspicaciously), with the aristocracy caring for both its own interests and those of the working class.[70] The "two nations," rather than being united by a common way of life, would be united by a national feeling. The empire would be the expression overseas of the national unity that was to be expressed at home in paternal social legislation. This empire was designed to be a source of power for Britain, not a work justified by its humanitarian effects (what Gladstone would call its promotion of national freedom or self-government).[71]

Disraeli's actual policies were inevitably much more limited than his ideological program, but his social legislation did include minimal union rights and welfare legislation. Although Disraeli was prepared to constrain both the totally free operation of the market and the untrammeled rule of the factory boss, there were also limits, those of landed property rights and the natural leadership of the aristocracy in party and country, beyond which the Conservative party would not go.[72]

Gladstone had refused just such special welfare measures on the grounds

69. Excerpted in R. Koebner and H. Schmidt, *Imperialism* (Cambridge, 1964), p. 111.

70. See Robert McKenzie and Allan Silver, *Angels in Marble: Working Class Conservatives in Urban England* (London, 1968).

71. Shannon, pp. 94–95; E. J. Feuchtwanger, *Disraeli, Democracy, and the Tory Party* (Oxford, 1968), p. 12. See also Justin McCarthy, *A History of Our Times* (New York, 1886): 2:575, for the importance of national power.

72. Paul Smith, *Disraelian Conservatism and Social Reform* (London, 1967).

that they represented inefficient paternalism and a denial of the potential equality—liberal, competitive equality—of the rising portion of the working class. The Conservatives were hampered by no such ideology. Seeing paternalism as itself a virtue, they gave away Liberal property (control of the factories) as, later, Liberals would give away Conservative and Whig property (control of land). The voting working class maintained strong ties to the Liberals in nonconformist religion, but they were prepared to express electoral gratitude to the Conservatives, particularly when the Liberals were in disarray.[73]

External policy reflected similar initiatives and limits. One major source of Disraeli's electoral victory was the shift to conservatism of the dissatisfied national public, Palmerston's foreign-policy constituency. Disraeli gratified them with a program aimed at the growth of British power and prestige in Europe, to be achieved through the agency of the empire and the power resources it provided. The self-governing colonies were "millstones, which [accurately] we do not govern," and his vision was of a settlement empire that Britain did govern, linked (in later years) to Britain with a colonial tariff and its foreign affairs directed by Whitehall.[74]

Little could be done with the existing self-governing colonies, as Chamberlain was to discover twenty years later, but elsewhere one can see a difference between the practices of Disraelian Toryism and Gladstonian Liberalism. A significant part of the difference was simply a matter of style. Disraeli sought what Justin McCarthy called imperial "sensationalism" or "gorgeous imperial fancies."[75] In the first two years of his ministry, Disraeli sent the romantic historian J. A. Froude to form a South African federation from the dour Boer republics, and he sent Lord Lytton, a writer of showy verse, as viceroy of India, spurring him to pursue a "forward" policy there. The Prince of Wales was packed off in 1876 for a state visit to the rajahs of the domain of the newly titled Empress of India, and in the same year he startled the French and

---

73. Shannon, pp. 104–5.

74. C. C. Eldridge, *England's Mission* (Chapel Hill, N.C., 1974), p. 183. Disraeli expressed his idea of imperialism as early as 1866: "It can never be our pretense or our policy to defend the Canadian frontier against the United States. . . . Power and influence we should exercise in Asia; consequently in Eastern Europe, consequently also in Western Europe; but what is the use of these colonial deadweights *which we do not govern*? . . . Leave the Canadians to defend themselves; recall the African squadron; and we shall make a saving which will at the same time enable us to build ships and have a good budget." As excerpted in Blake, *Disraeli*, p. 455; see also Harcourt, "Disraeli's Imperialism."

75. McCarthy, 2:575.

the British public with the surreptitious purchase of the khedive's Suez Canal shares.[76]

The difference between Gladstonian and Disraelian policies in the African tropics was practically nonexistent. Disraeli's was an imperialism of power, and West Africa had little power to offer in the 1870s. But both men were committed to the protection of an informal empire based if possible on the collaboration of "strong native powers" who would provide the security that profitable commerce required.[77] When the powerful Ashanti Confederacy attacked Britain's clients, it was Gladstone who sent a punitive expedition (its success redounded, however, to the political credit of the newly elected Disraeli). Disraeli was determined to avoid even these minor costs.

Disraeli's government continued the general exchange of territories with France in West Africa which the Liberals had inaugurated. The exchange reflected the lack of importance both Disraeli and Gladstone attached to British interests in West Africa and both leaders' desire to reduce conflicts with France, which both sought as an ally.[78] Nonetheless, French special interests and British merchants interested in the West Africa trade, philanthropists (an important factor in West African politics), and various chambers of commerce were too formidable to be overcome.[79] In West Africa the pursuit and protection of commerce,

76. Ibid., 2:577–79.

77. Hargreaves, p. 167. Reflecting on British policy in West Africa, a Colonial Office official named Wylde commented in 1876: "Where there is money to be made our merchants will be certain to intrude themselves, and . . . if they establish a lucrative trade public opinion in this country practically compels us to protect them." Quoted in ibid., p. 197.

78. Ibid., pp. 167–68.

79. Ibid., p. 330. In one instance Sir Percy Anderson, a member of the Foreign Office, minuted that he had been called upon by a committee of merchants to request that the British government recognize the Congo Free State (memorandum by Anderson, 4 November 1884, F.O. 403/47, in the Public Record Office, Kew, Surrey [hereafter PRO]). Hutton, president of the Manchester Chamber of Commerce, wrote extensive letters to the Foreign Office giving his organization's views on matters that came up for decision, such as official protection for traders in the Niger Delta (memorandum by Lister, 4 April 1884, F.O. 403/31 [PRO]). Members of Parliament were also prepared to present the interests of their influential constituents to the department of the government. Royden, M.P. for Liverpool, spoke frequently for the commercial interests of his city in order to protect and promote their extensive business with Africa. And Lord Salisbury, recently appointed foreign minister, declared: "The commerce of a great industrial country like this will only flourish—history attests it again and again—under the shadow of an empire, and those who give up an empire in order to make commerce prosper will end by losing both." Knightsbridge speech of 27 July 1878, quoted in G. Cecil, *Salisbury* (London, 1921–32), 2:302–3.

whether by Liberals or by Conservatives, led to steady expansion of influence and sometimes control into the interior, in a rivalry with the French.

In South Africa, on the other hand, the Conservative program and the previous and later Liberal policies clearly differed. The difference lies in how and why the empire expanded.

British policy in South Africa had traditionally followed a Palmerstonian policy of imperial paramountcy: Britain would retain control of the coastline to secure the route to India while the Boers, who had fled British rule on the southern coast to avoid humanitarian interference with their treatment of the black population, would be allowed independence in the remote interior. The Liberals, seeking imperial paramountcy in strategic matters, were prepared to tolerate confederated self-rule in local matters, which would reduce metropolitan administrative costs and endow the population with the moral benefits of political autonomy.[80] To secure a pro-British confederacy, they annexed Basutoland and Griqualand West, giving the Cape Colony defensible borders and the economic resources of the diamond fields.

Disraeli's administration appeared to be more ambitious. It pursued an activist, expansionist policy to effect a long-term confederal solution for the whole of South Africa by annexing the independent Boer republics of the Transvaal and the Orange Free State. The price of their governments' consent to annexation (rapidly disavowed by the majority of the Boer nationalists) was protection from the Zulus, and inevitably the Conservatives found themselves with another costly African war.[81]

The Conservatives profoundly differed from the Liberals in accepting the annexation of a self-ruling people on grounds of expediency, of power politics. Colonial self-government to the Conservatives was a technique of imperial power, to be judged by its contribution to imperial power. Self-government to the Liberals, by previous declaration and later action, was an *end*, an end that itself was an important justification for empire. Thus for the Conservatives no principled stand could counterbalance the expediency of annexation.

It was in the Orient that Disraeli's conception of empire was to find its clearest expression. Where power was to be harvested, Disraeli most thoroughly implemented his imperial idea—an empire of eastern power

80. Robinson and Gallagher, *Africa and the Victorians*, pp. 54, 57. The Conservative Cabinet, however, severely criticized Sir Bartle Frere, governor of Cape Colony, for provoking a war.
81. Eldridge, pp. 195–97.

based in India, linked to the China trade, and secured through the eastern Mediterranean. In 1875 Disraeli took over the Fiji Islands to secure its trade and stability in the face of German rivalry.[82] However, his strategy as a whole centered on India, for there was his coherent eastern base for Britain's future worldwide role. With that base Britain was equal or superior to the continental powers of the future.

At the Indian pivot, Disraeli consciously rejected the previous Liberal policy of "masterly inactivity." India presented two problems that would not disappear. One was its external security, primarily with respect to Russia, and the other its internal stability, disturbed by the rising nationalism of the Indian middle class.[83] The two were connected: a domestically unstable India was prone to Russian interference, an external threat undermined British influence over the "native mind," on which the Raj rested.[84]

Disraeli focused on the second relationship. Russian influence in Afghanistan, if it were to progress, could create a true military frontier problem for North West India. He appointed the adventurous Lord Lytton to take an active approach to the problem: "We wanted a man of ambition, imagination, some vanity and much will—and we have got him."[85]

Lytton's policy was to maintain the political balance of the permanent Raj. Although Britain had early in the nineteenth century fostered the westernization ("civilization") of the Indian middle class, now Lytton sought to suppress their consequent claims for self-governing equality. Beginning as a response to the Indian Mutiny, this policy seemed determined to make the British the "lords of human kind," unwilling to share the governance of India with any but the conservative ruling elite of rajahs. The Royal Titles Bill of 1876, which made the Queen the Empress of India, supported this conservative internal dominance of India by providing a figurehead for the collaborating Indian aristocracy.[86]

A frontier defeat could have destroyed imperial prestige. Thus, in pursuit of external security, Lytton sent a mission to Kabul to oust the Russians, who also had sent a diplomatic mission. When the British

82. H. Brunschwig, *L'expansion allemand d'outre mer* (Paris, 1957), pp. 102–3.

83. Anil Seal, *The Emergence of Indian Nationalism* (Cambridge, 1968), pp. 14–16.

84. Keith Jeffrey, "The Eastern Arc of Empire," *Journal of Strategic Studies* 5 (December 1982), 531–45.

85. Disraeli to Salisbury, 1 April 1877, quoted in G. E. Buckle and W. Moneypenny, *Disraeli* (New York, 1913–20), 6:379.

86. R. Hutchins, *The Illusion of Permanence* (Princeton, 1967), chap. 7. And see V. G. Kiernan, *Lords of Human Kind* (London, 1969).

were refused entry, Lytton precipitately declared war. Although Disraeli and the Cabinet did not seek war, they sought a controlling British influence over this border state, and in 1878–79 war resulted.

India was the pivot.[87] India was the entrepôt for all eastern operations, for the economic and political foundations of the China trade, and for the protection of British interests throughout the East. In India the British government had a European-quality army at no cost to the British taxpayer and with no responsibility to the Parliament. In 1878, for example, Disraeli was able to reinforce Malta with Indian troops without obtaining the approval of Parliament.[88]

The Indian pivot also had a western link, the vital link to the British homeland, in Suez and the eastern Mediterranean. The Russians again presented the threat, a threat to the link that made eastern power British power. Disraeli phrased the eastern connection of imperial power emphatically in these words: "Power and influence we should exercise in Asia; *consequently* in Eastern Europe; *consequently* also in Western Europe."[89] The music halls announced the same connection more memorably, reflecting popular approval of Disraeli's transfer of Indian troops to meet moves against Turkey in 1878. One version of the Jingo refrain was bombastic and became famous:

> "We don't want to fight,
> But, by Jingo, if we do,
> We've got the ships, we've got the men,
> We've got the money too."

The other was a tribute to the popular sense of humor:

> "We don't want to fight,
> But, by Jingo, if we do,
> We'll stay at home and sing our songs
> And send the mild Hindoo."[90]

Gladstone had seen European cooperation as making eastern (imperial) competition unnecessary. Disraeli reversed the conception; he saw eastern power making Britain's power in Europe more weighty—which

87. Robinson and Gallagher, *Africa and the Victorians*, p. 13.
88. Eldridge, p. 223.
89. Blake, *Disraeli*, p. 455.
90. McCarthy, 2:602; Sir Henry Lucy, *A Diary of Two Parliaments* (London, 1885–86), 1:419, as excerpted in Donald C. Gordon, *The Dominion Partnership in Imperial Defense* (Baltimore, 1965), p. 61.

required a secure eastern Mediterranean. As a step in this direction Disraeli bought the khedive's share of the Suez Canal, but Egypt was not enough. Its historic and constitutional links with and strategic proximity to the Ottoman empire, combined with the experience of the Crimean War, required Britain to aid Turkey in containing the Russian advance toward Constantinople.[91]

British aid to Turkey under Disraeli was primarily diplomatic. A blind eye was turned on the forcible suppression of a Bulgarian rising against Ottoman rule.[92] Later Disraeli waged a thoroughgoing diplomatic battle against the "Big Bulgaria" that the victorious Russians imposed on a defeated Turkey. At the resulting Congress of Berlin, Disraeli wrested a reduction in Bulgaria from the assembled powers and their acquiescence in British annexation of Cyprus (insurance in case Turkey did collapse).[93] The price was France's acquisition of Tunis and the beginnings of the Scramble.

The central question that this recounting of Disraeli's imperial policy raises is to what extent policy was determined externally or internally, by foreign crises and British defense or by British initiatives and foreign responses. Disraelian initiatives were evident, and there is evidence that they were not accidental: Disraeli set an imperial tone for his administration, he would not recall or rebuke galloping proconsuls in Africa and India, and the direction of his administration, his coalition of support, became more and more imperial.[94]

To clarify the question of domestic politics we need to examine one more, and a strange, phase—the Liberals during the Scramble.

Gladstone amidst the Snows of Afghanistan, 1880–1886

Gladstone's victory of 1880 was his greatest. It was a victory over the forces of jingoistic wars and high taxation. Yet despite a seemingly

---

91. Eldridge, pp. 209–11; P. Knaplund, *Gladstone's Foreign Policy* (New York, 1935), p. 68.

92. Eldridge, p. 214.

93. Hinsley, p. 225; Cecil, *Salisbury*, 2:288; and J. Grenville, *Salisbury and Foreign Policy* (London, 1967), p. 79.

94. Derby, a "Little Englander" Conservative, felt forced to resign and later joined the Liberals. He was replaced by the more imperially oriented Salisbury. On the other hand, Lord Caernarvon, who was also forced to resign, was a more active imperialist. He resigned as a consequence of his blunders in execution, not of his goals. Eldridge, p. 185.

overwhelming vote of confidence in his international liberalism, Gladstone was soon embroiled in the colonial scramble.

Gladstone had attempted to assemble a great coalition of his own supporters and those elements of the Disraelian coalition alienated by six years of costly adventure and deepening depression. The main plank in his indictment of Disraeli's administration was foreign policy. As an antidote to Disraelian aggression, Gladstone put forward "six right principles" that should guide Britain: strengthen the empire by "just legislation and economy at home"; defend the cause of peace; maintain the Concert; avoid "needless and entangling engagements"; recognize the equal rights of all nations; and ensure that the foreign policy of Britain shall always be inspired "by the love of freedom."[95] He urged his audiences to "Remember the rights of the savage, as we call him. Remember the happiness of his humble home, remember that the sanctity of life in the hill villages of Afghanistan, among the winter snows, is as inviolable in the eye of Almighty God as can be your own."[96]

This was a call to retrieval, a demand that the Liberals remake foreign policy upon the principles of traditional liberalism, freed of all trace of national vanity and aggression. But though the programs sounded familiar, the composition of the party was rapidly changing. Despite the political momentum that the 1880 victory and the upsurge of the middle-class conscience against Disraelian aggression gave the Liberals, divisions within the party showed a growing chasm in the left of British politics. The Whigs clung to their defense of property and oligarchical influence. Gladstonian liberals remained determined to create one nation, a nation of individuals ruled by independent, enlightened self-interest—a nation of the middle class. The Radicals, however, directed their principles and platform toward the abandonment of liberal laissez-faire and toward state intervention designed to promote the welfare and independence of the majority of the newly enfranchised working class.[97] Radicals sought better housing, a progressive income tax, and free elementary education. To the mainstream liberal view, they presented the danger of putting the people's welfare before their liberty. The two main tendencies within liberalism—Radicalism and Whiggery—were separating one from the other.

Gladstone was most gratified by the state of British relations with the self-governing colonies. Bonds formally imperial were in fact freely

95. Quoted in Shannon, pp. 139–41.
96. Quoted in Magnus, p. 262.
97. Shannon, p. 178.

chosen bonds of friendship. Southern Africa, on the other hand, caused him great distress. Significant reforms in policy were needed to correct Disraelian aggression. British troops had been defeated at the Battle of Majuba Hill—a battle fought by Britain to annex the Transvaal. Defying his own Whigs, Gladstone decided to negotiate a settlement. The Boers would receive a degree of self-government very close to full independence, with Britain retaining only suzerain authority over foreign relations.[98]

In India he attempted a nearly equal reversal. The Liberal viceroy, Lord Ripon, was committed to "good government and the development of Indian resources," which the Liberals felt to be more effective security against Russia "than the fortification of all the frontier towns of Afghanistan."[99] Withdrawal from the outpost at Kandahar soon followed, but Afghanistan had been weakened by invasion. Influence now had to be maintained or Afghanistan actually would become a Russian puppet. More significantly Ripon's administration advocated Indianization of the Indian Civil Service, trampling on the Conservative concept of the permanent Raj. The vernacular press was unmuzzled, the first Indian representative bodies in local administration were permitted, and official sanction was removed from the racism practiced in the courts (whereby only white judges and juries could try cases against white subjects). Despite the protests of the white civil servants and settlers, Ripon's leadership clearly inspired the development of the Indian National Congress.

These clear differences from Conservative policy in India make Liberal participation in the Scramble, first in Egypt, later in tropical Africa, seem all the more anomalous. In Egypt, Gladstone and the Liberal cabinet were divided between liberal principles and minimal British interests. Here a nationalist movement under Colonel Arabi claimed the very rights of national independence which had to be suppressed in order to ensure the security of the Suez Canal, Britain's link to India. The Liberals tried to make the best of the dilemma.[100] International liberal standards were assuaged by promoting a Concert approach (particularly

---

98. Robinson, "Imperial Problems in British Politics," p. 137.

99. Ibid., p. 147.

100. W. S. Blunt, *Secret History of the English Occupation of Egypt* (New York, 1922), chap. 10, describes the various factions within the Liberal Cabinet, including Dilke's crucial commitment to the French in order to obtain French acquiescence in a trade treaty (seen as vital for the Birmingham Radical wing of the party due to its machinery-exporting constituents). He together with Chamberlain pressured Gladstone into the naval expedition: "We have got the Grand Old Man into a corner now, and he *must* fight" (p. 277).

with France), and domestic liberal principles were addressed by promising a merely temporary intervention (to prop up a reformed khedival regime). Both plans collapsed. The mercurial French Assembly withdrew approval for joint intervention, and the khedival regime was too weak to stand.[101]

Britain became mired in Egypt. A formal pledge to cooperate in directing Egyptian finance gave France continual occasions for complaining over its lost opportunity and Bismarck a counter to be played for British goodwill. Worse, Gladstone had committed Britain to rule Egypt informally, in order to create the appearance of sovereignty under which it could some day abandon it. In political terms these constraints bound the consul general hand and foot, yet he had to reform Egyptian finance if Egypt was ever to pay its debt and be free of European financial control. Liberal imperialism of free trade, the residue of Palmerstonian intervention, here reached its disastrous apotheosis.[102]

In West Africa there was more continuity but little more success for the Liberals. The search for "strong native powers" had proceeded unabated. So had French rivalry and the expansion of trade, which helped weaken the very coastal powers that Britain relied upon for the security of its merchants. Competition brought chaos in its train. German "treaty making" sparked the already heated competition between France and Britain, igniting a scramble that the Berlin West Africa Conference of 1884–85 spent months straightening out. By refusing the National Africa Company a charter to rule Nigeria, however, Gladstone did try to keep commitments to a minimum.[103]

In both West and South Africa and in Egypt Gladstone resisted expansion. He saw the necessity of defending the Liberal status quo of informal empire to protect the route to India and to protect a growing trade. In neither case did he seek out new fields for expansion, but in both cases his liberal principles bent. In Ireland, however—fast becoming the dominant issue of imperialism at home—his principles were inflexible, his initiatives revolutionary, and the results for the Liberal party disastrous. It was the Irish question that created the clear division on the imperial issue which he had long avoided. It forced upon the Liberals a rankling choice between empire and liberalism, and it reduced the party to a shambles.

Gladstone began with appeasement in Ireland as in the Transvaal. Just

101. Shannon, pp. 148–49; Robinson and Gallagher, *Africa and the Victorians*, chap. 4.
102. Robinson, "Imperial Problems in British Politics," pp. 150–53.
103. Ibid., pp. 162–64.

as the Liberals sought the cooperation of "strong native powers" in tropical areas and ties of affection from self-governing colonies, so Gladstone sought to transform British rule in Ireland from the narrow base of Anglo-Irish landlords to a wider yeomanry led by their own Catholic landlords. He sought another O'Connell, but thirty years too late; he found Parnell and the radical Land League.[104] Coercion was no solution, for the coercion of a whole people to prevent their acquiring self-government was exactly what Gladstonian liberalism was committed to prevent.[105] Full Home Rule, first through a powerful system of local government (Chamberlain's proposal to "Birminghamize" Ireland), later through a wider, national self-government, inexorably became the only Liberal solution.

Liberalism had run up against British nationalism and imperialism, and in forcing a choice Gladstone lost Chamberlain's Radicals and the Whig landlords. His new and old opponents became the Unionists, and Ireland thus paved the way for nearly twenty years of Unionist, imperialist rule of the British empire.[106]

The desertion of Chamberlain's Radicals on the Irish imperial issue helped defeat Gladstone's liberalism, but the deeper causes are not far to seek. Gladstone's stunning coalition of 1880 ranged from Whig aristocrats, through Dissent and the middle class, to principled liberalism of the national and Cobdenite variety, and to skilled working-class radicalism led by Chamberlain. This wide coalition had assumed that an identity existed between property, liberty of persons and states, democracy, and Britain's own interests. That identity collapsed when the underpropertied actively voted, when liberty was proposed for hostile colonies such as Ireland, and when foreign powers no longer followed British merchants into new markets but instead competed for the division of England's informal imperial patrimony.

104. Shannon, p. 153.
105. Robinson, "Imperial Problems in British Politics," pp. 156–57.
106. Chamberlain had favored political reform in Ireland, extending the sort of reform he had promoted in Birmingham; but independence, the dissolution of the empire, was a different matter. For the empire was not an organization of convenience, it was the national patrimony of all the British people, of the masses whom the Irish were (in his view) permitted to join but not to subvert. To the Whigs, Britain's power and their own estates were threatened by a truly self-ruling Ireland. Their youthful adventures in liberating Greece were not to be repeated at home. Chamberlain's ideas were close to "social imperialism" as described by Semmel, *Imperialism and Social Reform*, p. 12.

The Imperial Coalition, 1886–1906

The imperial coalition of Conservatives and Unionists that replaced the Liberals in 1886 forms the endpoint of this comparative analysis of imperial policies. It was united by *interests*, not by abstract principles. (No Tory coalition still revering Burke and Disraeli could be united by abstract principles.) These interests were, within a range, elastic enough to produce cohesion.[107]

Chamberlain's Radicals demanded social reform at home to strengthen the empire. The Whigs required a more thoroughgoing defense of the fundamental rights of property at home and of the interests of Britain abroad than Gladstone had provided. The Tory aristocrats now differed little from their Whig cousins, except for a more reverential attitude toward the established church, and indeed a few Tory Democrats, Churchill among them, found Chamberlain sympathetic. The new force of "Tory Villadom"—converted members of the once liberal middle class—raucously adopted the new creed of Disraelian imperialism: maximum noise abroad and utmost quiet at home.[108]

With Salisbury at the helm, however, the touch of an utterly careful diplomat was applied to all questions at home and abroad. Each interest had to sacrifice something, but it was Chamberlain who had to sacrifice the most.[109] To keep the coalition together, social reform at home had to be shelved; only abroad could Chamberlain exercise his great capacities for social engineering. Even in the empire he had to wait for better, more stable times. Salisbury described the linchpin of his party in these words: "It is a party shackled by tradition; all the cautious people, all the timid, all the unimaginative, belong to it. . . . Yet the Conservative Party is the Imperial Party."[110] Indeed, the protection and promotion of the empire was to him part of a broader commitment to resist the disintegration of Britain: "It [disintegration] menaces us in the most subtle and in the most glaring forms—in the loss of large branches and limbs of our Empire [presumably a reference to the Transvaal and the growing crisis in Ireland], and in the slow estrangement of the classes which make up the *nation* to whom the Empire belongs."[111]

107. Fraser, chap. 4.
108. Robinson, "Imperial Problems in British Politics," pp. 158–59.
109. Thornton, *The Imperial Idea*, p. 113.
110. Quoted in Shannon, p. 229.
111. Quoted in Cecil, *Salisbury*, 3:70–71.

To Salisbury, imperial and domestic disintegration, both products of Liberal and Radical policies, were intimately connected. He thus appealed directly to the nation as a whole, a nation he saw as a balance of classes led by the Conservative aristocracy, for electoral support to avoid the collapse of the empire and divisive social reform.[112] Salisbury and the Unionists focused on Disraeli's imperial vision, a decade and a half old, as a way to bring Britain back together again.

They rejected self-government for the formally ruled colonies, and Ireland, though it possessed a wide franchise exercised at Westminster, was not allowed self-determination. Indian national efforts towards the development of self-government were vetoed, and the permanent Raj was to be defended.[113] In South Africa the separatism of the Boers was contained by foreign policy and later by a war of annexation against a country to which Gladstone's Liberals had granted effective independence.[114] Where Liberalism had sought political development leading to what we would now term a free commonwealth, the Unionists sought a permanent empire.

They sought to integrate both the defense and the commerce of the already self-governing colonies, replacing liberalism's policies of "natural affection" with imperial exhortation. Among the more extreme Unionists, and particularly among the Birmingham Unionists who followed Chamberlain, this movement culminated in the endorsement of an imperial tariff.[115]

They decidedly shifted the Liberal consensus on the defensive protection of trade in their dealings with the new tropical territories. Beginning about 1888, in Ronald Robinson's words, "For the first time the Foreign Office was carrying out a deliberate expansion according to a long-term conception of the Empire's strategic needs. Previous annexations by comparison had been haphazard expedients for the protection of existing interests. . . . "[116] Egypt joined the list of proposedly

112. "In imperialism (including in this not only the question of Empire but also of union with Ireland) the party had found a cause with a mighty appeal to the voter. Indeed, only from the election of 1886, at which Gladstone raised the 'cry' of Home Rule, did the party win those majorities of the popular vote which had eluded even Disraeli." Beer, p. 272.

113. Hutchins, *Illusion of Permanence*, chap. 9.

114. E. Halevy, *A History of the English People in the Nineteenth Century*, trans. E. I. Watkins, 2d rev. ed. (London, 1949–52), 5:33.

115. W. P. Morrell, *British Colonial Policy in the Mid-Victorian Age* (London, 1969), p. 39.

116. Robinson, "Imperial Problems in British Politics," p. 167.

permanent acquisitions, and chartered companies were encouraged to effect a cheap expansion of rule. The increased importance of the colonies was reflected in Chamberlain's decision to take the secretaryship for the colonies. He turned this formerly humdrum office into a hive of activism. He attempted, with new programs aimed at future development, to justify the empire's current cost and to provide the economic and military power that Disraeli had called for in his initiation of a constructivist imperialism.[117]

By 1892 Gladstonian liberalism was in full rout. The Liberal government of 1892 was dependent upon the Irish Nationalists, and thus Home Rule was their first item of business. But the Liberals also depended upon the liberal imperialists and were required, therefore, to bring in Lord Rosebery as foreign secretary. He was able to rely upon his imperialist faction of the Liberal party (a remnant of the Whigs) and the full support of the Unionists to conduct a holding operation for Unionist imperial policy.[118] The return of the old liberalism had to wait for Unionist mistakes to reunify Liberals and Radicals in a great coalition in 1905. In that year the costs of the Boer War, the alienation of Dissent, and the threat to free trade posed by Conservative endorsements of tariffs brought in Sir Henry Campbell-Bannerman's Liberal-Radical ministry. That ministry once again appeased Boer nationalists, revived the Radical social program that Chamberlain had been required to shelve, and took further steps toward Irish Home Rule.

The years between 1886 and 1906, however, had been the years of the imperial coalition. Then, as never before and never since, the imperial idea ruled British politics. The Conservatives, not mired in inconvenient principles, seemed to offer Britain an imperial solution to international competition in a world of continental states.[119]

The Political Economy of Metropolitan Imperialism

Transnational and Metropolitan Effects

The simple dichotomy between left and right, reform and reaction, is inadequate for understanding the metropolitan roots of imperialism. Nor is the dichotomy between those who favored imperialism and those who opposed it an adequate touchstone—one needs to ask what type

117. Shannon, p. 293.
118. R. James, *Rosebery* (London, 1963), pp. 281, 317.
119. Thornton, *The Imperial Idea*, p. 125.

of empire and where, for all were imperialists of one stamp or another. Yet it does not follow that domestic factors played little role in the nature and development of the empire, nor that some nearly homogeneous state or official position defined Britain's policy toward empire. The various strains of late-Victorian imperialism were thoroughly grounded in the domestic political economy of the British metropole, which helped to shape the rate of expansion and the form of empire.

Two conclusions emerge from the preceding analysis of the historical evolution of imperial policy. Both the Liberals and the Conservatives were imperialists. Both were determined to defend Britain's massive stake in India from attack and armed subversion. Both were prepared to protect the worldwide spread of British trade and investment. Both were prepared to exercise substantial informal influence or, where needed, informal control. And both were prepared to see the empire grow if growth were necessary to maintain these commitments. Britain's economic interests called for the expansion of empire irrespective of international strategic rivalry; empire expanded in the Niger Delta even before French and German rivals made themselves felt, though eventually foreign rivalry did escalate support for transnational expansion.

Yet Conservatives, later joined by the Unionists, were the party of the "empire." But for their dominance of late nineteenth-century metropolitan politics, the empire would have been very different. They created more empire, accelerated imperialism, and encouraged and sustained formal imperialism.

Indeed, the similarity and continuity between the imperial policies of the two parties appear in large measure the product merely of the nature of two-party politics, the minimal stability of bureaucratic administration, and the consequent near-impossibility of more than marginal policy changes.[120] The Tories' aggressive gambit soon became the Liberals' status quo; the turmoil of Liberal management of the status quo, the Tories' mandate for active imperial extension. Fear of a Cabinet breakup, and thus of a Conservative victory, seems to have pushed the Liberals into a forward imperialism in the 1880s. Yet the Conservatives seem not to have been pulled back. The political, social, and economic elites seemed eager to endorse imperial successes, provided they did not result in an expensive colonial war. The continuity of expansion was the continuity of a line drawn between the top and the bottom of a flight of

120. See Robert Dahl, *Polyarchy* (New Haven, 1971), chap. 2.

stairs. The line will be straight, but it will fail to register the steps in between.

The difference in "push" for imperial expansion lay in the parties' differing commitments to different sectors of the empire. In India the Liberals envisaged growing self-government, the Conservatives a permanent Raj. In Africa the Liberals sought to protect trade informally while after about 1890 the Unionists, envisaging "another India," pursued a miniscramble to acquire formally ruled territory. With regard to the self-governing colonies, the Liberals aimed at no more than ties of affection and an eventual commonwealth, the Unionists a closer military and economic integration. And in China the Liberals aimed at the expansion of trade, the Unionists at securing territory and spheres for investment.[121] Some of these effects are also explicable in terms of pericentric and international systemic factors. Yet Britain's independent metropolitan drives shaped the periphery (where there was the high salience of transnational trade) and the international system (as other states felt *they* were responding to Britain).

The Roots of Political Difference

In the crucial domestic politics of Victorian Britain the differences in attitude toward and interest in empire among Liberal, Conservative, Radical, Whig, Unionist, and other groups can be traced to four features of political change. The first two are the values and the material interests that drive political action. They can preserve a political order but they can also be a force for change.[122] As economic change creates tensions and mobilizes hitherto subject groups, these groups make new and different demands on the established political system which have to be

121. The complexity of these differences is well suggested by Marshall, "Imperial Factor in the Liberal Decline." Each individual developed a particular slant on imperial questions covering differences in priority, goals, and means. Reflecting some of these particular differences, Dilke once wrote, "I'm as great a jingo in Central Asia as I am a scuttler in South Africa" (quoted in Marshall, p. 133). Despite these individual differences, politicians acted as if and contemporary observers saw definable factions that distinguished groups of individuals from each other and provided the cement for political coalitions. See Justin McCarthy, *A History of Our Times*, vol. 3 (New York, 1903), pp. 2–38, for a striking portrait of these policy currents, and see Beer, *British Politics*, and G. Kitson Clark, *The Making of Victorian England* (New York, 1971). For a discussion of these differences in the context of British policy in Egypt see Agatha Ramm, "Great Britain and France in Egypt, 1876–1882," in Prosser Gifford and W. Roger Louis, eds., *France and Britain in Africa* (New Haven, 1971), pp. 73–75. For British policy in China, see W. L. Langer, *Diplomacy of Imperialism* (New York, 1951), chap. 12.

122. Beer, *British Politics*, Conclusion.

either accommodated or suppressed.[123] Each regrouping reshapes the political process, thereby reforming policy.

The other two features are institutional context, which shapes political action (most simply by the size of the electorate), and the strategies of leaders trying to assemble coalitions that can allocate values and interests. From the rise of a newly mobilized class, political entrepreneurs can draw a variety of coalitions, coalitions that reflect the variety of cleavages within the class as well as possible combinations with other subgroups already mobilized.[124]

In this perspective the political evolution of nineteenth-century Britain can be summarized as follows. Mid-Victorian popular politics were dominated by the liberalism of laissez-faire and the principled politics of Gladstone. In the cabinet and the House of Lords Whig ideas of discrete, balanced interests and interested policy still held sway under the leadership of Palmerston. For the empire, this Whig-Liberal mixture meant grudging tolerance of formal rule in India, encouragement of self-government in the white colonies to reduce costs, and active promotion of informal influence in peripheral regions to secure the expansion of trade. These policies combined the interests of the Whig oligarchy, the moderate Liberals, and the Radicals. The last two political factions were composed of the gentry and the middle classes—professional and business—admitted to the franchise in 1832.[125] They were sustained by the cheap daily provincial press, militant religious nonconformity, and the beginnings of organized labor.[126] Gladstone both represented the Whigs and, in a remarkably personal way, embodied the hopes of the Liberals and Radicals.

The Conservative party, on the other hand, spent much of the period between 1850 and 1874 in the political wilderness, the rump of a once great party. It still adhered to its ideology of a conservative social hierarchy and paternalism, and it was based on the landed interest—the aristocracy and squires of Britain—that still retained great influence in the county electorate of Parliament and in the House of Lords.

Political institutions in Britain mirrored these political currents. The Reform Act of 1832 opened the franchise to the wealthy middle classes

123. S. Huntington, *Political Order in Changing Societies* (New Haven, 1968), chaps. 1, 2; see F. Schurman, *The Logic of World Power* (New York, 1974), for a model. For Victorian Britain, see Kitson Clark, p. 240.

124. J. Schumpeter, *Capitalism, Socialism, and Democracy* (New York, 1950), chap. 22.

125. Beer, chaps. 1, 2.

126. Paul Adelman, *Gladstone, Disraeli, and Later Victorian Politics* (London, 1970), p. 5.

in the cities. These classes adhered to the Whigs, whose political culture accepted urban values and policies promoting industrial and commercial development, national economic power, and worldwide free trade. None of these values or policies were compatible with the interests of the Old Tories' bedrock of support, the landed and less wealthy gentry.[127]

After a vigorous campaign launched by the Whigs, and under the threat of revolutionary changes from lower down the social spectrum, Parliament had admitted the middle classes. The result was the dominant Whig-Liberal coalition of the early and mid-Victorian years. Whig landlords led commercial expansion abroad through free trade. At home the New Poor Law, the Bank Act (to protect business from excessive, exogenous, monetary fluctations), and the suppression of Chartism reflected the composition of a coalition that rallied all but the Tory squires and aristocracy. British industry boomed, exporting manufactured cotton and wool to the underdeveloped countries and machines and investments to the developing.

The late 1860s to the mid 1880s was, by contrast, a period of considerable confusion. The strength of Gladstonian liberalism appeared greater than before, but the appearance masked a growing tension as Whig ideas diminished in influence while democratic radicalism rose in strength. The Radicals sought greater liberty for the individual, particularly the underpropertied individual, at the expense of laissez-faire and the property rights of the aristocracy. At the same time the old Tory ideology was being refined under Disraeli's urgings into a broader sense of national patriotism, of a society united to promote the joint interests of all, led by the governing classes of Britain (still primarily the aristocracy of the land). The advantages of Whig liberalism were in imperial and international terms reversed. Previously, Tory ideas of conflicting interests that required negotiation had appeared quaint in a world characterized by a harmony of international free trade and an empire ruled through informal influence; now, Tory ideas seemed made for constructing coalition out of confusion. Their ideas were needed to cope with a world that rejected harmony as a British ideology. They appeared a newly efficient means to manage an empire that required formal rule because the "strong native powers" that had sustained informal rule either collapsed or became too strong.

Conservative ideology admitted both the balance of power and "native" populations that had to be ruled. Liberal ideology found the former

---

127. Cain and Hopkins, "Political Economy of British Expansion Overseas."

a problem, a discrepancy awaiting a "Concerted" solution, and the latter a contradiction of the principles of individual freedom which required either equality or slavery.[128] In domestic politics, where liberalism called for an amalgamation of classes (in fact, a widening of the middle class), conservatism called for an alliance of separate classes within the unity of the nation.[129]

Political institutions experienced equally significant developments. In 1867, the lower middle and upper working classes were finally admitted to the ballot. Seventeen years later the agricultural labor force similarly joined the constitution. The reform of 1832 had doubled the electorate, but it still comprised only about 10 percent of the male population; in 1867 the "leap in the dark" trebled the electorate. An enormous mass of new voters lacked the social and economic power that previously had accompanied the widening of the franchise. Their political interests were, moreover, profoundly ambiguous. Liberalism offered full acceptance in the middle class and a religious link in Dissent, but its ranks included those with whom the working class were in economic rivalry.[130] The Conservatives, on the other hand, were the party of the classes least likely to accept labor, and long hostile to the extension of the franchise. But they were also prepared to claim the unity of nation and actually to legislate specific measures in the interests of labor even if those measures hampered the free interplay of market forces.[131]

The farm laborer who entered the suffrage in 1884 faced a similar dilemma. Should he express his hostility to the landlords as ill-paying employers or recognize his agricultural solidarity with them? In the cases of both the urban working classes and the agricultural laborers new methods of mobilizing these amorphous social interests were required. No longer would parliamentary clubs suffice; party organizations were needed and developed on a local basis. The successes of the National Liberal Federation and the Conservative Primrose League began to determine the outcome of the political contest.[132]

Changes were occurring not merely at the lower end of the electoral-social spectrum but also in a "New Gentry" at the top of the middle

128. See C. V. Woodward, *The Strange Career of Jim Crow* (New York, 1955), concerning the United States and the Philippines; and N. Machiavelli, *The Discourses*, trans. L. Ricci (New York, 1950), bk. II, chap. 2, on the special oppression of being ruled by republics.

129. H. J. Hanham, *Elections and Party Management* (London, 1959), e.g. pp. 108–9.

130. H. Pelling, *The Social Geography of British Elections* (London, 1967), e.g. pp. 208–10.

131. Paul Smith, *Disraelian Conservatism and Social Reform* (London, 1967), p. 202.

132. Adelman, chap. 3.

class. This transformation was in part due to the same economic development that was raising the poor above subsistence.[133] Steady and
lengthy affluence removed the Victorian middle classes from their revolutionary origins and created the sense of permanence needed for gentry
status. Professionalization had similar effects as it removed lawyers,
doctors, and others from the marketplace. The middle class became a
conservative social defense against public interference with property.
Reinforcing its social conservatism was the reform of the public schools.
Aspiring upper middle-class youths could now join the old gentry both
in school and in the burgeoning bureaucracy. There also appeared an
artificial revival of ancient values—an "English way of life" resting on
the supposed harmonies of the traditional countryside. However much
this pastoral vision clashed, and perhaps because it clashed, with the
realities of continuing urbanization, it became an ideal to which the
middle class increasingly aspired.[134] Now tamed, the middle classes became aware that Britain and they no longer faced a world amenable to
both Britain's power and general rules of peaceable competition. New,
strong powers were growing and demanding a share in Britain's markets
and Britain's place in the world political system.

The outlines of the actual political combination that the Conservatives
would make were not clear in advance. Despite Disraeli's assiduous
wooing of Tory democracy, it appeared likely that the great mass of
working-class voters would follow the Radical leadership of such men
as Joseph Chamberlain and enter the Liberal ranks. Gladstone's victory
of 1868, wasted through political confusion by 1874 but resoundingly
reaffirmed after Disraeli's adventurism in 1880, seemed to indicate so.
Strains were growing, however. A realignment along new social lines
became possible.

The Economics and Strategy of the Imperial Coalition

Disraeli, Salisbury, and Gladstone were the political entrepreneurs
who competed to construct an effective coalition during these years.
The Conservatives won, primarily because their ideological and institutional position was flexible. Unlike the Liberals, their party did not
rest upon the presupposition of harmony. In a world where increasing
rivalry was becoming manifest, this was a vital asset.

133. Kitson Clark, p. 240.
134. Martin J. Wiener, *English Culture and the Decline of the Industrial Spirit, 1850–1980*
(Cambridge, 1981), chap. 3.

Although the Conservatives failed in their appeal to the "Tory" working man, the appeal did mobilize some local working-class grievances against Liberal capitalists, such as the anti-immigrant vote in Lancashire and parts of London. More importantly, the Tory welfare program, limited as it was, provided an ideological base for the assimilation of the Chamberlain Radicals in 1886. Some measure of social concern for the poor made the Unionists' shift possible, and the party remained a sufficient bulwark of privilege to attract the Whigs when Gladstone attacked Whig property in Ireland. More important still, after 1874 the upper middle class began to sense the threat to property represented by liberalism's flirtation with radicalism.

It was not financiers, or monopoly capitalists, or war machines that appear to have been driving imperialism, but indirect economic imperialism was, I believe, at work. The industrial revolution mobilized new social classes, the industrial workers and villa bourgeois that the Liberals had such difficulty in capturing. More directly, the shape of the opposing coalitions emerged in large part from the evolution of sectors in the transnational economy.

Sectors and classes, as noted above, divided into groups that leaned toward the domestic, the international, and the imperial economies. Domestic sectors and classes (service and much of the working class) seem to have been swayed by particular ties or by such consumer interests as the price of bread, which threatened Conservative schemes for an imperial tariff. Internationally efficient industries retained, not surprisingly, an international outlook, promoting free trade, antimilitarism, and actual free trade imperialism to protect trade from noneconomic disruption. They also retained their Liberal allegiance. Economic internationalism drove the coal industry, especially in Wales and the north, and the shipping industry (until the 1890s) toward liberalism. But the evolution of the economy produced great defections: wool manufacturers, for example, shifted to the Conservatives as foreign efficiency and tariffs in their overseas markets rose. The free-trading vision offered little in the way of solution to their contracting markets, while the Conservative's empire preference might. Most significantly, the Midlands machine industries, headquarters of Chamberlain's once radical liberalism, made a similar switch, also hoping for better results from imperial Unionism. Much of this economic pressure was complex: for the great cotton industry, home of Manchester liberalism, both the Conservatives' vision of an integral empire and the Liberals' free-trading empire-commonwealth would protect their Indian and tropical markets.

Cross-pressured, they divided on other lines. Lastly, international finance, Hobson's bugbear, shifted to the Conservative camp, though probably due more to the assimilation of their members into the new gentry than to any special financial interest in the empire.[135]

Strategic imperialism also drove Britons to the Conservatives. In a multipolar international system and empire, liberal principles and methods seemed, as in Ireland and Egypt, no longer a source of power but rather a catalyst of chaos. The rise of Germany and Italy, the recovery of France, and the growth of the United States and Russia—and their decisions to compete in the global periphery—made the global liberal vision appear, even at home, merely one ideological and national vision, and not a very effective one at that.[136]

This situation did not produce an inevitable, formal imperialism that only the Conservatives, representing the real British economic and strategic interest, could rule. Economic coalitions also had purely political roots. Gladstone's great reforming government of 1868–74 was defeated as much by alienating Dissent through its Education Act as by any other factor. Disraeli's "new imperialism" thus rested in part on religious disagreement. Much of the vote in Lancashire shifted to the Conservatives at the same time, not because informal imperialism failed to serve its textile interests but because working-class voters opposed the use of immigrant labor by local Liberal capitalists. Disraeli's coalition of 1874–80 came apart when depression mobilized both middle-class and working-class opposition, but that opposition was also galvanized by his callous dismissal of concern for the rights of foreign peoples brutally suppressed by the Ottoman empire.[137] The British working class was too close, historically, to the time of Peterloo when they too had feared—however exaggerated we may now judge that fear to have been—being the targets of aristocratic sabers. The Whig landlords found Gladstone's attack on their property in Ireland far from congenial, but they, the families that had founded the British empire in the eighteenth century, were also distressed by his vacillations. He seemed to be wasting the public legacy of international predominance which their ancestors had deeded to the nation. The strategic roots of the imperial coalition that the Conservatives won also were not inevitable gifts. The U.S. liberal

135. F. S. C. Northedge, *One Hundred Years of International Relations* (New York, 1971), pp. 50–51; Cecil, *Salisbury*, 2:263; Adelman, chap. 5.

136. This argument is made by P. M. Kennedy in a chapter entitled "Weakening of Liberalism," in his *The Rise of the Anglo-German Antagonism* (London, 1980), pp. 150–51.

137. Trevor Lloyd, *The General Election of 1880* (London, 1968), pp. 142–43.

regime was able to meet multipolar competition and successfully manage its imperialism.

The construction of coalitions was never a simple matter of economic or strategic addition. Other values and interests entered into coalition making. Nor were economic interests themselves straightforward. Combinations of material interest, traditional standards, and hopes for the future, they were capable of producing odd bedfellows. Among the oddest was the alliance of radical Unionists, many of whom had been vehement in the attack on the landed aristocracy, with those very landed aristocrats.

Disraeli and Salisbury, and Chamberlain, eventually created their coalition by capitalizing on three particular advantages. First, the attempt to rule an empire liberally in an age of nationalism helped produce a threat to property in Ireland, which alienated the Whigs, and created the chaotic management of imperial and international relations characteristic of the Gladstonian ministry from 1880 to 1886. Second, much of the middle-class public was alarmed by the threat to national power which liberalism seemed to represent. Disraeli had been insensitive to middle-class values before 1880; the more careful Salisbury was able to capitalize on Gladstone's repeated failures after 1880, in Egypt, in the Sudan (and particularly Gordon's death), in the matter of Boer appeasement, and most significantly in Ireland. Third, the Radical leaders, particularly Chamberlain, were not wedded to abstract Liberal principle. Determined to promote the democratization of British society, they saw Liberal principles as a threat to British power and economic welfare. And if liberalism reduced national and imperial resources, it would preclude the social efficiency and democratic redistribution that they ultimately sought.

Out of this variety of material the Conservatives created the imperial coalition. Its foundations were a changed economy and an altered focus abroad, reorientations of ideology, new developments in international and imperial politics, and the political skill of Conservative leaders. The coalition created a Conservative empire, an empire that would have existed anyway but whose specific development, whose formal character of rule, whose rapid and preemptive extension, and especially whose evolution away from self-government and toward a permanent Raj reflect the Tory-imperial imprint. The Tories gloried in the exercise of power and welcomed its expansion. A lingering commitment to social hierarchy at home made them more comfortable with formal rule abroad.

Their empire reflected British interests, but particularly those interests formed and amalgamated in the imperial coalition.

Empires, in short, are not the inevitable product of competing national interests. Nor are they the straightforward sum of the economic interests that they may incorporate. But they are the product of the interests, material and ideal, of the dominant domestic coalition. The operations of domestic politics do not create empires. They do, however, significantly shape them, and abroad in the colonies, if in fragmented form, they reproduce the ideas, the institutions, and the interests of the imperial coalition.

CHAPTER 12

France, Germany, and Spain

Britain's was hardly the only empire of the nineteenth century. France and Germany established empires in a century that also saw the disintegration of Spain's imperial pretensions. Was the building of political coalitions the key to these imperial expansions also, or were more fundamental economic or strategic forces determining? In this chapter we shall be exploring those aspects of the size, form, or rate of expansion of the nineteenth-century imperialisms of these metropoles which transnational and metropolitan forces explain. Particularly interesting is the case of Spain. Did Spain lose the structural prerequisites of metropolitan imperialism, or did it simply encounter an effective rebellion?

French Imperialism

The French empire in the nineteenth century was to all appearances the second empire of the times. It lacked an equivalent to Britain's Indian diadem, which France had fought for and lost in the colonial wars of the eighteenth century. Moreover, it had lost the most profitable colony of the eighteenth century, Saint Domingue, during the Revolution and the Napoleonic Wars.[1] But in the nineteenth century France conquered

---

1. D. K. Fieldhouse, *The Colonial Empires* (New York, 1966), chap. 8.

a new colonial empire of a most impressive geographical extent. Algeria and Indochina were this empire's most substantial centers. And the bulk of France's colonial real estate was gained in the early 1880s.[2]

Four features of French imperialism attracted the notice of contemporary observers. First, the empire was less substantial than Britain's. It contained fewer people; it was comparatively poor. Second, French economic activity was much less substantial. Trade and investment were much less focused on the empire than they were in Britain, in part because only Algeria was a colony of extensive settlement.[3] Third, the French emphasized direct rule; the British, indirect rule. Although France did rely on local, indigenous elites, it generally relied upon lower-level elites. As a result, French colonies had more administrators per capita than did British colonies. Fourth, the French held to an ideology and a partial reality of assimilation as opposed to Britain's policy of dual mandate (separate development).[4]

The Early Empire

Algiers, the later core of a great African empire, was acquired as a desperate last-minute venture by Charles X. He hoped by this Napoleonic stroke to regain the loyalty of the legislative chamber; he failed and was replaced by Louis Philippe, the bourgeois king, in 1830.[5] But the new regime kept Algiers and was forced to expand its holdings to provide a secure hinterland for the coastal city. Despite governmental revolutions in 1820, 1830, and 1848, France retained sufficient homogeneity of political identification (and its periods of instability were sufficiently short) to remain capable of directing and maintaining an empire.[6]

Under Napoleon III (1851–1870) metropolitan forces and institutions played a more consistently dynamic role in encouraging not merely the maintenance but also the expansion of empire. The empire was extended into Cochin China, inland from Senegal, and most spectacularly, across

---

2. D. W. Brogan, *France under the Republic* (New York, 1940), p. 217, and Fieldhouse, pp. 302–5.

3. R. Robinson, "Introduction," to H. Brunschwig, *French Colonialism, 1871–1914,* trans. W. G. Brown (New York, 1966).

4. By 1940 there were 1,315 Europeans for 20 million Africans in British Nigeria, 3,660 Europeans for 15 million Africans in French West Africa. R. Delavignette, *Freedom and Authority in French West Africa* (London, 1950), pp. 50–51.

5. J. B. Bury, *France, 1814–1940* (Philadelphia, 1949), pp. 43–44.

6. There was no sustained period of civil war such as occurred in the United States in the 1860s.

the Atlantic to the French-dominated empire of Mexico.[7] Napoleon's coup brought him formal supremacy in offices akin to that of Augustus in Rome, but he lacked the transnational, political, and military bases of power that Augustus had exercised. The possession of the form without the substance generated a tense dynamism: attempting to live up to the appearance of both the Napoleonic legend and the imperial tradition, Napoleon III exhausted the slender resources of France and brought about his own deposition in 1870.

Napoleon's historical task, as he conceived it, was to maintain the social order of French property against the disorders of republican factions and to maintain the glory of the united nation against the restraints of a Concert system erected to counter a revival of French Napoleonism of the very sort he represented.[8] Domestically, however, his power base was weak. The regime rested on a stalemate between the republican left and the monarchist right. Napoleon appealed to their minimal common interests in law, order, and international prestige. Napoleon, the second choice of every class, was especially dependent on the apparent support of the peasantry. Peasants, although they may form an ultimate reservoir of power, do not make governments or a court society, and for the latter Napoleon looked to financial and mercantile elites as *nouveaux* as himself. To supply governments, he fostered nationalistic ministries able to mollify both the right and the left.[9]

He maintained this balance by promoting French prestige in Europe. French arms and diplomacy achieved a new stature by their successful participation in the Crimean War. He pleased the left by being anti-Russian, the right by being pro-Catholic (the war originated in a dispute between Orthodox and Catholic clergy for the control of Christian sites in Palestine). His regime paid the price of tenuous political support by promoting special interests. Among these special-interest policies were the support of Catholic missionaries under attack in Cochin China and the debt-collecting expedition to Mexico.[10] Both were costly and merely temporary successes: the first appeased doubtful supporters on the Catholic right, the second, his court circle in the center. His Italian policy in the 1860s, however, met an even less happy fate as the unharmonious

---

7. Bury, p. 104.

8. Ibid., pp. 88–89.

9. Theodore Zeldin, *France, 1848–1945*, vol. 1: *Ambition, Love, and Politics* (London, 1973), pp. 511–13.

10. D. W. Brogan, *The Development of Modern France, 1870–1939*, vol. 1 (New York, 1966), p. 233.

coalition supporting the emperor was fatally strained by his awkward juggling of interests. He attempted to further French power and glory by establishing a French hegemony in Italy, with the help of the Sardinian monarchy, at the same time extending France's boundaries to include Savoy and Nice.[11] Moreover, he hoped to satisfy the right by supporting papal direction of Italy and the left by aiding Italian, liberal (that is, anticlerical) nationalism. He grossly underestimated the contradictions among these aims. Instead, a unified Italy emerged potentially to rival France's Mediterranean hegemony, the Pope was stripped of much temporal power, and Italian nationalists became anti-French.

Napoleon's jury-rigged regime began to split open. His disastrous bid for control over southern Germany was called by a more astute and more powerful Bismarck. Napoleon's desperate bid for European hegemony collapsed in the Franco-Prussian War.[12]

The Republican Empire

The residue of Napoleon III's imperialism included Cochin, an expanded Algeria, and Senegal. What was a republic pledged to universal rights to do with colonial possessions? Yet more strangely, Republicans now engaged in a geographic scramble to extend the conquests of the Napoleon whose adventurism they had decried. The republic added, in the course of the age of imperialism, Tonkin, Annam, Cambodia, and Laos in southeast Asia; the expansion of French control in North Africa; French West Africa; and Madagascar. Reasons for this imperial scramble appear variously in France's international position, her domestic and international economy, and her political system.

The entrance of new colonial powers in the peripheral world overwhelmed the Pax Britannica, ending the tacit arrangement that left to Britain the management 'of the periphery in the interest of European commerce. It became more advantageous for each country to maintain its own security in the periphery. The Scramble and the formalization of imperial rule followed in part from this change in the structure of international competition in the periphery. At the same time, however, each state also had more particular reasons to promote a foreign policy of imperial expansion.

France seems to have been a improbable candidate for metropolitan imperialism. The defeat in 1870 and the loss of Alsace-Lorraine focused

---

11. W. L. Langer, *European Alliances and Alignments* (New York, 1950), pp. 6–7.
12. Ibid., chap. 2.

French attention forcibly upon the European balance of power.[13] Although it is a common opinion that France sought empire as direct or sufficient compensation for the loss of Alsace-Lorraine, in fact the new territories could not be compared to the lost provinces. "I have lost two children, and you offer me twenty domestic servants," Paul Déroulède, poet member of the Assembly retorted when just such an exchange was suggested.[14] Moreover, no colonial adventures could be undertaken which would reduce France's ability to stand up to future German threats or to fail to take advantage of future German weakness. In order to regain Alsace-Lorraine, France had to nourish both its military and its diplomatic strengths. The army had to be reorganized, allies reassembled. The former required the absence of exhausting colonial wars, the latter, few colonial diplomatic squabbles. The Blue Line of the Vosges formed a constant horizon for French consciousness, even if the lure of a colonial adventure occasionally distracted politicians, as it would in Egypt in 1882.[15]

Two international factors did, however, play significant roles in promoting French imperialism. First was a special sensitivity to national prestige prevalent in the period. Prestige is to power as credit is to money (a rational basis exists for the pursuit of both).[16] The basis of this new sensitivity appears to have been the rise of new participants in power, the crumbling of old hierarchies, and the need to establish new order in an arena that lacked institutionalized hierarchy. Leveling took place both domestically and internationally. Hierarchies had to be based on the consent of formal equals, a consent that lacked permanent and institutional form, and the result was a concern for contingent and relative fame—prestige.[17] Colonies were prestigious because they were one of the attributes of Britain, which had been at the top and was still a leading state.[18]

13. G. P. Gooch, *Franco-German Relations* (New York, 1922), p. 24.

14. G. Chapman, *The Third Republic of France* (London, 1962), p. 247.

15. Brogan, 1:117; the colonial empire, although secondary, was a source of diplomatic tension.

16. R. Aron, *Peace and War*, trans. R. Howard and A. B. Fox (Garden City, N.Y., 1966), chap. 1.

17. H. Speier, "Honor," in his *Social Order and the Risks of War* (Cambridge, Mass., 1952), chap. 4.

18. Thus Georges Leygues, an ardent colonialist, reminded a colonial congress in 1906: "Just after 1870 it was colonial policy which gave us fresh energy, renewed our courage and once more brought to our spirits a taste of action and life. It enabled us to prove that our trials had not deprived us of sufficient confidence in ourselves for us to embark on the greatest undertakings and to carry them to fruition." Quoted in Brunschwig, pp. 175–77.

The second international factor was the need to obtain Germany's support for any French policy not directed against Germany. As France's only real strategic threat, Germany could veto all other French initiatives by raising tension over Alsace-Lorraine. France, moreover, needed Germany's positive diplomatic support to pursue foreign policies elsewhere. Since other policies were likely to bring France into conflict with potential anti-German allies, such as Britain and Russia, France would have become totally isolated without German support—a fate reminiscent of the disaster of 1870. In the 1880s Germany also held a crucial vote on the Egyptian Caisse whose acquiescence Britain required to rule and reform Egypt. Making this trump card available to France reduced the threat of colonial confrontation with Britain. Yet these strategic interests in imperialism are altogether slight. France, unlike Britain, had no choice but to be strategically dependent on the European balance of power. It was in the French economy, society, and political process that one finds the forces driving French imperialism.

The French economy was still preponderantly agricultural, and small farms, raising grain and wine, dominated the landscape. Under Napoleon III, however, the French economy had experienced substantial growth.[19] With the spread of the railroad, the price of wheat rose near to world (that is, British) levels as markets were opened to previously isolated farmers. British imports, made much more substantial by the Cobden-Chevalier Treaty of 1860, which opened the British and French markets to each others' products, brought boom conditions to wine and certain industrial products.[20] The silk industry, a labor-intensive sector typical of the first phase of the industrial revolution, found 65 percent of its output flowing to the British market. Napoleon, a man of the bankers and the merchants, helped shake the French economy out of years of isolated stagnation and loosed the forces of the industrial revolution.[21] (Other industries suffered from competition with more efficient British producers, of course, and helped remove him from power in 1870.) Napoleon also encouraged and defended French investment projects abroad.

After 1870 the French economy developed a special relationship to

19. Chapman, p. 84; more than one-half of the population was working in agriculture. See also Claude Fohlen, "The Industrial Revolution in France, 1700–1914," in Carlo Cipolla, ed., *The Fontana Economic History of Europe*, vol. 1 (London, 1973), p. 29.

20. J. H. Clapham, *The Economic Development of France and Germany, 1815–1914* (London, 1961), pp. 178–80.

21. C. Kindleberger, *Economic Growth in France and Britain* (Cambridge, Mass., 1964), pp. 282–83.

the empire which was characterized by two factors. One was the persistent reality of the meagerness of its connection with the empire. The other was a growing demand by certain sectors for an economic policy of imperialism.

The reality was hardly conducive to extensive imperialism. French overseas trade was considerably less than half of Britain's, and foreign investment, both stock and flow, bore no comparison to that of Britain's highly internationalized economy.[22] Moreover, while 45 percent of British foreign investment before 1914 wound up in the empire, only 9 percent of French foreign investment followed the flag (25% went to Russia).[23] India was Britain's largest prewar foreign market, and its trade was a crucial prop of the British balance of payments, The French empire could provide no equivalent in importance. Finally, as Chapter 11 argued, the empire was a growing factor in the British economy throughout the nineteenth century; France's trade with its empire, by contrast, was proportionally less at the end of the nineteenth century than it was at the time of the Revolution.[24]

It is not surprising that France, having neither a strategic commitment nor an economic orientation toward empire, developed much less of an imperial presence than did Britain.[25] Where, then, did French imperialism originate? Special economic sectors, rampant soldiers, and expansionist bureaucrats, all operating in a political environment that rewarded their particular interests, filled the imperialist gap. In particular, in the late 1870s and early 1880s, four new factors discredited the Napoleonic program of international competition and increased the interest of some economic sectors in a policy of imperial protection.

Just as the French economy was integrated by railroads, so a global economy was integrated by the combined impact of railroads and improved shipping.[26] Comparative advantage and disadvantage replaced geographical isolation as bases for trade. French agriculture, with the exception of wines, did not compare favorably with the production of

22. D. K. Fieldhouse, *Economics and Empire* (London, 1973), pp. 55–57, 18.

23. Christopher Andrew and A. S. Kanya-Forstner, *France Overseas* (London, 1981), p. 14.

24. Ibid., pp. 14–15. See also Winfried Baumgart, *Imperialism: The Idea and Reality of British and French Colonial Expansion, 1880–1914* (Oxford, 1982), pp. 114–16.

25. Brunschwig, p. 90; H. Feis, *Europe, the World's Banker* (New York, 1965), p. 55. N. Choucri and R. C. North, *Nations in Conflict* (San Francisco, 1975), pp. 36–37.

26. G. Barraclough, *Introduction to Contemporary History* (Harmondsworth, 1967), p. 59.

the American, Argentinian, or Russian plains. France's wines succumbed to phylloxera. An agricultural trade crisis followed.[27]

In industrial terms the uneven rate of economic development challenged the benefits of free trade. As the French economy in the 1870s and 1880s began to move into the second phase of the industrial revolution—capital goods, steel, and so forth—its products competed with the greater efficiency of Britain and the even greater efficiency of Germany and the United States.[28] Its infant industries demanded protection against foreign competition. The Third Republic, for reasons we shall examine below, listened to these demands against the free trade interests of merchants and financiers. The Méline Tariff of 1892 defeated the old free trade faction that had supported Napoleon's empire. But within the empire protection was introduced as early as 1877 and 1881–82 to aid French textile and other products against foreign competition.[29]

These pressures for protection coincided with the Atlantic trade depression of 1873 to 1896, which began to affect France in the late 1870s. The international and peripheral trade "pie" appeared to be shrinking. In these circumstances, competition for a constant or expanding share lent force to protection; an expanding pie might not have done so.

In the final analysis, however, protection and colonialism are not the same. Protectionists can benefit from a protected colonial market, but the investment in colonies, as one protectionist noted, may not be worthwhile: "On the trade which France does with its colonies as a whole, France loses 23 million francs a year [a negative trade balance]: to achieve which result the country spends 80 million francs."[30] Nonetheless, particular industries under the pressure of increasing international competition found the colonies a useful preserve for challenged exports. Silk manufacturers centered about the city of Lyon sought a stable source of raw silk in the empire. Sugar exporters found there a market for 68 percent of their exports.[31]

27. For this period see Peter Gourevitch, "International Trade, Domestic Coalitions, and Liberty: The Crisis of 1873–1896," *Journal of Interdisciplinary History* 8 (Autumn 1977), 281–314. See also James R. Kurth, "The Political Consequences of the Product Cycle," *International Organization* 33 (Winter 1979), 1–34.

28. E. Hobsbawm, *Industry and Empire* (New York, 1968), chaps. 9.

29. C. W. Newbury, "The Protectionist Revival in French Colonial Trade: The Case of Senegal," *Economic History Review*, 2d ser., 21 (August 1968), 337–48.

30. Brunschwig, pp. 138–39.

31. J. Laffey, "The Roots of French Imperialism: The Case of Lyon," *French Historical Studies* 6 (Spring 1969), 78–92.

These particular economic interests benefited from and agitated for a policy of imperialism. Some but not all of these industries were well represented in the pressure groups lobbying for colonial expansion.[32] But most colonialists complained, quite correctly, of the indifference of the business class. The army, however, together with much of the bureaucracy and certain political coalitions of the Third Republic, gave imperialism a much stronger welcome.

The particularly weak French state of the late 1870s and early 1880s permitted an expansion of the French empire. Both the Opportunist coalition of the Republican movement and the overseas army exploited this weakness.[33] After the extremes of 1870, when the commune of new Jacobins and communists was suppressed by an alliance of new Girondins and monarchists led by Thiers, the "republic" seemed little more than a constitutional convention for a monarchist restoration.[34] But monarchist factions could not agree, and the Opportunists—a conservative-bourgeois faction of the Republican movement—inherited the political stalemate. The Opportunists rigorously disciplined the pursuit of national prestige with a deep small-town caution. They were simultaneously determined to promote national economic development and yet to do so in a fashion that did not disturb a secure bourgeois economic society.[35]

After the temptations of a new restoration in the early 1870s, the French bourgeoisie shifted their votes to the Republicans. Though they sought stability, they were not averse to adding to the glory of the *grande nation*. The nation was the first religion of the secular bourgeoisie and the second of the practicing Catholics of the countryside. Théophile Delcassé, later colonial and foreign minister of France and a good representative of the leadership of these Republicans, captured the French national pride evoked by the disaster of 1870: "I had passed my baccalaureat and yet the glory I had so long looked forward to seemed far away . . . Wissenbourg, Forbach, Sedan, France herself torn asunder!

---

32. L. Abrams and D. J. Miller, "Who Were the French Colonialists? A Reasssessment of the Parti Colonial, 1890–1914," *Historical Journal* 19, 3 (1976), 685–725. See also the response of C. M. Andrew and A. S. Kanya-Forstner, "French Business and the French Colonialists," ibid., 19, 4 (1976), 981–1000.

33. It is to these groups (omitting "Republican," which for him goes without saying) that Jules Ferry, premier of France, refers when he warns the Chamber of Deputies, "Do not touch France, do not touch the Army." Quoted in F. L. Schurman, *War and Diplomacy in the French Republic* (Chicago, 1931), p. 74.

34. Chapman, pp. 160–61.

35. Zeldin, chap. 20.

These were moments I should never be able to forget. It was then I vowed to devote myself to my country, to make it my ambition to serve her, and to make my contribution to the reconstruction of her stricken edifice."[36]

Imperial Opportunists such as Jules Ferry sought to spread France's "language, her culture, her arms, and her genius." The order is significant—French prestige required the promulgation of a cultural and technical civilization, in the "conquests" of de Lesseps the engineer and de Brazza the explorer. Prestige also meant the export of political ideas. Military rule was not sought for its own sake. Rather, cultural assimilation, without rule, and political assimilation, when rule already existed or was necessary, were France's imperial goals. Civilization—an affirmation of universalistic republicanism—was France's equivalent of British free trade.

The Republic of the Opportunists demanded glory in foreign affairs to redress 1870. But the Republic also demanded prudence, for its electorate would suffer directly from foreign policy disasters. The Opportunist faction of the Republican movement excluded the monarchists and Napoleonists of the far right as well as the Radicals (Jacobins) and Socialists of the left. Members of the Parti Colonial, composed of pro-imperialist deputies in the Assembly and public lobbying organizations of businessmen, retired military officers, intellectuals, and civil servants, were especially prominent in the ranks of the Opportunists.[37] The Opportunist ministers sought colonialism because it seemed to promote prestige and more importantly because, being the preeminently bourgeois faction, they sought the prestige involved in the spread of France's bourgeois civilization. But the Opportunists were constrained in their pursuit of both goals. Expansion had to be truly prestigious, not adventures in the style of Napoleon III. Expansion also had to be politically cheap, not detracting from the long-term goal of revanche against Germany, and economically cheap, to protect a small-town bourgeoisie against massive military taxation.

The second Republican goal behind empire was rapid, nationalist-bourgeois development. Colonialism, Opportunists believed, would promote Republican and bourgeois interests by encouraging exports and tropical imports, by adding new opportunities for investment, and by protecting previous investments in Tunisia, Egypt, and Cochin China.

36. Speech by Delcasse, 30 July 1911, in C. Andrew, *Theophile Delcasse and the Making of the Entente Cordiale* (New York, 1968).

37. Abrams and Miller, "Who Were the French Colonialists?"

That this policy did not reflect the later realities of French trade was irrelevant; this was a program for the bourgeois Republic, a program for *future* profits as foreign competition increased and trade depression deepened. Moreover, this colonial program did reflect the interest of certain industrial sectors, sectors associated with the Opportunist faction of the Republican movement and its general orientation toward industrial capital and employment.[38]

In the late 1870s the Opportunists came to power, and France established colonial tariffs and joined the Scramble. This connection was not accidental. The old monarchial right had been anticolonial, and the Radicals saw colonialism as a distraction from revanche. To the Opportunists, however, imperialism was a part both of France's glory and of national, bourgeois, economic development.[39] Yet the connection was not itself sufficient to create an empire. Empire was not the only avenue to national glory.[40] As the public demanded nationalism, the imperialist agitators— the Parti Colonial—demanded that the empire be a part of French national glory. Sometimes they succeeded, but when empire became expensive they failed. The empire nevertheless expanded, despite costly misadventures, and often appeared costless. It did so because of the army.

Opportunism emerged unscathed from the Franco-Prussian War; so did the army. The army was crushed, but it had fought, and in fighting it gathered the devotion of the nation. It combined, to a degree not possible in the political sphere, the diverse elements of France. It drew upon aristocratic Catholic officers, the Republican elites of the Polytéchnique, and the citizen who fought in the ranks. The strength of the national sentiment on which it relied can be seen during the Dreyfus

38. Delcasse, when minister of the colonies, expressed this policy in his instructions to his colonial administrators: "Whilst remaining firmly attached to its professional duty, I believe that the administration can and must consider itself the appointed protector and auxiliary of men of goodwill who devote their energy, their strength, and their capital to the exploitation of our overseas possesions" (quoted in Andrew, p. 31). For Paul Leroy-Beaulieu's argument see Brunschwig, chap. 9, and T. Powers, *Jules Ferry and the Renaissance of French Imperialism* (New York, 1966), p. 17. Feis, p. 35; S. Elwitt, *The Making of the Third Republic* (Baton Rouge, La., 1975), pp. 238–52.

39. C. W. Newbury and A. S. Kanya–Forstner, "French Policy and the Origins of the Scramble of West Africa," *Journal of African History* 10, 2 (1969), 253–76; Zeldin, 1:424.

40. Andrew and Kanya-Forstner, *France Overseas*, p. 17. An interesting discussion of the range of views on imperialism in French politics is in E. M. Carroll, *French Public Opinion and Foreign Affairs* (New York, 1931), chap. 5.

Affair, when the government believed unsupported allegations and stood by the general staff even after its abuse of law became evident.[41]

The home army was condemned to be ever ready, always inactive—German strength precluded revanche. The army in the colonies, by contrast, offered a field of action for the energetic military officer, and a tradition grew of quick advancement through the professional colonial troops. These troops, such as the French Foreign Legion and other units under the nominal supervision of the Ministry of Marine, were capable of flexible employment and active service because they did not rely on politically costly drafted troops. Moreover, to the active officer, such as General Louis-Alexandre-Esprit-Gaston Brière de l'Isle or General Joseph Gallieni in Senegal, service in the colonies was an ideal stepping-stone from colonel to general, jumping the slow promotion ladder of the garrison army at home. The reluctance of the legislature to assume a new financial burden could be circumvented by *fait accompli*.[42] The recipe was simple: an expedition against marauding natives, a battle against high odds, a conquest, and an urgent demand for reinforcements. Thus de Lanessan, a former colonial governor, wrote (in a statement that resonates with Schumpeterian imperalism) "What drove us to expand in far-away places was above all the need to find something to occupy the army and navy."[43]

The Opportunists and the army were the driving forces behind French imperialism, but we still need to know what gave them the license to conduct an imperial policy so remote from the needs of the French economy or the demands of the French electorate.

The army could not be defeated again. The costs had to be met, or else the ministry—always unstable amidst the political tides of the Assembly—would fall to charges from the right or the left of cowardice. In the later 1880s and early 1890s, moreover, a group led by the colonial deputies from Algeria vigorously championed colonial interests in the Assembly.

Political majorities in France after 1870 tended to be confused and patchwork coalitions of special interests. Yet these coalitions were all subject to the grand principle of nationalism. As a consequence, special interests appear exceptionally influential in overall state policy yet also

41. Brogan, *Development of Modern France*, chap. 7.

42. A. S. Kanya-Forstner, "French Expansion in Africa: The Mythical Theory," in E. R. J. Owen and R. B. Sutcliffe, eds., *Studies in the Theory of Imperialism* (London, 1972).

43. Cited by X. Yacono, *Histoire de la colonisation française* (Paris, 1973), p. 47.

historically fragile.[44] Each coalition had to rescue military adventurers in increasingly unlikely spots across the Western Sudan or Tonkin; each had to respond to such special interests as the Lyons silk manufacturers or the Comité d'Afrique with its demand for larger budget for Senegalese development. But it took little more than a plausible appeal to the "nation in danger" by the colonial interest to wash away the delicate coalition of the moment.[45] If a military expedition appeared to be too costly or adventuristic, however, the tide of the Assembly would shift the other way. The left would lead the condemnation of the waste of national resources and the distraction from the true national concern—Alsace-Lorraine.[46]

Au Secours, Genevieve: The Process of French Expansion

> The heartfelt support of all Frenchmen accompanies our
> brave soldiers, carriers of individual liberty and
> commercial security marching under the flag of the
> Republic. . . .[47]

There were two major sources of French imperialism. First, the military made expansion by the cautious, bourgeois Republic possible, and promotion-producing victories made expansion a necessity for the colonial army. The army's necessity was translated by the call to national honor into national policy. The cornerstone of this honor was the integrity of the army, which would one day have to settle the score with Germany, and the army's position pulled the Opportunists into repeatedly answering the trumpet calls of adventurous colonels. Second, and independently, the Opportunist faction could rely upon the army and the nation to promote its view of the empire as a commercial development enterprise. The professional army made this policy cheap, and while the nation of farmers and bourgeois Republicans demanded nationalism, the structure of politics in the Third Republic gave them no direct control over its content.

These two sources help us account for the four special features of

44. Zeldin, 1:571–79. France averaged eight months per government between 1870 and 1940; Britain averaged three years per government between 1801 and 1937. But the French span was typical for the Continent.

45. Brunschwig, chap. 8; J. J. Cooke, *The New French Imperialism* (Newton Abbot, Devon, 1971), pp. 15–19.

46. See the essays by Agatha Ramm and G. N. Sanderson in P. Gifford and W. Louis, eds., *France and Britain in Africa* (New Haven, 1971), and also Carroll, p. 102.

47. An account of the Tunisian expedition from *Union Républicaine de Paris*, 5 April 1881, quoted in Elwitt, p. 294.

French imperialism. Its limited extent has partly to be explained by the "gap" in French overseas imperialism. But it also flows from the second feature.

Compared to the extensive British roots of imperialism—primarily the transnational-imperial economy—France's economic connection with the peripheral world was limited. The army and to a much lesser extent the missionaries were France's "imperial economy," but not being cost-less or profitable tools of transnational, imperial integration (as was Britain's economy), they were less effective than Britain's imperial econ-omy in extending imperial influence. The economy was limited largely because of the comparative inefficiency of the sectors focused on com-merce with the periphery. Britain was more efficient in the old indus-tries, such as most textiles; Germany and the United States were rapidly becoming more efficient in the new industries of steel and mass pro-duction. Moreover, French agriculture, though not as efficient as that of Russia or the United States, was more capable of providing a live-lihood for a large number of small farmers than was British agriculture. Hence the pressure to emigrate was much lower. Little migration would have gone to France's colonies under any circumstances, because most of the colonies were tropical and thus unattractive to European migration.

France's preference for direct as opposed to indirect rule, to the extent that this difference is real, reflects the difference in means of influence. Soldiers tend to produce hierarchical rule; French soldiers expected obe-dience and were unaccustomed to manipulation and cooperation among formal equals. Moreover, a military expansion was not likely to employ as allies the defeated opposing leaders. Britain's merchants and diplo-mats, contrariwise, found a continuation of commercial relationship in a new guise of rule more suited to their interests and habits.

Finally, only in assimilation could the ideology of universal repub-licanism find imperialism acceptable. The extent to which this policy changed into "association" in the later prewar period, however, illus-trates both the isolation of colonies from ongoing French politics and the increasing influence of the colonial party of the settlers.

German Imperialism

German imperialism has long interested historians and theorists of im-perialism. This interest is to a significant extent less a product of the German empire than of the crucial role of Germany in the great events of the past century: in the origins of the world wars, in monopoly capitalism, and in nazism. Nineteenth-century German imperialism is to many scholars a kite held aloft by the wind of these powerful concerns.[48] The German empire is also interesting because Germany evolved Augustan metropolitan institutions, in which domestic autocracy complemented international imperialism. But both concerns need to be approached with caution, for few metropoles acquired so little territory or population. The historian of Germany observes a small kite whose flight path may indicate the direction in which great forces were pushing Germany. For the theorist of imperialism, however, the interest of German imperialism is the limited ability of those forces to create an extensive empire.

Germany had a surfeit of some of the metropolitan conditions for empire but a dearth of others, permitting us to assess the importance of the combination of factors which empire requires. In the nineteenth century the German combination was weak. Even in the twentieth, despite an enhanced capability in all respects and a spectacular strength in the military respect, this still weak combination contributed to the defeat of the nazi bid for empire over Europe.

Four features characterize the German empire prior to World War I.[49] The empire was of very limited extent: Togo, the Cameroons, South-West Africa, Tanganyika, and small islands in the Pacific—a million square miles with a population of about 15 million. Most of this expansion occurred in Africa after 1884, although aspects of informal imperialism could be found in the Pacific before this date.[50] These territories had an extremely slight economic connection to Germany. The colonial empire developed in three phases. The first was characterized by chartered company rule and a burst of acquisition between 1884 and 1886; the second, 1890–1906, by a *Weltpolitik* of adventurism in the Far East and military rule in Africa; and the third, 1906–1914, by a regularization of direct rule over the African colonies. Finally, and unlike the French tendency, there was little assimilation and much pure administration.

The search for the sources of German imperialism has led scholars in

48. Thus Lenin, Schumpeter, Hannah Arendt, A. J. P. Taylor, Eckhart Kerr, and Fritz Fischer all felt a need to explain German imperialism as a stepping stone to their more central concerns with monopoly capitalism, militarism, totalitarianism, and the struggle for mastery of a declining Europe. See Wolfgang Mommsen, "Domestic Factors in German Foreign Policy before 1914," in James J. Sheehan, ed., *Imperial Germany* (New York, 1976), pp. 223–68.

49. Fieldhouse, *Colonial Empires*, p. 365.

50. M. Townsend, "Commercial and Colonial Policies of Imperial Germany," in G. Nadel and P. Curtis, eds., *Imperialism and Colonialism* (New York, 1964).

three directions: The *Primat der Aussenpolitik* most clearly exemplified in the diplomatic theory of A. J. P. Taylor; the primacy of economic forces found in Mary Townsend's work and, less directly, in Hans Ulrich Wehler's studies; and the *Primat der Innenpolitik*, focusing on domestic politics, which is exemplified in the work of Erick Eyck and others.

The "Primat der Aussenpolitik"

A succinct and single-minded diplomatic explanation of colonial imperialism ascribes the German acquisition of colonies in the 1880s as a "move in Bismarck's European policy." A. J. P. Taylor advances the interpretation thus:

> Bismarck quarrelled with England in order to draw closer to France; and . . . the method of the quarrel was the deliberately provocative claim to ownerless lands, in which the German government had hitherto shown no interest. These lands had a certain negative value to Great Britain, in that they adjoined existing British colonies or lay near British strategic routes; but their value was not such as to provoke the English government into a war. Moreover, they were of no concern to any other power, and claims to them would not cause any international complications, such as would have been occasioned by German demands in China or Persia. The German colonies were the accidental by-product of an abortive Franco-German entente.[51]

Bismarck's Egyptian policy before British intervention in 1882 was designed to encourage Anglo-French cooperation and competition. He sought cooperation to avoid exacerbating France's sense of isolation and thereby to contain the more extreme revanchist forces in France, and he sought competition to ensure that no Western Entente would form against Germany.[52] Hence Bismarck supported the joint Anglo-French intervention in Egypt. After France failed to intervene militarily in consort with Britain, he encouraged France's diplomatic efforts to have British forces withdrawn from Egypt. At the same time Bismarck supported France's scramble for colonies in Africa, hoping thereby to divert its attention from the Blue Line of the Vosges.

These efforts to isolate and to woo France also provide a plausible explanation for German colonialism. Bismarck's demarches in west and south-west Africa appear as moves designed to encroach on Britain's

---

51. A. J. P. Taylor, *Germany's First Bid for Colonies* (New York, 1970), p. 6.
52. N. Rich, *Friedrich von Holstein*, vol. 1 (Cambridge, 1965), p. 125.

African preserves. By encouraging France and by claiming German areas in Africa, Bismarck planned to annoy the British lion. Convinced of Bismarck's sincere commitment to a Franco-German entente, France, so the idea went, would be confident of and dependent on German goodwill.

Several aspects of German diplomacy do not, however, accord well with this *Aussenpolitik* thesis. First, it is not clear that Bismarck felt that such a strategy would be a significant step in isolating France and making it dependent on Germany. In fact, France had no great need for German support in pursuing its colonial policy, for in most areas of conflict England appeared, as Bismarck recognized, to be appeasing France.[53] Indeed, Bismarck appeared to fear an Anglo-French entente against German colonial claims more than he anticipated a Franco-German understanding on colonies. Second, Bismarck was unlikely to believe that entente on colonial questions would substantially divert France from revanche. Third, and more significantly, if diplomatic entente was Bismarck's motive, he passed up an opportunity to achieve it when he deserted France at the Berlin West African Conference on the question of tariff barriers in the Congo area.[54] If entente was worth antagonizing Britain, it was certainly worth a reduction in the trivially small potential for German trade in the Congo—but he promoted German colonial expansion even at the risk of annoying France.[55] As Bismarck's remarks at the time show, German imperialism was by no means an accidental by-product of the Franco-German entente; the temporary closeness of the entente, rather, was the by-product of German colonialism.[56]

Taylor is in general correct: Bismarck was supporting French colonial expansion, and diplomatic factors do play a supporting and a constraining role. The diplomacy of the appeasement of France did limit Bismarck's imperialism.[57] England's dependence on international diplomatic acquiescence to stabilize Egyptian finances led to Gladstone's partial appeasement of France in West and Central Africa, and it also opened Britain to German blackmail on colonial issues. The multipolar structure of international politics in the last quarter of the nineteenth century

53. R. Lucius in F. B. M. Hollyday, ed., *Bismarck* (Englewood Cliffs, N.J., 1970), pp. 75–76.

54. S. E. Crowe, *The Berlin West Africa Conference* (London, 1942), pp. 72–73.

55. Ibid., pp. 194–95.

56. H. Turner, "Bismarck's Imperialist Venture: Anti-British in Origin?" in P. Gifford and W. Louis, eds., *Britain and Germany in Africa* (New Haven, 1967), p. 75.

57. A. J. P. Taylor, *Bismarck: The Man and the Statesman* (New York, 1967), pp. 215–16.

created incentives for exclusive and preclusive acquisition of international resources. But the reasons for thinking colonies worthy of competition also need to be sought inside Germany's economy and polity.

Economic Imperialism

Bismarck referred frequently enough to a domestic concern for commercial expansion and colonialism to cast doubt on Taylor's "accidental by-product" theory, but evidence also suggests that before 1884 and after 1886 Bismarck was not a convinced imperialist. The position of colonial empire in German economic and political development remains complex.

The economic determinist of the Leninist variety would interpret German imperialism as a necessary evolution of the capitalist system and its inherent economic and political expansionism. Mary Townsend also notes a long-term (secular) development of overproduction in German industry which required foreign expansion.[58] Bismarck, in her view, engaged in an extended preparation for colonial expansion from 1871 to 1876, a period of cooperation with private companies from 1876 to 1884, and finally came into the open with state support after 1884.[59]

A somewhat different position is taken by Hans Ulrich Wehler. He stresses the importance of informal and formal economic imperialism as a necessary (although perhaps small) aspect of managing the dangerous fluctuations inherent in economic growth. Bismarck, he notes, saw "our colonizing efforts (as) measures designed to help German exports."[60] Furthermore, the German government lacked the ability to pursue monetary, exchange-rate, and fiscal policies because of restrictions imposed by the Reichstag. It had to rely on foreign economic expansion to moderate both the swings of the business cycle and the revolutionary pressures on the conservative social fabric which such erratic swings would otherwise create.[61] We shall return to this broader thesis, but for the moment let us examine economic factors.

Considerable evidence suggests large-scale strains and change in the German economy during these decades. Germany was experiencing very rapid industrial growth: internal free trade, a wide resource base (especially after the inclusion of Lorraine ores), high levels of technological

---

58. M. E. Townsend, *The Rise and Fall of Germany's Colonial Empire* (New York, 1930), p. 58.

59. Ibid., pp. 59–64.

60. H. U. Wehler, "Bismarck's Imperialism," *Past and Present*, no. 48 (August 1970), 124–26.

61. H. U. Wehler, "Industrial Growth and Early German Imperialism," in Owen and Sutcliffe, chap. 3.

innovation, and a rapidly developing railroad network brought the German economy through the stages of the industrial revolution at a quick step.[62] In 1870 the shipbuilding industry was smaller than Spain's; by 1890 it was beginning to rival Great Britain's. In the 1880s the second phase of the industrial revolution (iron and steel) was already being overtaken by the third (electrical and chemical products). Like France and Britain, Germany was also experiencing the strains of development. Iron and steel and agriculture suffered particularly, the former from British competition and French subsidies, the latter from American and Russian grains.[63] In 1879 Bismarck protected these two sectors by establishing a general tariff. As a result of these various developments the overall structure of German trade was shifting, away from Europe and toward the Americas and the Orient. In 1880, 80 percent of German exports went to Europe; in 1914, 50 percent.[64]

In fact, however, the real economic importance of German imperialism was slight. The German economy as a whole was much less internationally oriented than the British: trade, though growing, was a much smaller proportion of gross national product, and foreign investments were considerably less significant (and they declined after the 1880s).[65] Very little of what trade and investment did take place went to areas of formal or informal imperialism. Nor were South-West Africa, Togo, the Cameroons, and Tanganyika likely to become major markets for Germany's specialty steels and electrical generators (though they did absorb a good deal of Hamburg gin). Indeed, between 1894 and 1913 the German colonies cost considerably more in budgetary support than their gross trade value.[66]

Whatever push did exist in German capitalism it was not pushing toward imperialism. Townsend's interpretation has an elephant giving birth to a field mouse. Nor can it be surprising that Germany's empire was insignificant given the small involvement of the German economy

62. Hans Rosenberg, "Political and Social Consequences of the Great Depression of 1873–1896 in Central Europe," in Sheehan, *Imperial Germany*.

63. J. H. Clapham, *The Economic Development of France and Germany*, 4th ed. (Cambridge, 1961), pp. 210–11, 279, 286, 303, 311, 316.

64. F. Fisher, *Germany's Aims in the First World War* (London, 1967), p. 12.

65. Feis, pp. 61–62; and Fieldhouse, *The Colonial Empires*, pp. 330–31.

66. Colonial trade represented no more than 0.5% of Germany's overseas trade. And at the highest possible estimate, German investment overseas in informally or formally controlled areas was about one-eighth of its total foreign investment by 1914. See Feis, p. 74; and even of this one-eighth, more than one-half was in the Rand district of South Africa, an area over which Germany had no control.

in peripheral lands. The transnational economic basis for extensive empire was missing. Moreover, Bismarck's colonialism occurred in a burst, from 1884 to 1886. After 1886 he scoffed at colonies, and before 1883 he was even declaring of South-West Africa that Germany "would be only too happy to see England extend her efficacious protection to the German settlers in those regions."[67] Given these observations, it becomes difficult to credit the crucial importance of colonial imperialism to Bismarck as a means of stabilizing the trade cycle.[68] If colonialism were so important a long-term secular policy tool, one would expect a continuing pursuit of colonial expansion and the building of a fleet to protect them. But the resumption of colonial politics in the 1890s under Wilhelm II followed a significant decline in interest in the colonies during the later 1880s.[69]

This is not to say that Bismarck had no economic interest in colonialism. In fact he did. But his interest was particularistic and tentative. Bismarck was concerned with the stabilization of steady growth, to which end he introduced the tariff of 1879 and social welfare programs. Colonialism was a much more experimental tool where the gain was very speculative. To cut costs and pacify England, Bismarck allowed colonial expansion to drop from his arsenal of political economy.

As Bismarck stated when defending his colonial policy before the Reichstag on 26 June 1884, the colonies were "due to the enterprise of the Hanseatic people," to which Bismarck had added the support of the German government.[70] Hamburg, Bremen, and the other North German cities had long traded with far-flung areas in the Pacific and more recently Africa, and this trade had become quite important to leading merchant houses in these cities.[71] For the importance of Bismarck's colonial speculation, the reasons for his support of private Hanseatic interests, and his decision to respond to the clamorings of colonial lobbies, we need to turn to the political arena.[72]

---

67. Quoted in Fritz Stern, *Gold and Iron: Bismarck, Bleichroder, and the Building of the German Empire* (New York, 1977), p. 410.

68. P. M. Kennedy, "German Colonial Expansion," *Past and Present* no. 54 (February 1972), 138.

69. Felix Gilbert, *End of the European Era* (New York, 1979), pp. 78–90. And see H. Turner, "Bismarck's Imperialist Venture," in Gifford and Louis, p. 52.

70. P. S. Hammerow, ed., *The Age of Bismarck* (New York, 1973), p. 305.

71. M. Townsend, in Nadel and Curtis, *Imperialism and Colonialism.*

72. There also lies the answer to why he did not choose to support other, especially anticolonial interests.

The "Primat der Innenpolitik"

There are three main contending political explanations for the rise of German colonial imperialism. One stresses the role of nationalism. A second ties imperialism to short-term maneuvers by Bismarck to preserve his political leadership. And a third is Wehler's "manipulated social imperialism."

Germany has acquired among scholars a reputation for nationalistic fervor as strong as France's. Was German expansion a product of direct or indirect nationalist pressure? The election of 1884 witnessed a considerable amount of procolonialist agitation, it is true, but one finds no consistent nationalist pressure for colonial expansion throughout the 1880s. If nationalism is an indirect explanation, one wants to know the proximate cause (the role played by the army and the Opportunists in France), and that leads us into specifically political analysis.[73]

One of the political interests at stake was the political support of the old Hanseatic towns, which benefited from overseas trade with those peripheral areas which were now becoming objects of international preemption. Another and more thoroughly explored reason for Bismarck's adoption of colonial policy was the political usefulness of the colonial lobbies.[74] These lobbies, agitating for solutions to the "emigration problem," claimed that the acquisition of colonies would provide lands for settlement for German emigrants who would otherwise be lost to the Reich. Composed of businessmen, intellectuals, and retired civil servants, they had some impact on the popular press, but their use to Bismarck was that they appealed to the same middle-class audience that provided the core of political support for his major rivals—the anticolonial, liberal, and free-trading Progressives. A third source of Bismarck's colonial strategy was his relationship with the future emperor. According to Herbert Bismarck, Otto's son, a crucial political interest was at stake: "When we entered upon a colonial policy, we had to reckon with a long reign of the Crown Prince. During this reign *English influence would have been dominant.* To prevent this, we had to embark on a colonial policy, because it was popular and conveniently adopted to *bring us into conflict with England at any given moment.*"[75]

---

73. Fieldhouse, *Economics and Empire*, p. 74; H. Pogge von Strandmann, "Domestic Origins of Germany's Colonial Expansion under Bismarck," *Past and Present* no. 42 (February 1969), 19.

74. E. Eyck, *Bismarck and the German Empire* (New York, 1964), p. 275.

75. Quoted in Woodruff Smith, *The German Colonial Empire* (Chapel Hill, N.C., 1978), p. 275. But see Stern, p. 400: the crown prince also supported the colonial move-

A colonial quarrel with Britain capable of mobilizing national fervor in the Reichstag and discrediting the liberal Progressive party associated with the prince would restrain the independence of the next emperor and keep Bismarck in office. In 1884 the emperor was eighty-seven years old, and rapid action seemed necessary.[76] Bismarck's waning interest in imperialism after 1886 can be explained by the return to health of the old emperor and the later death of the crown prince.

Political motivations may help explain the circumstances of Bismarck's initiation of formal colonialism in 1884–85, but none is satisfactory as a complete answer. At least one wants to know why the support of special interests was important and why Bismarck, once allied with the Liberals, now opposed them.

Wehler has one answer: "Bismarck's Bonapartist and dictatorial regime together with the social forces that supported it, and later on particularly the exponents of Weltpolitik, expected that economic and social imperialism would legitimate their authority."[77] Imperialism, he argues, preserved the conservative social fabric of Germany by preserving the political coalition of Junker and industrialist rule, dominated by the former. This coalition was part of a tripartite relationship: imperialism provided markets for the trade sector and nationalistic legitimation for the conservative ruling alliance.[78]

But Bismarck, had he thought colonialism a center piece in the preservation of the status quo, would have continued to press for colonial aggrandizement. He would have built a fleet to protect colonies (and to demonstrate the Reich's prestige), and he would have exulted in the role of the state in ruling foreign parts. Instead, he abandoned colonialism and limited the state's role by the use of chartered companies.[79] Social-imperialist characteristics are apparent later, under Bismarck's successors, but not under the Bismarckian system, which was much more tenuous and experimental.

In the 1880s the connection between the specific colonial interests that Bismarck pursued and the domestic political structure appears to have been indirect. Bismarck was attempting to contain the democratic forces unleashed by the industrial revolution; colonial policy was only a tem-

---

ment. A quarrel might nonetheless serve to embarrass him in an association with liberal Britain and thus be sufficient for Bismarck's purposes.

76. N. Simon, *Germany in the Age of Bismarck* (London, 1968), pp. 84–85.

77. Wehler, "Bismarck's Imperialism," p. 122.

78. Ibid., p. 130. And Wehler, *The German Empire*, trans. K. Traynor (Dover, N H., 1985), pp. 171–76.

79. Kennedy, p. 138.

porary expedient in that containment.[80] Containment evolved in stages. Both a conservative Junker and a German nationalist, Bismarck attempted to shape the changes required by the latter to the needs of the former. In 1871 he allied with the leading nationalist party, the Liberals, to pass his budgets and to build the legal structure of the new Reich. His Liberals were prepared to suppress religious reaction—the Catholic Center party—but not to crush the Social Democrats, with whom they shared the goals of freedom and legality.[81] The Liberals were a dangerous long-term ally, and steering a conservative path amidst upsurges of radicalism and parliamentarism required exceptional skill and constant extraparliamentary ploys. The War in Sight Crisis of 1875 was one such method of stampeding Liberal allies; the exploitation of an attempted assassination of the kaiser to push through laws aimed against the Social Democrats was another.[82]

The Liberals still threatened parliamentary rule by their reluctance to adhere to a conservative, monarchical Germany. To avert this parliamentary threat, Bismarck revolutionized his coalition. First, he sought alliance with the Catholic Center party.[83] Second, in 1879 he split the Liberal party into conservative and progressive wings over the issue of protection for agriculture and industry. Bismarck guaranteed the autonomy of the state (that is, the monarchy) against the legislature by using tariffs to persuade the industrial wing of the Liberals (the conservative Liberals) to join him in an alliance with the conservatives (both landholding Junkers and the Center).[84] He undermined the ideological basis of the Liberals and in addition acquired a source of state revenue less subject to legislative control, thus weakening parliamentary sovereignty. As in the Disraelian coalition, a politics of international power and the manipulation of domestic interest from the top replaced a politics of principle and class from below.

But the 1881 elections did not produce a majority for Bismarck, and the Center party could be relied upon only for tariff issues.[85] On other issues, Bismarck was in danger of defeat. He needed sections of the less

80. Eyck, p. 269.

81. Ibid., pp. 195, 203, 241. See also Gordon Craig, *Germany, 1866–1945* (New York, 1978), pp. 69–78.

82. Craig, p. 238.

83. Ibid., p. 230. Bennigsen refused a ministerial portfolio unless he could also bring in two liberal colleagues.

84. See Rosenberg, "Political and Social Consequences"; H. Brunschwig, *L'expansion allemand d'outre-mer* (Paris, 1957), p. 99; and Simon, pp. 60–62.

85. Simon, p. 65.

committed parts of the Liberal party and in particular the colonial interest, the towns with an interest in overseas trade.[86] Colonial preemption against European rivals was one means of securing their support, and colonial conflict with England would also help discredit the crown prince and his English wife, both progressive liberals.[87]

Colonial policy was a temporary patch for the Bismarckian coalition. The permanent cement was found in another war scare directed at France, which required a detente with Britain on colonial claims. In 1887 Bismarck formed his Kartell party, finally burying effective parliamentary democracy and securing Bismarck's conservative state. He had designed a state that would guard the status quo without needing an aggressive colonial policy. Indeed, the new kaiser, Wilhelm II, dropped Bismarck for failing to acquiesce in social imperialism, which Bismarck refused to pursue. He rejected both radical, democratic social welfare and an interventionist policy designed to lure the working class away from socialism. The latter disturbed his delicate system of alliance, the former threatened the very social conservatism he had committed himself to preserve.[88]

In the roots of the empire that Germany created in the 1880s, one finds a conjunction of separate but related forces and constraints. The international system provided much of the constraint, limiting colonial policy to avoid a conflict with more important strategic interests. But the increasingly tense multipolarity of the international system also provided an important incentive for colonialism. The most important drive for colonies combined a general economic interest in trade expansion and particular private interests in the protection of foreign trade. These forces attained significance because in the middle 1880s Bismarck's political conservatism required the support of private imperial interests and an issue with which to discredit the anglophile Liberal party associated with the crown prince. Wehler's social-imperialist triangle seeks to make too much of the general connections; it is only the *particular* links that can account for German imperialism in the 1880s.

Yet the flexible diplomatic structure of Bismarckian imperialism became in the hands of Wilhelm II the social-imperialist machine that Wehler dates ten years too early. Inspired by the parts of Bismarck's

86. Bismarck owned, coincidentally, four distilleries supplying Hamburg exporters; Craig, p. 123–38. But Hamburg, although the home of such colonial exporters as the Godeffroy firm, favored a laissez-faire policy (Stern, p. 399).

87. Strandmann, "Domestic Origins of Germany's Colonial Expansion"; Eyck, p. 275.

88. Eyck, pp. 314, 422.

structure, Wilhelm attempted to make them a whole. He forgot that diplomatic flexibility was crucial to the preservation of more important German interests in the stability of the European balance of power.[89] He forgot that political flexibility at home was equally important to the foundations of the conservative order in which monarch and civil service united in an effective but limited state.[90] Wilhelm attempted to link management of the economy, provision of social welfare, extreme nationalism, militarism, and transformation of monarchy into Bonapartism with an expansive, imperial *Weltpolitik*. In so doing, he made monarchy a radical authoritarian force and took the German state over the Augustan threshold into autonomous, autocratic rule.[91] As Admiral Alfred von Tirpitz, Wilhelm's coadjutor in the building of an imperial fleet, expressed their strategy, "In this new and important national task of imperialism and in the economic gain that will result from it, we have a powerful palliative against both educated and uneducated social democrats."[92] The colonial empire was bureaucratized to meet its new importance (and local revolts). Despite the efforts of missionaries and Hamburg merchants, however, it never acquired an extensive transnational presence. But the imperialists of the 1890s failed fully to integrate the forces of order against socialism and democracy. Disputes between agrarian Junkers and industrial middle classes remained live and divisive.[93] The effort to achieve manipulated social imperalism in a stalemated political society did have one significant effect; it helped lead Germany to militarism, the destruction of representative government, and the disaster of World War I.[94]

The German empire, in sum, was small because the Germans had few previous economic or social connections to the periphery in Africa and Asia. A transnational connection did emerge before and in the course of the Scramble. The economic connection remained slight, however, because German overseas trade was small and focused overwhelmingly on exporting advanced industrial goods. There was little assimilation and much direct rule because of the empire's brief span and because it

89. Langer, *European Alliances*, chap. 13.

90. John Rohl, *Germany without Bismarck* (Berkeley, 1967), p. 246.

91. Kennedy, "German Colonial Expansion."

92. Wehler, "Bismarck's Imperialism."

93. Ian Forbes, "Social Imperialism and Wilhelmine Germany," *Historical Journal* 22, 2 (1979), 331–49.

94. Mommsen, "Domestic Factors in German Foreign Policy." See also T. Veblen, *Imperial Germany and the Industrial Revolution* (1915; rpt. Ann Arbor, 1968), chap. 7.

was primarily bureaucrats who were interested in its development. Its acquisition and development were sporadic because imperialism was necessary to neither the German economy nor the social triangle. And, finally, it was brief (1885–1914) because Wilhelm II's efforts to make it fundamental to his *Weltpolitik* destroyed the diplomatic and strategic stability of Europe.

The Collapse of Spanish Imperialism

In our examination of the metropolitan roots of imperialism we have considered only cases of imperial expansion. All have satisfied the structural conditions of the metropolitan threshold (political unity and transnational forces). The process of imperialism has varied, in some cases being more economic, in others more strategic or political. But in all these cases we have been investigating "dogs that barked." The examination of a "dog that didn't bark" is to test these various arguments. The decline of the Spanish empire in the nineteenth century is a case in point.

The Spanish case is interesting because it provides a strong test of theories that stress the independent motor of the international system or the multipolar balance of power as *the* creative force behind empire in the nineteenth century. Spain participated in the diplomacy of the time but did not acquire an extensive empire and, indeed, lost extensive possessions in the Americas at the beginning of the century and in the Antilles and the Philippines at the end. At the same time Portugal, a state no more powerful or active in the international system, held on to much of its paper empire and expanded its effective control in Angola and Mozambique. Spain and Portugal confirm that international factors and peripheral collapse are insufficient as sole causative agents; we need to look into domestic structure and process.[95]

Three factors helped separate the Americas from Spain. The first was the isolation created by the Napoleonic Wars—specifically, the blockades and embargoes of Britain and the Continental System. The second was the long-term frustration of the Creole elite over the continuing restrictions of Spanish mercantilism, combined with the poor market that Spain offered for colonial exports and imports. The third factor was a dispersal of Creole political allegiance among three possible claimants

95. In this section I am re-examining in a modern context the arguments advanced in connection with the collapse of the Athenian empire.

to their loyalty: the Napoleonic regime in actual control of the metropole, the liberal junta fighting for Spanish independence, and the Spanish king held in captivity by the French.[96] The king they perceived as their legitimate sovereign, but he was also the least accessible. Loyalty to him required temporary independence from the other two claimants.

The appetite for independence grew. The new Creole states, with British aid, opposed a restoration of Spanish imperial rule. The Mexican elite attempted to preserve the old order, first by wartime independence from the reforming liberal junta in Spain, and then by reunification with the restoration regime of King Ferdinand. The liberal coup in Spain of 1820 upset the guarantee of stability,[97] however, and to preserve the social order, the Creoles supported independence. Forty years later Cuba also attempted to revolt, in order to avoid the reformist policies of another liberal republican regime in Spain, and thirty years after that Cuba's successful rebellion illustrates similar causes—the Creole elite, whose sugar exports went to the American market, was unwilling to support a Spanish tariff. The conflict that began in 1895 soon escaped the control of the elite, however, and Spanish policy inadvertently contributed to the populist cause by alternating between concessions and repression.[98] The coup de grace to the last substantial remnants of the Spanish empire, here and in the Philippines, was delivered by the superior firepower of the U.S. fleet.

Clearly, the revolt of the periphery itself and the support that these revolts received from Britain and the United States were important to the end of empire. But Spain's domestic environment also helped account for the fall of empire. It may, moreover, help explain why Spain, unlike other metropoles in the nineteenth century, did not found another empire in Africa or in Asia.

Spain's economy and political system were, briefly, not adequate for imperial maintenance and expansion. The economy was unable to integrate the empire transnationally by providing incentives for imperial collaboration and resources for imperial influence. The polity, due to its domestic instability, was unable either to direct the empire or to inspire wider imperial loyalty.

Spain's economy, far from being transnational and imperial, was nearer to becoming a peripheral economy dependent on France and Britain. Extensive agricultural development began only in 1837 when the prop-

96. Fieldhouse, *Colonial Empires*, chap. 6.
97. R. Carr, *Spain, 1808–1939* (Oxford, 1966), p. 145.
98. Ibid., pp. 306–9, 381, 185–86.

erty of the church was nationalized and sold to large landowners.[99] A textile industry grew in Catalonia, but it was made up of many small and politically powerful firms. The result was high-cost tariff-protected production. A mining boom in the Basque provinces was soon taken over by the French and the British; the French also took a leading role in organizing and financing the railroad system. Foreign capital contributed to growth, but heavy import dependence and repatriation of profits reduced the manifold growth connections associated with a domestically owned and directed leading sector.[100]

Though certain Spanish industries, cotton among them, relied heavily on colonial markets (60 percent of Barcelona's exports), the Spanish colonies did not rely on Spain. The metropole was both a poor market and high-cost producer. Indeed, the structure of Spain's exports resembled that of a raw-material-producing colony.[101] Over 50 percent of Spain's exports in 1883 were in wine, grapes, and raisins, and another 20 percent in minerals. As a result, Spain's imports were not particularly complementary with the products of its colonies in the Antilles and the Philippines.

The Spanish economy lacked the transnational attraction of Britain's economy. Its exports were not sought by the colonies, and it did not provide a market for their exports sufficient to justify the mercantile system it imposed on them. Some Spanish industry benefited from the empire, in particular the textiles of Catalonia, but it would be hard to argue that Spain as a whole benefited economically. The colonies, on the other hand, experienced no marked private or public economic benefit from the imperial connection. Spain maintained rule only through bureaucratic and military means, sometimes supported by the Creoles' fear of social revolution and by the allegiance of recent migrants from Spain who were intent upon making as rapid a fortune as possible and retiring to Spain.[102]

One should not make too much of these failings in the economics of imperialism. Although Spain's attractiveness as a market for colonial exports and imports had declined relative to its condition in the sixteenth and seventeenth centuries, there appears to have been no absolute decline in the Spanish metropolitan economy. Indeed, Spain's economy had never been the primary integrating force of its empire. Its empire was

99. J. V. Vives, *Approaches to the History of Spain* (Berkeley, 1967), pp. 128–29.
100. J. V. Vives, *An Economic History of Spain* (Princeton, 1969), pp. 723–24.
101. Carr, p. 200.
102. Carr, pp. 306–9.

always an extension of the culture and society of Spanish settlers who adventured overseas ambitious for God, glory, and gold. The true significance of increased economic strains lies in the pressure they added to an imperial political system that was already in serious difficulties.

Political fluctuations in Spain registered as tidal waves in the colonies, and Spain's nineteenth-century politics fluctuated dramatically. Spain began the century under the heel of Napoleon and in the grip of civil war. No sooner was independence achieved than Spain collapsed in repressive monarchical reaction. The end of the century witnessed another political revolution, this time bringing in constitutional monarchy. But there had been little change at the roots of Spanish political life. Local landowners still were above and beyond the law and disposed of the use of the land as they did the "votes" of the electorate.[103] Spain throughout the century was divided into a bewildering variety of both vertical and horizontal layers. Royalists (Carlists vs. Isabellistas), liberals (Moderados, Exaltados), and democrats (republicans, anarchists, and socialists) comprised the vertical layers. Basque separatists, Catalan nationalists, and movements from the other provinces that reacted to the first two comprised the horizontal layers.[104] And these horizontal and vertical divisions reinforced each other. The radical federal republic collapsed when part of the lower middle class it was supposed to represent broke away into Catalan cantonalism.

Spanish politics lost consensus on social ideology and on national identity. This disintegration resulted primarily from the very rapid mobilization in 1808 of *all* the people—aristrocracy, middle classes, and peasantry—against both the Napoleonic invader and the corrupt ministers of the Bourbon regime. All were mobilized by participation in guerrilla war, but no two held the same goal. The people and the elite became soldiers and officers before either had become citizens or politicians. With peace came many radical demands, from the top to the bottom of the social hierarchy, but economic power was still focused at the very top. Bossism, the rule of the landowner in privatized politics, responded to the lack of widespread political participation and to the lack of any general public vision. These imbalances produced a continuing stream of military pronunciamentos, monarchical cameralists, and oligarchic manipulation of republican elections.[105]

France also experienced instability in this century, of course, but none

103. G. Brenan, *The Spanish Labyrinth*, 2d ed. (Cambridge, 1950), pp. 2–3.
104. C. A. M. Hennessey, *A Federal Republic in Spain* (Oxford, 1962), pp. 247–53.
105. Vives, *Approaches to the History of Spain*, chap. 19.

of its domestic conflicts involved extended military campaigns as did the thirty years of intermittent Carlist wars. Moreover, none of France's governments reflected as extreme and as narrow a privatization of the political process as was habitual in Spain, no matter which regime was in power.[106]

Not surprisingly, few of Spain's policies were consistently pursued and little political energy was available for foreign expansion. Spain's army followed adventure *inside* Spain. (The French Army's Sudanese temptations appear small beside the Spanish Army's opportunities to stage a successful coup at home.)[107] Spanish metropolitan politics lacked not only the consistency and energy to expand but also the stability to provide a focus for an ongoing empire. The importance of these metropolitan factors is suggested by comparison. Spain failed to develop a Spanish commonwealth akin to the British, and Britain held on to Ireland for twenty years longer than Spain held Cuba, the Caribbean remnant of what had once been the most extensive empire in the world.

The root causes of Spain's imperial collapse lay not in the absence of economic motive but in the insufficiency of that interest to provide the links needed to smooth the path of imperial rule. As what transnational economy did exist deteriorated (in relative terms), the political mechanism at home which supposedly directed the empire and inspired the loyalty of the colonial Spaniard became even further strained. This political mechanism was, moreover, crumbling under the impact of domestic instability. The decline of either Spanish overseas venturesomeness or Spanish political stability might themselves have been disastrous, but the simultaneous deterioration of both proved decisive.

Metrocentric Theory

Metropolitan structures and forces tell us only half the story. All the metropolitan vigor of Britain or France or Germany could not establish colonies over the European nation-states of the nineteenth century. The observation diverts us outward again, to examine what makes a society an imperializable periphery. Nor do metrocentric factors help us explain the striking generality of the Scramble for Africa. Factors specific to no one state or society are needed to account for the rush of so many into colonial expansion, and systemic and transnational factors are superior.

106. Carr, pp. 184–95.
107. Ibid., pp. 260–61.

Yet even when we assume for analytic purposes the existence of an imperializable periphery, significant weaknesses affect the metrocentric models. In Britain's expansion over the Niger and the Nile, for example, no single overriding drive—whether commercial, financial, military, or religious—dominated the process. On the Niger, commercial and re-ligious (missionary and humanitarian) factors predominated; on the Nile, strategic and financial factors seemed paramount. While no one motive clearly dominated, however, the impact of one without the other would probably have been markedly different. The slave trade was profitable and strengthened West Africa's local oligarchs (and probably increased their resistance to missionary penetration). Without an additional need to protect the missionaries, the palm-oil trade alone might not have sustained a British commitment to a naval and consular presence. In Egypt the British government, unlike the French, was not prepared to interfere in a "bondholders' quarrel" until the quarrel implicated the safety of British subjects and the control of a strategic and commercial route to the east.

There was, moreover, no steady metrocentric drive to expand. Con-trary to the presuppositions of Lenin, Hobson, or Schumpeter, Britain even tried to withdraw from West Africa in 1865; refused at first to invest in the Suez Canal; and rejected at first the naming of a public member of Egypt's debt commission in order to protect the interests of British bondholders. The "push" was too sporadic to play the part of a deep metropolitan drive or to have been a fundamental part of stabilizing the domestic politics of the metropole. And the metrocentric approach neglects the "pull" of "men on the spot" and of unstable local competition in the periphery.

Still, the metropolitan half of the story, when seen in interaction with the periphery, is a necessary and influential half. The collapse of the Athenian empire, which followed upon the revolution inside Athens, clearly indicates one crucial and limiting role of metropolitan political forces and institutions in maintaining an empire. An equally fundamental role involves the very distinction between the imperializers and the imperialized, for this is a distinction between different types of domestic society. And the tendency of colonial societies to mirror the society of their metropoles also illustrates an effect of domestic political and social forces.

Particular differences among societies each of which has crossed the metropolitan threshold—had a state, some substantial differentiation, and communal identification—do not seem even to determine whether they acquired an empire. Nor do they determine whether an empire grew if transnational forces, for example, were expanding and drawing more and more peripheries into contact with the metropolitan state. Metropoles in contact with peripheries "always" establish an empire.

Those which lack these features either lose their established empire or fail to expand. Thus in the nineteenth century, when Denmark's transnational economy turned away from the periphery and toward exporting meat and dairy products to Europe, its empire actually shrunk.[108] Its industrial development focused on many small firms (such as furniture making); large firms concentrated in brewing and shipbuilding.[109] None of these interests stood to lose when Denmark sold its last colonial holdings in Africa to Britain in 1850. The Dutch empire merely consolidated within its previous boundaries. The Portuguese experienced a substantial decline of their "paper empire" in Africa, and throughout the century Spain's empire disintegrated colony by colony.[110]

Differences among metropoles do influence the size, style, or form of empire. In the 1880s the United States, for example, established "effective occupation" of the massive territory in the center of the American continent by subduing the native population. But lacking the transnational pull of Britain, it did not stake out claims in distant spots as did many of the European metropoles.

It was Britain that acquired the lion's share of Africa in the 1880s and 1890s. Much of Britain's imperial presence was commercial, conducted by and for commercial companies, some chartered as actual agents of rule. France acquired "light soils" (deserts), and military proconsuls ruled many of the new possessions. Germany acquired very little, neglected what it did acquire, and only later, at the turn of the century, began to develop the territories economically. Each empire experienced spurts and halts in imperial acquisition, a variability that can in part be accounted for by differences in the respective peripheries. Even in similar areas of West Africa, however, the British, French, and German versions of imperialism differed in form and rate.[111] These differences find their

---

108. Lennart Jorberg, "The Industrial Revolution in the Nordic Countries," in *The Fontana Economic History of Europe*, C. Cipolla, ed., *The Emergence of Industrial Societies*, *1* (London, 1973), p. 398.

109. Alan S. Milward and S. B. Saul, *The Economic Development of Continental Europe* (Totowa, N.J., 1973), p. 511.

110. J. E. Duffy, *Portugal in Africa* (Harmondsworth, 1962), and Fieldhouse, *The Colonial Empires*, chap. 15.

111. D. K. Fieldhouse, *Colonialism, 1870–1914: An Introduction* (New York, 1981), pp. 29–41. The debate on indirect rule best captures these differences. The key sources are

roots in differing domestic ideologies, domestic interests, and domestically based transnational actors. And, importantly, these features need to be explained by metropolitan political coalitions. In the conclusion we shall assemble these interacting elements of the imperial scramble.

Hubert Deschamps, "Et maintenant, Lord Lugard," *Africa* 33, 4 (1963), 293–306, which argues that the differences between British and French colonialism were minor. Michael Crowder replied in "Indirect Rule—French and British Style," *Africa* 34, 3 (1964), 197–205, arguing that differences were real. A. I. Asiwaju showed that even in a similar part of the periphery differences between French and British colonialism were evident, in *Western Yorubaland under European Rule, 1889–1945* (Atlantic Highlands, N.J., 1976).

CHAPTER 13

The Politics of Nineteenth-Century Imperialism

Metropolitan forces shaped imperialism, but the dispositional imperialisms of Hobson, Lenin, and Schumpeter do not explain nineteenth-century imperialism. At the most basic level the dispositions do not account for what made a metropole a metropole, a periphery a periphery. Dispositions did not lead to empires over western Europe. And some of the societies of Asia and Africa, Menelik's reformed Ethiopian monarchy among them, managed a successful resistance.

Nor do dispositions fully account for the metropolitan sources of nineteenth-century imperialisms. Nowhere was Hobson's "Finance" the governor of an imperial engine. Lenin's finance capital, such as it was, came after, not before, the Scramble for Africa. Britain had a large and growing commercial stake in its empire, and it also had the largest financial stake of all European metropoles in imperialism. Commercial and financial interests were influential in both of Britain's political parties, but they controlled neither. No "Reactionary Coalition" was exclusively responsible for British imperialism. Instead, both parties pursued imperialism, fitfully. Neither party supported it strongly in the 1860s; both supported it in the 1880s—but then their imperialisms were not the same. The Conservatives supported their imperialism more, and more enthusiastically; the Liberals supported their imperialism less, and less wholeheartedly. Nowhere was there a Schumpeterian war machine.

339

Even though the colonial army was a crucial force in French imperialism, its influence came not from its hold over French politics but from the inability of French politics to hold a stable governing coalition together. French tariff politics, which did have an influence in imperialism, were less a corruption induced by monarchical residues than a self-interested escape by eminently bourgeois commercial interests from the free trade imposed by Napoleon III. Social imperialism in Germany came after the Scramble. German imperialism of the 1880s was the least rooted— whether domestically or internationally—of the three. It was a purely political stratagem, a minor ploy designed by Bismarck to strengthen his domestic coalition, upset the crown prince, and woo France. Economic interests certainly shaped the process of imperialism, but the degree of their influence depended on the country in question (much in Britain, less in France and Germany in this period). They help explain outcomes only when we understand how economic forces were combined in political coalitions and allied to bureaucratic factions; the shape they took cannot be fully understood without taking into account such noneconomic sources of cleavage as the Anglican church's distrust of Gladstone's educational reforms, or Bismarck's need to heal the political wounds caused by the *Kulturkampf*, or the French army's importance to the Opportunist coalition.

Geopolitical rivalry among the European metropoles influenced the Scramble, but nineteenth-century imperialism cannot be described adequately as a reflection of multipolar strategic rivalries. Here too, rather than focus solely on international systemic effects, we need to account for the identity of the actors (the European metropoles) and the acted upon (the peripheries). Empires persisted and grew in the first half of the century when multipolar rivalry was at a minimum. Germany, most powerful within Europe at the time of the Scramble, acquired the smallest imperial presence. Spain lost and Portugal retained colonies, though both were of equivalent (small) weight in the European balance of power. Most important, the central (European) balance-of-power game, real as it was among the great powers of Europe, was not the only game for imperial powers to play. For Britain and to a lesser degree for France, the imperial game had standing beyond considerations of the European balance. For them, the European balance could be sacrificed for imperial security, as it seems to have been in the Scramble.

The sporadic resistance and collapse of the periphery also contributed to nineteenth-century imperialism. Some peripheries collapsed without ever finding a metropole, as did some Caribbean islands able to tempt neither the United States nor Britain. Most peripheries, however, do not collapse on their own; most tribal, patrimonial, and feudal societies seem to have been fully able to manage their affairs in isolation and to adapt (albeit violently) to transnational contact when free from coercive pressures and interventions. Metropoles determined when and where they would pick up the pieces and, to a large degree, what would happen to the peripheral society under imperial rule.

These conclusions drawn from nineteenth-century imperialism basically confirm the experience of the classical and early modern empires. No one explanation was sufficient. Imperialism involves kinds of power and actors different from the fungible power and similar actors presupposed by systemic models. Systemic models, to be adequate to explain imperialism, would have to be "thickened" to the extent that the systemic determination which is their prime strength would disappear, becoming one among many factors. Metropolitan and peripheral models likewise fail to account each for the reactions of the other. To do so, they would have to be put in context, thereby losing the explanatory power of their dispositions.

Although industrialism, nationalism, and the more virulent forms of racism introduced massive changes, the foundations of empires remained a combination of causes. Imperial rule in the nineteenth century called, as earlier empires did, for the combination of a metropole, a periphery, and transnational contact. Nineteenth-century imperialism rested on an interaction, not a disposition of the metropoles, nor a simple collapse of peripheries, nor a structural crisis of the international system. It reflected, like the earlier empires, not only geopolitical and economic forces but also metropolitan party politics and peripheral collapse and collaboration. These factors combined to account for the processes of imperialism—for the forms empire took and for the persistence, accretion, and acceleration of nineteenth-century imperialism.

Comparative Statics, or the Forms of Empire

The two major forms of imperial rule are formal and informal empire. Formal empire signifies rule by annexation and colonial governors supported by metropolitan troops and local, low-level collaborators in the colonial bureaucracy and army. Informal empire means the exercise of control, by such indirect means as bribes, over the domestic and external politics of a legally independent peripheral regime. The major differences between the sources of formal and informal imperialism in the nineteenth century lay in variations among transnational forces, metropolitan standards of legitimacy, international systemic pressures, and vulnerabilities of peripheral societies.

Nongovernmental transnational forces encouraged informal empire where other factors did not preclude it. Government's transnational forces, moreover, its bureaucrats and soldiers, encouraged formal imperialism even when international and peripheral conditions favored informal empire. Bureaucrats and armies generally sought to replace rather than persuade or control local authorities in the periphery. Among nongovernmental transnational forces, merchants who worked on commission and multinational companies were somewhat more conducive to informal empire because their stake in the periphery was adjustable. Portfolio investors and national corporations with capital invested directly in the periphery tended to lead to formal empire, calling in, where they could, the metropole to protect their hostage capital. (So the bondholders agitated for protection from the perceived dangers of Colonel Arabi.) Settlers had similar stakes—their property, their lives, and their "sacred honor"—that required formal rule or independence.

Metropolitan regimes, and even factions or coalitions, were split between those legitimated by authority (traditional monarchy, technocracy or charisma) and those legitimated by participation (such as constitutional oligarchies and liberal democratic republics). The first associate themselves more easily with, and indeed seek to promote, formal rule, as did the Conservative party under Disraeli. They subjected foreigners to their own substantive ideas of authority. The second tended to encourage informal rule, as did Gladstone's Liberals. They shared, albeit with an elite, the task of political accommodation. But where the collaborating elite did not yet exist, liberals with a fixed idea of the citizen were occasionally prepared to educate foreigners to it forcibly, as the French did with *assimilation*, as the Macaulayite and Palmerstonian Liberals seemed eager to do in India.

Any tendency toward formal rule seemed to overwhelm a tendency toward informal rule, largely because the former was perceived as more secure. Patrimonial peripheries tended to be associated with informal rule (sovereignty rested with a peripheral elite) and with indirect rule (local administration by the peripheral, collaborating elite). Tribal peripheries tended to be associated with both formal rule (colonial governor and troops) and direct rule (colonial bureaucrats).

The limited social differentiation of patrimonial society, with its quasi-autonomous economic and political roles, permitted collaboration without social collapse. Merchants of the periphery aligned themselves with metropolitan merchants to their mutual (though not equal) advantage. Peripheral political factions similarly perceived benefits in a client relationship with the metropole. Yet limited social differentiation necessitated political intervention by the metropole to sustain their merchants in the face of the linkages between politics and economics characteristic of a patrimon's governance. Informal control was thus possible, advantageous, and required: possible, because collaboration was possible; advantageous, because it reduced administrative costs and generally met with less resistance than did formal rule; and required, because to support trade the metropole had to engage in political interference to match the patrimonial politicization of economic relationships.

In tribal peripheries metropolitan transnational forces generally were highly disruptive. A metropolitan merchant's dealings could produce an automatic and specific shift in the balance of local political power, a slight to a religious authority, even a profanation of ritual. Collaboration was thus unstable, and formally institutionalized rule was necessary. Once established, this rule tended to rely on a relatively more intense bureaucracy—direct rule—than was necessary in a patrimonial periphery to administer colonial regulations. Tribes often had no differentiated rulers to start with and administrators from the metropole therefore ruled the new "natives" of the periphery.

Another important determinant of the mode of empire was the structure of the international system. Multipolar systems tended to require formal institutions of imperial rule; bipolar and unipolar systems, to permit informal arrangements.

Unipolar domination or bipolar rivalry between metropoles over the control of the periphery allowed stable collaboration to form between each governing, collaborating faction in a periphery and a single metropole. This stable identification was furthered by the oft-noted tendency of a bipolar system to internationalize domestic politics in a transnational extension of ideological conflict and factionalism. Since the periphery was ruled by either one domestic faction or another, associated with one metropole or the other, the stability of international alignments was reinforced by the domestic costs of change. Since the faction out of power in each periphery would attempt to establish links to the metropole not already linked to its governing collaborators, a change of allegiance would tend to require a domestic "revolution," replacing the governors with their opponents. Stable collaboration thus leads to informal rule. Both are reinforced—domestically and internationally—in a bipolar system, as they were by Athenian and Spartan competition in the ancient Aegean, and this without the formal imposition of metropolitan rule.

In a multipolar system, by contrast, no such stability between particular peripheral governments and particular metropoles developed. Each governing, peripheral faction could improve its bargaining position by playing metropole against metropole. Each metropole consequently had an incentive to establish more formal, more direct, and closer supervision of the periphery. It was when African chiefs in Britain's traditional region began to bargain with French and German emissaries that the incentives for formal acquisition climbed.

Dynamics of the Scramble

The factors influencing the forms of imperialism also combined to account for the inherited persistence of imperial rule over the peripheries, the steady expansion (accretion) of empire between the 1820s and the 1860s and the sharp acceleration of the Scramble of the 1880s.

Empire persisted throughout the nineteenth century because three basic elements of empire persisted. No major metropole fell back from the metropolitan threshold of political centralization and socioeconomic differentiation. On the other side of the imperial relationship there was no general development of peripheral societies beyond the peripheral threshold. Despite the political and economic development of Japan, the United States, Ethiopia, and others, much of the non-European world (as well as localities within European states) remained tribal or patrimonial in character across the century. Lastly but crucially, the metropoles continued to provide sound foundations for a widespread transnational economy and society.

Transnational penetration under these circumstances required empire, which the peripheries were incapable of effectively resisting. The metropoles supported a penetration leading to control because it appears to offer advantages in trade and strategy, because it seemed just (protection of nationals overseas), and because it was cheap.

The three elements of the imperial relationship also account for the accretion of empire. Empires slowly grew throughout the century as Britain added Australia, South Africa, Lagos, and Penang; France added Algeria, Senegal, and Annam; and Russia expanded eastward, the United States westward. In this growth one notes an increase in the number and centralization (and thus power) of the metropoles in Europe and North America. At the same time, transnational contact spread and intensified under the stimulus of the industrial revolution, which enhanced specialization in the world economy. As Nazli Choucri and Robert North have argued, the more extensive a metropole's involvement in trade and investment with the periphery, the larger its empire became, irrespective of the strategic significance of the metropole. Maritime Britain, hub of a massive transnational economy, in this respect vastly outranked Germany, dominant power on the continent, and so did France. On the other side of the imperial relationship the periphery progressively succumbed as economic, cultural, and religious forces of the metropoles penetrated and dislocated their societies.

The imperial growth that peaked in 1882–85 was differentiated from the steady, piecemeal growth of the earlier period by two features. The Scramble involved the *rapid* acquisition of large peripheral areas to be ruled on a *formal* basis. The Scramble was a land rush for the most extensive frontiers possible and all the formal trappings of empire seemed both necessary and welcome. Clearly something new had been added.

Looking at the peripheries, one might expect in the early 1880s a continuing collapse of tribal societies disrupted by market exchange and naval interventions. One might also expect a crisis to develop a generation or so after the first mid-century contact of patrimonial societies with European culture and capitalism. This latter crisis, in countries such as Tunisia and Egypt, stemmed as Ronald Robinson and John Gallagher have argued from a proto-nationalist revolt against the earlier commercial and financial collaboration with the Europeans. It was resolved in the early 1880s by increased, formal control by France and Britain, and it accounts for some aspects of the Scramble: the timing and the formality. However, the simultaneous rush of formal rule into the wastes of the Sudan and the hinterlands of sub-Saharan Africa can be seen as only tenuously connected to these Mediterranean developments.

The character of the transnational linkages between peripheries and metropoles was also changing. Metropolitan trading firms represented by local "factors" in the peripheries began to amalgamate under the pressure both of competition from their metropolitan rivals and of chaos stemming from the collapse of peripheral societies. The stability of the old, informal, collaborative system was destroyed. In the Niger Valley these new companies established their own rule—near to formal bureaucratic rule but as yet on a private basis—while still calling upon their home governments to confirm their acquisitions by official charter.

Elsewhere, transnational competition revolved about the varying fortunes of missionaries, their security from peripheral attack, and their rivalry against competing sects. In East Africa each sect called in its metropole for formal military protection.

This transnational factor, added to our preceding discussion of peripheral collapse, illuminates the force drawing metropoles into sub-Saharan Africa and Indochina. But the actual timing of the Scramble is still obscure, as is its generality. These last two qualities can, however, be explained by bringing into our explanation a consideration of the changes in the structure of the international system and in the composition of the ruling regimes of the metropoles.

The diplomatic system around 1880 responded to the guidance of Bismarck. His genius for diplomacy combined with Germany's military might to turn what might have been a multipolar European coalition against German power into a rivalry for colonial real estate which Bismarck himself brokered. He did so by focusing diplomatic arrangements on Balkan and colonial conflicts among the European powers. This new rivalry pulled out the supports from beneath the preceding system in which the British managed metropolitan contacts with the peripheral world. Britain's naval patrols, cartography, and commercial finance had been supporting free trade in the periphery and thus had provided a quasi-collective good for the European economy—Britain, of course, extracting for itself private returns in port dues and private advantages in official, colonial purchases. With the advent in the late 1870s of an active multipolar system in Europe, the net benefit to the continental European countries of the Pax Britannica declined, and the net cost to Britain increased. The Pax Britannica collapsed, its legs pulled out from under it: the cost to Britain had risen with more competition, other metropoles now provided their own security in the periphery. The shift to a multipolar international system, combined with Bismarck's reorientation of conflict towards peripheral issues, encouraged preemption. More imperial control became desirable and more formal control became necessary, either to keep out other metropoles or, in the British case, to prevent other metropoles from excluding one's own trade. Tariffs and taxes were needed to defray the added administrative costs and guarantee the maximum economic return, and they became salient aspects of the new imperialism.

But one more step is necessary to our explanation, if for no other reason but that calculations of national advantage in the late nineteenth century were, as they are now, both ambiguous and reactive. Strategy, economic interest, and national pride were interpreted variously by different domestic factions. One country's external strategic challenge was another's sop to its domestic interests, and one thus needs to know the domestic context of particular decisions. Who or what were the nations, and why did they do what they were doing? The composition of the imperial coalition in the metropole, especially its socioeconomic and political sources, is important in accounting for the form and the timing of imperialism.

Domestic sources differed in each country. In France the Opportunist faction attempted to channel the tides of Republican politics, frequently affected by the interests of the armies at home and overseas. The Opportunists rested upon a foundation of small-town bourgeoisie, Parisian finance, industrial capitalism, and anticlericalism; they subscribe to imperialism as economic policy and to empire as civilizing mission. The army, for its part, rested upon a grandiose conception of its role as savior of the nation, and officers in search of promotion "saved the nation" in increasingly unlikely places in the western Sudan and on the Annamese coast. The combination of Opportunist leadership, a fluctuating nationalist Assembly, and the army made imperialism seem both desirable and necessary to France's *gloire*, industry's progress, and the army's promotions.

In Britain, imperialism was in the 1880s more problematic as a policy and much more significant as a reality. Disraeli had largely preempted the imperial identification for the Conservative party, Gladstone being elected in 1880 after what had appeared to be an anti-imperialist campaign. In the 1870s a political realignment had brought large parts of the middle class from liberalism to Tory "Villadom" in reaction to increased radicalism within the Liberal party, hints of "Little Englandism" in Gladstonian foreign policy, and new waves of foreign competition, both economic and strategic. This shift was driven home in 1886 with the defection of Joseph Chamberlain and the Birmingham engineering industry from liberalism. The Conservatives would enjoy dominance for twenty years as the party of "governors," of empire and power, and of a Britain that the Conservatives hoped would be reinvigorated by trade preference in the dominions and a permanent Raj in India. Liberalism, however, entered office in 1880 seeking to retain the free cooperation and free trade of the dominions together with the liberal development of India and Ireland. It rejected Disraeli's imperial glory. But it also sought to maintain the free trade ascendancy, in certain areas amounting to informal empire, which protected the sale of British goods—particularly the cotton of its Manchester wing—in the periphery. Gladstone restrained expansion in India and South Africa, but his attempts at high principle may have so disconcerted France and Germany as to spur them to step up their challenges to what remained of the Pax Britannica. Gladstone's Liberals thus found themselves in the difficult position of defending liberal nationalism and condemning imperial aggression but ruling Ireland, invading Egypt, and engaging in the Scramble for Africa to preserve informally ruled or commercially influenced areas from other metropoles.

While the Opportunists were strategists of formal empire and Gladstone was the defender of informal and commercial empire (but now by formal means), Bismarck's was an instigator of the rush for territory. His reasons, however, had little to do with the periphery. He sought to embroil Germany's rivals in colonial disputes that were nongermane because non-German. He sought to manage domestic "cabinet" politics by embarrassing the anglophile successor to the throne with a British, colonial quarrel that would make it impolitic for the crown prince, once kaiser, to dismiss Bismarck. After Bismarck's dismissal, imperialism as a distinct policy would become a linchpin of Wilhelmine politics—the external branch of social imperialism designed to mobilize chauvinist support in a divided society. But in the 1880s Bismarck's own interest in empire appears to have been ephemeral, a ploy in his cabinet politics and European diplomacy. This ploy did nevertheless accelerate the competition between France and England. Germany, the new participant, made the peripheral world shrink. Staking claims became a requirement for future trade, raw materials, coaling stations, military employment, votes, and power—but not for any one of these goods singly.

International systemic pressures and transnational crises in the periphery did not make Spain, Portugal, and Denmark expand their empires. These pressures, it is true, did encourage most metropoles to acquire more empire and more formally, but the empire that they actually acquired was the empire for which their metropolitan coalitions were prepared to pay. The French Opportunists thus acquired the Western Sudan for its colonial army and Tonkin for its missionaries, but involvement in Egypt threatened too great a dependence on Germany. Gladstone's Liberals rejected Disraeli's imperial strategy of advances against the Transvaal and Afghanistan but succumbed in Egypt to the more general, imperial, strategic interests of the route to India and to the need to protect the lives and property of British citizens put at risk by Arabi's rising. They also supported, albeit after much hesitation,

Goldie's claims for the commerce of the Niger Valley. Bismarck, meanwhile, first supported and then neglected the claims of his merchants and explorers, for Bismarck's purposes lay not in the periphery but in his European diplomacy.

These sources of the Scramble of the 1880s can themselves be understood only as the culminations of a steady growth of informal and formal empire, a growth rooted in the continuing crisis of peripheral societies in contact with metropolitan transnational extensions of industrial capitalism backed by an increasing number of politically more powerful metropoles. This steady growth of empire, in turn, rests on an understanding of the combination of political institutionalization, social differentiation, and political integration which lends strength to metropoles. The partial absence of this combination engenders in peripheries political fragility when the peripheries become subject to transnational forces and organizations, such as nineteenth-century merchants and missionaries, emanating from the metropoles.

PART III

CONCLUSION

CHAPTER 14

Imperial Development:
The End of Empire?

The course of modern empire has been determined by changes in the character of the international environment, in the domestic society of the metropole, and in the development of social change and the balance of collaboration in the peripheries. The historical alternatives have divided between persistence, which necessitated imperial development in both the metropole and the periphery, and decline and fall. Persistence in an extensive empire required that the metropole cross the Augustan threshold to imperial bureaucracy, and perhaps the Caracallan threshold to integration as the periphery became in effect an equal political partner with the metropole. But of European examples only the Roman and the Spanish empires developed in this direction.

Most have followed another path. Their colonies have been redistributed after defeat in metropolitan wars. The balance of collaboration in the periphery, in other cases, has shifted against continued metropolitan control, and sufficient coordination and legitimacy has emerged in these peripheries to effect an anti-imperial revolution. In the metropoles themselves the coalitions in favor of empire have declined as the interests seeking empire were defeated, electorally or otherwise.

By the middle of the twentieth century these three factors had destroyed the edifice of formal imperialism. The German, Italian, and Japanese empires had been repartitioned. Following World War II, the

European metropoles were ruled by political coalitions committed in principle to the abolition of empire and for whom, strategically and economically, empire seemed no longer worth the cost. Finally, yet crucially, the peripheries themselves underwent political mobilization that made imperial collaboration increasingly unacceptable, imperial rule increasingly costly. The result was the end of formal colonial empires as they had been known for over a century.

The course of imperial development began after an officer raised a flag over a new formal acquisition or after a diplomat gained a grip over the sovereign of an informally ruled periphery. Then imperial rule had to create both change and order. But social change could not easily be halted, and in the modern empires change itself led to decolonization. But would decolonization led to actual independence—or to a new informal imperialism, neoimperialism?

The Gold Coast and Imperial Control

The striking anomaly of the imperial order is that it surmounted two societies.[1] Laws developed over ages and through violent and profound social revolutions in the metropolitan society were transplanted to control the evolution of a radically different society. The law became a tool in the hands of the western power limited only by the need to prevent massive resistance by the native peoples. A legal model and some of the political skills had been developed by Britain in the ruling of India where laws, while remaining unobtrusive in a populous land, had also had to provide stability. Native legal orders were partially integrated into the uniquely adaptable common law system, but before this delicate integration could take place, political control and its accompaniment, constitutional law, was needed.

During the eighteenth century, according to Brodie Cruickshank (a colonial official), Britain already exercised "a certain kind of mediatorial influence, with the view of preventing any interruptions to the trade, arising out of the squabbles of the different tribes" on the Gold Coast, now Ghana.[2] At this early stage Britain relied on African courts for local

---

1. For general sources on tribal and colonial law see M. Gluckman, *Ideas in Barotse Jurisprudence* (New Haven, 1965); C. K. Meek, *Land Tenure and Land Administration in Nigeria and the Cameroons* (London, 1957); P. C. Lloyd, *Yoruba Land Law* (Oxford, 1962); H. Kuper and L. Kuper, eds., *African Law* (Berkeley, 1965); and E. A. Hobel, *The Law of Primitive Man* (Cambridge, Mass., 1961).

2. Brodie Cruickshank, *Eighteen Years on the Gold Coast of Africa* (1853; London, 1966), 1:30. This book is an important first-hand account of the beginning of colonial rule.

justice, but in 1803 the governor of the colony began to exert imperial legal jurisdiction by imprisoning one of the chiefs.

Meanwhile the larger tribes of the interior were conducting periodic raids on the coast. When Mr. Meredith, a British subject, was killed in February 1812, the governor chose to impose collective responsibility on the African village; it was destroyed. The introduction of schooling and the governor's intervention to save maltreated slaves also served to undermine the local political order. Soon African villagers were asking the governor, by his account, to "moderate the claims and pretensions of either party, and his happy tact enabled him to do this with effect." By arbitrating African disputes, he enhanced his political power.

In 1835 missionaries arrived. Governor MacLean provided a fitting companion to a foreign and revolutionary religion in his campaign for imperial political order. Of the state of affairs in this year, Cruickshank commented: "Indeed we had no legal jurisdiction in the country whatever. It had never been conquered or purchased by us, or ceded to us. The chiefs, it is true, had, on several occasions, sworn allegiance to the Crown of Great Britain; but, by this act, they only meant the military service of a vassal to a superior. Native laws and customs were never understood to be abrogated or affected by it."[3]

Yet a select committee of Parliament in 1842 recognized the "practically and necessarily, and usefully . . . irregular jurisdiction" of MacLean's adjudications, which employed his own version of equity and were reinforced by the influence he acquired in his manipulation of African rivalries.[4] Over time, British power grew. The governor forced the chiefs to pledge gold for their good behavior and stationed a soldier in every town to serve as a communications and control link. Furthermore, MacLean set up modern rules of credit, liberating contracts and purchas-

---

3. Ibid., pp. 36, 100, 129, 184; quotation at pp. 186–87.
4. A. N. Allott, "Native Tribunals in the Gold Coast," *Journal of African Law* 1, 3 (1957), 164. As Cruickshank explained, "The peculiar circumstances of our position on the Gold Coast have hitherto rendered a large military force unnecessary. The very important part which we played in the war which led to their [coastal chiefs'] independence, and the indication of the exhaustless nature of our pecuniary resources, apparent in the great recklessness of expense during the progress of the war; the necessity of a protector against the power and ambition of the Ashantees, and their own inability to maintain their independence; the mutual fear and jealously of rival chiefs, which made a common superior necessary to prevent discord; the tyranny of chiefs over their dependents, and of masters over their slaves; and a general belief in the rectitude of our intentions, and the impartiality of our justice; all conspired to influence the minds of every class, to elevate us into power, and to make common cause in maintaining our authority." Cruickshank, 2:10–11.

ing agreements from the traditional penalty for default (slavery) and the need to secure every contract with property. He thus became "federal" head of the coast chiefs through an adjudication system that provided settlement of disputes, security of travel, and a means of British control.

As the number of Christian converts grew, they incited the slaves to mutiny and insulted the holy ground of Fetishes. In 1846 several Fetish priests and chiefs joined to kidnap the Christian offenders.[5] MacLean fined both sides. The Fetishists refused to pay, but the chiefs accepted his decision. The assessor then sent his African levies after the Fetishists, apprehended them, and exposed the "tricks" of their religion to the public in his court.[6]

In steady increments MacLean thus began to create a basic, "constitutional" order of colonial rule. Intertribal rivalries and pressures for social change helped break the bonds of the tribal system of rules. From the social fragments Britain then built a political coalition behind the colonial system of law and order.

Following the establishment of colonial rule, Britain formed a Gold Coast Legislative Council. All British ordinances as of 1874 were adopted for the Gold Coast. In 1878 and in 1883 London passed the Native Jurisdiction Ordinances, in order to set up official tribunals of African law that would begin the integration of legal orders at the lowest level.[7] In addition, the higher British courts on the Gold Coast began to sift tribal law in order to adapt it to modern conditions wherever possible.[8] The development of "constitutional" colonial order soon led to substantive colonial law governing crime, commerce, and property.

Some compromises became necessary. London demanded the freeing of all slaves, including those employed in transporting the commerce of coastal chiefs. Colonial officials knew that freedom for slaves would destroy the economic base of the newly rich chiefs who were the main prop of African acquiescence to British rule. Local colonial officials urged

---

5. Cruickshank, chap. 11.

6. Ibid., pp. 328–30. See also George Metcalfe, *MacLean of the Gold Coast* (London, 1962), p. 323.

7. Allott, p. 166.

8. N. M. Ollennu, "The Influence of English Law on West Africa," *Journal of African Law* 5, 1 (1961), 30–31. See also J. C. Anene, *Southern Nigeria in Transition* (Cambridge, 1966), pp. 304–7. D. Forde, "Justice and Judgment among the Southern Ibo under Colonial Rule," in Kuper and Kuper, eds., pp. 89–96, analyzes the way in which early British jail sentences for crimes seemed to the Ibos to reward criminals with good bed and board.

a compromise with the London authorities. The slaves were freed, but they were required to be affiliated with one of the chiefs in order to trade. Since many small traders did not have an affiliation, this law actually increased the power of the chiefs while, in practice, it did very little for former slaves because its provisions for emancipation were unenforceable.[9]

But why did Britain create a new (primary) legal order? One reason undoubtedly was humanitarian. But perhaps the clearest reason was that the commercial capitalism which sustained the colony required an extensive and modern legal order. It required universality of application and equality in a free market, specific and rigidly fixed standards for the commodity trade, specific relationships of contract and conveyance to finance firms, and government and regular courts to provide an efficient means of enforcement of western legalism.[10]

Land tenure and its evolution illustrate the development of colonial law. The shift from traditional, communal land tenure to modern tenure under the notion of fee simple—full individual ownership—is a profound shift. It corresponds to the progression from status to contract put forward by Sir Henry Maine. An expanding market and a demand for nonagricultural land and labor mobility resulted in a demand for full ownership that sought to bypass or crush the traditional system of communal tenure. Yet law holds to the general principle of *nemo dat quod non habet* (no one can give that which he does not own). Since African tenure was communal, shared by kin, there could be no fee simple tenure because no conveyance (e.g., sale) could transfer nonexistent rights.[11] This was a true dilemma for the colonial courts. Two tactics were followed to remove the obstacle.

First, in *Balogun v. Oshodi* (1931) Judge Berkeley ruled that fee simple could be derived from *dominum directum*—the supreme power of the sovereign, which held ultimate ownership of the soil through cession by African rulers. Fee simple lay dormant in *dominum directum* (the original colonial conquest) and could be "revived" by a conveyance from the apparent holder, often a collaborating chief appointed or sustained by the colonial authority. The second rationale was more straightfor-

---

9. T. O. Elias, *Government and Politics in Africa* (New York, 1963), p. 147.

10. Max Weber, "The Principal Modes of Capitalistic Orientation," in Talcott Parsons, ed., *The Theory of Social and Economic Organization*, trans. A. Henderson and Parsons (New York, 1947), pp. 446–47. Sidney Simpson and J. Stone, eds., *Cases and Readings on Law and Society*, vol. 1 (St. Paul, Minn., 1948), pp. 319–30, 347–52.

11. A. E. W. Park, "A Dual System of Land Tenure," *Journal of African Law* 9, 1 (1965), 17.

ward. C. J. Kingdon, in a dissenting opinion to the same 1931 case, argued that since land tenure was communal, the community as a whole could convey fee simple by ceding all its rights to the land. The Privy Council supported Kingdon's rationale in 1936 when it reconsidered the earlier case on appeal from the colonial court.[12] Each specific tribal community would receive recompense for its land, generating little political unrest, but a fundamentally different form of legal tenure would be created. This controlled social transformation meant the destruction of tribal society. Land tenure as a compact between the dead, the living, and the yet-to-be-born was broken. Communities no longer chose their chiefs; rather, Britain imposed property, capitalist economic development, the patrimonialization of tribal society, and the appointment of "native authorities."

We have seen how a metropole develops an imperial order in tribal society, on the Gold Coast. Let us turn to another periphery, the patrimonial society of Zanzibar, to see how decolonization develops from imperial rule itself.

Zanzibar and Decolonization

In the early nineteenth century Seyyid ("Sultan") Said led a revival of the sultanate of Muscat and Zanzibar that coincided with Mehemet Ali's strengthening of Egypt. Said relied heavily and, as it would turn out, ironically on an alliance with Britain to defeat the Indian Ocean pirates who were preying upon Zanzibari trade to India. Once Said had cleared the sea of pirates, Zanzibar's exports of cloves and slaves to India and the Persian Gulf grew rapidly and the foundations of Zanzibar's booming plantation-entrepôt economy were laid. In 1824 the British further aided Said by refusing to recognize a rebellious governor of one of Zanzibar's East African mainland ports.[13]

The disproportionate alliance between Zanzibar and Britain was transformed by humanitarian pressure to use British naval supremacy in the Indian Ocean to stop the slave trade. The treaty that prohibited the trade to the Americas was signed in 1822. A second treaty, banning the more important Persian Gulf trade, followed in 1845. These exercises in naval hegemony had far-reaching implications, for by the middle of the century the Zanzibari regime was completely based on export-oriented

---

12. Ibid., pp. 14–17.
13. Lawrence Hollingsworth, *Zanzibar under the Foreign Office, 1890–1913* (London, 1953), pp. 8–9, and F. B. Pearce, *Zanzibar* (London, 1920), chap. 8.

plantation agriculture. The income of Said's major followers—Arab settlers from Muscat—flowed from slave-tended clove plantations and the slave trade itself. Much of Said's private income came from his own plantations, and his and his public export revenues stemmed from taxes on the slave and clove trades. Since Black Zanzibaris (Shirazis) and the slaves formed a majority of the population, emancipation struck at the ideological and legal basis of Arab rule. When the British forced Said to ban the slave trade, therefore, they were striking at both the political and the economic bases of his patrimonial authority.[14]

British aims, both during and for a while after the protectorate was formally announced in 1890, were to control Zanzibar's foreign relations, leaving domestic politics intact. The British planned a hegemony to avoid Zanzibar's falling to another European state. But a hands-off policy proved impossible, and inevitably the sultan's regime became more unstable and British power in Zanzibar grew.[15] When Britain changed its international relationship with Zanzibar from alliance to hegemony, it began to change the relationship of the ruler of Zanzibar to his people, from autocratic patrimon to foreign-supported puppet. Before this new relationship could become informal empire, however, a more reliable mechanism of influence was needed to supplement British naval power and commercial preeminence.[16]

The British Navy and commerce influenced the formulation of Zanzibari policy. A newly established consul general more directly controlled political decisions, and he became the effective sovereign. Consul Sir John Kirk (the "Cromer of Zanzibar") spread his influence into the implementation of Zanzibari policy by having British officers appointed to train and command the army and by having British subjects take over the more directly political offices of the patrimonial regime. Eventually a British subject—the general of the army—became prime minister, and the independent ruler of Zanzibar became a ruler in little more than name.

The announcement of the protectorate in 1890 did little more than legitimate Britain's existing predominance. In 1893 the British consul picked the successor to the Zanzibari throne. This control was further strengthened in 1896 when the seyyid had the temerity to rebel. Retri-

---

14. M. Lofchie, *Zanzibar: Background to Revolution* (Princeton, 1965), pp. 50–57.

15. See R. J. Gavin, "The Bartle Frere Mission to Zanzibar," *Historical Journal* 5, 2 (1962), 122–48.

16. See Consul Holmwood, *Memorandum*, F.O. 403:48, December 1884, in the Public Record Office, Kew, Surrey.

bution followed a year later: his palace was leveled by naval bombardment. That lesson of British invincibility sank in, and Britain achieved the full control required to reform the foundation of Zanzibari society. Slavery was abolished.[17]

Imperial development had radical social aims and conservative political ends. Given a limited commitment of resources, the politics of control governed development. Since Britain relied upon the Arab governing class and the purely formal rule of the seyyid for political support in Zanzibar, the fundamental interests of the landlords, while subject to some change, could not be undermined. The Black African population, despite emancipation, remained tied to the soil.

British policy attempted to maintain a delicate balance between control and economic progress, and management of this balance soon required more administration than the consul and informal rule allowed. Between 1913 and 1915 the control of Zanzibar was moved from the Foreign Office to the Colonial Office, the island becoming a part of British East Africa. In 1926 Arab landlord members of the protectorate council were allowed to share colonial rule in "responsible government"—to the collaborating sultan the British added the collaborating landlord.

After 1945 the balancing became even more complex as Britain committed itself to eventual independence for the colonies and Zanzibar experienced the rise of Arab-Zanzibari nationalism and African social mobilization. The British, still hoping to balance local politics with pro-British Arabs in a dominant position, arranged for the council to have a continuing Arab majority despite the African majority in the colony.[18] But Islamic nationalism became vehement, both in response to the continued affronts of colonial status and in response to the fear that decolonization might one day lead to African majority rule. Thus the 1950s saw not only the formation of a party (the ZNP) to achieve Arab-led independence but also, and in reaction, the formation of both the Afro-Shirazi Union (ASU) for Africans and some Shirazis, and the ZPPP to reflect the allegiances of Shirazi groups who considered themselves distinct from exslaves.[19]

In the end the Arab collaborators chose independence to avoid majority rule; the majority chose national independence to end Arab-British rule. The result was an Arab-Shirazi coalition (ZNP and ZPPP) in 1961,

---

17. Hollingsworth, p. 125; R. N. Lyne, *Zanzibar in Contemporary Times* (New York, 1909), chap. 17.

18. Lofchie, pp. 129–39.

19. Ibid., pp. 187–96.

followed soon afterward by a military coup. A radical military group came to power committed to African (ASU) interests; it subsequently united Zanzibar with the excolony of Tanganyika to form Tanzania.[20]

The Growth of Imperial Control

Establishing imperial control over a tribal society such as the Gold Coast required formal empire and direct rule because tribal instability required complete authority. Patrimonial societies, such as Zanzibar, led to informal empire. Indigenous political authority could collaborate, and both the metropole and the periphery preferred this relationship. The same reasons that led to informal empire led toward indirect rule when, for other reasons (such as multipolar competition) the empire was formal. Then, rather than bureaucratic *direct* rule, there emerged *indirect* rule through the supervision of traditional indigenous notables.[21] In Northern Nigeria the emirs ruled for Britain; in Princely India, the rajas; in Uganda, the kabaka. Even the French, who for other (bureaucratic) reasons preferred direct rule, established more fully direct rule over tribal societies than over patrimonial societies. Both forms required local collaboration; the distinguishing factor between tribal and patrimonial colonies was the social level of collaboration (clerks as against emirs).

However various the form in which imperial control was established, the process of imperial development was much the same. The builders of empire all sought the creation and maintenance of a favorable balance of collaboration. Given the pressures of social mobilization engendered by economic change in the colonial periphery and the desire to maintain the metropolitan support needed to sustain imperial rule, a favorable balance was never easy to achieve.

The long-term economic consequences of transnational economic contact under conditions of empire have long been a subject for debate. Karl Marx, no admirer of precapitalist economic formations, saw both

---

20. Ibid., p. 216.

21. For the distinctions between the policies of direct and indirect rule see Frederick Lord Lugard, *Dual Mandate in British Tropical Africa*, 5th ed. (London, 1965), chap. 10, "Methods of Ruling Native Races." For French colonial policy, see Robert Delavignette, *Service africain* (Paris, 1946). The actual importance of local conditions in shaping the character of rule is discussed by A. S. Kanya-Forstner, "Military Expansion in the Western Sudan—French and British Style," and Boniface Obichere, "The African Factor in the Establishment of French Authority in West Africa," both in Prosser Gifford and W. Roger Louis, eds., *France and Britain in Africa* (New Haven, 1977).

formal and informal economic colonialism as highly progressive.[22] He noted that imperial commerce and the railroads broke the feudal and "Asiatic" communal structures of economic life that enshackled man to complete hierarchies and pervasive superstition.[23]

The domestic political consequences of social and economic change, Samuel Huntington has argued, should be conceived of as a series of relations.[24] Economic development both stimulates social mobilization and soothes some of the demands of the mobilized with the economic rewards of upward social mobility—or, as Albert Hirschman has added, the promise of future reward.[25] If these demands are not met, social frustration results in increased political participation, which in turn needs to be met with political institutionalization (the assimilation of new political participants). If assimilation fails, political instability, including perhaps revolution, will arrive. Though much of this model holds for imperial development, modifications are needed to recognize the foreign and forceful authoritarianism of imperial development.[26]

The less differentiated the peripheral society, the more traumatic will be the initial social mobilization stimulated by transnational forces. Still, change will occur. Transnational trade differentiates the social roles of the tribal population, and petty traders, colonial clerks, and small farmers replace the communal tribesman. Trade and colonial administration widen the bounds of peripheral society, giving the tribal periphery, within a context of colonial order, the social characteristics of a patrimonial society.

The most significant difference between independent and colonial political development was the metropole's control of adjustments in the political institutionalization of the periphery. The end of colonial rule was preventing those major institutional changes which would prevent the metropole's controlling the periphery. The result, relative to social change, was a highly uneven political development: while colonial po-

22. See his *New York Daily Tribune* article, "On Imperialism in India," in R. Tucker, ed., *The Marx-Engels Reader* (New York, 1972).

23. Karl Marx, *Pre-Capitalist Economic Formations*, trans. J. Cohen (New York, 1965), pp. 81, 105.

24. S. Huntington, *Political Order in Changing Societies* (New Haven, 1968), p. 55.

25. Albert Hirschman, "The Changing Tolerance for Income Inequality in the Course of Economic Development," *Quarterly Journal of Economics* 87 (November 1973), 544–65.

26. In addition to the other sources cited, this section relies on Thomas Hodgkin, *Nationalism in Africa* (New York, 1957), Rupert Emerson, *From Empire to Nation* (Cambridge, 1967), and Richard N. Lebow, *White Britain and Black Ireland* (Philadelphia, 1976). The last explicitly develops the significance of contradictions between mobilization and imperial control in the Irish context, pp. 90–98.

litical strategy was fundamentally conservative, in that it could not allow mass national participation, it was also economically, and often socially, progressive. Moreover, it was prepared to make often radical shifts in collaborating elites (the very social groups that would resist political change if the country were independent). The metropole sought economic development skewed toward its own interests, and it often promoted religious conversion and social change. Both, however, mobilized society and, in undifferentiated social systems, created social frustration that the inhabitants of the periphery were forced to internalize.

While direct constraints on noninstitutionalized participation were the linchpin of colonial control, other methods also played their part. Mobilization itself was often restricted: the hostility of the colonial civil service to missionaries in Lord Lugard's Northern Nigeria and restrictions on white settlement in Southern Nigeria both illustrate this concern to avoid mobilizing the native population. Some attention was directed to institutionalization in the recruitment of clerks and soldiers, and later, as a response to nationalist pressure, to the Indianization and Africanization of the civil services. In addition to these "colonial outputs," some changes in the institutions of "colonial input" appeared in the 1920s and 1930s in the formation of advisory legislative councils.[27]

The other side of this dynamic of rule and collaboration was the process of resistance and independence. Each failure in the former was a push toward the latter. In fact, imperial development, just as it created collaboration, also created the basis for resistance and revolt: it spread technical and organizational skills, it widened political horizons as it built larger national political units, and it recruited new strata into political participation.[28]

Imperial political development is thus the dynamic balance between collaboration and resistance. The first brings constrained and skewed socioeconomic development under a technically and organizationally efficient state that is highly institutionalized in administration but not institutionalized in colonial participation. The second merges the continuing power of tradition with the tensions springing from mobilization and the new horizons of unity and progress to which the colonial state gives rise.

The motives of both the collaborators and the metropoles were di-

27. Martin Kilson, "The Emergent Elites of Black Africa, 1900 to 1960," in L. H. Gann and P. Duignan, eds., *Colonialism in Africa*, vol. 2: *History and Politics of Colonialism, 1914–1960* (Cambridge, 1970), pp. 351–98.

28. Michael Adas, *Prophets of Rebellion* (Chapel Hill, N.C., 1979), pp. 40–42.

verse.[29] Imperial strategies, though playing on a common theme of divide-and-rule, varied as well. The metropole usually sought a path of imperial development which joined metropole and current collaborators to restrain the masses while winning over parts of the newly mobilized. This was Lord Lugard's strategy of the dual mandate.

The metropole might, however, choose a strategy of rapid imperial development, in which the metropole appealed to the colonial elite or even the peripheral masses in order to achieve rapid change. Often followed to curb the demands of existing collaborators, this dangerous strategy risked the defection of existing collaborators to the anti-imperial elite. Britain employed this form of "vertical" division in India in the early nineteenth century, appealing to the Indian elite to adopt British liberalism. Lord Cromer toyed with the idea, at least rhetorically, in Egypt. Britain threatened both the Arabs of Zanzibar and the white settlers of Rhodesia with the strategy in the 1960s.[30]

The third variant employs "horizontal" divisions: exploiting traditional tensions between one region, ethnic group, religion, or race and the rest of the inhabitants of the periphery. Coastal tribes on the Gold Coast played this role to Britain's advantage and against their enemies in the interior. The Gurkhas epitomized this role in the Indian empire. But combinations of vertical and horizontal division seemed the most frequent, and such was the effect of castes in India and trade diasporas more generally.

The danger most feared by the metropole lay in the strategy most desired by the anticolonial elite of the periphery: a united front of native patriots consisting of defectors from the collaborating elite, the newly mobilized, and the anti-imperial elite. Under such conditions, imperial rule comes to rest on force alone, as in the American Revolution. The great planters of the South and the compradorial merchants of New England joined with small farmers newly mobilized by the Great Awakening to oppose colonial rule.

The Stages of Imperial Development

Political change within an empire seems to evolve in a recognizable sequence or set of stages. We must, nonetheless, allow for local variation

29. Jorge Dominguez, "Responses to Occupations by the United States: Caliban's Dilemma," *Pacific Historical Review* 48 (November 1979), 591–605.

30. See D. K. Fieldhouse, *The Colonial Empires* (New York, 1967), chap. 12; F. Hutchins, *Illusion of Permanence* (Princeton, 1967), pp. vii–xi.

and for individual leadership; for they have enabled some nationalist movements to jump or combine stages and some metropoles to renew, coercively, imperial authority.[31]

The sequence of political change in tribal societies began at first confrontation and developed until the tribal society, with the development of landed property and commerce, became patrimonial. In patrimonial societies this sequence of crises began when patrimonial landlords and merchants confronted metropolitan merchants.

In the crisis of Caliban the transnational merchants and missionaries were usually welcomed by tribal societies. "Water with berries in it" was traded for the "qualities of isle," and the process of imperial expansion began.

In the crisis of the compradors the merchant-tribesmen, although they adjusted to the revolutionary demands made by foreign intrusion, were nonetheless made redundant by subsequent economic and organizational changes in the transnational economy. Resistance usually fails because the compradors' political power is insufficiently broad.

As in tribal society, metropolitan commercial contact with patrimonial society engenders compradorial merchants who depend on metropolitan commerce. This relationship is likely to be more stable, however, because the merchants are better able to serve metropolitan commerce. They are already a distinct, differentiated sector in society, and they offer access to a considerable market. Furthermore, they are protected (and exploited) by a more powerful patrimonial regime. The metropole has both less incentive and less ability to bypass them. When the metropole more fully penetrates patrimonial society, however, beginning to rely on the landlords for political collaboration, a crisis ensues. When the compradors are no longer politically useful, they become economically inefficient. But because merchants do not hold a central political position in patrimonial society, a revolt led by them will not gain sufficient support to create a rebellion.

In the crisis of the convert marginal elites or social pariahs (or the personally inspired), having accepted European religion, learn that they are not truly liberated, only converted. Since their numbers are generally

31. This use of sequence draws on Leonard Binder, "The Crises of Political Development," in Binder et al., eds., *Crises and Sequences in Political Development* (Princeton, 1971). Many contemporary developmentalist strategies, including Maoism, have been premised on the idea of skipping stages. For a brilliant discussion of an imperial strategy (Britain's during World War I) designed to reestablish imperial authority, see John Gallagher, "The Decline, Revival, and Fall of the British Empire," in his *Decline, Revival, and Fall of the British Empire*, ed. Anil Seal (Cambridge, 1982), pp. 73–153.

small and they are isolated from the mass of the people who hold fast to traditional religion, they remain dependent on colonial protection. These groups frequently develop messianic and separatist variants of the established colonial religion. These movements do not, however, directly challenge the political basis of colonial rule. For most, conversion means education; they become colonial clerks.

In the crisis of the "landlord" some inhabitants of the tribal periphery, having sold their land or been expelled, fight fierce but rarely successful campaigns against colonial encroachment. As for the American Indians, so it is generally: lack of organization and unity, low levels of military technology, and the ruthlessness of settlers usually spell tribal defeat. Where imperialism is not accompanied by settlers, others may become a new class of agricultural landlords, deriving their wealth from land seized from the tribal community. Chiefs become actual landlords, and in these "native authorities" the metropole has new groups of strong collaborators for agricultural development and colonial stability.[32] Where natives of the metropole do settle on formerly tribal land, the settlers establish themselves as patrimons and collaborate with imperial rule.[33]

This stage of empire over tribal societies also forms the first and essential step in the development of empire over patrimonial societies, for it is the landlords—both the largest, the patrimon, and his followers—who constitute the economic and political foundations of these societies. They also constitute the most salient vertical cleavage; indeed, Consul General Baring of Egypt and others consciously based their rule on collaborating classes.[34] Britain and France attempted to restrain the actions of the khedive by making him, in 1878, partially responsible to a constitutional assembly of landlords led by Nubar Pasha. These landlords were closely tied to the European market and sought, through foreign help, to secure their property against khedival whims. Britain rewarded their role in maintaining political stability, providing economic support by such means as improving irrigation. In Zanzibar a similar relationship was created with the Arab planters. In India the establishment of British rule rested preeminently on the collaboration of the Zamindari, transformed by the governor general, Lord Cornwallis, from

32. Martin Kilson, "British Colonialism and Transformation of Traditional Elites," in W. Cartey and M. Kilson, eds., *The Africa Reader: Colonial Africa*, 1st. ed. (New York, 1970), 1:115–21.

33. R. Robinson, "Non-European Foundations of European Imperialism: Sketch for a Theory of Collaboration," in R. Owen and Bob Sutcliffe, eds., *Studies on the Theory of Imperialism* (London, 1972).

34. Ibid.

tax collectors to landlords to insure the stability and direction of the countryside in the British interest.[35]

Collaboration between the landed elite and the imperial power has been of the utmost significance in the history of imperial development. It enabled the metropole to rule at relatively little cost to itself. At the same time it permitted the metropole to extract a considerable income from the peripheral area through marketing agricultural produce, through mining, and through taxation. Should the metropole desire to go beyond this social level of collaboration, however, or should newly mobilized nonlanded groups demand a voice in peripheral politics, a crisis ensues. The landlords may aid the metropole in repressing the newly mobilized or join them in revolt against imperial rule. The landlords may also be superseded, partly or totally, by collaboration between the metropole and a new group, the bourgeoisie.

In the crisis of the bourgeoisie we encounter the need of almost every empire for educated, middle-class support to staff the lower levels of colonial bureaucracies. Literate native clerks from the periphery were required in the Roman and all subsequent empires. Moreover, most modern empires engendered in the very process of imperial economic development a native trading and artisan class that filled in the interstices of the imperial, transnational economy. Such were the market women of colonial Africa and, on a larger scale, according to Marx, the cotton spinners of Bombay.[36]

The intellectual and economic bourgeoisie has, however, only rarely formed the center of peripheral collaboration. The Athenian empire sought the democratic (antioligarchic and patrimonial) faction of the Aegean island states as its collaborators.[37] In the early stages of the Roman empire a number of urban communities were played off against the opposing countryside. In the early twentieth century the radicals in temporary control of the French government sought the assimilation of the colonial bourgeoisie.[38] The United States, in its policies toward the Philippines, Cuba, and Santo Domingo, seemed to be planning in a similar direction. The preponderance of the experience of modern empire was, however, quite different.

35. See Barrington Moore, *Social Origins of Dictatorship and Democracy* (Boston, 1966), pp. 345–470.

36. Marx, "On Imperialism in India," and "The Future Results of British Rule in India," both in Tucker, *Marx-Engels Reader*, pp. 577–88.

37. Thucydides, *The Peloponnesian War*, trans. Rex Warner (Baltimore, 1954).

38. See G. Wesley Johnson, "Blaise Diagne: African Politics in the Colonial Era," in Cartey and Kilson, pp. 211–16.

The metropole more usually engages the collaboration of the patrimonial landlords and a small number of educated members of the
bourgeoisie. Education is restricted where it can be, and those who are
educated attract great suspicion.[39] The reasons for this antipathy are
not far to seek. First, most metropoles had aristocratic classes in influential positions in their home governments. Because the metropole seeks
to reaffirm its own political culture and promote its own interests in the
periphery, a preference for patrimonial collaboration and abhorrence for
the colonial bourgeoisie is quite understandable. (For the same reason
the larger tolerance in France, the United States, and Athens for the
colonial bourgeoisie should not be surprising.) A second reason sup-
plements the first: bourgeois leadership in the metropoles, including
England, saw the rise of a colonial bourgeoisie in a mixed light. Imitation
may have been flattering, but the economic threat of colonial infant-
industry tariffs was real. Manchester was alarmed at the prospect of
Indian duties on cotton imports. The third reason affected all metropoles:
the mobilization of middle-class intellectuals and businessmen endan-
gered continued rule. Danger to empire lay in a nationalist bourgeoisie
too radical in its aims and too large in its numbers (in comparison to
landlords) to be institutionalized into the imperial system of collaboration.

The middle classes are typically recalcitrant collaborators, and they
often foment nationalist revolutions. If the potential middle classes are
mobilized en masse to confront the metropole and landed collaborators,
they will probably hold the overwhelming balance of political power.
But history does not work quite so neatly. Parts of the urban working
classes and the peasantry (small farmers) tend to be mobilized at the
same stage as the middle classes.[40] The crisis of the middle classes will
be determined by the degree of unity between the two wings of the
bourgeoisie (the intellectuals and the merchants/industrialists). If the
industrialists have as yet had little social effect—if they are still "early
capitalists" and not the organizers of large dehumanizing factories—
intellectuals are likely to support them. Otherwise, intellectuals may
join the workers and peasants. If they do, bourgeois collaboration
becomes not only possible but likely. When a mobilized working class
or peasantry appears, it may be too late for the bourgeoisie itself to lead
a colonial revolution.

The working class and peasants, when mobilized, have a large influ-

39. See Hutchins, chap. 5; Anil Seal, *The Rise of Indian Nationalism* (Cambridge, 1968).
40. See T. Hodgkin, *Nationalism in Africa* (New York, 1957), chaps. 4–5; Moore,
chaps. 7–9, for a discussion of the variety of routes to modernity.

ence on the behavior of the crucial middle classes. But their own role in imperial collaboration is insignificant. No metropole can politically assimilate, or institutionalize, the mass of a peripheral population (unless the population is almost purely colonial in origin, such as settlers in the U.S. West and Russian settlers in Siberia). This difficulty results from their numbers—how could they be "bought?"—and from an observation: if they did effectively collaborate, the imperial aspect of empire would have disappeared and the Caracallan threshold of political integration would have been crossed.

These groups can, however, have a significant role in the destruction or maintenance of empire. A truly mobilized peasantry or working class makes empire unsustainable, raising the costs of rule far beyond the metropolitan benefits of empire. But the mobilization of an ethnically divided peasantry can lead to separate and competing nationalisms, which can severely weaken the anticolonial movement. Indeed, Indian independence was hampered by these conflicts as were nationalist movements in Africa, Asia, and Europe (e.g., Ireland).

Decolonization

Throughout this political evolution, the maintenance of imperial rule depended upon a favorable balance of political collaboration within the periphery (a balance occasionally supplemented by the use of force). Independence became possible, no matter what the stage of development, when the balance shifted to the opponents of continued rule and when the metropole was not in a position to apply overwhelming force. Independence could be led by patrimons such as Mehemet Ali, who separated Egypt from Turkey. But independence was more likely where collaboration was more difficult, where a nationalist consciousness developed after the mobilization of the middle classes. The Indian independence movement, for example, drew its strength from an alliance of nationalist middle-class intellectuals, some of them landlords, and a partially mobilized urban working class. The Zanzibar independence movement was formed from an alliance of Arab landlords and Arab, middle-class, nationalist intellectuals. Their longer-term failure stemmed from the fact that the African and Shirazi masses of Zanzibar had also been mobilized, mobilized into their own nationalism, which was as much anti-Arab as anti-British. As Tony Smith has noted: "Every war of national liberation carries within it a civil conflict, so that in fact the nationalist elite is fighting on two fronts: against the imperial power and against other local groups striving to replace it."[41]

The stage of institutionalization at which independence takes place depends on several structural factors. One is the diplomatic constellation. Foreign support for an independence movement can reduce the level of nationalist mobilization required to lead an effective revolt. The task of the American nationalist leaders of 1776 was made easier by French military assistance, and after 1945 U.S. and Soviet pressure on the colonial metropoles also had considerable, though indirect, effect. Britain in particular responded to U.S. pressure, largely due to its close ties to the United States.[42] France was noticeably less attuned to American wishes, but U.S. financial and economic pressures had their effect.[43]

Another structural factor is the level of institutionalization of the metropole, for that level determines the stage of independence of the periphery. When the periphery threatens to institutionalize more participation than the metropole, a profound crises challenges both the domestic legitimacy of the metropolitan regime and the metropole's transnational interests in the periphery. The usual result is either independence or a crushing demobilization of the peripheral society. Russia's attempt in 1815 to allow a more liberal, participatory constitution for Poland than in Russia itself led to subsequent, violent repression.[44] More subtle metropolitan traditions are also at work. Miles Kahler has shown that the institutional strength of political parties played a vital role in the successful, less violent decolonization of the British as contrasted to the French empire.[45] The French not only faced more radical national movements; their resistance made decolonization more difficult. Trans-

41. Tony Smith, *The Pattern of Imperialism: The United States and Great Britain in the Late Industrializing World since 1815* (New York, 1981), p. 120. See chap. 3 for a thorough comparative analysis of varieties of contemporary decolonization.

42. Ibid., pp. 102–3. And see Margery Perham, *The Colonial Reckoning* (New York, 1962), pp. 58–59; Gallagher, *Decline, Revival, and Fall*, on the other hand, describes the U.S. role as more that of a facilitator of a British decision to decolonize made for other, primarily peripheral, reasons.

43. Richard Neustadt, *Alliance Politics* (New York, 1970), for an analysis of alliance diplomacy during the Suez crisis.

44. B. Dmytryshyn, ed., *Imperial Russia* (New York, 1967), reprints the Polish Constitution of 1815 and the eventual abrogation of 1831. See also J. Kurth, "Modernity and Hegemony: The American Way of Foreign Policy" (paper delivered at the Harvard Center for International Affairs, Cambridge, Mass., 1971), where a more general argument is made with respect to levels of modernization.

45. Miles Kahler, *Decolonization in Britain and France* (Princeton, 1984), pp. 356–57, covers in careful argument the domestic consequences of decolonization on Britain and France.

national interests also affect decolonization, of course, settlers being the classic case.[46]

Lastly, independence does not depend just on the level of mobilization, discussed above. It also depends on the rates at which different social groups in peripheral society mobilize and also on the speed of mobilization of society as a whole. The faster the rate, the more likely is a nationalist rebellion at an early stage.[47]

Independence has two keys. First, the independence movement needs to create a sense of national identity strong enough to withstand subnational pressures toward divisions which the metropole could exploit. Second, it needs to develop a central political organization to coordinate and control the national movement and organize effective resistance against both the metropole and divisive tendencies in the periphery. In the nineteenth century and today control of the capital, the colonial army, or a coalition of leading landlords often served to ward off imperial counterattack or raise the costs of empire above what the metropole would pay. But in order to ensure that its formal independence remains actual independence, the national movement needs to find ways to institutionalize the participation of its newly mobilized, potential citizenry. In the contemporary Third World, it may even need the active support of the peasantry.[48] Only a competing political organization—another nation state—seems to guarantee a successful challenge to imperial domination.

The stronger the imperial institutions were, the stronger the national institutions had to be in order to achieve independence. A new regime needs effective institutions to govern and develop its economy. Ironi-

---

46. Ibid., chap. 5, discusses settler politics in the two metropoles.

47. See Huntington, chaps. 5 and 7, for the relative rates of mobilization and institutionalization and the resulting prospects for revolution. Gallagher emphasizes the peripheral factor in independence, calling colonial political development the "one constant factor in decolonization" (p. 153). But he also emphasizes that the peripheral factor should not be thought of as a revolutionary surge from the colonial masses. In most cases decolonization came to the fore when Britain made new, and unacceptable, fiscal and political demands on the collaborators who were managing imperial (and their own) development in the colonial periphery. Jorge Dominguez, referring to Latin American independence movements in the early nineteenth century, also makes a strong case that decolonization can take place at stages before the full mobilization and institutionalization of the population of the periphery. See J. Dominguez, "Political Participation and the Social Mobilization Hypothesis: Chile, Mexico, Brazil, and Cuba, 1800–1825," *Journal of Interdisciplinary History* 5, 4 (1974), 257–66.

48. Smith, p. 112.

cally, therefore, one of the greatest unintended gifts a metropole could give its periphery was the refusal to grant "easy" independence.[49] Too easy a peripheral independence can set up the peripheral conditions for neo-imperial rule.

The reverse of anticolonial revolution is the possibility of continued collaboration and imperial development. The Caracallan integration has seemed in the modern age of nationalisms an anachronism, but in the far past it was the culmination of the empires of Rome, China, and Islam, and the Holy Roman Empire. In these empires the metropolitan level of political institutionalization fell as empire evolved beyond the Augustan threshold of bureaucratic imperial rule. Though domestic autocracy dimmed their civilizations, these empires created zones of global order that have inspired ideals of internationally organized peace.

Imperial integration completes this sketch of the evolution of the periphery. From tribe to patrimony to national independence, from formal rule to informal rule to anticolonial revolution, the peripheral half of the imperial relationship plays a necessary and active role in determining the outcome of empire. It begins as the object of metropolitan activity. If it ends in authentic independence, it has all the metropolitan characteristics required to become an imperial metropole in its own right. So Vietnam, after a long struggle for independence, now acquires a grip over the sovereignty of Cambodia. And so the newly independent United States once struggled out of Britain's imperial grip and set itself on a course of continental and, some say, global empire.

49. John Strachey, *The End of Empire* (London, 1959), chaps. 19–20, discusses decolonization and the transition to either independence or neoimperial status in a particularly interesting way.

Bibliography

Abrams, L., and D. J. Miller. "Who Were the French Colonialists? A Reassessment of the Parti Colonial, 1890–1914." *Historical Journal* 19, 3 (1976), 685–725.

Adas, M. *Prophets of Rebellion*. Chapel Hill: University of North Carolina Press, 1979.

Adelman, P. *Gladstone, Disraeli, and Later Victorian Politics*. London: Longman, 1970.

Albertini, A. von. *Decolonization*. New York: Doubleday, 1971.

Aldcroft, D. H., ed. *The Development of British Industry and Foreign Competition*. London: Allen & Unwin, 1968.

Allen, W. A., and H. D. Trotter. *Expedition to the Niger*. London: Bentley, 1848.

Allott, A. N. "Native Tribunals in the Gold Coast." *Journal of African Law* 1, 3 (1957), 163–71.

Almond, G., and G. Powell. *Comparative Politics: A Developmental Approach*. Boston: Little, Brown, 1966.

Al-Sayyid, A. *Egypt and Cromer*. New York: Praeger, 1968.

Amin, S. *Accumulation on a World Scale*. New York: Monthly Review, 1974.

——. *Neo-Colonialism in West Africa*. Harmondsworth: Penguin, 1973.

Anderson, M. S. *The Ascendancy of Europe*. London: Longman, 1972.

Anderson, P. *Passages from Antiquity to Feudalism*. London: New Left Books, 1974.

373

Andrew, C. M. *Theophile Delclasse and the Making of Entente Cordiale.* New York: Macmillan, 1968.

Andrew, C. M., and A. S. Kanya-Forstner. "French Business and the French Colonialists." *Historical Journal* 19, 4 (1976), 981–1000.

———. *France Overseas.* London: Thames & Hudson, 1981.

Andrewes, A. "Spartan Imperialism?" In P. D. A. Garnsey and C. R. Whittaker, eds., *Imperialism in the Ancient World.* New York: Cambridge University Press, 1978.

Andrews, G. R. "Spanish American Independence: A Structural Analysis." *Latin American Perspectives* 12, 1 (Winter 1985), 105–32.

Anene, J. C. *Southern Nigeria in Transition.* London: Cambridge University Press, 1966.

Arbuthnot, Sir A. *Memories of Rugby and India.* London: Fisher Unwin, 1910.

Arendt, H. *The Origins of Totalitarianism.* Cleveland: World, 1958.

Aristotle. *Politics.* Trans. Sir Ernest Barker. London: Oxford University Press, 1962.

Aron, R. *Peace and War.* Trans. R. Howard and A. B. Fox. Garden City, N.Y.: Doubleday, 1966.

Arrighi, Giovanni. *The Geometry of Imperialism.* Trans. P. Camiller. London: New Left Books, 1978.

Art, R., and R. Jervis, eds. *International Politics.* Boston: Little, Brown, 1973.

Ascherson, N. *The King Incorporated.* London: Allen & Unwin, 1963.

Ashley, A. E. M. *Life and Correspondence of Palmerston.* 2 vols. London: Bentley, 1879.

Ashton, T. S., and R. S. Sayer, eds. *Papers in English Monetary History.* Oxford: Oxford University Press, 1973.

Asiwaju, A. I. *Western Yorubaland under European Rule, 1889–1945.* Atlantic Highlands, N.J.: Academic, 1976.

Ayandele, E. A. *The Missionary Impact on Modern Nigeria, 1842–1914.* London: Longmans Green, 1966.

Badian, E. *Foreign Clientelae, 264–70 B.C.* Oxford: Clarendon, 1967.

———. *Roman Imperialism in the Late Republic.* Witwatersrand: University of South Africa Press, 1967.

Baer, G. *A History of Landownership in Modern Egypt, 1800–1950.* London: Oxford University Press, 1962.

———. "Social Change in Egypt: 1890–1914." In P. M. Holt, ed., *Political and Social Change in Modern Egypt.* London: Oxford University Press, 1968.

Bagehot, W. *Lombard Street: A Description of the Money Market.* London: King, 1875.

Bailyn, B. "The Origins of American Politics." *Perspectives in American History* 1 (1967), 9–122.

Balandier, G. "The Colonial Situation." In I. Wallerstein, ed., *Social Change: The Coloinal Situation.* New York: Wiley, 1966.

Baran, P. *The Political Economy of Growth*. New York: Monthly Review, 1957.

Baran, P., and P. Sweezy. *Monopoly Capital*. New York: Monthly Review, 1966.

Barraclough, G. *Introduction to Contemporary History*. Baltimore: Penguin, 1967.

Barratt-Brown, M. *After Imperialism*. Rev. ed. New York: Humanities, 1970.

——. *The Economics of Imperialism*. Harmondsworth: Penguin, 1974.

——. *Essays on Imperialism*. Nottingham: Bertrand Russell Peace Foundation/ Spokesman, 1972.

Barry, B. "An Economic Approach to the Analysis of Power and Conflict." *Government and Opposition* 9, 2 (Spring 1974), 189–223.

Baster, A. S. J. *Imperial Banks*. London: King, 1929.

Baumgart, W. *Imperialism: The Idea and Reality of British and French Colonial Expansion, 1880–1914*. New York: Oxford University Press, 1982.

Baynes, N. H. "The Decline of the Roman Empire in Western Europe: Some Modern Explanations." In D. Kagan, ed., *Problems in Ancient History*. New York: Macmillan, 1975.

Beenstock, Michael. *The World Economy in Transition*. London: Allen & Unwin, 1983.

Beer, S. *British Politics in the Collectivist Age*. New York: Vintage, 1969.

Bendix, R., ed. *State and Society*. Berkeley: University of California Press, 1968.

Benians, E. A., Sir J. Butler, and C. E. Carrington, eds. *The Cambridge History of the British Empire*. Vol. 3: *The Empire Commonwealth*. Cambridge: Cambridge University Press, 1959.

Bernardi, A. "The Economic Problems of the Roman Empire." In C. Cipolla, ed., *The Economic Decline of Empires*. London: Methuen, 1970.

Berque, J. *Egypt: Imperialism and Revolution*. London: Faber & Faber, 1972.

Betts, R. *The False Dawn*. Minneapolis: University of Minnesota Press, 1976.

Bhagwati, J. "The Pure Theory of International Trade." *Economic Journal* 74 (March 1964), 1–84.

Binder, L., et al. *Crises and Sequences in Political Development*. Princeton: Princeton University Press, 1971.

Biobaku, S. O. *The Egba and Their Neighbours, 1842–1872*. London: Oxford University Press, 1957.

Birley, Anthony. *Septimius Severus*. London: Eyre Spottiswoode, 1971.

Blake, R. *Disraeli*. New York: St. Martins, 1967.

——. *The Conservative Party*. New York: St. Martins, 1970.

Blakemore, H. *British Nitrates and Chilean Politics, 1886–1896*. London: Athlone, 1974.

Blaug, M. "Economic Imperialism Revisited." In K. Boulding and T. Mukerjee, eds., *Economic Imperialism*. Ann Arbor: University of Michigan Press, 1972.

Bloch, M. *Feudal Society*. Trans. L. A. Manyon. Chicago: University of Chicago Press, 1964.

Bloomfield, A. *Patterns of Fluctuation in International Investment before 1914.* Princeton: Princeton University, International Finance Section, 1968.

Blunt, W. S. *Secret History of the English Occupation of Egypt.* New York: Knopf, 1922.

Bodelsen, C. A. *Studies in Mid-Victorian Imperialism.* London: Heinemann, 1960.

Bodenheimer, S. "Dependency and Imperialism: The Roots of Latin American Underdevelopment." In K. T. Fann and D. C. Hodges, eds., *Readings in U.S. Imperialism.* Boston: Porter Sargent, 1971.

Bohannan, P. "Africa's Land." In G. Dalton, *Tribal and Peasant Economies.* Garden City, N.Y.: Natural History, 1967.

Boulding, K., and T. Mukerjee, eds. *Economic Imperialism.* Ann Arbor: University of Michigan Press, 1972.

Bourne, K. *The Foreign Policy of Victorian England, 1830–1902.* Oxford: Clarendon, 1970.

Bourne, K. *Palmerston: The Early Years.* New York: Macmillian, 1982.

Bowersock, G. "Gibbon on Civil War and Rebellion in Rome." *Daedalus* 105, 3 (1976), 63–88.

Bozeman, A. P. *Politics and Culture in International History.* Princeton: Princeton University Press, 1960.

Bradeen, D. "The Popularity of the Athenian Empire." In D. Kagan, ed., *Problems in Ancient History,* vol. 1. New York: Macmillan, 1975.

Braudel, F. *The Mediterranean,* vol. 2. Trans. Sian Reynolds. London: Collins, 1973.

Brenan, G. *The Spanish Labyrinth.* Cambridge: Cambridge University Press, 1950.

Brewer, A. *Marxist Theories of Imperialism.* London: Routledge & Kegan Paul, 1980.

Briggs, A. *Victorian People.* Chicago: University of Chicago Press, 1955.

Brodie, B. "Technological Change, Strategic Doctrine, and Political Outcomes." In Klaus Knorr, ed., *Historical Dimensions of National Security Problems.* Lawrence: Regents Press of Kansas, 1976.

Brogan, D. W. *The Development of Modern France, 1870–1939.* New York: Harper & Row, 1966.

——. *France under the Republic.* New York: Harper & Row, 1940.

Brown, B. H. *The Tariff Reform Movement in Great Britain, 1881–1895.* New York: Columbia University Press, 1943.

Brown, Peter. *The World of Late Antiquity.* London: Thames & Hudson 1971.

——. *The Making of Late Antiquity.* Cambridge: Harvard University Press, 1978.

Bruell, C. "Thucydides' View of Athenian Imperialism." *American Political Science Review* 68 (March 1974), 11–17.

Brunschwig, H. *L'expansion allemand d'outre-mer.* Paris: Presses Universitaires de France, 1957.

——. *French Colonialism.* Trans. W. G. Brown. New York: Praeger, 1966.

Brunt, P. A. "Laus Imperii." In P. D. A. Garnsey and C. R. Whittaker, eds., *Imperialism in the Ancient World*. New York: Cambridge University Press, 1978.

———. *Social Conflicts in the Roman Republic*. London: Oxford University Press, 1971.

Buckle, G. E., and W. Moneypenny. *Disraeli*, vol. 6. New York: Macmillan, 1920.

Bull, Hedley. *The Anarchical Society*. New York: Columbia University Press, 1972.

Bullen, R. "Anglo-French Rivalry and Spanish Politics, 1846–1848." *English Historical Review* 89 (January 1974), 25–47.

Burns, Sir Alan. *History of Nigeria*. London: Allen & Unwin, 1963.

Bury, J. B., et al. *The Cambridge Ancient History*, vol. 5. Cambridge: Cambridge University Press, 1927.

———. *France, 1814–1940*. Philadelphia: University of Pennsylvania Press, 1949.

Buxton, T. F. *The African Slave Trade and Its Remedy*. London: Murray, 1840.

Cady, J. F. *Foreign Intervention in the Rio de la Plata*. Philadelphia: University of Pennsylvania Press, 1929.

Caesar, Julius. *The Conquest of Gaul*. Trans. S. A. Handford. Baltimore: Penguin, 1951.

Cain, P. J. "J. A. Hobson, Cobdenism, and the Radical Theory of Economic Imperialism, 1898–1914." *Economic History Review*, 2d ser., 31 (November 1978), 463–90.

Cain, P. J., and A. G. Hopkins. "The Political Economy of British Expansion Overseas, 1750–1914." *Economic History Review*, 2d ser., 32 (November 1980), 463–90.

Cairncross, A. *Home and Foreign Investment*. Cambridge: Cambridge University Press, 1953.

Caporaso, J., and M. B. Dolan. "Dependence, Dependency, and Power in the Global System." *International Organization* 32 (Winter 1978), 13–43.

Cardoso, F., and E. Faletto. *Dependency and Development in Latin America*. Trans. M. M. Urquidi. Berkeley: University of California Press, 1979.

Carr, R. *Spain, 1808–1939*. London: Oxford University Press, 1966.

Carroll, E. M. *French Public Opinion and Foreign Affairs*. New York: Century, 1931.

Cartey, W., and M. Kilson, eds. *The Africa Reader: Colonial Africa*. New York: Vintage, 1970.

Caves, R., and H. Johnson, eds. *Readings in International Economics*. Homewood, Ill.: Irwin, 1968.

Cecil, Gwendolen. *Life of Robert, Marquis of Salisbury*, vols. 1 and 2. London: Hodder & Stoughton, 1921–32.

Checkland, S. G. *The Rise of Industrial Society in England, 1815–1855*. London: Longman, 1964.

Choucri, N., and R. C. North. *Nations in Conflict*. San Francisco: Freeman, 1975.

Cipolla, C. *The Economic Decline of Empires*. London: Methuen, 1970.

——. *Guns, Sails, and Empires*. New York: Minerva, 1965.

——, ed. *The Fontana Economic History of Europe*, vol. 1. London: Collins, 1961.

Clapham, J. H. *The Economic Development of France and Germany, 1815–1914*, 4th ed. London: Cambridge University Press, 1961.

Clark, G. K. *The Making of Victorian England*. New York: Atheneum, 1971.

Clarke, P. F. "Hobson, Free Trade, and Imperialism." *Economic History Review*, 2d ser., 34, 2 (1981), 308–12.

Cohen, B. J. *The Question of Imperialism*. New York: Basic, 1973.

Colson, E. "African Society at the Time of the Scramble." In L. H. Gann and P. Duignan, eds., *Colonialism in Africa, 1870–1960*, vol. 1. Cambridge: Cambridge University Press, 1969.

Connor, W. R. *Thucydides*. Princeton: Princeton University Press, 1984.

Cook, J. M. *The Greeks in Ionia and the East*. New York: Praeger, 1963.

Cook, S. A., et al., eds. *The Cambridge Ancient History*, vol. 11. Cambridge: Cambridge University Press, 1936.

Cooke, J. J. *The New French Imperialism*. Newton Abbot: David & Charles, 1971.

Cooney, S. "Political Demand Channels in the Processes of American and British Imperial Expansion." *World Politics* 27 (January 1975), 227–55.

——. "The Rosecrance Model." *British Journal of International Studies* 1, 2 (1975), 131–47.

Cornewall-Lewis, Sir George. *On the Government of Dependencies*. London: Murray, 1841.

Coser, Lewis. *The Functions of Social Conflict*. New York: Free, 1956.

Cottam, R. *Competitive Interference and World Politics*. Pittsburgh: University of Pittsburgh Press, 1967.

Cottrell, P. L. *British Overseas Investment in the Nineteenth Century*. London: Macmillan, 1975.

Coupland, R. "The Abolition of the Slave Trade," In J. H. Rose, ed., *The Cambridge History of the British Empire*, vol. 2. Cambridge: Cambridge University Press, 1940.

Craig, Gordon. *Germany, 1866–1945*. New York: Oxford University Press, 1978.

Cromer, Earl (Evelyn Baring). *Modern Egypt*. London: Macmillan, 1911.

Crowder, Michael. "Indirect Rule—French and British Style." *Africa* 34, 3 (1964), 197–205.

——. *The Story of Nigeria*. London: Faber & Faber, 1966.

Crowe, S. E. *The Berlin West Africa Conference*. London: Longmans, 1942.

Crowther, S. *The Gospel on the Banks of the Niger: The Niger Expedition, 1857–9* (1859). London: Dawsons, 1968.

Cruickshank, B. *Eighteen Years on the Gold Coast of Africa* (1853). London: Cass, 1966.

Curtin, Philip. *Cross-Cultural Trade in World History.* New York: Cambridge University Press, 1984.

——. *Economic Change in Pre-Colonial Africa.* Madison: University of Wisconsin Press, 1975.

Dacey, W. M. *The British Banking Mechanism.* London: Hutchinson, 1951.

Dahl, R. *Modern Political Analysis.* Englewood Cliffs, N.J.: Prentice-Hall, 1963.

——. *Polyarchy.* New Haven: Yale University Press, 1971.

Dahrendorf, R. *Society and Democracy in Germany.* Garden City, N.Y.: Doubleday, 1967.

Dangerfield, G. *The Strange Death of Liberal England* (1935). New York: Capricorn, 1961.

Davidson, B. *The African Genius.* Boston: Little, Brown, 1969.

Davidson, B., and F. K. Buah. *A History of West Africa, To the Nineteenth Century.* New York: Doubleday/Anchor, 1966.

Davis, L., and R. Huttenback. "The Political Economy of British Imperialism." *Journal of Economic History* 42 (March 1982), 119–32.

de Cecco, M. *Money and Empire.* Totowa, N.J.: Rowman & Littlefield, 1975.

Delavignette, R. *Freedom and Authority in French West Africa.* London: Oxford University Press, 1950.

de Romilly, J. *Thucydide et l'impérialisme Athénien.* Paris: Belles Lettres, 1947.

Deschamps, Hubert. "Et maintenant, Lord Lugard." *Africa* 33, 4 (1963), 293–306

de Ste Croix, G. E. M. *The Origins of the Peloponnesian War.* Ithaca: Cornell University Press, 1972.

de Tocqueville, A. *Democracy in America.* Trans. H. Reeve and F. Bowen. New York: Vintage, 1945.

——. *Recollections.* Trans. G. G. Lawrence. New York: Doubleday, 1970.

Deutsch, K. *The Analysis of International Relations.* Englewood Cliffs, N.J.: Prentice-Hall, 1968.

——. *Nationalism and Social Communication.* Cambridge: MIT Press, 1966.

Diaz, Bernal del Castillo. *The Discovery and Conquest of Mexico.* Trans. A. P. Maudslay. New York: Farrar, Strauss, & Cudahy, 1956.

Diehl, Charles. "The Economic Decay of Byzantium." In C. Cipolla, ed., *The Economic Decline of Empires.* London: Methuen, 1970.

Dike, K. O. *Trade and Politics in the Niger Delta.* Oxford: Oxford University Press, 1959.

Dmytryshyn, B. *Imperial Russia.* New York: Holt, Rinehart & Winston, 1967.

Dole, Gertrude. "Anarchy without Chaos." In M. Schwartz, V. Turner, and A. Tuden, eds., *Political Anthropology.* Chicago: Aldine, 1966.

Dominguez, Jorge. *Insurrection or Loyalty: The Breakdown of the Spanish American Empire.* Cambridge: Harvard University Press, 1980.

Doyle, Michael W. "Kant, Liberal Legacies, and Foreign Affairs," Pts. 1 and 2. *Philosophy and Public Affairs*, 12, 3–4 (June and October 1983).

Duffy, J. E. *Portugal in Africa*. Harmondsworth: Penguin, 1962.

Dumett, Raymond E. "Pressure Groups, Bureaucracy, and the Decision-making Process: The Case of Slavery Abolition and Colonial Expansion in the Gold Coast, 1874." *Journal of Imperial and Commonwealth History* 9 (January 1981), 193–215.

Easton, S. C. *Rise and Fall of Western Colonialism*. New York: Praeger, 1964.

Eckstein, H. "Authority Patterns: A Structural Basis for Political Inquiry." *American Political Science Review* 67 (December 1973), 1142–61.

Edelstein, M. "Rigidity and Bias in the British Capital Market, 1870–1913." In D. N. McCloskey, ed., *Essays on a Mature Economy*. Princeton: Princeton University Press, 1971.

———. *Overseas Investment in the Age of High Imperialism*. New York: Columbia University Press, 1982.

Eisenstadt, S. N. *The Political Systems of Empires*. New York: Free Press, 1969.

Eldridge, C. C. *England's Mission*. Chapel Hill: University of North Carolina Press, 1974.

Elias, T. O. *The Government and Politics of Africa*. New York: Asia, 1963.

Elliott, J. H. *Imperial Spain*. Harmondsworth: Penguin, 1970.

———. "The Decline of Spain." In C. Cipolla, ed., *The Economic Decline of Empires*. London: Methuen, 1970.

Elvin, Mark. *The Pattern of the Chinese Past*. Stanford: Stanford University Press, 1973.

Elwitt, L. *The Making of the Third Republic*. Baton Rouge: Louisiana State University Press, 1975.

Emerson, R. *From Empire to Nation*. Cambridge: Harvard University Press, 1967.

Engels, F. *The Origins of the Family, Private Property, and the State*. New York: International, 1942.

Etherington, Norman. "Reconsidering Theories of Imperialism." *History and Theory* 21, 1 (1982), 1–36.

Evans, Peter. *Dependent Development*. Princeton: Princeton University Press, 1979.

Evans-Pritchard, E. E. *The Nuer*. Oxford: Clarendon, 1940.

Fairbank, J. K. et al. *East Asia: The Modern Transformation*. Boston: Houghton Mifflin, 1965.

Fanon, Frantz. *Wretched of the Earth*. Trans. C. Farrington. New York: Grove, 1968.

Farmer, P. "The Second Empire." In J. P. T. Bury, ed., *The Cambridge Modern History*, vol. 10. Cambridge: Cambridge University Press, 1960.

Feinstein, C. H. *National Income, Output, and Expenditure of the United Kingdom*. Cambridge: Cambridge University Press, 1972.

Feis, H. *Europe, the World's Banker*. New York: Norton, 1965.

Ferguson, William Scott. *Greek Imperialism*. Boston: Houghton Mifflin, 1913.

Ferns, H. S. *Britain and Argentina in the Nineteenth Century*. London: Oxford University Press, 1960.

Fetter, Frank. *The Development of British Monetary Orthodoxy*. Cambridge: Harvard University Press, 1965.

Feuchtwanger, E. J. *Disraeli, Democracy, and the Tory Party*. Oxford: Clarendon, 1968.

Fieldhouse, D. K. *The Colonial Empires*. New York: Delacorte, 1965.

——. *Colonialism, 1870–1914: An Introduction*. New York: St. Martins, 1981.

——. *Economics and Empire*. London: Weidenfeld & Nicholson, 1973.

——. "Imperialism: An Historiographical Revision." *Economic History Review*, 2d ser., 14, 2 (December 1961), 187–217.

——. *The Theory of Capitalist Imperialism*. London: Longman, 1967.

Finkle, J., and R. N. Gable. *Political Development and Social Change*. New York: Wiley, 1971.

Finley, J. *Thucydides*. Ann Arbor: University of Michigan Press, 1963.

Finley, M. I. *The Ancient Economy*. London: Chatto & Williams, 1973.

——. *Economy and Society in Ancient Athens*. Ed. B. Shaw and R. P. Saller. New York: Viking, 1982.

——. "The Fifth Century Athenian Empire: A Balance Sheet." In P. D. A. Garnsey and C. R. Whittaker, eds., *Imperialism in the Ancient World*. Cambridge: Cambridge University Press, 1978.

——. "Manpower and the Decay of Rome." In C. Cipolla, ed., *The Economic Decline of Empires*. London: Methuen, 1970.

——. *Politics in the Ancient World*. New York: Cambridge University Press, 1983.

Fischer, F. *Germany's Aims in the First World War*. London: Chatto & Windus, 1967.

Fischer, L. *Lenin*. New York: Harper & Row, 1964.

Fliess, Peter J. *Thucydides and the Politics of Bipolarity*. Baton Rouge: Louisiana State University Press, 1966.

Flint, J. *Sir George Goldie and the Making of Modern Nigeria*. London: Oxford University Press, 1960.

——, ed. *The Cambridge History of Africa*, vol. 5. London: Cambridge University Press, 1976.

Flint, J., and G. Williams, eds. *Perspectives of Empire*. London: Longman, 1973.

Fogel, R., and S. Engerman. "A Model for the Explanation of Industrial Expansion in the Nineteenth Century." *Journal of Political Economy* 77 (May 1969), 306–28.

Forbes, Ian. "Social Imperialism and Wilhelmine Germany." *Historical Journal* 22, 2 (1979), 331–49.

Ford, A. G. *The Gold Standard, 1880–1914: Britain and Argentina*. Oxford: Clarendon, 1962.

———. "Notes on the Role of Exports in British Economic Fluctuations, 1870–1914." *Economic History Reivew*, 2d ser. 16 (December 1963), 328–37.

Forde, D. "Justice and Judgment among the Southern Ibo under Colonial Rule." In H. Kuper and L. Kuper, eds., *African Law*. Berkeley: University of California Press, 1965.

Forde, D., and Mary Douglas. "Primitive Economics." In George Dalton, ed., *Tribal and Peasant Economies*. Austin: University of Texas Press, 1967.

Forrest, W. G. *A History of Sparta*. London: Hutchinson, 1968.

Frank, A. G. *Capitalism and Underdevelopment in Latin America*. New York: Monthly Review Press, 1967.

———. *Lumpenbourgeoisie: Lumpendevelopment*. New York: Monthly Review, 1972.

Frank, Tenney. *Roman Imperialism*. New York: Macmillan, 1921.

Fraser, P. *Joseph Chamberlain, Radicalism and Empire*. London: Casset, 1966.

French, A. *The Growth of the Athenian Economy*. New York: Barnes & Noble, 1964.

Furnivall, J. S. *Colonial Policy and Practice*. Cambridge: Cambridge University Press, 1948.

Furtado, C. *Obstacles to Development in Latin America*. Garden City: Doubleday-Anchor, 1970.

Galbraith, J. S. "Gordon, MacKinnon, and Leopold: The Scramble for Africa." *Victorian Studies* 14, 4 (June 1971), 369–88.

———. "The Turbulent Frontier as a Factor in Btitish Expansion." *Comparative Studies in Society and History* 1 (1960), 150–68.

Gallagher, John. *The Decline, Revival, and Fall of the British Empire*. Ed. Anil Seal. Cambridge: Cambridge University Press, 1982.

Gallagher, John, and Ronald Robinson. "The Imperialism of Free Trade," *Economic History Review*, 2nd. ser., 6, 1 (1953), 1–25.

Galtung, J. "A Structural Theory of Imperialism." *Journal of Peace Research* 8, 2 (1971), 81–117.

Ganiage, Jean. *L'expansion coloniale et les rivalités internationales*, vol. 1. Paris: C.D.U., 1964.

Gann, L. H., and P. Duignan, eds. *Colonialism in Africa, 1870–1960*, vol. 1. New York: Cambridge University Press, 1961.

Garnsey, P. D. A., and C. R. Whittaker., ed. *Imperialism in the Ancient World*. Cambridge: Cambridge University Press, 1978.

Garvin, J. L. *The Life of Joseph Chamberlain*. London: Macmillan, 1935.

Gavin, R. J. "The Bartle Frere Mission to Zanzibar." *Historical Journal* 5, 2 (1962), 122–48.

Geertz, Clifford. *Negara: The Theatre State in Nineteenth Century Bali*. Princeton: Princeton University Press, 1980.

Gerth, H., and C. W. Mills, eds. *From Max Weber*. New York: Oxford University Press, 1946.

Gibbon, E. *Decline and Fall of the Roman Empire*. In D. Saunders, ed., *The Portable Gibbon*. New York: Viking, 1952.

Gifford, P., and W. Louis. *Britain and Germany in Africa*. New Haven: Yale University Press, 1967.

———. *France and Britain in Africa*. New Haven: Yale University Press, 1971.

Gilbert, Felix. *End of the European Era*. New York: Norton, 1979.

———. *To the Farewell Address*. Princeton: Princeton University Press, 1961.

Gilpin, Robert. *War and Change in World Politics*. New York: Cambridge University Press, 1981.

Gladstone, W. E. "Aggression in Egypt and Freedom in the East." *Nineteenth Century* 2, 6 (August 1877), 149–66.

Gluckman, M. *The Ideas in Barotse Jurisprudence*. New Haven: Yale University Press, 1965.

Gongara, M. *Studies in the Colonial History of Spanish America*. Trans. R. Southern. Cambridge: Cambridge University Press, 1975.

Gooch, G. P. *Franco-German Relations*. New York: Russell & Russell, 1922.

Gordon, Donald C. *The Dominion Partnership in Imperial Defense*. Baltimore: Johns Hopkins Press, 1965.

Gossman, L. *The Empire Unpossess'd*. Cambridge: Cambridge University Press, 1981.

Gourevitch, Peter. "International Trade, Domestic Coalitions, and Liberty: The Crisis of 1873–1896." *Journal of Interdisciplinary History* (Autumn 1977), 281–314.

Graham, G. *Tides of Empire*. Montreal: McGill University Press, 1972.

Graham, R. *Britain and the Onset of Modernization in Brazil*. London: Cambridge University Press, 1968.

Grampp, W. D. *The Manchester School of Economics*. Stanford: Stanford University Press, 1966.

Green, P., and S. Levinson, eds. *Power and Community*. New York: Random, 1969.

Greene, J. "An Uneasy Connection." In S. Kurtz and J. Huston, eds., *Essays on the American Revolution*. Chapel Hill: University of North Carolina Press, 1967.

Greenfield, Richard. *Ethiopia*. New York: Praeger, 1965.

Grenville, J. A. S. *Lord Salisbury and Foreign Policy*. London: University of London Press, 1964.

Gross, J., ed. *Age of Kipling*. New York: Simon & Schuster, 1972.

Groves, C. P. "Missionary and Humanitarian Aspects of Imperialism from 1870 to 1914." In L. H. Gann and P. Duignan, eds., *Colonialism in Africa*, vol. 1. Cambridge: Cambridge University Press, 1969.

Gulick, E. *The Classical Balance of Power*. New York: Norton, 1955.

Gunderson, G. "Economic Change and the Demise of the Roman Empire." *Explorations in Economic History* 13 (1976), 43–68.

Hailey, Lord. *An African Survey*. London: Oxford, 1957.

Halevy, E. *History of the English People in the Nineteenth Century*, vol. 5: *Imperialism and the Rise of Labor*. Trans. E. I. Watkins. London: Benn, 1968.

Hall, A. R., ed. *The Export of Capital from Britain, 1860–1914*. London: Methuen, 1968.

Hammerow, P. S., ed. *The Age of Bismarck*. New York: Harper & Row, 1973.

Hancock, W. K. *Survey of British Commonwealth Affairs*, vol. 2. New York: Oxford University Press, 1940.

Hanham, H. J. *Elections and Party Management*. London: Longmans, 1959.

Hansson, Karl. "A General Theory of the System of Multilateral Trade." *American Economic Review* 42 (March 1952), 59–88.

Harcourt, Freda. "Disraeli's Imperialism, 1866–68." *Historical Journal* 23, 1 (1980), 87–109.

Hargreaves, J. D. *Prelude to the Partition of West Africa*. London: Macmillan, 1963.

——. "Towards a History of the Partition of Africa." *Journal of African History* 1, 1 (1960), 97–109.

——. *West Africa Partitioned*, vol. 1: *The Loaded Pause, 1885–1889*. Madison: University of Wisconsin Press, 1974.

Harris, M. *Culture, Man and Nature*. New York: Crowell, 1971.

Harris, S., ed. *Schumpeter: Social Scientist*. Cambridge: Harvard University Press, 1951.

Harris, William V. *War and Imperialism in Republican Rome, 327–70 B.C.* Oxford: Clarendon, 1979.

Hart, J. "Three Approaches to the Measurement of Power in International Relations." *International Organization* 30 (Spring 1976), 289–308.

Headrick, Daniel. *Tools of Empire*. New York: Oxford University Press, 1981.

Heitland, W. E., and R. Kagan, ed. *Decline and Fall of the Roman Empire*. Boston: Heath, 1962.

Hennessey, C. A. M. *A Federal Republic in Spain*. Oxford: Oxford University Press, 1962.

Herz, J. *International Politics in the Atomic Age*. New York: Columbia University Press, 1959.

Hess, R. *Ethiopia*. Ithaca: Cornell University Press, 1970.

Hicks, J. *A Theory of Economic History*. London: Oxford University Press, 1969.

Hilferding, R. *Capital financier* (1910). Paris: Minuit, 1970.

Hinsley, F. H. *The New Cambridge Modern History*, vol. 11. Cambridge: Cambridge University Press, 1962.

——. *Power and the Pursuit of Peace*. London: Cambridge University Press, 1963.

Hirschman, A. "Hegel, Imperialism, and Structural Stagnation." *Journal of Development Economics* 3, 1 (July 1976), 1–8.

——. *National Power and the Structure of Foreign Trade.* Berkeley: University of California Press, 1945.

Hoag, Malcolm. "On Stability in Deterrent Races." In R. Art and K. Waltz, eds., *The Use of Force.* Boston: Little, Brown, 1971.

Hobsbawm, E. *Industry and Empire.* New York: Pantheon, 1968.

Hobson, J. A. "Capitalism and Imperialism in South Africa." *Contemporary Review*, January 1900, 1–17.

——. *Confessions of an Economic Heretic.* London: Allen & Unwin, 1938.

——. *Imperialism: A Study* (1902). Ann Arbor: University of Michigan Press, 1965.

Hodgart, Alan. *The Economics of European Imperialism.* New York: Norton, 1977.

Hodgkin, T. *Nationalism in Africa.* New York: New York University Press, 1957.

Hoebel, E. A. *The Law of Primitive Man.* Cambridge: Harvard University Press, 1961.

Hoffman, J. R. S. *Great Britain and the German Trade Rivalry, 1875–1914.* Philadelphia: University of Pennsylvania Press, 1933.

Hoffman, S. *Gulliver's Troubles.* New York: McGraw-Hill, 1968.

——. "Obstinate or Obsolete?" In J. Nye, ed., *International Regionalism.* Boston: Little, Brown, 1968.

Hollingsworth, Lawrence. *Zanzibar under the Foreign Office, 1890–1913.* London: Macmillan, 1953.

Hollyday, F. B. M. *Bismarck.* Englewood Cliffs, N.J.: Prentice-Hall, 1970.

Holt, P. M. "Egypt and the Nile Valley." In J. Flint, ed., *The Cambridge History of Africa*, vol. 5. London: Cambridge University Press, 1976.

Holt, P. M., ed. *Political and Social Change in Modern Egypt.* London: Oxford University Press, 1968.

Hopkins, A. G. *An Economic History of West Africa.* New York: Columbia University Press, 1974.

——. "Economic Imperialism in West Africa: Lagos, 1880–1892." *Economic History Review*, 2d ser., 21 (December 1968), 580–606.

——. "Property Rights and Empire Building: Britain's Annexation of Lagos, 1861." *Journal of Economic History* 40, 4 (December 1980), 777–98.

Hopkins, K. *Conquerors and Slaves.* Cambridge: Cambridge University Press, 1978.

Howard, Michael. "The Armed Forces." In F. H. Hinsley, ed., *The New Cambridge Modern History*, vol. 11. Cambridge: Cambridge University Press, 1962.

Humphreys, R. A. "The States of Latin America." In J. P. T. Bury, ed., *The New Cambridge Modern History.* Cambridge: Cambridge Univesity Press, 1960.

Humphreys, R. A., and J. Lynch. *The Origins of the Latin American Revolutions.* New York: Knopf, 1965.

Huntington, S. "The Change to Change." *Comparative Politics* 3, 3 (1971), 283–322.

——. *Political Order in Changing Societies*. New Haven: Yale University Press, 1968.

Huntington, S., and Z. Brzezinski. *Political Power: U.S.A.:U.S.S.R.* New York: Viking, 1964.

Hutchins, R. *The Illusion of Permanence*. Princeton: Princeton University Press, 1967.

Hyam, Ronald, and Ged Martin. *Reappraisals in British Imperial History*. London: Macmillan, 1975.

Hynes, W. G. "British Mercantile Attitudes towards Imperial Expansion." *Historical Journal* 19, 4 (1976), 969–79.

Hynes, W. G. *The Economics of Empire*. London: Longman, 1983.

Igbafe, P. A. "The Fall of Benin: A Reassessment." *Journal of African History* 11, 3 (1970), 385–400.

Imlah, Albert. *Economic Elements in the Pax Britannica*. Cambridge: Harvard University Press, 1958.

Inalcik, I. "The Emergence of the Ottomans." In P. M. Holt, A. Lambton, and B. Lewis, eds., *The Cambridge History of Islam*, vol. 1. Cambridge: Cambridge University Press, 1970.

Isichei, E. *The Ibo People and the Europeans*. London: Faber & Faber, 1973.

Issawi, Charles. *Egypt in Revolution*. London: Oxford University Press, 1963.

James, R. *Rosebery*. London: Weidenfeld & Nicholson, 1963.

Jeffery, Keith. "The Eastern Arc of Empire." *Journal of Strategic Studies* 5, 4 (December 1982), 531–45.

Jenks, Leland. *The Migration of British Capital to 1875*. New York: Knopf, 1927.

Jervis, Robert. "Cooperation under the Security Dilemma." *World Politics* 30, 2 (January 1978), 167–214.

Jesurun, C. "The Anglo-French Declaration of 1896 and the Independence of Siam." *Journal of the Siam Society* 58, 2 (1970), 105–26.

Jones, A. M. *The Decline of the Ancient World*. London: Longmans, 1966.

Jones, G. I. *Trading States of the Oil Rivers*. Oxford: Clarendon, 1953.

Jorberg, Lennart. "The Industrial Revolution in the Nordic Countries." In C. Cipolla, ed., *The Fontana Economic History of Europe: The Emergence of Industrial Societies*, 1. London: Fontana, 1973.

Judd, D. *The Victorian Empire, 1837–1901*. New York: Praeger, 1970.

Jullian, C. *Histoire de la Gaule*, vol. 3. Paris: Hachette, 1926.

Kagan, Donald. *The Outbreak of the Peloponnesian War*. Ithaca: Cornell University Press, 1969.

Kagan, Donald, ed. *Problems in Ancient History*, vols. 1–2. New York: Macmillan, 1975.

Kahler, Miles. *Decolonization in Britain and France*. Princeton: Princeton University Press, 1984.

Kahn, A. *Great Britain and World Economy*. New York: Columbia University Press, 1946.

Kanya-Forstner, A. S. *The Conquest of the Western Sudan*. London: Cambridge University Press, 1969.

———. "French Expansion in Africa: The Mythical Theory." In E. R. J. Owen and R. Sutcliffe, *Studies in the Theory of Imperialism*. London: Longman, 1972.

Kaplan, M. *System and Process*. New York: Wiley, 1957.

Kautsky, John H. *The Politics of Aristocratic Empires*. Chapel Hill: University of North Carolina Press, 1982.

———. "J. A. Schumpeter and Karl Kautsky." *Midwest Journal of Political Science* 5 (May 1961), 101–28.

Kemp, T. *Theories of Imperialism*. London: Dobson, 1967.

Kennan, George F. *The Decline of Bismarck's European Order*. Princeton: Princeton University Press, 1979.

Kennedy, P. M. "German Colonial Expansion." *Past and Present* no. 54 (1972), 134–41.

———. *The Rise and Fall of British Naval Mastery*. London: Lane, 1967.

———. *The Rise of the Anglo-German Antagonism, 1860–1914*. London: Allen & Unwin, 1980.

Keohane, R. "Theory of World Politics: Structural Realism and Beyond." In Ada W. Finifter, ed., *Political Science: The State of the Discipline*. Washington, D.C.: A.P.S.A., 1983.

Keohane, Robert, and Joseph Nye. *Power and Interdependence*. Boston: Little, Brown, 1977.

Kiernan, V. G. *From Conquest to Collapse*. New York: Pantheon, 1982.

———. *The Lords of Human Kind*. Boston: Little, Brown, 1969.

Kindleberger, C. *Economic Growth in France and Britain*. Cambridge: Harvard University Press, 1964.

———. *Economic Response: Comparative Studies in Trade, Finance and Growth*. Cambridge: Harvard University Press, 1978.

Kissinger, H. *A World Restored*. New York: Universal, 1964.

Kitson-Clark, G. *The Making of Victorian England*. New York: Atheneum, 1971.

Klein, I. "British Expansion in Malaya." *Journal of Southern Asian History* 9, 1 (1968), 53–68.

Knaplund, P. *Gladstone's Foreign Policy*. New York: Harper & Row, 1935.

Knorr, Klaus. *British Colonial Theories*. Toronto: University of Toronto Press, 1944.

———. *Power and Wealth*. New York: Basic, 1973.

Koebner, R., and H. Schmidt. *Imperialism: The Story and Significance of a Political World, 1840–1860*. Cambridge: Cambridge University Press, 1964.

Kuhn, T. *The Structure of Scientific Revolutions*. 2d ed. Chicago: University of Chicago Press, 1970.

Kurth, J. "The Political Consequences of the Product Cycle." *International Organization* 33 (Winter 1979), 1–34.

LaFeber, W. *The New Empire*. Ithaca: Cornell University Press, 1963.

Laffey, J. "The Roots of French Imperialism: The Case of Lyon." *French Historical Studies* 6, 1 (Spring 1969), 78–92.

Laitin, David. "Capitalism and Hegemony." *International Organization* 36 (Autumn 1982), 687–713.

Landes, D. *Bankers and Pashas.* Cambridge: Harvard University Press, 1958.

——. "Some Thoughts on the Nature of Economic Imperialism." *Journal of Economic History* 21, 4 (December 1961), 496–513.

Langer, W. L. *The Diplomacy of Imperialism*. New York: Knopf, 1935.

——. *European Alliances and Alignments*. New York: Vintage, 1950.

Langer, W. L., ed. *Encyclopedia of World History*. 5th ed., rev. Boston: Houghton Mifflin, 1972.

Latham, A. J. *Old Calabar, 1600–1891*. Oxford: Clarendon, 1973.

Leach, E. R. *The Political Systems of Highland Burma*. Boston: Beacon, 1954.

Lebow, Richard N. *White Britian and Black Ireland*. Philadelphia: Institute for the Study of Human Issues, 1976.

Lenin, V. I. *Collected Works*. Trans. Institute of Marxism-Leninism. 45 vols. New York: International, 1960–70.

——. *Imperialism: The Highest Stage of Capitalism*. New York: International, 1939.

——. *Selected Works*. London: Lawrence & Wishart, 1968.

——. *State and Revolution* (1917). New York: International, 1943.

Levy, M. *The Structure of Society*. Princeton: Princeton University Press, 1952.

Lewis, Bernard. *The Emergence of Modern Turkey*. London: Oxford University Press, 1961.

Lewis, W. A. *Growth and Fluctuations*. London: Allen & Unwin, 1978.

Lichtheim, G. *Imperialism*. New York: Praeger, 1971.

——. *Marxism*. London: Routledge & Kegan Paul, 1961.

Lijphart, A. *The Politics of Acommodation*. Berkely: University of California Press, 1975.

Lipson, C. *Standing Guard*. Berkeley: University of Califoria Press, 1985.

Liska, George. *Career of Empire*. Baltimore: Johns Hopkins Press, 1978.

Lloyd, P. C. *Yoruba Land Law*. London: Oxford University Press, 1962.

Lockhart, J., and S. Schwartz. *Early Latin America*. New York: Cambridge University Press, 1983.

Lofchie, M. *Zanzibar: Background to Revolution*. Princeton: Princeton University Press, 1965.

Louis, W. R. "Sir Percy Anderson's Grand African Strategy." *English Historical Review* 81 (April 1966), 292–314.

Louis, W. R., ed. *Imperialism: The Robinson and Gallagher Controversy*. New York: New Viewpoints, 1976.

Lowe, C. J. *The Reluctant Imperialists*. New York: Macmillan, 1967.

———. *Salisbury and the Mediterranean, 1885–1896*. London: Routledge & Kegan Paul, 1965.

Lowe, R. "The Value to the U.K. of the Foreign Dominions of the Crown." *Fortnightly Review* 28 (1 November 1877), 618–30.

Luttwak, Edward N. *The Grand Strategy of the Roman Empire*. Baltimore: Johns Hopkins Press, 1976.

Luxemburg, R. *The Accumulation of Capital* (1913). Trans. A. Schwarzchild. London: Routledge & Kegan Paul, 1951.

Lynch, J. *The Origins of the Latin American Revolutions*. New York: Knopf, 1965.

Lyne, R. N. *Zanzibar in Contemporary Times*. New York: Negro Universities Press, 1909.

Lynn, M. "Change and Continuity in the British Palm Oil Trade with West Africa." *Journal of African History* 22, 3 (1981), 331–48.

———. "Consuls and Kings: British Policy, 'the Man on the Spot' and the Seizure of Lagos, 1851." *Journal of Imperial and Commonwealth History* 10 (January 1982), 150–67.

Machiavelli, N. *The Prince and the Discourses*. Trans. L. Ricci. New York: Modern Library, 1950.

MacLean, D. "Commerce, Finance, and British Diplomatic Support in China." *Economic History Review* 26, 3 (August 1973), 464–76.

Magdoff, H. *The Age of Imperialism*. New York: Monthly Review, 1970.

Magnus, P. *Gladstone*. London: Murray, 1954.

Mahler, Vincent. *Dependency Approaches to International Political Economy*. New York: Columbia University Press, 1980.

Maine, H. *Ancient Law*. London: Murray, 1880.

Mair, L. *Primitive Government*. Baltimore: Penguin, 1964.

Mannoni, Otare. *Prospero and Caliban*. London: Methuen, 1956.

Mansfield, P. *The British in Egypt*. London: Weidenfeld & Nichcolson, 1971.

Maquet, J. "African Society: Subsaharan Africa." In D. L. Sills, ed., *International Encyclopedia of the Social Sciences*. New York: Macmillan, 1968.

Marlowe, John. *Anglo-Egyptian Relations, 1800–1956*. 2d ed. London: Cass, 1965.

———. *Spoiling the Egyptians*. New York: St. Martins, 1975.

Marx, K. *Pre-Capitalist Economic Formations*. Trans. J. Cohen. New York: International, 1965.

———. *Selected Works*. New York: International, 1968.

Mason, P. [P. Woodruff.] *The Men Who Ruled India*. London: St. Martins, 1954.

Mason, P. *Patterns of Dominance*. London: University Press, 1971.

Mathias, P. *First Industrial Nation*. London: Methuen, 1964.

May, E., and J. Thompson, Jr. *American–East Asian Relations*. Cambridge: Harvard University Press, 1972.

McCarthy, Justin. *A History of Our Times*, vol. 2. New York: Harper, 1886.

McCloskey, D., ed. *Essays in a Mature Economy*. Princeton: Princeton University Press, 1971.

McFarlan, D. M. *Calabar: The Church of Scotland Mission*. London: Nelson, 1957.

McGowan, P., and B. Kordan. "Imperialism in World-System Perspective." In W. L. Hollist and J. Rosenau, eds., *World System Structure*. Beverley Hills: Sage, 1981.

McIntyre, W. D. *The Imperial Frontier in the Tropics*. London: Macmillan, 1967.

McKenzie, Robert, and Allan Silver. *Angeles in Marble: Working Class Conservatives in Urban England*. London: Heinemann, 1968.

McNeil, William H. *A World History*. New York: Oxford University Press, 1967.

Medlicott, W. *Bismarck, Gladstone, and the Concert of Europe*. London: Athlone, 1956.

Meek, C. K. *Land Tenure and Land Administration in Nigeria and the Cameroons*. London: H.M.S.O., 1957.

Meiggs, Russell. *The Athenian Empire*. London: Oxford University Press, 1972.

Memmi, A. *The Colonizer and the Colonized*. Boston: Beacon, 1965.

Metcalfe, George. *MacLean of the Gold Coast*. London: Oxford University Press, 1962.

Milward, A., and S. B. Saul. *The Economic Development of Continental Europe, 1780–1870*. Totowa, N.J.: Rowman & Littlefield, 1973.

Mommsen, Wolfgang. "Domestic Factors in German Foreign Policy before 1914." In James J. Sheehan, ed., *Imperial Germany*. New York: Franklin Watts, 1976.

——. *Theories of Imperialism*. New York: Random, 1980.

Montesquieu, Charles L. de Secondat. *Considerations on the Causes of the Greatness of the Romans and Their Decline* (1734). Trans. D. Lowenthal. New York: Free, 1965.

Moore, B. *Social Origins of Dictatorship and Democracy*. Boston: Beacon, 1966.

Moore, R. "Imperialism and Free Trade Policy in India, 1853–1854." *Economic History Review*, 2d ser., 17, 3 (August 1964), 135–45.

Morgan, E. V., and W. A. Thomas. *The Stock Exchange*. London: Elek, 1962.

Morgenbesser, S. "Imperialism: Some Preliminary Distinctions." *Philosophy and Public Affairs* 3 (Fall 1973), 3–44.

Morgenthau, H. *Politics among Nations*. 5th ed. New York: Random, 1975.

Morrell, W. P. *British Colonial Policy in the Mid-Victorian Age*. London: Oxford University Press, 1969.

Morris, James. *Pax Britannica*. New York: Harcourt, Brace & World, 1968.

Moses, R. *The Civil Service in Great Britain.* New York: Columbia University Press, 1914.

Mowat, R. C. "From Liberalism to Imperialism: Egypt, 1875–1887." *Historical Journal* 16, 1 (1975), 109–24.

Murphey, R. *Treaty Ports and China's Modernization: What Went Wrong?* Ann Arbor: University of Michigan Center for Chinese Studies, 1970.

Murphy, G. "On Satelliteship." *Journal of Economic History* 21, 4 (December 1961), 641–51.

Nadel, G., and P. Curtis, eds., *Imperialism and Colonialism.* New York: Macmillan, 1964.

Nemmers, E. E. *Hobson and Underconsumption.* Amsterdam: North-Holland, 1956.

Neustadt, R. *Alliance Politics.* New York: Columbia University Press, 1970.

Newbury, C. W. "The Development of French Policy on the Lower and Upper Niger, 1880–1898." *Journal of Modern History* 31, 2 (1959), 16–26.

———. "The Protectionist Revival in French Colonial Trade." *Economic History Review*, 2d ser., 21, 2 (August 1968), 337–48.

———. "Trade and Authority in West Africa from 1850 to 1880." In L. H. Gann and P. Duigan, eds., *Colonialism in Africa*, vol. 1. Cambridge: Cambridge University Press, 1969.

———. *The Western Slave Coast and Its Rulers.* London: Oxford University Press, 1961.

Newbury, C. W., and A. S. Kanya-Forstner. "French Policy and the Origins of the Scramble for West Africa." *Journal of African History* 10, 2 (1969), 253–76.

North, D. C. *Growth and Welfare in the American Past.* Englewood Cliffs, N.J.: Prentice-Hall, 1974.

Northedge, F. S. C. *One Hundred Years of International Relations.* New York: Praeger, 1971.

Northrup, D. *Trade without Rulers.* Oxford: Clarendon, 1978.

Nwabara, S. N. *Iboland: A Century of Contact with Britain.* Atlantic Highlands: Humanities, 1978.

Nye, J., ed. *International Regionalism.* Boston: Little, Brown, 1968.

Nye, J., and R. Keohane, eds. *Transnationalism and World Politics.* Cambridge: Harvard University Press, 1972.

Oliver, R. *Sir Harry Johnston and the Scramble for Africa.* London: Chatto & Windus, 1957.

Ollennu, N. M. "The Influence of English Law on West Africa." *Journal of African Law* 5, 1 (1961), 21–35.

Olson, M. *The Logic of Collective Action.* Cambridge: Harvard University Press, 1971.

Oman, Sir Charles. *Memoirs of Victorian Oxford.* London: Methuen, 1941.

Owen, E. R. J. *Cotton and the Egyptian Economy, 1820–1914.* London: Oxford University Press, 1969.

Owen, E. R. J., and R. B. Sutcliffe, eds. *Studies in the Theory of Imperialism.* London: Longman, 1972.

Park, A. E. W. "A Dual System of Land Tenure." *Journal of African Law* 9, 1 (1965), 1–19.

Parry, J. H. *The Establishment of European Hegemony, 1415–1757.* New York: Harper Torchbooks, 1959.

——. "Colonial Development and International Rivalries." In R. B. Wernham, ed., *The New Cambridge Modern History*, vol. 3. Cambridge: Cambridge University Press, 1968.

Parsons, T., and E. Shils, eds. *Toward a General Theory of Action.* New York: Harper Torchbooks, 1951.

Payer, Cheryl. *The Debt Trap.* Harmondsworth: Penguin, 1974.

Pearce, F. B. *Zanzibar.* London: Cass, 1920.

Pelling, H. *The Social Geography of British Elections.* London: Macmillan, 1967.

Penrose, E. F., ed. *European Imperialism and the Partition of Africa.* London: Cass, 1975.

Perham, M. *The Colonial Reckoning.* New York: Knopf, 1962.

——. *Lugard: The Years of Adventure.* London: Collins, 1956.

Pfeffer, Alan. "The Rise of the Imperialist System." Harvard University, 1974.

Phillip, J. "The Function of Land in a Colonial Society." *Victorian Historical Magazine* no. 39 (1968), 46–50.

Platt, D. C. M. *Finance, Trade and Politics in British Foreign Policy, 1815–1914.* London: Oxford University Press, 1968.

——. "Further Objections to an Imperialism of Free Trade." *Economic History Review*, 2d ser., 26 (February 1973), 77–91.

——. "The Imperialism of Free Trade: Some Reservations." *Economic History Review*, 2d. ser., 21 (August 1968), 296–306.

——. *Latin America and British Trade, 1806–1914.* New York: Harper & Row, 1973.

Plutarch, "Pericles." Trans. I. Scott-Kilvert. *The Rise and Fall of Athens: Nine Greek Lives.* Harmondsworth: Penguin, 1960.

Polanyi, K. *The Great Transformation.* Boston: Beacon, 1944.

Polybius, *Histories.* Trans. Evelyn Shuckburgh. Bloomington: Indiana University Press, 1962.

Porter, B. *Critics of Empire.* London: Macmillan, 1968.

Potter, G., ed. *The New Cambridge Modern History*, vol. 1. Cambridge: Cambridge University Press, 1962.

Powers, T. *Jules Ferry and the Renaissance of French Imperialism.* New York: Octagon, 1966.

Pressnell, L. S. *Studies in the Industrial Revolution.* London: Athlone, 1960.

Priestley, H. I. *France Overseas.* New York: Appleton-Century, 1938.

Ramm, Agatha. "Great Britain and France in Egypt, 1876–1882." In P. Gifford and W. R. Louis, eds., *France and Britain in Africa*. New Haven: Yale University Press, 1971.

Ranger, T. O. "Connections between 'Primary Resistance' Movements and Modern Mass Nationalism in East and Central Africa: Part 1." *Journal of African History* 9, 3 (1968), 437–53.

Reischauer, Edwin O., and John K. Fairbank. *East Asia: The Great Tradition*. Boston: Houghton Mifflin, 1958.

Remer, C. F. *Foreign Investment in China*. New York: Fertig, 1968.

Reynolds, C. *Modes of Imperialism*. New York: St. Martins, 1981.

Rich, N. *Friedrich von Holstein*, vol. 1. Cambridge: Cambridge Unviersity Press, 1965.

Ridley, Jasper. *Lord Palmerston*. London: Constable, 1970.

Robinson, Ronald. "Imperial Problems in British Politics." In Sir E. Benians, ed., *The Cambridge History of the British Empire*, vol. 3. Cambridge: Cambridge University Press, 1959.

——. "Introduction." H. Brunschwig, *French Colonialism, 1871–1914: Myths and Realities*. New York: Praeger, 1966.

——. "The Non-European Foundations of European Imperialism: Sketch for a Theory of Collaboration." In E. R. J. Owen and R. Sutcliffe, eds., *Studies in the Theory of Imperialism*. London: Longman, 1972.

Robinson, R. E., and J. Gallagher, with Alice Denny. *Africa and the Victorians* (1961). Garden City, N.Y.: Doubleday/Anchor, 1968.

——. "The Partition of Africa." In F. H. Hinsley, ed., *The New Cambridge Modern History*, vol. 11. Cambridge: Cambridge University Press, 1962.

Rohl, J. *Germany without Bismarck*. Berkeley: University of California Press, 1967.

Rose, J. H., ed. *The Cambridge History of the British Empire*, vol. 2. London: Cambridge University Press, 1940.

Rose, J. H., and J. Baster. *Imperial Banks*. London: King, 1929.

Rosecrance, R. *Action and Reaction in World Politics*. Boston: Little, Brown, 1963.

Rostovtzeff, M. *Rome*. London: Oxford University Press, 1960.

Rostow, W. *The British Economy in the Nineteenth Century*. London: Oxford University Press, 1948.

——. *The World Economy: History and Prospect*. Austin: University of Texas Press, 1978.

Rotberg, R., ed. *Africa and Its Explorers*. Cambridge: Harvard University Press, 1970.

Roth, G. "Personal Rulership, Patrimonialism, and Empire Building in the New States." *World Politics* 20, 2 (January 1968), 194–206.

Rubenson, Sven. *The Survival of Ethiopian Independence*. London: Heinemann, 1976.

Rustow, D., ed. *Philosophers and Kings*. New York: Braziller, 1970.

Sanderson, George. *England, Europe, and the Upper Nile, 1882–1899*. Edinburgh: Edinburgh University Press, 1962.

——. "The European Partition of Africa: Coincidence or Conjuncture?" In E. F. Penrose, ed., *European Imperialism and the Partition of Africa*. London: Cass, 1975.

Sargent, A. J. *Anglo-Chinese Commerce and Diplomacy*. London: Oxford University Press, 1907.

Saul, S. B. *The Myth of the Great Depression, 1873–1896*. London: Macmillan, 1972.

——. *Studies in British Overseas Trade*. Liverpool: Liverpool University Press, 1960.

Schelling, T. *Arms and Influence*. New Haven: Yale University Press, 1966.

Schlote, W. *British Overseas Trade from 1700 to the 1930s*. Oxford: Blackwell, 1952.

Scholch, Alexander. "The 'Men on the Spot' and the English Occupation of Egypt in 1882." *Historical Journal* 19, 3 (1976), 773–85.

Schroeder, P. "Alliances, 1815–1945: Weapons of Power and Tools of Management." In K. Knorr, ed., *Historical Dimensions of National Security*. Lawrence: Regents Press of Kansas, 1976.

Schumpeter, J. *Capitalism, Socialism, and Democracy*. New York: Harper & Row, 1950.

——. *Imperialism and Social Classes*. Cleveland: World, 1955.

Schurman, F. L. *War and Diplomacy in the French Republic*. Chicago: University of Chicago Press, 1931.

Schurman, F. *The Logic of World Power*. New York: Pantheon, 1974.

Schwartz, M. V., V. Turner, and A. Tuden. *Political Anthropology*. Chicago: Aldine, 1966.

Seal, A. *The Emergence of Indian Nationalism*. London: Cambridge University Press, 1968.

Seeley, J. R. *The Expansion of England*. London: Macmillan, 1883.

Semmel, B. *Imperialism and Social Reform*. Cambridge: Harvard University Press, 1960.

——. *The Rise of Free Trade Imperialism*. London: Cambridge University Press, 1970.

Shannon, R. *The Crisis of Imperialism*. London: Hart-Davis, 1974.

Sheehan, J., ed. *Imperial Germany*. New York: Franklin Watts, 1976.

Simon, N. *Germany in the Age of Bismarck*. London: Allen & Unwin, 1968.

Simpson, S., and J. Stone. *Cases and Readings on Law and Society*. St. Paul, Minn.: West, 1948.

Singer, H. "The Distribution of Gains between Investing and Borrowing Countries." In R. Caves and H. Johnson, eds., *Readings in International Economics*. Homewood, Ill.: Irwin, 1968.

Smith, Paul. *Disraelian Conservatism and Social Reform.* London: Routledge & Kegan Paul, 1967.

Smith, R. E. *The Failure of the Roman Republic.* London: Cambridge University Press, 1955.

Smith, Robert. *The Lagos Consulate, 1851–1861.* Berkeley: University of California Press, 1979.

Smith, Tony. *The Pattern of Imperialism.* New York: Cambridge University Press, 1981.

Smith, Woodruff. *The German Colonial Empire.* Chapel Hill: University of North Carolina Press, 1978.

Spalding, W. F. *The London Money Market.* London: Pitmans, 1922.

Speier, H. *Social Order and the Risks of War.* Cambridge: MIT Press, 1951.

Staley, E. *War and the Private Investor.* Chicago: University of Chicago Press, 1935.

Starr, Chester. *The Beginning of Imperial Rome, Rome in the Mid-Republic.* Ann Arbor: University of Michigan Press, 1980.

———. *The Roman Empire, 27 B.C.–A.D. 476: A Study in Survival.* New York: Oxford University Press, 1982.

Stein, Stanley, and Barbara Stein. *The Colonial Heritage of Latin America.* New York: Oxford University Press, 1970.

Steiner, Z. *The Foreign Office and Foreign Policy.* London: Cambridge University Press, 1969.

Stengers, J. "The Congo Free State and the Belgian Congo before 1914." In L. H. Gann and P. Duignan, eds., *Colonialism in Africa,* vol. 1. London: Cambridge University Press, 1969.

Stern, Fritz. *Gold and Iron: Bismarck, Bleichroder, and the Building of the German Empire.* New York: Vintage/Random, 1977.

Steward, Julian H., ed. *Handbook of South American Indians,* vol. 2: *The Andean Civilizations.* New York: Cooper Square, 1963.

Stokes, Eric. "Late Nineteenth Century Colonial Expansion and the Attack on the Theory of Economic Imperialism: A Case of Mistaken Identity." *Historical Journal* 12, 2 (1969), 285–301.

Strachey, E. J. *The End of Empire.* London: Gollancz, 1959.

Strandmann, H. Pogge von. "Domestic Origins of Germany's Colonial Expansion under Bismarck." *Past and Present* no. 42 (1969), 140–59.

Stretton, H. *Policy Sciences.* New York: Basic, 1969.

Sutherland, L. *The East India Company in Eighteenth Century Politics.* London: Oxford University Press, 1952.

Syme, R. *Colonial Elites: Rome, Spain, and the Americas.* London: Oxford University Press, 1958.

———. *The Roman Revolution.* London: Oxford University Press, 1960.

Szymanski, A. *The Logic of Imperialism.* New York: Praeger, 1981.

Tacitus. *The Agricola and the Germania.* Trans. H. Mattingly and S. A. Hanford. Harmondsworth: Penguin, 1970.

Tanter, R., and R. H. Ullman. *Theory and Policy in International Relations.* Princeton: Princeton University Press, 1972.

Tarling, N. *Britain, the Brookes, and Brunei.* New York: Oxford University Press, 1971.

Taylor, A. J. P. *Bismarck: The Man and the Statesman.* New York: Vintage, 1967.

———. *Germany's First Bid for Colonies.* New York: Norton, 1970.

———. *Struggle for the Mastery of Europe.* Oxford: Clarendon, 1954.

Temperley, H. "Capitalism, Slavery, and Ideology." *Past and Present* no. 75 (May 1977), 94–118.

Thomas, Brinley. *Migration and Economic Growth.* Cambridge: Cambridge University Press, 1963.

Thompson, E., and G. Garratt. *The Rise and Fulfillment of British Rule in India.* Allahabad: Central Book Depot, 1962.

Thornton, A. P. *Doctrines of Imperialism.* New York: Wiley, 1963.

———. *The Imperial Idea and Its Enemies.* New York: St. Martins, 1959.

Thucydides. *The Peloponnesian War.* Trans. Rex Warner. Baltimore: Penguin, 1954.

Tignor, R. L. *British Colonial Rule in Egypt, 1882–1914.* Princeton: Princeton University Press, 1966.

Townsend, M. "Commercial and Colonial Policies of Imperial Germany." In G. Nadel and P. Curtis, eds., *Imperialism and Colonialism.* New York: Macmillan, 1964.

———. *The Rise and Fall of Germany's Colonial Empire.* New York: Macmillan, 1930.

Tucker, Irwin St. John. *A History of Imperialism.* New York: Rand School of Social Science, 1920.

Tucker, R. C., ed. *The Marx-Engels Reader.* New York: Norton, 1972.

Tucker, R. W. *Nation or Empire?* Baltimore: Johns Hopkins Press, 1968.

Tucker, Robert W., and David G. Hendrickson. *The Fall of the First British Empire.* Baltimore: Johns Hopkins Press, 1982.

Turan, O. "Anatolia in the Period of the Seljuks and the Beyliks." In P. M. Holt, A. Lambton, and B. Lewis, eds., *The Cambridge History of Islam,* vol. 1. Cambridge: Cambridge University Press, 1970.

Turner, H. "Bismarck's Imperialist Venture." In P. Gillford and W. Louis, eds. *Britain and Germany in Africa.* New Haven: Yale University Press, 1965.

Turner, V., ed. *Colonialism in Africa,* vol. 3. London: Cambridge University Press, 1971.

Uzoigwe, G. N. *Britain and the Conquest of Africa.* Ann Arbor: University of Michigan Press, 1974.

Van Alstyne, R. *The Rising American Empire.* New York: Oxford University Press, 1960.

Veblen, T. *Imperial Germany and the Industrial Revolution* (1915). Ann Arbor: University of Michigan Press, 1968.

Vernon, R. "International Investment and International Trade in the Product Cycle." *Quarterly Journal of Economics* 80, 2 (May 1966), 190–207.

——. *Sovereignty at Bay.* New York: Basic, 1971.

Vives, J. V. *Approaches to the History of Spain.* Berkeley: University of California Press, 1967.

——. "The Decline of Spain." In C. Cipolla, *The Economic Decline of Empires.* London: Methuen, 1970.

——. *An Economic History of Spain.* Princeton: Princeton University Press, 1969.

Walbank, F. W. *The Awful Revolution.* Toronto: University of Toronto Press, 1968.

Wallerstein, I. *The Modern World System,* vol 1. New York: Academic, 1974.

——. *Social Change: The Colonial Situation.* New York: Wiley, 1966.

Waltz, K. *Man, the State, and War.* New York: Columbia University Press, 1959.

——. *Theory of International Politics.* Reading, Mass.: Addison-Wesley, 1979.

Walzer, Michael. *Just and Unjust Wars.* New York: Basic, 1977.

Weber, Max. *The Agrarian Sociology of Ancient Civilizations.* Trans. R. I. Frank. London: New Left Books, 1976.

——. *Economy and Society.* Ed. G. Roth and C. Wittich. Trans. E. Fischoff. Berkeley: University of California Press. 1978.

——. *The Theory of Social and Economic Organization.* Ed. T. Parsons. Trans. A. M. Henderson. New York: Free, 1964.

Wehler, H. U. "Bismarck's Imperialism." *Past and Present* no. 48 (August 1970), 119–55.

——. "Industrial Growth and Early German Imperialism." In E. R. Owen and R. Sutcliffe, *Studies in the Theory of Imperialism.* London: Longman, 1972.

——. *The German Empire: 1871–1918.* Trans. K. Traynor. Leamington Spa and Dover, N.H.: Berg, 1985.

Welbourne, F. B. "Missionary Stimulus and African Response." In V. Turner, ed., *Colonialism in Africa,* vol. 3. Cambridge: Cambridge University Press, 1971.

Welles, S. *Naboth's Vineyard.* New York: Payson & Clarke, 1928.

Wesson, R. *The Imperial Order.* Berkeley: University of California Press, 1967.

Wheare, K. C. *Federal Government.* New York: Oxford University Press, 1964.

Wiener, Martin J. *English Culture and the Decline of the Industrial Spirit, 1850–1980.* New York: Cambridge University Press, 1981.

Williams, E. *Capitalism and Slavery* (1944). New York: Russell & Russell, 1961.

Winch, D. *Classical Political Economy and Colonies.* Cambridge: Harvard University Press, 1965.

Winslow, E. M. *The Pattern of Imperialism.* New York: Columbia University Press, 1948.

Wittek, Paul. *The Rise of the Ottoman Empire.* London: Royal Asiatic Society, 1965.

Wittfogel, Karl. *Oriental Despotism.* New Haven: Yale University Press, 1957.

Woddis, J. *Introduction to Neo-Colonialism.* New York: International, 1971.

Wolff, R. D. *The Economics of Colonialism.* New Haven: Yale University Press, 1974.

——. "Modern Imperialism: The View from the Metropolis." *American Economic Review* 60, 2 (1970), 225–30.

Woodward, C. V. *The Origins of the New South, 1877–1913.* Baton Rouge: Louisiana State University Press, 1971.

Woodward, Sir L. *The Age of Reform.* Oxford: Clarendon, 1962.

Yacono, X. *La colonisation française.* Paris: PUF, 1973.

Yates, E. *Recollections and Experiences.* London: Bentley, 1884.

Zeldin, F. *France.* London: Oxford University Press, 1974.

Zevin, R. "The Interpretation of American Imperialism." *Journal of Economic History* 32, 1 (1972), 316–60.

Index

Adowa, 218, 220
Afghanistan, 286–287, 290
Africa. *See* Scramble for Africa; South Africa; West Africa
Agents, imperial, 167–179, 201–207, 342; administrators, 178; colonial settlers, 168–170, 201–202; consuls, 39, 177, 184, 185, 188, 206–207, 211, 219; financiers, 203, 205–206, 211, 215; merchants and companies, 172–177, 201–205, 215, 365; missionaries, 170–172, 181–182, 185, 187, 203, 219; soldiers, 177–178, 207
Alabama dispute, 280, 281
Alcibiades, 77
Alexander VI (Pope), 111
Algeria, 307, 309, 318
Alsace-Lorraine, 309–310, 311, 318
Ambassador. *See* Consuls
America. *See* United States
Americas, 110, 112, 114–116, 331. *See also* Latin America
Amery, Leopold, 236
Anarchy, international, 126
Anderson, Percy, 191
Annexation, 32, 135, 251–253. *See also* Formal rule
Antonines, 98

Arabi, A., 210, 214–217, 290
Argentina, 120, 196, 223–225, 265, 269–271
Aristotle, 73, 88
Armed forces. *See* Military
Aron, Raymond, 125
Ashanti, 166, 175, 184, 284
Assimilation, 315, 319. *See also* Integration, social
Athenian empire, 28, 30, 40, 54–58, 60–81, 129; adventurous spirit of, 65–67, 70–71; and democracy, 56–59, 66–67, 73, 80, 136; economy of, 57–63, 67–68, 71–73; history and description of, 55–58; military of, 56–57, 67, 76–78; motives of, 60–64; political unity of, 58, 70–75; popularity of, 57–58; resistance to, 58, 76–81; sources of power of, 65–68. *See also* Sparta
Augustan threshold. *See* Centralization
Augustus, 93–97, 137
Aussenpolitik, 321–323
Austria-Hungary, 234–235, 241
Ayandele, E. A., 171
Aztecs, 115–116

Badian, Ernest, 25–26
Bailyn, Bernard, 117

Balance of payments, 264–265
Balance of power, 146, 244, 310, 311, 330, 340. *See also* International system
Bali, 221
Baring, Evelyn (Earl Cromer), 39, 206, 211, 212, 217, 218, 229, 366
Barry, Brian, 41
Baumgart, Winfried, 32
Beecroft, John, 185–186
Belgium, 247, 252
Berlin West Africa Conference, 141–143, 233, 251, 253, 291, 322
Bismarck, Herbert, 326
Bismarck, Otto von, 239, 240, 245, 247, 276, 280; and diplomatic system, 234–235, 241, 248–255, 346, 348; and metropolitan motives, 321–329. *See also* Germany
Blockade, 25, 38–39, 228, 331
Blunt, W. S., 215
Boers, 145, 148, 283, 285, 290, 294
Bonaparte, Louis, 240
Bonny, 180, 181, 183, 184, 186, 187–188
Boundaries: international, 26, 127–128, 148; trade, 173, 176, 178
Bourgeoisie, crisis of, 367–369
Brazil, 223
Britain. *See* English empire
Brown, Peter, 100
Bulgaria, 288
Bureaucracy, 107–108, 220, 330; Roman, 95–97, 100–101, 137; Spanish, 118–121, 137. *See also* Centralization
Buxton, T. F., 171, 181

Caesar, Julius, 30, 89–90
Caisse de la Dette Publique, 211–212
Calabar, 180, 181, 182, 183, 185–186
Calgacus, 177
Caliban, 191–192; crisis of, 365
Capitalism, 22–24, 124, 150–155, 158–159, 200
Caracallan threshold, 97–98, 137. *See also* Integration, social
Carthage, 84, 85, 87
Catherine the Great, 158
Catholic Center party, 328
Catholicism, 308, 314
Centralization, 128–129, 136–137, 344; English, 119, 137; German, 330; Ottoman, 107–108; peripheral, 78–79, 132–

133, 220–222, 371; Roman, 93–97, 100–101, 137; Spanish, 118–121, 137
Chamberlain, Joseph, 216, 275, 276, 283, 292–295
Chile, 222–223
China, 113–114, 130, 143, 203, 204, 297; Cochin, 307–309; dependency of, 225–226
Choucri, Nazli, 345
Civil War, American, 278–279
Clayton-Bulwar Treaty, 242
Coalitions, political, 150, 339–340, 347–348; British, 276–279, 289, 292–305, 339, 347–348; and economic system, 295–305; French, 308–309, 314–318, 340, 347; German, 326–331, 340, 348; Spanish, 334. *See also* Political institutions
Cobden, Richard, 235, 277–280
Cobden-Chevalier Treaty, 311
Cohen, Benjamin J., 27, 28, 125, 259
Collaboration, 38–39, 84–85, 90–91, 114–116, 136, 361–369; African, 169, 192–194; Egyptian, 217–218; with England and Spain, 114, 115–116; and horizontal and vertical divisions, 364; patrimonial, 207, 226–229, 361–363; and stages of imperialism, 365–369
Collective goods international, 236–237, 242, 246–248, 346
Colson, Elizabeth, 164
Columbus, Christopher, 109, 110, 111, 132
Colvin, Auckland, 206, 215
Commercial companies, 172–177, 204–205, 215
Community, sense of, 35, 78, 116–118, 121–122, 128–129, 233–234, 334; lack of, 79–80, 100; peripheral, 218–221. *See also* Integration, social; Social and cultural forces; Unity
Comparative statics, 135–136, 341–344
Competition, international, 196–197, 215, 230, 262–263, 274–275, 291; and French empire, 309, 312–313, 322–324; multipolar, 236–237, 242–248, 251–256, 346. *See also* Transnational economy, British
Compradors, crisis of, 365
Concert of Vienna, 234–238, 280, 281, 289, 291
Confucianism, 114

Congo, 247–248, 252, 322
Congress of Berlin, 191, 288
Conservative party, British, 258, 266, 276–279; and Disraeli, 281–288; and political coalitions, 296–304, 339
Consuls, 39, 145, 177, 184, 185, 188, 206–207, 211, 219, 355–366
Control, political, 30–45; definition of empire as, 51; and dependency, 222–226; development of, 354–364; domain of, 35–36; formal and informal, 32–39, 90, 109, 135–136, 168–170, 274, 319, 341–344; scope of, 36–37; weight, range, and duration of, 40–45. *See also* Formal rule; Informal rule
Converts, crisis of, 365–366
Cook, J. M., 79–80
Cooperation, economic, 247–248, 251–252. *See also* Competition, international
Corcyra, 58, 79
Corinth, 59, 60, 61, 62, 64, 68
Cornewall-Lewis, George: *On the Government of Dependencies*, 31
Coser, Lewis, 227
Cotton, 260–262
Courts of equity, 185 186
Creole elite, 120, 331–333
Cruickshank, Brodie, 354–355
Cuba, 118–119, 120, 332, 335

Dahl, Robert, 34
Dahomey, 175
Decolonization, 353–354, 358–361, 369–372
de Lanessan, Governor, 317
Delcassé, Théophile, 314–315
Delian League. *See* Athenian empire
Democracy: Athenian, 56–59, 60–67, 73, 80, 136; British, 150
Denmark, 337
Dependency, 12, 43–44, 205–207, 211, 222–228
de Romilly, Jacqueline, 28
Déroulède, Paul, 310
Destabilization, African, 170–172, 174–175, 183–184, 186–187, 193–194
de Tocqueville, Alexis, 168
Deutsch, Karl, 41
Development, imperial, 353–372; and decolonization, 353–354, 358–361, 369–372; and establishment of law, 354–

361; process of, 361–364; stages of, 364–369
Diaz, Bernal, 115
Differentiation, social, 128–134, 344, 362–363; feudal, 201; patrimonial, 198–200, 203–204, 342–343; tribal, 89–90, 105–106, 107, 132–133, 163–164, 194, 198
Dilke, Charles, 216, 256
Diplomacy, 147, 221, 248–254, 332, 370–371. *See also* International system; Systemic analysis
Dispositional models. *See* Metrocentric analysis
Disraeli, Benjamin, 211, 230, 244, 258, 266, 277–278; policies of, 281–288, 304
Domestic system: and international system, 35–36, 40, 95–96, 136; and weight of power, 41, 45. *See also* Coalitions, political; Political institutions
Don Pacifico, 277–278
Dorians, 76–79
Dreyfus Affair, 316–317
Dual Control, 211–212, 215
Duration, 45, 136–138, 145; of English empire, 116–117; of Ottoman empire, 107–108; of Roman empire, 92–98; of Spanish empire, 117–118, 331–335
Durkheim, Emile, 131
Dynamics, 52–53, 54, 136–138, 344–349

East India Company, 145, 173
Economic reciprocity, 113, 117–120
Economist, 266
Economy, 44, 110–113, 117–118; Athenian, 57, 61–63, 67–68, 71–73; British, 109–113, 258–305; Egyptian, 209–212; French, 311–313, 322–324; German, 323–325; in Hobson, 149–150; imperial, 172–177, 188–191, 196–197, 211, 262–267, 311–314, 324–325; international, 25, 109–110, 236–237, 242–248, 344–345; and intervention, 168–170, 175–176, 184–190, 196, 205–207, 255–256, 259, 273–275; in Lenin, 150–155; and multipolar competition, 236–237, 242–248, 251–256, 262–263, 274–275, 291, 346; patrimonial, 203–206; and political coalitions, 295–305; Roman, 86–87, 95, 97–98, 100–103, 121; in Schumpeter, 155–159; Spanish, 109–113, 331–335; Spartan, 69, 72; tribal,

Economy *(cont.)*
164, 171–172, 173–174, 180–181. *See also* Transnational economy, British
Egbo cult, 181, 182, 183, 186
Egypt, 157, 206, 208–218, 229–230; Anglo-French control of, 211–216; and British domestic politics, 287–288, 290–291, 294–295; collaboration in, 217–218; and debt, 205; and Germany, 310, 321–322; history and description of, 208–211; military intervention in, 214–217, 255–256
Eisenstadt, S. N., 94, 99
Empire, definitions of, 11–12, 19–47, 81; formal and informal, 32–39; Hobson's, 150; Lenin's, 150–152; metrocentric, 22–24, 33, 123–124; pericentric, 25–26; as political control, 30–34, 45; Schumpeter's, 156; systemic, 26–28, 125–127; and weight, range, and duration, 40–45. *See also* Imperialism, theories of
English empire, nineteenth century, 22–23, 162–197; development of, 232–248; in Egypt, 208–218, 229; in Ethiopia, 219–220; and European diplomacy, 248–256; imperial agents of, 167–179, 201–207; and Latin America, 222–226; military intervention by, 183–191, 214–217; in Niger Delta, 179–191, 296; in South Africa, 145, 148, 283, 285, 290, 294. *See also* Pax Britannica; Transnational economy, British
English empire, pre-nineteenth century: duration of, 116–117, 137; economy of, 109–113; fall of, 118–119, 121–122, 137; peripheries of, 108, 112–115; political institutions of, 117, 119; rise of, 108–109, 112–113
Entrepreneurs, colonial, 110–113
Ethiopia, 212, 217, 218–221
Ethiopianism, 172
Export monopolism, 24
Eyck, Erick, 321
Eyre controversy, 279

Fabians, 276
Ferguson, William Scott, 57
Ferns, H. S., 223–224
Ferry, Jules, 315
Feudalism, 133–134, 135, 200–201, 220–221; merchant, 174, 180–181. *See also* Patrimonial societies

Fieldhouse, David, 146, 259
Finance, 203, 205–206, 267–271, 272, 275, 311
Financiers, 203, 205–206, 211, 215
Finley, John, 73
Foreign debt, patrimonial, 205–206, 211, 228
Formal rule, 32, 135, 168–170, 319; causes of, 273–275, 341–344, 361–363; from informal, 176–177, 183–195, 207–208; and multipolar competition, 251–253, 255–256, 340. *See also* Control, political
Fractionated polity, 80, 134, 135, 238
France, 306–319; in Africa, 178, 188–191, 195, 220, 288; domestic politics, 308–309, 314–318, 340, 347; and economic factors, 311–313; in Egypt, 208–218, 229–230, 291; and Germany, 240, 309, 310, 311, 321–322; history and description of, 306–309, 318–319; and international system, 234–254; and national prestige, 308, 310, 314–315; possessions of, 306–307, 309, 318; Republican, 309–318; and trade competition, 196–197, 262, 267, 284–285, 291, 309, 312–313
Franco-Prussian War, 309, 316
Free trade, 243–244, 312–313; imperialism of, 25–26, 32–33, 143–145, 147–148; and informal rule, 143–145, 147–148, 273–275. *See also* Competition, international; Transnational economy, British
Frontier: fluid, 26, 127–128, 148; trade, 173, 176, 178
Froude, J. A., 283

Gallagher, John, 21, 25, 32, 143–145, 147, 345
Geertz, Clifford, 221
Germany, 234–235, 276, 319–331; and Aussenpolitik, 321–323; and economic factors, 323–325; and France, 240, 309, 310, 311, 321–322; history and description of, 319–321; and Innenpolitik, 326–331; and international system, 239–240, 248–256; possessions of, 320; predominance of, 242–248; and trade competition, 188–191, 196–197, 261–264, 268. *See also* Bismarck, Otto von
Ghana. *See* Gold Coast

Ghazi fanaticism, 106–107

Gibbon, E., 82–83, 85, 98

Gladstone, William, 215, 245, 249–250, 255–256; policies of, 277, 279–283, 288–292, 298–299, 301–304

Gold Coast, 178, 354–358

Goldie-Taubmann, George, 189–191, 196–197, 255

Great(er) Britain. *See* English empire; Transnational economy, British

Greeks, and Roman empire, 84–85, 91. *See also* Athenian empire; Sparta

Gulick, Edward, 27–28

Habbakuk, H. S., 269

Hailey, Malcolm: *African Survey*, 11

Harcourt, Freda, 127, 160

Harris, William, 24, 30

Hegemony, 12, 40, 129–130; definition of, 81; Spartan, 54, 59–60, 70–75, 130

Hermocrates, 77–78

Hewett, E. H., 177, 191

Hicks, John, 67

Hirschman, Albert, 362

Hispaniola, 110, 117

Hobsbawm, Eric, 261

Hobson, John A., 12, 13, 20, 22–24, 31, 141, 148–150, 259

Holland, 109, 113

House system, 174, 180–181

Huntington, Samuel, 362

Ibn Khaldun: *Prolegomena*, 105–106

Imperial coalition, British, 293–295, 301–304. *See also* Coalitions, political

Imperialism: nineteenth-century politics of, 339–349; as process, 161; theories of, 11–13, 123–128, 145–161. *See also* Empire, definitions of

Incas, 115–116

Independence. *See* Decolonization

India, 113, 114, 133–134, 196, 236, 369; and British domestic politics, 264–265, 284–284, 286–287, 290, 297; Egypt as route to, 208, 214, 217, 230, 287–288

Indians, American, 115, 132, 168, 193, 366

Inequality. *See* Control, political

Influence, 34, 213, 228–229. *See also* Control, political; Informal rule

Informal rule, 22–23, 25–26, 32–39, 56, 90, 168–170; causes of, 341–344; and

collaboration, 207, 226–229, 361–363; definition of, 135–136, 341; and dependency, 222–226; in Egypt, 214–218; and free trade, 143–145, 147–148, 273–275; and shift to formal rule, 176–177, 183–195, 207–208; in Zanzibar, 358–361. *See also* Control, political

Instability. *See* Unity

Integration, social, 35–36, 131–132, 137, 225, 315, 319, 372; Ottoman, 107–108; patrimonial and feudal, 200, 201; Roman, 96–98, 100, 137; of settlers, 116–117, 121–122, 137. *See also* Community, sense of; Differentiation, social; National identity; Unity

Interdependence, 44

International Association of the Congo, 247, 252

International relations theory, 11, 13, 34–35, 126. *See also* Systemic analysis

International system, 109, 146, 232–256; and the Concert, 234–238; and domestic systems, 35–36, 40, 95–96, 136; predominance of Germany in, 242–248; and Realpolitik, 238–242; unipolar, bipolar, and multipolar, 20, 136, 146, 244, 310, 311, 330, 340, 343–344; and weight of power, 41, 45. *See also* Diplomacy

Interstate politics, definition of, 134

Investment, 205–206, 267–271, 272, 275, 311

Ionian colonies, 55, 58, 61, 79–81

Ireland, 281, 291–292, 294–295, 302, 304

Ismail, 205, 209–212

Italy, 111, 146, 218, 220, 308–309

Jaja, 187–188, 191

Jamaica, 112, 279

Japan, 113–114, 203, 221

Jefferson's Rule, 39–40

Jingoism, 287

Johnston, Harry, 171, 177

Junkers, 327–328

Kahler, Miles, 370

Kanya-Forstner, A. S., 159–160

Kaplan, Morton, 27

Kartell party, 329

Kautsky, John, 151, 155

Kennedy, Archibald, 119

Kirk, John, 39, 206, 359

Lagos, 175, 180, 184, 185–186, 187
Land acquisition, 168–170, 202, 270, 357–358
Landes, David, 209, 210
Landlord, crisis of, 366–367
Langer, William, 34
Latin America, 25, 115–116, 222–226, 262, 264. *See also* Americas; Argentina; Cuba; Mexico
Law: colonial, 354–358; tribal, 165
Leibniz, Gottfried von, 30–31, 220–231
Lenin, Nikolai, 12, 13, 20, 22–24, 31, 46, 124, 150–155, 259
Leopold, 247, 252
Lesbos, 79
Liberal party (British), 258, 266, 276–279, 339; and Gladstone, 279–285, 289–292; and political coalitions, 296–304
Liberal party (German), 328–329
Liberia, 170
Little Englanders, 276
Loans, 205–206, 211, 228
Louis XIV, 158
Luxemburg, Rosa, 153
Lyons, Viscount, 215–216, 230
Lytton, E., 283, 286–287

McCarthy, Justin, 283
Machiavelli, N., 36–37, 85, 86, 88, 92
MacLean, Consul, 145, 177, 355–356
Maecenas, 93–94
Maine, Henry, 357
Malet, Edward, 206
Malinowski, Bronislaw, 165
Manufacturing, 204–205
Maquet, Jacques, 166, 200
Markets, imperial: British, 262–267, 311–312; French, 313–314 German, 324–325
Marx, Karl, 134, 151–152, 155, 240, 361–362, 367
Mehemet Ali, 208–209, 229
Melos, 58, 71, 76, 131
Menelik II, 218–221
Merchants, 172–177, 201–205, 215, 365; Goldie-Taubmann, 189–191, 196–197, 255
Metals, 260–264
Metrocentric analysis, 20, 22–24, 33, 60; inadequacy of, 123–125, 335–341; of modern imperialism, 145, 146–147, 148–159, 229–230

Metropole: definition of, 11, 19, 128–129; threshold of, 70–76, 128–130
Mexico, 110, 115–116, 120, 196, 202–203, 262, 332; debt of, 242, 308
Middle class, 367–369
Middlemen, African, 173–176
Military, 107, 126; Athenian, 56–57, 67, 76–78; French, 178, 195, 244, 314, 316–319, 340; as imperial agent, 177–178, 207; patrimonial, 202, 213–214; Roman, 84–85, 86, 88, 90, 91, 95, 100–101; Spartan, 69, 72. *See also* Naval power
Mill, John Stuart, 278, 279
Ming Dynasty, 114, 130
Mining, 204
Missionaries, 170–172, 203, 219, 365–366; in Niger Delta, 181–182, 185, 187
Monarchists, 314–316
Mongol empire, 106
Monson, Mr., 178
Montesquieu, C., 90
Motives, metropolitan, 60–64, 108–113, 339–341; economic development, 258–260, 273, 315–316, 323–325; glory and honor, 62–63, 64, 85–86, 308, 310, 314–315; material interest, 61, 63–64, 86–87, 109–113; religion, 85, 105–107, 110, 114, 157–158; security, 61–62, 64, 109, 125–126, 255–256
Multipolar competition. *See* Competition, international

Napoleon III, 239, 240, 244, 307–309, 311
Narvaez, Manuel, 238
National identity, 218–220, 334, 371. *See also* Community, sense of
Nationalism, 368–370; Egyptian, 213–214, 217; European, 275–276, 326–331; Islamic, 213, 360
National liberation movements, 154–155
Nation-states, European, 238–246
Naval power, 104, 113–114, 235–237; in Africa, 178, 181, 182–186, 188; Athenian, 56–57, 62, 67
Niger Delta, 164, 171, 175, 179–191, 296
North, Robert, 345
Nubar Pasha, 212, 213, 214, 366
Nuer, 164, 166

Oligarchy, 59, 72, 136
Opportunist party, 314–318, 347
Ottoman empire, 106–108, 208–209, 214–216

Pace. *See* Rate of imperial expansion
Palmerston, Lord, 214, 229, 237, 277–279
Palm oil trade, 173, 174, 182–183, 187, 189–190
Paris, Ferdinand, 117
Parry, J. H., 109–110
Parti Colonial, 315, 316
Parties. *See* Coalitions, political
Patrick Henry's Rule, 40
Patrimonial societies, 133, 135–136, 198–231; collapse of, 202–203; and decolonization, 358–361; definition of, 199; development of, 200–201; imperial agents in, 201–207; Latin American, 115–116; social organization of, 198–200, 203–204, 342–343
Pausanias, 55, 60, 61, 80
Pax Britannica, 235–237, 242, 246–247, 254, 264, 274, 309, 346
Peasants, 368–369
Peloponnesian League. *See* Sparta
Pepple, Anna, 183, 186
Pepple, William Dappa, 183, 184, 186
Pericentric analysis, 21, 25–26, 127, 340–342; of modern imperialism, 147–148, 195–198, 229–231, 255
Pericles, 56, 62, 65, 67, 73, 74
Periphery: definition of, 11, 19; social organization of, 130–134, 163–167, 174–175, 194, 198–200, 203–204, 342–343; subordination of, 76–81, 88–91, 113–116, 218–221; threshold of, 76–81, 131–134. *See also* Collaboration; Patrimonial societies; Tribal societies
Persia, 55, 57, 61, 74
Peru, 110, 115–116, 117, 120, 202–203
Philippines, 118–119, 332
Plantation agriculture, 110, 168, 359
Plato, 80
Platt, D. C. M., 32, 196
Plutarch, 56
Political institutions, 69, 362–363, 370–372; Athenian, 56–59, 66–67, 73, 80, 136; British, 117, 119, 298–301; French, 308, 314–318; Ottoman, 107–108; Roman, 88, 92, 95–98, 100–101; Spanish, 118–121, 331–332, 334–335;

tribal, 164–166, 174–175. *See also* Coalitions, political
Polybius, 70–71, 85
Portugal, 108, 110, 111, 113, 114, 180, 331, 337
Prussia, 234–235, 241. *See also* Bismarck, Otto von; Germany

Radical party (British), 277, 289, 292, 293, 297–299, 301–302, 304
Radical party (French), 315, 316
Railroads, 25, 268–271
Rate of imperial expansion, 188, 196–197, 230, 344–345, 364
Realpolitik, 238–242
Rebellion. *See* Resistance
Reductionist analysis. *See* Metrocentric analysis
Religion, 219–221, 365–366; Christianity, 98, 110, 219–220; Islam, 213, 360; as metropolitan motive, 85, 105–107, 110, 114, 157–158; and missionaries, 170–172, 181–182, 185, 187, 203, 219, 346, 355, 365–366; and tribal organization, 163–164
Republicanism: French, 309–318; Roman, 88, 92–95
Resistance, 40, 43–44, 117–118, 124, 138, 340–341, 363–364; African, 169, 184, 187, 192–194; against Athens, 58, 76–81; Egyptian, 214, 217; against England and Spain, 115–116, 119, 120, 331–335; Ethiopian, 218–220; and international diplomacy, 332, 370–371; Japanese, 221; in Lenin, 154–155; patrimonial, 203–204; against Rome, 90–91, 98–99; and social organization, 368–369
Revolution: American, 364; European, 234–235, 238–240
Ripon, Lord, 290
Robinson, Ronald, 21, 25, 32, 143–145, 147, 169, 218, 294, 345
Roman empire, 24, 25–26, 30, 82–103; and Augustan threshold, 93–97, 137; and Caracallan threshold, 97–98, 137; decline and fall of, 98–103; duration of, 92–98; economy of, 86–87, 95, 97–98, 100–103, 121; history and description of, 83–85; military of, 84–85, 86, 88, 90, 91, 95, 100–101; peripheries of, 88–91; political institutions of, 88, 92, 95–

Roman Empire *(cont.)*
98, 100–101; resistance to, 90–91, 98–99; rise of, 83–92; transnational connections of, 87, 96–98
Rosebery, Lord, 295
Rostovtzeff, M., 84
Rule. *See* Formal rule; Informal rule
Russia, 234–235, 241, 286–288
Rwanda, 200

Said, Seyyid, 358
Salisbury, Lord, 213, 230, 233, 258, 274, 293–294, 304
San Martín, José de, 224
Schumpeter, Joseph, 12, 13, 20, 31, 46, 155–159, 259; and definition of empire, 22–24, 123–124
Scramble for Africa: and the international system, 232–233, 252–254; sources of, 345–349; theories of, 141–161; and tribal peripheries, 162–197. *See also* West Africa
Self-government, colonial, 289–290, 294, 297
Senegal, 178, 195
Settlers, colonial, 108–109, 116–118, 134, 319; entrepreneurial, 110–113; as imperial agents, 168–170, 201–202
Severus, 100–101
Sharp, Granville, 181
Siam, 221
Sicily, 66–67, 74, 76–79
Sidney, Philip, 30–31
Sierra Leone, 170
Slave revolts, 120, 182, 183–184
Slavery: African, 168, 355, 356; Athenian, 60, 63; Ottoman, 107–108; Roman, 87, 90, 102; suppression of, 170, 178, 181–184, 356–357, 358–360; trade in, 172, 174, 175, 180–181
Smith, Tony, 369–370
Social and cultural forces: for Athenian expansion, 65–67, 68–69; and attachment to metropole, 116–118; and domestic British politics, 297–303; and international systems, 233–234; of peripheries, 76–81, 89–90, 218–221; for Roman expansion, 85–87, 97–98, 100, 102–103; for Spartan expansion, 70–73; transnational extension of, 128, 129–130. *See also* Community, sense of; Differentiation, social; Integration, social; Transnational connections

Social Democratic party, 328
Social organization, 130–134, 368–369; patrimonial, 198–200, 203–204, 342–343; tribal, 163–167, 174–175, 194, 198
Social reform, 279–283, 302
Soldier. *See* Military
Sources of power, 64–69, 84–88, 101–103; allies and subordinates, 65; social character, 65–73, 85–87, 97–98, 100, 102–103, 233–234
South Africa, 145, 148, 283, 285, 290, 294
Sovereignty, 106
Spanish empire, 235, 237–238; duration of, 117–118, 137; economy of, 109–113, 331–335; fall of, 118–122, 331–335; peripheries of, 108, 110, 112–116; political institutions of, 118–121, 331–332, 334–335; rise of, 108–112. *See also* Latin America
Sparta, 28, 54, 68–70, 72–81, 129; and Athens, 61, 70; economy of, 69, 72; and hegemony, 58–60; history and description of, 58–60, 68–69, 72–73; military of, 69, 72; motives of, 64; sources of power, 68–69; spirit of, 68–71, 72–73
Special interests, 313, 318, 326–327
Spenser, Edmund: *Faerie Queene*, 169
Statics, 52–53, 54, 128–135; comparative, 135–136, 341–344
Suez Canal, 208, 214, 217, 230
Suzerainty, 42–43, 119
Swarming, 60, 64
Syracuse, 77–78
Systemic analysis, 21, 26–28, 60; inadequacy of, 125–127, 341; of modern imperialism, 145–147, 229–230, 231–256

Tacitus, 82, 89, 131, 132
Tanzania. *See* Zanzibar
Taylor, A. J. P., 146, 239, 321–322
Technology, 115, 131; and African destabilization, 170–171, 187, 192; industrial, 261–263, 271–272; military, 238–241, 243, 244; Roman, 87–88, 102
Tewfik, 212, 217
Tewodros, 219
Textiles, 260–264, 274
Thucydides, 30, 40, 54–61, 65–67, 73, 76, 78, 80–81, 125, 129, 131
Tirpitz, Alfred von, 330

Tocqueville, Alexis de, 168
Tory party. *See* Conservative party
Townsend, Mary, 321, 323–324
Trade diaspora, 172–173
Trade frontier, expansion of, 173, 176, 178
Trade restrictions, 109, 112, 117, 121
Transnational connections, 107, 128–130, 137, 345–346; Greek, 52, 71–74; Roman, 87, 96–98. *See also* Agents, imperial; Integration, social; Social and cultural forces
Transnational economy, British, 258–305; and domestic politics, 275–305, 339, 347–348; expansion of, 271–275; and imperial markets, 262–267, 311–312; and investment and finance, 267–271, 272, 275; rise of, 258–260; and textiles and metals, 260–264, 274. *See also* Economy; Pax Britannica
Treaty of Tordesillas, 111
Tribal empire, 105–108
Tribal societies, 132–133, 135, 162–197, 343, 365; American, 115, 168, 193, 366; definition of, 163; and imperial agents, 167–179; social and political organization of, 163–167, 174–175, 194, 198, 354–358; types of, 166–167
Tribal warfare, 186, 174–175, 187, 193
Triple Alliance, 248–254
Trobriand Islands, 200
Tucker, Irwin St. John, 51
Tunisia, 207, 288
Turkey, 288

Unionist party, 292–297, 301–304
United Africa Company, 190

United States, 242, 260–266, 278–279, 332; colonial, 39–40, 112, 117–119, 196, 364
Unity: Athenian, 58, 70–75; Ottoman, 105–106; peripheral, 76–81; Roman, 90, 100; Spanish, 111. *See also* Centralization; Community

Venezuela, 120
Vivian, Mr., 213

Waddell, Hope, 182
Waltz, Kenneth, 27
War machine, 157, 159, 339–340. *See also* Military; Schumpeter, Joseph
Warner, Rex, 78
War Scare, 245, 248
Wealth, 128, 131
Weber, Max, 199, 201
Wehler, Hans Ulrich, 159, 276, 321, 323, 326, 327, 329
Weight of power, 40–45
West Africa, 170, 175, 279, 284–285, 291. *See also* Ashanti; Bonny; Calabar; Gold Coast; Lagos; Niger Delta; Senegal
Whig party, 277, 278, 289, 292, 293, 297–299, 302–304. *See also* Liberal party (British)
Wilhelm II, 329–331
Wilson, Edmund, 125
Winslow, E. M., 31
Wolseley, G., 216

Yohannes, 219–220

Zanzibar, 358–361, 366–367, 369

Library of Congress Cataloging-in-Publication Data

Doyle, Michael W.
 Empires.

  (Cornell studies in comparative history)
  Bibliography: p.
  Includes index.
  1. Imperialism. 2. Imperialism—History. I. Title.
II. Series.
JC359.D69 1986   321.03   85-24257
ISBN 0-8014-1756-2
ISBN 0-8014-9334-X (pbk.)